TELECOMMUNICATIONS MODELING, POLICY, AND TECHNOLOGY

OPERATIONS RESEARCH/COMPUTER SCIENCE INTERFACES

Professor Ramesh Sharda
Oklahoma State University

Prof. Dr. Stefan Voß
Universität Hamburg

Bierwirth / *Adaptive Search and the Management of Logistics Systems*

Laguna & González-Velarde / *Computing Tools for Modeling, Optimization and Simulation*

Stilman / *Linguistic Geometry: From Search to Construction*

Sakawa / *Genetic Algorithms and Fuzzy Multiobjective Optimization*

Ribeiro & Hansen / *Essays and Surveys in Metaheuristics*

Holsapple, Jacob & Rao / *Business Modelling: Multidisciplinary Approaches — Economics, Operational and Information Systems Perspectives*

Sleezer, Wentling & Cude/*Human Resource Development And Information Technology: Making Global Connections*

Voß & Woodruff / *Optimization Software Class Libraries*

Upadhyaya et al / *Mobile Computing: Implementing Pervasive Information and Communications Technologies*

Reeves & Rowe / *Genetic Algorithms—Principles and Perspectives: A Guide to GA Theory*

Bhargava & Ye / *Computational Modeling And Problem Solving In The Networked World: Interfaces in Computer Science & Operations Research*

Woodruff / *Network Interdiction And Stochastic Integer Programming*

Anandalingam & Raghavan / *Telecommunications Network Design And Management*

Laguna & Martí / *Scatter Search: Methodology And Implementations In C*

Gosavi/ *Simulation-Based Optimization: Parametric Optimization Techniques and Reinforcement Learning*

Koutsoukis & Mitra / *Decision Modelling And Information Systems: The Information Value Chain*

Milano / *Constraint And Integer Programming: Toward a Unified Methodology*

Wilson & Nuzzolo / *Schedule-Based Dynamic Transit Modeling: Theory and Applications*

Golden, Raghavan & Wasil / *The Next Wave in Computing, Optimization, And Decision Technologies*

Rego & Alidaee/ *Metaheuristics Optimization via Memory and Evolution: Tabu Search and Scatter Search*

Kitamura & Kuwahara / *Simulation Approaches in Transportation Analysis: Recent Advances and Challenges*

Ibaraki, Nonobe & Yagiura / *Metaheuristics: Progress as Real Problem Solvers*

Golumbic & Hartman / *Graph Theory, Combinatorics, and Algorithms: Interdisciplinary Applications*

Raghavan & Anandalingam / *Telecommunications Planning: Innovations in Pricing, Network Design and Management*

Mattfeld / *The Management of Transshipment Terminals: Decision Support for Terminal Operations in Finished Vehicle Supply Chains*

Alba & Martí/ *Metaheuristic Procedures for Training Neural Networks*

Alt, Fu & Golden/ *Perspectives in Operations Research: Papers in honor of Saul Gass' 80th Birthday*

Baker et al/ *Extending the Horizons: Adv. In Computing, Optimization, and Dec. Technologies*

Zeimpekis et al/ *Dynamic Fleet Management: Concepts, Systems, Algorithms & Case Studies*

Doerner et al/ *Metaheuristics: Progress in Complex Systems Optimization*

Goel/ *Fleet Telematics: Real-time management & planning of commercial vehicle operations*

Gondran & Minoux/ *Graphs, Dioïds and Semirings: New models and algorithms*

Alba & Dorronsoro/ *Cellular Genetic Algorithms*

Golden, Raghavan & Wasil/ *The Vehicle Routing Problem: Latest advances and new challenges*

TELECOMMUNICATIONS MODELING, POLICY, AND TECHNOLOGY

Edited by

S. RAGHAVAN
University of Maryland

BRUCE GOLDEN
University of Maryland

EDWARD WASIL
American University

 Springer

Editors
S. Raghavan
University of Maryland
College Park, MD, USA

Bruce Golden
University of Maryland
College Park, MD, USA

Edward Wasil
American University
Washington, DC, USA

Series Editors
Ramesh Sharda
Oklahoma State University
Stillwater, Oklahoma, USA

Stefan Voß
Universität Hamburg
Germany

ISBN: 978-1-4419-4604-1   e-ISBN: 978-0-387-77780-1

Contents

Preface   vii

1

Single-Layer Cuts for Multi-Layer Network Design Problems   1
Arie M. C. A. Koster, Sebastian Orlowski, Christian Raack, Georg Baier,
and Thomas Engel

2

Optimal Multi-Channel Assignments in Vehicular Ad-Hoc Networks   25
Hanan Luss and *Wai Chen*

3

The Label-Constrained Minimum Spanning Tree Problem   39
Yupei Xiong, Bruce Golden, Edward Wasil, and *Si Chen*

4

Ex-Post Internet Charging   59
Joseph P. Bailey, Jose Nagel, and *S. Raghavan*

5

Error Bounds for Hierarchical Routing   81
Eric Rosenberg

6

An Entropy Based Method to Detect Spoofed Denial of Service (DoS)   101
Attacks
Willa K. Ehrlich, Kenichi Futamura, and *Danielle Liu*

7

Mobile Networks Competition and Asymmetric Regulation of   123
Termination Charges
Livio Cricelli, Francesca Di Pillo, Massimo Gastaldi, and *Nathan Levialdi Ghiron*

8

A Package Bidding Tool for the FCC's Spectrum Auctions, and its Effect   153
on Auction Outcomes
Karla Hoffman, Dinesh Menon, and *Susara A. van den Heever*

9

Comparison of Heuristics for Solving the GMLST Problem   191
Yiwei Chen, Namrata Cornick, Andrew O. Hall, Ritvik Shajpal, John Silberholz,
Inbal Yahav, and *Bruce L. Golden*

10

Optimizing the Node Degree in Wireless Multihop Networks with Single-   219
    Lobe Beamforming
Christian Hartmann, Moritz Kiese, and *Robert Vilzmann*

11

Fluid Model of an Internet Router Under the MIMD Control Scheme   239
Urtzi Ayesta, Alexei B. Piunovskiy, and *Y. Zhang*

12

Optimal Survivable Routing with a Small Number of Hops   253
Luís Gouveia, Pedro Patrício, and *Amaro de Sousa*

13

Communication Constraints and Ad Hoc Scheduling   275
Steven Weber

14

Topology Control in a Free Space Optical Network   291
Yohan Shim, Steven Gabriel, Stuart Milner, and *Christopher Davis*

15

A Local Search Hybrid Genetic Algorithm Approach to the Network   311
    Design Problem with Relay Stations
Sadan Kulturel-Konak and *Abdullah Konak*

16

Dynamic Bandwidth Reservation in a Virtual Private Network under   325
    Uncertain Traffic
Hélène Le Cadre and *Mustapha Bouhtou*

17

Evaluation and Design of Business Models for Collaborative Provision   353
    of Advanced Mobile Data Services: A Portfolio Theory Approach
Alexei A. Gaivoronski and *Josip Zoric*

Preface

This edited book serves as a companion volume to the Ninth INFORMS Telecommunications Conference held in College Park, Maryland, from March 27 to 29, 2008. The 17 papers in this book were carefully selected after a thorough review process.

Rapid advances in telecommunications technology have spawned many new innovative applications. These advances in technology have also fostered new research problems. In a certain sense, each one of the papers in this book is motivated by these advances in technology. Technologies considered range from free-space optical networks and vehicular ad-hoc networks to wave division multiplexing and multiprotocol label switching. The research contained in these papers covers a broad spectrum that includes the design of business models, tools for spectrum auctions, Internet charging schemes, Internet routing policies, and network design problems. Together, these papers address issues that deal with both engineering design and policy.

We thank all of the authors for their hard work and invaluable contributions to this book. We are very pleased with the outcome of this edited book, and hope these papers will give rise to new ideas and research in their respective domains.

S. RAGHAVAN, BRUCE GOLDEN, AND EDWARD WASIL

Chapter 1

SINGLE-LAYER CUTS FOR MULTI-LAYER NETWORK DESIGN PROBLEMS

Arie M.C.A. Koster

University of Warwick, Centre for Discrete Mathematics and its Applications (DIMAP), Coventry CV4 7AL, United Kingdom

Arie.Koster@wbs.ac.uk

Sebastian Orlowski, Christian Raack

Zuse Institute Berlin (ZIB), Takustr. 7, D-14195 Berlin

{orlowski,raack}@zib.de

Georg Baier

Siemens AG CT, Discrete Optimization, Munich, Germany

georg.baier@siemens.com

Thomas Engel

Nokia Siemens Networks GmbH & Co. KG, Munich, Germany

thomas.1.engel@nsn.com

Abstract   We study a planning problem arising in SDH/WDM multi-layer telecommunication network design. The goal is to find a minimum cost installation of link and node hardware of both network layers such that traffic demands can be realized via grooming and a survivable routing. We present a mixed-integer programming formulation for a predefined set of admissible logical links that takes many practical side constraints into account, including node hardware, several bit-rates, and survivability against single physical node or link failures. This model is solved using a branch-and-cut approach with cutting planes based on either of the two layers. On several realistic two-layer planning scenarios, we show that these cutting planes are still useful in the multi-layer context, helping to increase the dual bound and to reduce the optimality gaps.

Keywords: Telecommunication networks; multi-layer network design; mixed-integer pro-
              gramming; cutting planes.

1.   Introduction

During the last decade, dense wavelength division multiplexing (DWDM) has turned out to be the dominant network technology in high-capacity optical backbone networks. It provides a flexible way to expand capacity in optical networks without requiring new cabling. Current DWDM systems usually provide 40 or 80 different wavelengths on a single optical fiber to carry high capacity channels, e. g., 2.5, 10, or 40 Gbit/s per wavelength. Typically, these capacities exhibit economies of scale, such that, for instance, the cost of 10 Gbit/s is only three times the cost of 2.5 Gbit/s. Low-granularity traffic given, for instance, in units of 2 Mbps, can be routed through these high-capacity wavelength channels. Flexible optical network nodes selectively terminate a wavelength or let them pass through to the next fiber, provided that an add/drop multiplexer with sufficient switching capacity has been installed to handle the terminating traffic. Ultra long-haul transmission permits high capacity optical channels via several fiber segments requiring transponders only at the end of the whole path, whose cost depends on the data rate and the length of the chosen path.

The corresponding network design problem can be summarized as follows. Given is a set of network nodes together with potential optical fiber connections between them. This optical network is called the *physical layer*. On every fiber, a limited number of lightpath channels can be transmitted simultaneously, each of them corresponding to a capacitated path in the physical network. The nodes together with the lightpath connections form a so-called *logical network* on top of the physical one. Setting aside some technical limitations, any path in the physical network can be used for a lightpath, which leads to many parallel logical links. In practice, however, the set of admissible lightpaths is often restricted to several short paths between each node-pair. A lightpath can be equipped with different bandwidths, and lower-rate traffic demands have to be routed via the lightpaths without exceeding their capacities. A demand may be 1+1-protected, i. e., twice the demand value must be routed such that in case of any single physical link or node failure, at least the demand value survives. To terminate a lightpath, a sufficiently large electrical cross-connect (EXC) must be installed at both end-nodes. The EXC converts the wavelength signal into an electrical SDH signal and extracts lower-rate traffic from it. The latter is either terminated at that node or recombined with other traffic to form new wavelength signals which are sent out on other lightpaths. The goal of the optimization is to minimize total installation cost.

Like in any other publication where an integrated two-layer model is actually used for computations, we do not explicitly assign wavelengths to the lightpaths because finding a suitable wavelength assignment is an extremely hard problem on its own. Instead, we make sure that the maximum number of lightpaths on each fiber is not exceeded, and propose to solve the wavelength assignment and converter installation problem in a subsequent step, as done successfully in [23]. It has been shown in [24] that such an approach causes at most a marginal increase in the overall installation cost on practical instances.

The network planning task is particularly driven by two parameters: the bound on the number of wavelengths per fiber and the transponder prices. A shortage in wavelengths may force the network planner to employ optical channels with high data rates. To keep the total transponder cost low, a suitable set of lightpaths has to be chosen in order to make the best possible use of these high data rates. To draw the maximal benefit out of the optical and the aggregation equipment, both layers have to be optimized together.

Already the optimal design of a single layer network is a challenging task that has been considered by many research groups, see for instance [3, 18, 33, 34] and references therein. A branch-and-cut algorithm enhanced by user-defined, problem-specific cutting planes has been proven to be a very successful solution approach in this context. The combined optimization of two layers significantly increases the complexity of the planning task. This is mainly due to the combined network design problem with integer capacities on the logical layer and the fixed-charge network design problem on the physical layer, and due to the large number of logical links with corresponding integer capacity variables. In previous publications, mixed-integer programming techniques have been used for designing a logical layer with respect to a fixed physical layer [4, 14, 15] or for solving an integrated two-layer planning problem with some simplifying assumptions, like no node hardware or wavelength granularity demands [19, 25]. Recently, Belotti et al. [6] have used a Lagrangean approach for a two-layer network design problem with simultaneous mean demand values and non-simultaneous peak demand values. Orlowski et al. [30] present several heuristics for a two-layer network design problem, which solve a restricted version of the original problem as a sub-MIP within a branch-and-cut framework. Raghavan and Stanojevic [35] consider the case where all logical links are eligible and develop a branch-and-price algorithm with respect to a fixed physical layer for the case of unprotected demands and one facility on the logical links.

In this paper, we present a mathematical model for the described planning problem with a predefined set of logical links and solve it using a branch-and-cut approach with user-defined cutting planes. To our knowledge, this is the first time that so many practically relevant side constraints are taken into account in one integrated two-layer planning model. This includes node

hardware, several bit-rates on the logical links, and survivability against physical node and link failures. Despite its practical importance, survivability has
not been considered in any previous integrated solution approach for two network layers. This is probably due to the high complexity of the survivable
multi-layer network design problem, which is further discussed at the end of
Section 2.

On the algorithmic side, we show that a branch-and-cut approach is still
useful for an integrated planning of two network layers with all these side
constraints, provided that the MIP solver is accelerated by problem-specific
cutting plane routines. The algorithm is tested on several network instances
provided by Nokia Siemens Networks. By adding a variety of strong single-
layer cutting planes for both layers to the solver, we can significantly raise
the dual bounds on our network instances. Especially in the unprotected case,
most of the optimality gap is closed. With 1+1-protection, the problem is much
harder to solve due to the increased problem size and other effects discussed
in our computational results. However, the employed cutting planes turn out to
be useful also with protection.

The paper is structured as follows. In Section 2, we will present and discuss
our mixed-integer programming model. Section 3 describes the used cutting
planes and states some known results about their strength. We show in Section 4 how to generate these inequalities during the branch-and-cut algorithm,
and provide computational results in Section 5. Eventually, we draw some
conclusions in Section 6.

2.   Mathematical Model

We will now introduce the mixed-integer programming model on which our
cutting planes are based.

Parameters.   The physical network is represented by an undirected graph
(V, E). The logical network is modeled by an undirected graph (V, L) with the
same set of nodes and a fixed set L of admissible logical links. Each logical
link represents an undirected path in the physical network. In consequence,
any two nodes $i, j \in V$ may be connected by many parallel logical links corresponding to different physical paths, collected in the set $L_{ij} = L_{ji}$. Looped
logical links are forbidden, i. e., $L_{ii} = \emptyset$ for all $i \in V$. Let $\delta_L(i) = \cup_{j \in V} L_{ij}$ be
the set of all logical links starting or ending at i. Eventually, $L_e \subseteq L$ denotes
the set of logical links containing edge $e \in E$, and likewise, $L_i \subseteq L$ refers to
the set of logical links containing node $i \in V$ as an inner node.

We consider different types of capacities for logical links, physical links,
and nodes. Each logical link $\ell \in L$ has a set M_ℓ of available capacity modules
(corresponding to different bit-rates), each of them with a cost of $\kappa_\ell^m \in \mathbb{R}_+$
and a base capacity of $C_\ell^m \in \mathbb{Z}_+$ that can be installed on ℓ in integer multiples.

Similarly, every node $i \in V$ has a set M_i of node modules (representing different EXC types), at most one of which may be installed at i. Module $m \in M_i$ provides a switching capacity of $C_i^m \in \mathbb{Z}_+$ (e. g., in bits per second) at a cost of $\kappa_i^m \in \mathbb{R}_+$. On a physical link $e \in E$, a fiber may be installed at a cost of $\kappa_e \in \mathbb{R}_+$. Each fiber supports up to $B \in \mathbb{Z}_+$ lightpaths.

For the routing part, a set H of undirected point-to-point communication demands is given, which may be *protected* or *unprotected*. Protected demands are expected to survive any single physical node or link failure, whereas unprotected demands are allowed to fail in such a case. Each demand $h \in H$ has a source node, a target node, and a demand value d_h to be routed between these two nodes. Without loss of generality, we may assume the demands to be directed in an arbitrary way. For 1+1-protected demands, d_h refers to twice the original demand value that would have to be routed if the demand was unprotected. By adding constraints that limit the amount of flow for a protected commodity through a node or physical link to $\frac{1}{2}d_h$, it is guaranteed that at least the original demand survives any single physical link or node failure. This survivability model, called *diversification* [2], is a slight relaxation of 1+1-protection, but its solutions can often be transformed into 1+1-solutions.

From the demands, two sets K^p and K^u of protected and unprotected commodities are constructed, where $K := K^p \cup K^u$ denotes the set of all commodities. With every commodity $k \in K$ and every node $i \in V$, a net demand value $d_i^k \in \mathbb{Z}$ is associated such that $\sum_{i \in V} d_i^k = 0$. Every *protected commodity* $k \in K^p$ consists of a single 1+1-protected point-to-point demand, i.e., $d_i^k \neq 0$ only for the source and target node of the demand. In contrast, *unprotected commodities* $k \in K^u$ are derived by aggregating unprotected point-to-point demands at a common source node. Summarizing, every commodity $k \in K$ has a unique source node $s^k \in V$. Unprotected commodities may have several target nodes, whereas protected commodities have a unique target $t^k \in V$. The (undirected) emanating demand of a node $i \in V$, i. e., the total demand value starting or ending at node i, is given by $d_i := \sum_{k \in K} |d_i^k|$. The demand value d^k of a commodity is defined as the demand for k emanating from its source node, i. e., $d^k := d_{s^k}^k > 0$. Notice that for protected commodities, this value is twice the requested bandwidth to ensure survivability.

Variables.   The model comprises four classes of variables representing the flow and different capacity types. First, for a logical link $\ell \in L$ and a module $m \in M_\ell$, the logical link capacity variable $y_\ell^m \in \mathbb{Z}_+$ represents the number of modules of type m installed on ℓ. For a physical link $e \in E$, the binary physical link capacity variable $z_e \in \{0, 1\}$ indicates whether e is equipped with a fiber or not. Similarly, for a node $i \in V$ and a node module $m \in M_i$, the binary variable $x_i^m \in \{0, 1\}$ denotes whether module m is installed at node i or not. Eventually, the routing of the commodities is modeled by flow variables. In order to model diversification of protected commodities, we need fractional flow variables $f^k_{\ell,ij}, f^k_{\ell,ji} \in \mathbb{R}_+$ representing the flow for commodity $k \in K$ on logical link $\ell \in L_{ij}$ directed from i to j and from j to i, respectively. For notational convenience, $f^k_\ell := f^k_{\ell,ij} + f^k_{\ell,ji}$ denotes the total flow for $k \in K$ on $\ell \in L_{ij}$ in both directions.

In our model, a flow variable $f^k_{\ell,ij}$ for commodity k and logical link $\ell \in L_{ij}$ is omitted if any of the following conditions is satisfied: (i) $j = s^k$, (ii) $k \in K^p$ and $i = t^k$, and (iii) $k \in K^p$ and ℓ contains the source or target node of k as an inner node. The first two types of variables represent flow into the unique source node or out of the unique target node of a protected commodity. They are not generated in order to reduce cycle flows in the edge-flow formulation. For aggregated unprotected commodities, we have to allow flow from one target node to another, and thus flow out of target nodes. The third type of variables would allow flow to be routed through an end-node u of a protected commodity without terminating at that node, and then back to u on another logical link. As such routings are not desired in practice, we exclude flow variables whose logical link contains an end-node of the corresponding commodity as an inner node. Again, in the unprotected case, such variables have to be admitted because commodities may consist of several aggregated demands.

Objective and Constraints.   The objective and constraints of our mixed-integer programming model read as follows:

$$\min \quad \sum_{i \in V} \sum_{m \in M_i} \kappa^m_i x^m_i + \sum_{\ell \in L} \sum_{m \in M_\ell} \kappa^m_\ell y^m_\ell + \sum_{e \in E} \kappa_e z_e \tag{1}$$

$$\text{s.t.} \quad \sum_{j \in V} \sum_{\ell \in L_{ij}} (f^k_{\ell,ij} - f^k_{\ell,ji}) = d^k_i \qquad \begin{array}{l} \forall\, i \in V, \\ \forall\, k \in K \end{array} \tag{2}$$

$$\sum_{m \in M_\ell} C^m_\ell y^m_\ell - \sum_{k \in K} f^k_\ell \geq 0 \qquad \forall\, \ell \in L \tag{3}$$

$$\sum_{\ell \in L_i} f^k_\ell + \sum_{\ell \in \delta_L(i)} \frac{1}{2} f^k_\ell \leq \frac{1}{2} d^k \qquad \begin{array}{l} \forall\, i \in V, \\ \forall\, k \in K^p \end{array} \tag{4}$$

$$f^k_{\ell,s^k,t^k} \leq \frac{1}{2} d^k \qquad \begin{array}{l} \forall\, k \in K^p, \\ \ell = e = \{s^k, t^k\} \end{array} \tag{5}$$

$$\sum_{m \in M_i} x^m_i \leq 1 \qquad \forall\, i \in V \tag{6}$$

$$2 \sum_{m \in M_i} C_i^m x_i^m - \sum_{\ell \in \delta_L(i)} \sum_{m \in M_\ell} C_\ell^m y_\ell^m \geq d_i \qquad \forall i \in V \qquad (7)$$

$$B z_e - \sum_{\ell \in L_e} \sum_{m \in M_\ell} y_\ell^m \geq 0 \qquad \forall e \in E \qquad (8)$$

$$f_{\ell,ij}^k, f_{\ell,ji}^k \in \mathbb{R}_+, \ y_\ell^m \in \mathbb{Z}_+, \ x_i^m, z_e \in \{0,1\} \qquad (9)$$

The objective (1) aims at minimizing the total installation cost. The flow-conservation (2) and capacity constraints (3) describe a multi-commodity flow and modular capacity assignment problem on the logical layer. For protected commodities, the flow diversification constraints (4) restrict the flow through an intermediate node to half the demand value. In this way, the original demand is guaranteed to survive single node failures as well as single physical link failures, except for the direct physical link between source s^k and target t^k. This exception is covered by the variable bound (5). In fact, to reduce cycle flows in the LP, we set an upper bound of d^k and $\frac{1}{2}d^k$ on *all* flow variables for unprotected and protected commodities, respectively. The generalized upper bound constraints (6) guarantee that at most one node module is installed at each node. The node switching capacity constraints (7) ensure that the switching capacity of the network element installed at a node is sufficient for all traffic that can potentially be switched at that node. Since all traffic is counted twice, it is compared to twice the installed node capacity. Eventually, the physical link capacity constraints (8) make sure that the maximum number of modules on a physical link is not exceeded, and set the physical link capacity variables to 1 whenever a physical link is used.

Discussion of the model. There are three main challenges in solving this planning task using standard MIP techniques. First, lower granularity traffic has to be routed in integer capacity batches on the logical links, which in turn have to be supported by the physical network. This is a capacitated network design problem with modular integer capacities on the logical layer (see [3, 8, 27]) combined with an additional fixed-charge network design or Steiner tree problem (see [12, 13, 16, 17, 21, 32]) on the physical layer. Both types of problems are well studied and strong valid inequalities are known, but integrated approaches have been rarely considered. Second, the logical lightpath graph is complete and may even contain many parallel links corresponding to different paths on the fiber graph. This leads to a large number of integer capacity variables and an even larger number of flow variables. Even if these are fractional, the time required for solving the LP relaxations during the branch-and-cut process becomes a critical factor as the network size increases. Third, indirect interdependencies, e. g., between physical fibers and the switching capacity of a node module, are hard to detect for a black-box MIP solver.

Several particular design choices in our model deserve a brief discussion. First, we assume a fractional multi-commodity flow on the logical layer although SDH requires an integer routing in practice. This is motivated by our observation that in good solutions, the routing is often nearly integer even if this is not required, and by the fact that relaxing the integrality conditions on the flow variables significantly reduces the computation times. If an integral routing is indispensable, it can be obtained in a postprocessing step, which usually does not deteriorate the cost of the solutions very much if properly done. Notice that the lower bound computed for the model with fractional flow can also be used to assess the quality of the postprocessed integral solutions.

Second, we aggregate unprotected demands by their source node. Compared to using point-to-point commodities also in the unprotected case, this standard approach (see [8], for instance) reduces the number of commodities from $\mathcal{O}(|V|^2)$ to $\mathcal{O}(|V|)$, which leads to a much smaller ILP formulation. As every solution of the aggregated formulation can be transformed into a solution of the model with disaggregated commodities and vice versa, the aggregation does not affect the LP bound.

Third, we assume a predefined set of logical links for computational reasons. The consideration of all possible physical paths as logical links in combination with the practical side constraints and the survivability requirements would ask for a branch-and-cut-and-price approach with a nontrivial pricing problem already in the root node. Such an approach clearly can only be successful if the problem with a limited set of logical links can be solved efficiently. For a branch-and-price approach that deals with all possible logical links using a simplified model without survivability, the interested reader is referred to [35].

3.   Cutting Planes

Backed by theoretical results of polyhedral combinatorics, cutting plane procedures have been proven to be a feasible approach to improve the performance of mixed integer programming solvers for many single-layer network design problems. In this section we show how an appropriate selection of these inequalities can be adapted to our problem setting. Their separation and some computational results are given in Sections 4 and 5, respectively.

3.1   Cutting Planes on the Logical Layer

On the logical layer, we consider *cutset inequalities* and *flow-cutset inequalities*. These cutting planes have, for instance, been studied in [3, 8, 11, 26, 34] for a variety of network settings (e. g., directed, undirected, and bidirected link models, single or multiple capacity modules, etc.) and have been successfully used within branch-and-cut algorithms for capacitated single-layer network design problems [7, 8, 18, 33].

To be precise, the inequalities on the logical layer are valid for the polyhedron P defined by the multi-commodity flow constraints (2) and the capacity constraints (3). That is,

$$P := \text{conv} \left\{ (f, y) \in \mathbb{R}_+^{n_1} \times \mathbb{Z}_+^{n_2} \mid (f, y) \text{ satisfies (2), (3)} \right\},$$

where $n_1 := 2|K||L|$ and $n_2 := \sum_{\ell \in L} |M_\ell|$. As P is a relaxation of the model discussed in Section 2, the inequalities are also valid for that model.

We introduce the following notation. For any subset $\emptyset \neq S \subset V$ of the nodes V, let

$$L_S := \{ \ell \in L \mid \ell \in L_{ij}, \ i \in S, \ j \in V \setminus S \}$$

be the set of logical links having exactly one end-node in S. Furthermore, define $d_S^k := \sum_{i \in S} d_i^k \geq 0$ to be the total demand value to be routed over the cut L_S for commodity $k \in K$. By reversing the direction of demands and exchanging the corresponding flow variables, we may w. l. o. g. assume that $d_S^k \geq 0$ for all $k \in K$ (i.e., the commodity is directed from S to $V \setminus S$, or the end-nodes of k are either all in S or all in $V \setminus S$). This reduction is done implicitly in our code. More generally, let $d_S^Q := \sum_{k \in Q} d_S^k$ denote the total demand value to be routed over the cut L_S for all commodities $k \in Q$.

Mixed-integer rounding (MIR).   In order to derive strong valid inequalities on the logical layer we aggregate model inequalities and apply a strengthening of the resulting base inequalities that is known as *mixed-integer rounding* (MIR). It exploits the integrality of the capacity variables. Further details on mixed-integer rounding can be found in [28], for instance.

Let $a, c, d \in \mathbb{R}$ with $c > 0$ and $\frac{d}{c} \notin \mathbb{Z}$ and define $a^+ := \max(0, a)$. Furthermore, let

$$r_{a,c} := a - c(\lceil \tfrac{a}{c} \rceil - 1) > 0$$

be the remainder of the division of a by c if $\frac{a}{c} \notin \mathbb{Z}$, and c otherwise. A function $f : \mathbb{R} \to \mathbb{R}$ is called *subadditive* if $f(a) + f(b) \geq f(a + b)$ for all $a, b \in \mathbb{R}$. The MIR function

$$F_{d,c} : \mathbb{R} \to \mathbb{R} : a \mapsto \lceil \tfrac{a}{c} \rceil r_{d,c} - (r_{d,c} - r_{a,c})^+$$

is subadditive and nondecreasing with $F_{d,c}(0) = 0$. If $d/c \notin \mathbb{Z}$ then $\bar{F}_{d,c}(a) := \lim_{t \searrow 0} \frac{F_{d,c}(at)}{t} = a^+$ for all $a \in \mathbb{R}$; otherwise $\bar{F}_{d,c}(a) = a$ for all $a \in \mathbb{R}$ [33]. Because of these properties, applying this function to the coefficients of a valid inequality yields another valid inequality [29]. In particular, if a valid inequality contains continuous flow variables and integer capacity variables then applying $F_{d,c}$ to its capacity coefficients and $\bar{F}_{d,c}$ to its flow coefficients yields a valid inequality. More details and explanations can be found in [33] where it is also shown that the MIR function $F_{d,c}$ is integral if a, c, and d are integral, and that $|F_{d,c}(a)| \leq |a|$ for all $a \in \mathbb{R}$. Both properties are desirable from a numerical point of view.

Cutset inequalities.   Let L_S be a cut in the logical network as defined above. Obviously, the total capacity on the cut links L_S must be sufficient to accommodate the total demand over the cut:

$$\sum_{\ell \in L_S} \sum_{m \in M_\ell} C_\ell^m y_\ell^m \geq d_S^K. \tag{10}$$

Since all coefficients are nonnegative in (10) and $y_\ell^m \in \mathbb{Z}_+$, we can round down all coefficients to the value of the right-hand side (if larger). For notational convenience we assume from now on $C_\ell^m \leq d_S^K$ for all $\ell \in L_S$ and $m \in M_\ell$. Mixed-integer rounding exploits the integrality of the capacity variables. Setting $c > 0$ to any of the available capacities on the cut and applying the MIR-function $F_c := F_{d_S^K, c}$ to the coefficients and the right-hand side of (10) results in the *cutset inequality*

$$\sum_{\ell \in L_S} \sum_{m \in M_\ell} F_c(C_\ell^m) y_\ell^m \geq F_c(d_S^K). \tag{11}$$

A crucial necessary condition for (11) to define a facet for P is that the two subgraphs defined by the network cut are connected, which is trivially fulfilled if L contains logical links between all node pairs.

Flow-cutset inequalities.   Cutset inequalities can be generalized to flow-cutset inequalities, which have nonzero coefficients also for flow variables. Like cutset inequalities, flow-cutset inequalities are derived by aggregating capacity and flow-conservation constraints on a logical cut L_S and applying a mixed-integer rounding function to the coefficients of the resulting inequality. However, the way of aggregating the inequalities is more general. Various special cases of flow-cutset inequalities have been discussed in [3, 8, 11, 33, 34]. Necessary and sufficient conditions for flow-cutset inequalities to define a facet of P can be found in [34].

Consider fixed nonempty subsets $S \subset V$ of nodes and $Q \subseteq K$ of commodities. Assume that logical link $\ell \in L_S$ has end-nodes $i \in S$ and $j \in V \setminus S$. We will denote by $f_{\ell,-}^k := f_{\ell,ji}^k$ inflow into S on ℓ while $f_{\ell,+}^k := f_{\ell,ij}^k$ refers to outflow from S on ℓ. We now construct a base inequality to which a suitable mixed-integer rounding function will be applied. First, we obtain a valid inequality from the sum of the flow conservation constraints (2) for all $i \in S$ and all commodities $k \in Q$:

$$\sum_{\ell \in L_S} \sum_{k \in Q} (f_{\ell,+}^k - f_{\ell,-}^k) \geq d_S^Q$$

Given a subset $L_1 \subseteq L_S$ of cut links and its complement $\bar{L}_1 := L_S \setminus L_1$ with respect to the cut, we can relax the above inequality by omitting the inflow variables and by replacing the flow by the capacity on all links in L_1:

$$\sum_{\ell \in L_1} \sum_{m \in M_\ell} C_\ell^m y_\ell^m + \sum_{\ell \in \bar{L}_1} \sum_{k \in Q} f_{\ell,+}^k \geq d_S^Q. \tag{12}$$

Again we may assume $C_\ell^m \leq d_S^K$ for all $\ell \in L_1$ and $m \in M_\ell$.

Let $c > 0$ be the capacity of a module available on the cut and define $F_c := F_{d_S^Q, c}$ and $\bar{F}_c := \bar{F}_{d_S^Q, c}$. Applying these functions to the base inequality (12) results in the *flow-cutset inequality*

$$\sum_{\ell \in L_1} \sum_{m \in M_\ell} F_c(C_\ell^m) y_\ell^m + \sum_{\ell \in \bar{L}_1} \sum_{k \in Q} f_{\ell,+}^k \geq F_c(d_S^Q). \tag{13}$$

Notice that $\bar{F}_c(1) = 1$, so the coefficients of the flow variables remain unchanged. This inequality can be generalized to a flow-cutset inequality also containing inflow-variables [33]. By choosing $L_1 = L_S$ and $Q = K$, inequality (13) reduces to the cutset inequality (11).

3.2 Cutting Planes on the Physical Layer

If the fixed-charge cost values κ_e are zero then the corresponding variables z_e can be assumed equal to 1 in any optimal solution. If, on the other hand, this cost is positive, the variables will take on fractional values in linear programming (LP) relaxations. By the demand routing requirements, we know that certain pairs of nodes have to be connected not only on the logical layer but also on the physical layer. Consequently, the variables z_e have to satisfy certain connectivity constraints. Note that information of the physical layer is combined with the demands here, skipping the intermediate logical layer.

Connectivity problems have been studied on several occasions, in particular in the context of the Steiner Tree problem and fixed-charge network design, e. g., [10, 32]. Let $S \subset V$ be a set of nodes and $\delta(S)$ the corresponding cut in the physical network. If some demand has to cross the cut then the inequality

$$\sum_{e \in \delta(S)} z_e \geq 1 \tag{14}$$

ensures that at least one physical link is installed on the cut. If a protected demand has to cross the cut, the right-hand side can even be set to 2 because the demand must be routed on at least two physically disjoint paths.

If the demand graph (defined by the network nodes and edges corresponding to traffic demands) has p connected components (usually $p = 1$) then

$$\sum_{e \in E} z_e \geq |V| - p \tag{15}$$

is valid, because the installed physical links can consist of at most p connected components as well, each one being at least a tree. If protected demands exist and the demand graph is connected, inequality (15) can be strengthened by setting the right hand side to $|V|$. If protected demands exist for all demand end nodes, this inequality is however dominated by the inequalities (14) for all demand end nodes as single node subsets.

4.   Separation and Implementation

We used the branch-and-cut framework SCIP 0.90 [1] with CPLEX 10.1 [20] as the underlying LP solver to tackle the multi-layer problem introduced in Section 2. At every node of the search tree, SCIP applies various primal heuristics to compute feasible solutions, as well as built-in and application-specific separators to cut off fractional solutions. For the cutting planes described in Section 3, three *separation problems* are addressed: Given a fractional point, find a cutset inequality (11), a flow-cutset inequality (13) or one of the fixed-charge inequalities (14) and (15) cutting off this point, or decide that no such inequality exists. After calling all of its own and all user-defined separators, SCIP selects the best inequalities based on criteria such as the Euclidean distance to the current fractional point and the degree of orthogonality to the objective function. In the following we will describe the separation algorithm that we have implemented for each of the considered inequalities.

4.1   Cutset Inequalities

As explained in Section 3.1, a cutset inequality (11) is completely determined by its base inequality (10), which in turn depends only on the choice of the cut in the logical network. Our separation procedure works as follows:

1 Choose a subset S of nodes and compute the corresponding cut links L_S.

2 Compute the base inequality (10) corresponding to this logical cut.

3 For all different capacity coefficients c occurring in the base inequality, compute the cutset inequality (11) using the function $F_{d_S^K, c}$ and check it for violation.

In this way, the task reduces to finding a suitable cut in the logical network. In general, it is $\mathcal{NP}$-hard to find a cut where the cutset inequality is maximally violated, see [7]. We apply a heuristic shrinking procedure to the logical network, similar to what has been done in [7, 18, 33] for single-layer problems. Define the link weights $w_\ell := s_\ell + \pi_\ell$ where s_ℓ and π_ℓ are the slack and the dual value of the capacity constraint (3) for link ℓ with respect to the current LP solution. We iteratively shrink links with the largest weight w_ℓ, aggregating parallel logical links if necessary, until k nodes are left. Using a value of k between 2 and 6, we enumerate all cuts in the shrunken graph. The definition of w_ℓ is based on the heuristic argument that a cutset inequality is most likely to be violated if the slack of the base inequality is small. We thus want to keep links in the shrunken graph that have a small slack in the capacity constraints, i. e., we have to shrink links with a large slack s_ℓ. Since many capacity constraints are usually tight in the LP solutions, many slacks are 0. For those we use the dual values as a second sorting criterion. In addition to the described shrinking procedure we check all cutset inequalities for violation that correspond to single-node cuts, that is $S = \{i\}$ for all $i \in V$.

4.2 Flow-cutset Inequalities

For separating a flow-cutset inequality, a suitable set S of nodes, a subset Q of commodities, a capacity c, and a partition $(L_1, \bar{L}_1)$ of the cut links L_S have to be chosen. We apply two different separation heuristics. Both restrict the separation procedure to special subclasses of flow-cutset inequalities. However, already with this restriction a large number of violated inequalities is found.

The first heuristic considers commodity subsets Q that consist of a single commodity $k \in K$ and node-sets S consisting of one or two end-nodes of k. After fixing S and k and choosing an available capacity $c > 0$ on the cut, a partition of the cut links that maximizes the violation for flow-cutset inequalities is obtained by setting

$$L_1 := \left\{ \ell \in L_S \mid \sum_{m \in M_\ell} F_c(C_\ell^m)\bar{y}_\ell^m \leq \sum_{k \in Q} \bar{f}_{\ell,+}^k \right\}, \tag{16}$$

where $(\bar{f}, \bar{y})$ are flow and capacity values on the logical graph in the current LP solution, see Atamtürk [3]. The calculation of L_1 is done in linear time.

The second, more time-consuming heuristic finds a most violated flow-cutset inequality for a fixed single commodity $k \in K$ and a fixed capacity c, see [3]. The crucial observation is that once k and c are fixed, the two values compared in (16) are known, and thus the partition of the potential cut links into L_1 and $\bar{L}_1$. The only remaining question is which links are part of the cut. This question can be answered in polynomial time by defining the logical link weights $w_\ell := \min\{\sum_{m \in M_\ell} F_c(C_\ell^m)\bar{y}_\ell^m, \bar{f}_{\ell,+}^k\}$ and searching for a minimum-weighted cut between the end-nodes of the commodity with respect to these weights (introducing artificial super-source and super-target nodes if necessary).

Table 1.1.   Network instances used for testing cutting planes

instance	$\|V\|$	$\|E\|$	$\|L\|$	$\|H\|$	$\|M_i\|$	$C_\ell^1, C_\ell^2, C_\ell^3$	physical cost?
Germany17	17	26	674	121	16	1, 4, 16	no
Germany17-fc	17	26	564	121	16	1, 4, 16	yes
Ring15	15	16	184	78	5	16, 64, 256	no
Ring7	7	8	32	10	5	16, 64, 256	no

4.3   Physical Layer Cutset Inequalities

The single tree inequality (15) can simply be added to the initial MIP formulation. The number of components of the demand graph is determined using depth-first search.

The physical cutset inequalities (14) can be separated using a min-cut algorithm. The weight of a physical link e is set to its capacity value $\bar{z}_e$ in the current LP solution, which is exactly its contribution to the left-hand side of the inequality if the link is part of the cut. Then a minimum cut with respect to these weights is searched between every pair of nodes, and the corresponding cutset inequality is tested for violation. Assuming all demands are either protected or unprotected, the right-hand side of the inequality does not depend on the cut, and thus this procedure is exact, i. e., a violated inequality exists if and only if this algorithm finds it. In addition, we test all cuts defined by single nodes $i \in V$ in each iteration, as these cuts turned out to be quite important.

5.   Computational Results

5.1   Test Instances and Settings

For our computational experiments we used the network instances summarized in Table 1.1. In addition to the number of nodes, physical, and logical links, the number $\|H\|$ of communication demands is given from which the commodities were constructed ($\|K\| = \|V\| - 1$ if all demands are unprotected and $\|K\| = \|H\|$ if all demands are protected). Further we report the number $\|M_i\|$ of node modules installable at each node and the size of the installable logical link modules. Eventually, Table 1.1 indicates whether the instance has physical link cost or not. The first three instances are realistic scenarios provided by Nokia Siemens Networks, whereas the small ring network Ring7 has been constructed out of the larger instance Ring15 in order to study the effect of the cutting planes on the number of branch-and-cut nodes needed to prove optimality.

Germany17 and Germany17-fc are based on a physical 17-node German network available at SNDlib [31]. In both networks, the set of admissible

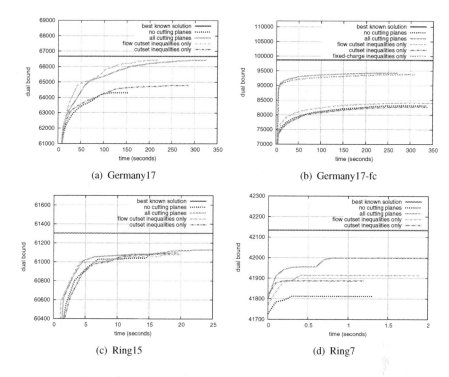

Figure 1.1.   Unprotected demands: dual bound at the root node

logical links consists of 3–5 short paths in the physical network between each pair of nodes. Ring15 consists of a physical ring with a chord, representing a regional subnetwork connected to a larger national network. The set of logical links consists basically of the two possible logical links for each node pair, one in each physical direction of the ring. Ring7 has been constructed from Ring15 by successively removing nodes with the smallest emanating demand value. Because in our ring instances, every node is a demand end-node and the demand graph is connected, nearly all physical links have to be used in any feasible solution. We thus do not consider ring variants with physical link cost because doing so would basically add a constant to the objective function. In all networks, up to three capacity modules corresponding to 2.5, 10, and 40 Gbit/s can be installed on each logical link, depending on its physical path length.

All computations were done on a Linux-operated machine with a 2×3 GHz Intel P4 processor and 2 GB of memory. In a first series of test runs, we assumed unprotected demands with physical fibers supporting $B = 40$ wavelengths. In a second series, we made all demands 1+1-protected, assuming $B = 80$ wavelengths in order to allow for feasible solutions with the doubled demand values. We have used extended versions of the MIP-based heuristics

Table 1.2.   Number of violated cutset inequalities (11), flow-cutset inequalities (13), and fixed-charge inequalities (14) found in the root node of branch-and-bound tree without separating SCIP's Gomory and c-mir cuts

	# cuts unprotected			# cuts protected		
instance	cutset	flow-cutset	fixed-charge	cutset	flow-cutset	fixed-charge
Germany17	37	1521	-	4	940	-
Germany17-fc	34	1046	35	7	844	20
Ring15	66	652	-	26	489	-
Ring7	41	98	-	15	24	-

from [30] in all tests. To reduce the complexity of the problem, we also applied preprocessing and probing techniques, as described in [22].

5.2   Unprotected Demands

As cutting planes are primarily thought to increase the lower bound of the LP-relaxation, we first consider the effect of the different types of cutting planes on the lower bound at the branch-and-bound root node. We separated each of the classes cutset inequalities, flow-cutset inequalities and fixed-charge inequalities on its own as well as all together. Figure 1.1 shows the improvement over time of the lower bound in the root node of the search tree for all test instances. The solid red line at the top marks the value of the best known solution, which cannot be exceeded by the dual bound curves. The line "no cutting planes" refers to the dual bound with SCIP's built-in general-purpose cuts only.

It can be seen that in the two Germany17 instances and on the small ring network, our cutting planes reduce the gap between the lower bound and the best known solution at the root node by 50–75%. In all three problem instances, flow-cutset inequalities performed better than cutset inequalities, which is in contrast to the results presented by Raack et al. [33] for a single-layer problem. There might be several reasons for this effect. A good candidate is the structural difference between single-layer networks and the logical layer in multi-layer problems: the logical layer graph (V, L) contains edges between almost all node pairs, whereas only a few links cross a cut in single layer graphs. Further, we have implemented our cutting planes as callbacks in SCIP, whereas in [33], CPLEX was used as the underlying branch-and-cut framework, which means that different general-purpose cutting planes have been used.

For the problem Germany17-fc with physical cost, most of the optimality gap comes from the z_e variables whose values are highly fractional and close to zero in the solution of the LP-relaxation. A major part of this gap is closed by the fixed-charge inequalities that operate on the physical layer. Of course,

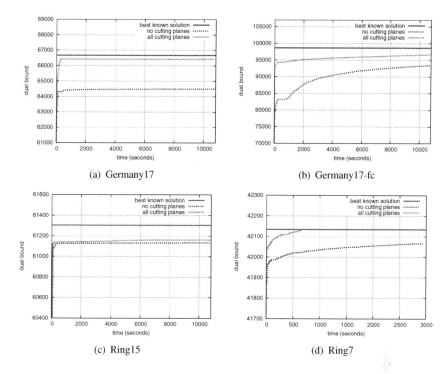

Figure 1.2. Unprotected demands: dual bound during 3h test runs

the contribution of these inequalities changes with the ratio of the cost of the physical fiber links on the one hand and the logical wavelength links and the node hardware on the other hand.

In contrast to these three instances, the problem-specific cutting planes have only a marginal effect on the dual bound for Ring15 compared to SCIP's built-in general-purpose cuts. This is probably due to the fact that already in SCIP's default settings, the dual bound at the end of the root node is within 0.4 % of the optimal solution value, so there is not much room for improvement at all. We also observed that on this instance, our cuts seem to interfere with the c-mir and Gomory cuts separated by SCIP. Both classes are based on a mixed-integer rounding procedure similar to the one described in Section 3. With these two classes of cuts disabled in SCIP, our inequalities could reduce the relative distance between the root dual bound and the best known solution from 3.8 % to 0.4 %, thus achieving the same dual bound as SCIP's cutting planes. The number of violated cutting planes found in this setting is reported in Table 1.2 for all instances.

In a second study, we have investigated the lasting effect of the cutting planes on the dual bound in longer computations. Figure 1.2 shows the development of the dual bound with and without all cutting planes from Section 3 during a computation with a time limit of 3 hours for all four test instances, compared to the best known solution. Similarly to most of SCIP's own cutting planes, we separated our inequalities only at the root node of the branch-and-cut tree.

By applying all separators we could solve the problem Ring7 to optimality within 10 minutes, whereas without our cutting planes the computation was aborted after nearly one hour with a nonzero optimality gap due to the memory limit of 2 GB. The size of search tree was 1.2 million unexplored nodes at this point (and 4 million explored nodes). Figure 1.4 shows the relative gap between the dual bound and the best known solution (defined as (*bestsol* − *dual*)/*dual*), which overestimates the relative distance of the dual bound to the optimal solution value. As the figure shows, this gap could be reduced by factor 10 on Germany17 and by factor 2 on Germany17-fc by raising the lower bound only. It can be seen from Figures 1.2 and 1.4 that the dual bounds obtained with our cutting planes are very close to their maximum possible value. In fact, as also the upper bound improved in both cases, the relative gap between the dual bound and the best solution found in that specific run (as opposed to the best solution known at all) could be improved from 4 % to 0.36 % and from 12.4 % to 3.1 %, respectively. For Ring15 the improvement of the dual bound by the cutting planes was much smaller than for the other instances, probably for the reasons discussed above.

5.3   Protected Demands

In the case of protected demands, we first of all would like to point out that the problem size drastically increases compared to the unprotected case. Instead of $|V| - 1$ commodities, $|H|$ commodities have to be routed, increasing the number of variables and constraints considerably. Consequently, solving the initial LP relaxation, as well as reoptimizing the LP after adding a cutting plane or a branching constraint, takes more time with protection than without.

With 1+1 protected demands, the cutting planes have only a marginal effect of the dual bound. Figure 1.3 shows the increase of the dual bound in a three hour test run with and without cutting planes (again, the solid red line at the top indicates the best known solution value). It can be seen that the dual bound always increases, but only by a very limited amount. Figure 1.4 shows the corresponding change in the relative gap between the dual bound after three hours and the best known solution. More detailed investigations revealed that the small progress is mainly due to the strength of the general-purpose c-mir and Gomory cuts generated by SCIP. Experiments where these cuts were turned off showed that our inequalities still contribute significantly to closing the optimality gap at the root node. Table 1.2 shows the number of violated inequalities found at the root node in this setting. Only slightly lower

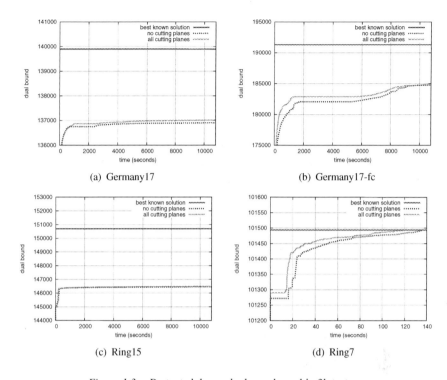

Figure 1.3. Protected demands: lower bound in 3h test runs

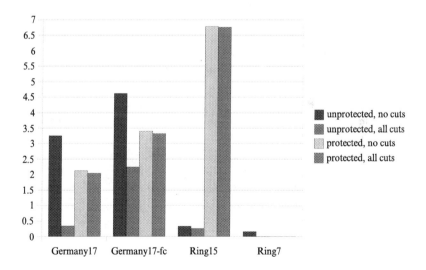

Figure 1.4. Relative gap (in %) between best dual bound after 3h and best known solution

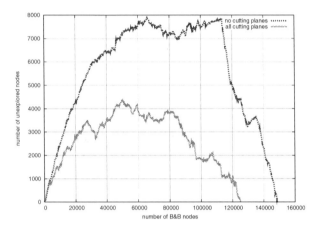

Figure 1.5.   Number of unexplored branch-and-cut nodes on the protected Ring7 network

numbers of violated inequalities are found with c-mir and Gomory cuts turned on, but their impact on the dual bound is limited in such a case, cf. Figure 1.3.

The strength of the general-purpose cuts originates from the potential to include all inequalities from the original formulation, as well as cutting planes added later in the solution process. In contrast, our cutting planes only take capacity and flow conservation constraints into account. The inclusion of survivability requirements into the generation of cutset and flow-cutset inequalities might accelerate the increase of the lower bound compared to SCIP. For this, the polyhedral studies of Bienstock and Muratore [9] and of Balakrishnan et al. [5] for single layer survivability network design could be a good starting point. We suspect that cuts that make use of such problem-specific information will outperform the general-purpose cuts of SCIP, as in the unprotected case.

Nevertheless, the cutset inequalities and flow-cutset inequalities seem to have a lasting effect on the performance of the branch-and-bound algorithm as can be shown for the small ring network Ring7. This instance could be solved to optimality in both cases. But as Figure 1.5 shows, the maximum number of unexplored nodes in the search tree was roughly halved by our cutting planes, even though they were added only in the root node. Moreover, optimality was proven about 13 % faster (cf. Figure 1.3(d)) and with 16 % less nodes.

6.   Conclusions

In this work, we have presented a mixed-integer programming model for a two-layer SDH/WDM network design scenario. The model includes many practically relevant side constraints like many parallel logical links, various bit-rates, node capacities, and survivability with respect to physical node and link failures. To accelerate the solution process for this planning task, we have applied a variety of network design specific cutting planes that are known to be strong in single-layer network design to either of the two layers, namely cutset inequalities and flow-cutset inequalities on the logical layer and fixed-charge inequalities on the physical one. These cutting planes have been used as callbacks within the branch-and-cut framework SCIP and tested on several realistic planning scenarios provided by Nokia Siemens Networks.

With unprotected demands, our cutting planes significantly raised the lower bounds until close to the optimal solution value. With 1+1 protection against physical failures, they also helped to improve the dual bounds, but less than in the unprotected case. This is partly due to the fact that with protection, many of our cutting planes were already found by SCIP alone, and partly due to the impact of the survivability constraints on the structure of the polyhedron. We expect that adapting previous results for survivable single-layer network design to the multi-layer setting could further raise the lower bound in these cases. Moreover, new classes of specific multi-layer cuts have to be found for multi-layer problems with protected demands.

References

[1] T. Achterberg. *Constraint Integer Programming*. PhD thesis, Technische Universität Berlin, 2007. http://opus.kobv.de/tuberlin/volltexte/2007/1611/.

[2] D. Alevras, M. Grötschel, and R. Wessäly. A network dimensioning tool. ZIB Technical Report SC-96-49, Konrad-Zuse-Zentrum für Informationstechnik Berlin, 1996.

[3] A. Atamtürk. On capacitated network design cut-set polyhedra. *Mathematical Programming*, 92:425–437, 2002.

[4] G. Baier, T. Engel, A. Autenrieth, and P. Leisching. Mehrperiodenplanung optischer Transportnetze. In *7. ITG-Fachtagung Photonische Netze, Leipzig, Germany*, volume 193, pages 153–160. VDE-Verlag, April 2006.

[5] A. Balakrishnan, T. Magnanti, J. Sokol, and Y. Wang. Modeling and solving the single facility line restoration problem. Technical report, MIT Press, 1998.

[6] P. Belotti, A. Capone, G. Carello, F. Malucelli, F. Senaldi, and A. Totaro. Design of multi-layer networks with traffic grooming and statistical multiplexing. In *Proceedings of the 3rd International Network Optimization Conference (INOC 2007), Spa, Belgium*, April 2007.

[7] D. Bienstock, S. Chopra, O. Günlük, and C.Y. Tsai. Mininum cost capacity installation for multicommodity flows. *Mathematical Programming*, 81:177–199, 1998.

[8] D. Bienstock and O. Günlük. Capacitated network design – polyhedral structure and computation. *INFORMS Journal on Computing*, 8(3):243–259, 1996.

[9] D. Bienstock and G. Muratore. Strong inequalities for capacitated survivable network design problems. *Mathematical Programming*, 89(1):127–147, 2000.

[10] S. Chopra. On the spanning tree polyhedron. *Operations Research Letters*, 8:25–29, 1989.

[11] S. Chopra, I. Gilboa, and S. T. Sastry. Source sink flows with capacity installation in batches. *Discrete Applied Mathematics*, 86:165–192, 1998.

[12] S. Chopra and M. Rao. The Steiner tree problem I: Formulations, compositions and extension of facets. *Mathematical Programming*, 64(2):209–229, 1994.

[13] S. Chopra and M. Rao. The Steiner tree problem II: Properties and classes of facets. *Mathematical Programming*, 64(2):231–246, 1994.

[14] G. Dahl, A. Martin, and M. Stoer. Routing through virtual paths in layered telecommunication networks. *Operations Research*, 47(5):693–702, 1999.

[15] M. Dawande, R. Gupta, S. Naranpanawe, and C. Sriskandarajah. A traffic-grooming algorithm for wavelength-routed optical networks. *INFORMS Journal on Computing*, 2006. To appear.

[16] M. Grötschel, C. Monma, and M. Stoer. Facets for polyhedra arising in the design of communication networks with low-connectivity constraints. *SIAM Journal on Optimization*, 2(3):474–504, August 1992.

[17] M. Grötschel, C. Monma, and M. Stoer. Design of survivable networks. volume Networks of *Handbooks in Operations Research and Management Science*, chapter 10, pages 617–672. North-Holland, Amsterdam, 1993.

[18] O. Günlük. A branch-and-cut algorithm for capacitated network design problems. *Mathematical Programming*, 86:17–39, 1999.

[19] H. Höller and S. Voss. A heuristic approach for combined equipment-planning and routing in multi-layer SDH/WDM networks. *European Journal of Operational Research*, 171(3):787–796, June 2006.

[20] ILOG CPLEX Division, 889 Alder Avenue, Suite 200, Incline Village, NV 89451, USA. *CPLEX 10.1 Reference Manual*, 2006.

[21] T. Koch and A. Martin. Solving steiner tree problems in graphs to optimality. *Networks*, 32(3):207–232, 1998.

[22] A. M. C. A. Koster, S. Orlowski, C. Raack, G. Baier, and T. Engel. Single-layer cuts for multi-layer network design problems. ZIB Report ZR-07-21, Konrad-Zuse-Zentrum für Informationstechnik Berlin, August 2007.

[23] A. M. C. A. Koster and A. Zymolka. Minimum converter wavelength assignment in all-optical networks. In *Proceedings of ONDM 2004*, pages 517–535, Ghent, Belgium, 2004. The 8th IFIP Working Conference on Optical Network Design & Modelling.

[24] A. M. C. A. Koster and A. Zymolka. Tight LP-based lower bounds for wavelength conversion in optical networks. *Statistica Neerlandica*, 61(1):115–136, 2007.

[25] E. Kubilinskas and M. Pióro. An IP/MPLS over WDM network design problem. In *Proceedings of the 2nd International Network Optimization Conference (INOC 2005), Lisbon, Portugal*, volume 3, pages 718–725, March 2005.

[26] T. L. Magnanti and P. Mirchandani. Shortest paths, single origin-destination network design and associated polyhedra. *Networks*, 33:103–121, 1993.

[27] T. L. Magnanti, P. Mirchandani, and R. Vachani. Modelling and solving the two-facility capacitated network loading problem. *Operations Research*, 43:142–157, 1995.

[28] H. Marchand and L. A. Wolsey. Aggregation and mixed integer rounding to solve MIPs. *Operations Research*, 49(3):363–371, 2001.

[29] G. Nemhauser and L. A. Wolsey. *Integer and Combinatorial Optimization*. John Wiley & Sons, 1988.

[30] S. Orlowski, A. M. C. A. Koster, C. Raack, and R. Wessäly. Two-layer network design by branch-and-cut featuring MIP-based heuristics. In *Proceedings of the 3rd International Network Optimization Conference (INOC 2007), Spa, Belgium*, April 2007.

[31] S. Orlowski, M. Pióro, A. Tomaszewski, and R. Wessäly. SNDlib 1.0–Survivable Network Design Library. In *Proceedings of the 3rd International Network Optimization Conference (INOC 2007), Spa, Belgium*, April 2007. http://sndlib.zib.de.

[32] F. Ortega and L. A. Wolsey. A branch-and-cut algorithm for the single-commodity, uncapacitated, fixed-charge network flow problem. *Networks*, 41:143–158, 2003.

[33] C. Raack, A. M. C. A. Koster, S. Orlowski, and R. Wessäly. Capacitated network design using general flow-cutset inequalities. ZIB Report 07-14, Konrad-Zuse-Zentrum für Informationstechnik Berlin, June 2007. Submitted to Networks.

[34] C. Raack, A. M. C. A. Koster, and R. Wessäly. On the strength of cut-based inequalities for capacitated network design polyhedra. ZIB-Report 07-08, Konrad-Zuse-Zentrum für Informationstechnik Berlin, June 2007.

[35] S. Raghavan and D. Stanojević. WDM optical design using branch-and-price. Robert H. Smith School of Business, University of Maryland, April 2007.

Chapter 2

OPTIMAL MULTI-CHANNEL ASSIGNMENTS IN VEHICULAR AD-HOC NETWORKS

Hanan Luss and Wai Chen
Telcordia Technologies, Piscataway, New Jersey 08854
hluss@telcordia.com, wchen@research.telcordia.com

Abstract: This paper focuses on establishing a communications path among an ordered sequence of moving nodes, representing vehicles. A channel is used to send information from one node to the next in the sequence on a wireless link. The set of available channels may differ from one node to the next node. Each of the available channels at a node can be used for receiving information from its predecessor node in the sequence or for transmitting information to its successor node in the sequence. However, the same channel cannot be used at a node for both receiving and transmitting information. We present algorithms that determine an optimal sequence of channels that establishes a communications path from the first node to the farthest node possible. We present a depth-first search algorithm that uses a "look-ahead" channel selection rule in order to decrease backtracking. We also present an algorithm that requires only a single pass through the sequence of nodes by identifying optimal channel assignments in subsequences of nodes without a need for backtracking. The latter algorithm requires computational effort that is proportional to the number of nodes in the ordered sequence of nodes.

Keywords: Channel assignments; mobile ad-hoc networks; vehicular ad-hoc networks; wireless communication.

1.   INTRODUCTION

A mobile ad-hoc network (MANET) is formed by multiple moving nodes equipped with wireless transceivers. The mobile nodes communicate with each other through multi-hop wireless links, where every node can transmit and receive information. Mobile ad-hoc networks have become increasingly important in areas where deployment of communications infrastructure is difficult. Such networks are used for communications in battle fields, natural disasters, fleets on the ocean, and so forth. Numerous papers have been published on this topic. Representative references include Lin and Gerla (1997), Lin and Liu (1999), and McDonald and Znati (1999). Xu, et al. (2006) describe a framework for multi-channel management in such networks. Earlier related work has focused on channel assignment for traditional packet radio networks with no mobility. Representative studies include Cidon and Sidi (1989), Ephremides and Truong (1990), and Lu (1993).

A vehicular ad-hoc network (VANET) refers to a mobile ad-hoc network designed to provide communications among nearby vehicles and between vehicles and nearby fixed equipment. Chisalita and Shahmehri (2002), Chen and Cai (2005) and Chen, et al. (2006) present a networking approach that uses local peer group architecture in order to establish communications among vehicles. The use of multiple channels allows for simultaneous communication sessions at the logical layer among a network of moving vehicles without partitioning available resources at the physical layer. Thus, the use of multiple channels would significantly increase the network throughput. Existing channel assignment methods use distributed decisions where each vehicle determines which channel to use based on local information on channel availability at neighboring vehicles.

In this paper, we focus on establishing a communications path among an ordered sequence of moving nodes, representing vehicles, using global information of channel availability. The ordered sequence of nodes can be viewed as a directed linear tree topology where a link interconnects a node only to its successor node in the ordered sequence. A channel is used to send information from one node to the next on a wireless link. The set of available channels may differ from one node to the next due to external interferences, other ongoing communications that involve some of these nodes, different equipment used at the nodes, and the like. Each of the available channels at a node can be used for receiving information from its predecessor node in the sequence or for transmitting information to its successor node in the sequence. However, the same channel cannot be used at a node for both receiving and transmitting information. Note that the channel used to transmit information from a node is the channel used to receive information at its successor node in the ordered sequence of nodes. The first node in the sequence, or some nearby system, has as input the information of the set of available channels at each of the nodes in the ordered sequence.

A sequence of channel assignments is called optimal if it establishes a communications path from the first node in the ordered sequence of nodes to the last node in that sequence, or, if such a feasible sequence of channels does not exist, it establishes a communications path from the first node to the farthest node possible. We present two algorithms that determine an optimal sequence of channel assignments. The first algorithm uses a depth-first search starting from the first node in the sequence. We present two versions of the Depth-First Search Algorithm, where the second version improves upon the channel selection rule at a node by using a "look ahead" scheme that may decrease the amount of backtracking, and thus reduce the computational effort. The second algorithm, referred to as the One-Pass Algorithm, requires only a single pass through the sequence of nodes by identifying optimal channel assignments in subsequences of nodes without a need for backtracking, resulting in computational effort that is proportional to the number of nodes in the ordered sequence of nodes.

2.   THE MULTI-CHANNEL ASSIGNMENT PROBLEM

Consider a sequence of nodes i, $i = 1, 2, ..., N$, where the nodes represent moving vehicles. The ordered sequence of nodes can be viewed as a directed linear tree topology where a link interconnects node i only to node $i+1$ in the ordered sequence. The sets S_i denote the channels available at node i, $i = 1$, 2, ..., N. The number of channels in each of the sets is expected to be quite small, say, between 2 to 4.

Consider the example in Figure 1 with $N = 5$. Each node has a set of channels available for receiving or transmitting information where the term channel is used as a logical entity. It may represent a frequency band (under FDMA), an orthogonal code (under CDMA), and so forth. The set of available channels may differ from one node to the next due to external interferences, other ongoing communications that involve some of these nodes, different equipment used at the nodes, and so forth. For example, node 1 can use channels 1 and 2 as depicted by the set $S_1 = \{1, 2\}$, and node 2 can use channels 1, 2 and 4 as depicted by the set $S_2 = \{1, 2, 4\}$. The information of all sets S_i, $i = 1, 2, 3, 4$ and 5, is provided as input to the channel assignment algorithms. Typically, the input will be available at node 1, however, it may be available at some other location, e.g., at nearby fixed devices. The channel assignment methods are generic and independent of the location of the input.

Each of the available channels at any node i can be used for receiving information from node i-1 or for transmitting information to node $i+1$. However, the same channel cannot be used at a node i for both receiving and transmitting information. The objective of the channel assignment algorithms is to establish a communications path from node 1 to the farthest node possible in the sequence of ordered nodes. Of course, if possible, the established communications path should reach node N, however, this may not always be possible.

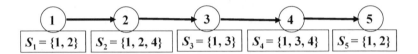

Figure 1. An Ordered Sequence of Nodes and the Available Channels

Let T_i denote the set of available channels at node i and at node $i+1$, i.e., $T_i = S_i \cap S_{i+1}$. The sets T_i for $i = 1, 2, \ldots, N\text{-}1$ are readily computed from the sets S_i for $i = 1, 2, \ldots, N$. Thus, in the example of Figure 1, $T_1 = \{1, 2\}$, $T_2 = \{1\}$, $T_3 = \{1, 3\}$, and $T_4 = \{1\}$. Since node i must use on its outgoing link a channel that is in S_i and node $i+1$ must use on its incoming link a channel that is in S_{i+1}, node i can interconnect with node $i+1$ only on channels that are in the set T_i. In addition, node i must use different channels for receiving information from node $i\text{-}1$ and for transmitting information to node $i+1$.

Let f represent index for channels. Let $x_{fi} = 1$ if channel f is selected at node i to interconnect node i to node $i+1$, and let $x_{fi} = 0$ otherwise. From the discussion above, $x_{fi} = 0$ if $f \notin T_i$. Let $z_i = 1$ if a channel is assigned at node i to interconnect node i to node $i+1$, and let $z_i = 0$ otherwise. The multi-channel assignment problem is formulated as follows.

The Multi-Channel Assignment Problem

$$Max[\ \sum_{i=1}^{N-1} z_i\ ] \tag{1}$$

$$z_i = \sum_{f \in T_i} x_{fi}, \quad i = 1, 2, \ldots, N-1 \tag{2}$$

$$x_{fi} = 0, \quad f \notin T_i, i = 1, 2, \ldots, N-1 \tag{3}$$

$$x_{fi} + x_{f,i+1} \le 1, \quad f \in T_i \cap T_{i+1}, i = 1, 2, \ldots, N-1 \tag{4}$$

$$z_{i+1} \le z_i, \quad i = 1, 2, \ldots, N-1 \tag{5}$$

$$x_{fi}, z_i = 0, 1, \quad f \in T_i, i = 1, 2, \ldots, N-1. \tag{6}$$

Constraints (2) express decision variables z_i in terms of decision variables x_{fi}, while constraints (3) state that channel f cannot be assigned at node i if $f \notin T_i$. Constraints (4) assure that a node cannot receive and transmit information on the same channel. Constraints (5) state that a channel can be assigned at node $i+1$ only if a channel is assigned at node i. Constraints (6) define the 0-1 decision variables that are not forced to 0 by constraints (3). Note that by constraints (2) and (6), the number of channels assigned at a node is at most one. Given the constraints above, objective function (1) maximizes the number of assigned channels, which is equivalent to assigning channels to the farthest possible node in the ordered sequence of nodes. Problem (1)-(6) is an integer program with significant structure. A similar formulation without variables z_i can also be provided. In Section 3, we present the Depth-First Search Algorithm for the Multi-Channel Assignment Problem that is not necessarily polynomial as it may require backtracking. In Section 4, we present the One-Pass Algorithm that finds an optimal solution in polynomial time; in particular, for given sets T_i, the computational effort is $O(N)$.

We present below several important observations that will be exploited by the algorithms.

- If each of the sets T_i has two or more channels, a sequence of channels that connects node 1 to node N can readily be assigned. Moreover, this still holds if either T_1 or T_{N-1} (but not both) have a single channel. Consider an example of five nodes with $T_1 = \{1\}$, $T_2 = \{1, 2\}$, $T_3 = \{1, 2\}$ and $T_4 = \{1, 2\}$. Then, we simply select channel 1 from T_1 and T_3 and channel 2 from T_2 and T_4.

- The challenge is to determine optimal assignments when some of the sets T_i include only one channel. Suppose $T_1 = \{1, 2\}$, $T_2 = \{1, 2\}$, $T_3 = \{1\}$ and $T_4 = \{1, 2\}$. Then, we must select channel 1 from T_1. If channel 2 is selected from T_1, we must select channel 1 from T_2 which, in turn, would prevent selection of channel 1 from T_3.

- Each of the sets T_i can be limited to at most three channels. This is easy to see through the following example. Suppose $T_1 = \{1\}$, $T_2 = \{1, 2, 3\}$ and $T_3 = \{2\}$. Although channels 1 and 2 cannot be selected from T_2, there is always another channel available for selection in T_2.

- If set T_i does not include any channel, a feasible communications path cannot be established beyond node i. Other infeasible cases can also be identified. For example, if sets $T_i = T_{i+1} = \{1\}$, or if sets $T_{i-1} = \{1\}$, $T_i = \{1, 2\}$ and $T_{i+1} = \{2\}$, a feasible communications path cannot be established beyond node $i+1$.

3.   THE DEPTH-FIRST SEARCH ALGORITHM

The search algorithm constructs a tree, while using backtracking when necessary. We first describe the basic version of the algorithm. From here on we use the notation f_i to denote the channel used for transmitting information from node i to node $i+1$. Let $FEAS_i$ denote the set of channels that can be used for interconnecting node i with node $i+1$, given that node i-1 communicates with node i on channel f_{i-1}. Since node i must use different channels for receiving information from node i-1 and for transmitting information to node $i+1$, $FEAS_1 = T_1$ and $FEAS_i = T_i - f_{i-1}$ for $i > 1$ (obviously, if $f_{i-1} \notin T_i$, then $FEAS_i = T_i$).

Starting from node 1, we select a channel $f_1 \in FEAS_1$. The selection can be done randomly or using any other arbitrary rule. Thereafter, the set T_2 is updated by deleting channel f_1 from T_2 (no update is needed if $f_1 \notin T_2$). The search then continues, attempting to assign a channel that would connect node 2 to node 3. The search continues until a channel successfully interconnects node N-1 to node N, in which case a communications path is established from node 1 to node N, or until at some node $i < N$ $FEAS_i = \varnothing$. In the latter case, backtracking in the search tree is needed. If at some stage $FEAS_1 = \varnothing$, node N cannot be reached for the specified sets S_i, and the search terminates with a communications path that connects node 1 to the farthest node possible.

We illustrate the search algorithm by solving the example shown in Figure 1. We compute the sets $T_i = S_i \cap S_{i+1}$. The resulting search tree is shown in Figure 2.

Starting with node 1, we select a channel from the set T_1 as the candidate channel on the link from node 1 to node 2, using some specified rule, e.g., random selection, the largest or smallest channel index, and so forth. Suppose we select channel 1. Channel 1 is now deleted from the set T_2 since the channel used on the outgoing link from node 2 must differ from the channel used on the input to the node. Since the set T_2 is now empty, there is no available channel to connect node 2 to node 3. So the search on this branch of the tree failed as depicted by in the right part of the tree in Figure 2.

We then backtrack to node 1 and delete channel 1 from set T_1. We now select the remaining channel in T_1, i.e., channel 2, to connect node 1 to node 2 as depicted in the left part of the tree in Figure 2.

Since channel 2 is not in T_2, the set T_2 remains unchanged. Next, we select channel 1 to connect node 2 to node 3. Channel 1 is deleted now from T_3 and we select channel 3 to connect node 3 to node 4. Since channel 3 is not in T_4, the set T_4 remains unchanged. We now select channel 1 to connect node 4 to node 5.

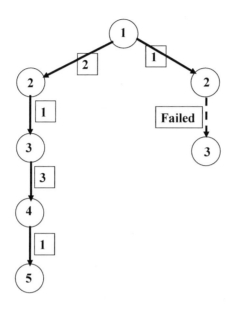

Figure 2. Example of the First-Depth Search Algorithm

We found an optimal sequence of channels that establishes a communications path that connects node 1 to node 5. The path uses channel 2 on the link from node 1 to node 2, channel 1 on the link from node 2 to node 3, channel 3 on the link from node 3 to node 4, and channel 1 on the link from node 4 to node 5.

The search algorithm can be improved by using a "look-ahead" rule to select a channel from among the channels in the set $FEAS_i$. We first examine whether the set $FEAS_i$ includes a channel that is not in the set T_{i+1}, and if so we select such a channel. This selection does not decrease the selection options at node $i+1$ since it does not affect $FEAS_{i+1}$; hence, it may lead to less backtracking in the search tree. If such a channel does not exist, we use the same selection rule as before.

Figure 3 illustrates the search algorithm by resolving the example shown in Figure 1.

We start by selecting a channel from the set $FEAS_1 = T_1$ as the candidate channel on the link from node 1 to node 2. Since channel 2 is the only channel in $FEAS_1$ that is not in T_2, we select channel 2. By using this "look-ahead" rule we did not select channel 1 which would lead to a failure to establish a connection from node 2 to node 3 as previously demonstrated in

Figure 2. The remaining steps of the search shown in Figure 3 are the same as those shown in the left part of the tree in Figure 2. The search with the "look-ahead" rule found the same optimal solution found by the basic search, but did not require any backtracking.

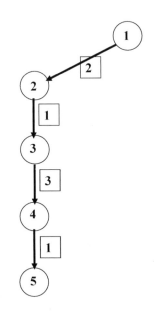

Figure 3. Example of the First-Depth Search Algorithm Using the "Look-Ahead" Rule

Note, however, that the search with the "look-ahead" rule may still require backtracking. This can be easily demonstrated by adding another node to the example of Figure 1, referred to as node 1A, between node 1 and node 2 with the set $S_{1A} = S_1$. Now, since $T_1 = T_{1A} = \{1, 2\}$, starting at node 1, the "look-ahead" rule does not provide any guidance at node 1. If channel 2 is selected at node 1, channel 1 must be selected at node 1A, and no channel would be available to connect node 2 to node 3. Backtracking on the search tree would then be required.

As mentioned in Section 2, we may limit the number of channels in each of the sets T_i to no more than three. Although not guaranteed, this will often reduce the effort spent on backtracking. We should attempt to keep channels that are likely to be selected by the "look ahead" rule; e.g., keep in T_i channels that are not in T_{i+1}.

We now present the search algorithm with the "look-ahead" rule.

The Depth-First Search Algorithm

Initialization

Compute sets $T_i = S_i \cap S_{i+1}$ for $i = 1, 2, ..., N-1$.

If T_i has more than three channels, keep only three. If available, keep in T_i channels that are not in T_{i+1}.

$N \leftarrow$ minimum[N, smallest i with $T_i = \varnothing$] (a communications path cannot be established from node 1 to a node beyond the revised N).

Initialize sets $TEMP = BEST = \varnothing$ ($TEMP$ is the interim sequence of channels from node 1 to the currently reached node, and $BEST$ records the longest sequence of channels found since the beginning of the search).

Initialize $i = 1$.

End of initialization.

While $i < N$

$FEAS_i = T_i - f_{i-1}$ (for $i = 1$, $FEAS_i = T_i$).

If $FEAS_1 = \varnothing$, STOP (the set $BEST$ provides the longest possible sequence of channels; at this stopping point the optimal communications path does not reach node N).

If $FEAS_i = \varnothing$ ($i > 1$), backtracking is needed:

Begin

If the sequence of channels in $TEMP$ is longer than that in $BEST$, then update $BEST \leftarrow TEMP$.

Update $T_{i-1} \leftarrow T_{i-1} - f_{i-1}$.

Update $TEMP \leftarrow TEMP - f_{i-1}$.

Update $i \leftarrow i-1$.

Go to beginning of the while loop.

End.

$FEAS_i \neq \varnothing$: Select channel on next link.

Begin

Select channel for transmitting from node i to node $i+1$ as follows:

If available, select some $f_i \in FEAS_i \backslash T_{i+1}$ (i.e., f_i is in $FEAS_i$ but not in T_{i+1}); otherwise, select some $f_i \in FEAS_i$.

Update $TEMP \leftarrow TEMP + f_i$.

Update $i \leftarrow i+1$.

If $i < N$, go to beginning of the while loop.

End.

End of while loop.

BEST ← *TEMP* (at this stopping point the set *BEST* provides a communications path that connects node 1 to node N).

STOP.

End of Depth-First Search Algorithm.

Each of the sets T_i can be obtained by sorting sets S_i and S_{i+1} and merging the sorted sets. Thus, the N-1 sets T_i are computed at an effort of $O(Nhlogh)$ where h is the number of channels in the largest set S_i. Recall that if all sets T_i include two or more channels, a sequence that connects node 1 to node N is obtained through arbitrary selection. The Depth-First Search Algorithm will then find a solution without any backtracking. Nevertheless, in general, the computational effort may grow exponentially with N, where in the worst case the entire search tree will be constructed. The computational effort (after computing the sets T_i and keeping up to three channels in each) is at most $O(3^N)$. We illustrate this through an example in which there is no path that connects node 1 to node N. Let $T_{N-3} = \{1\}$, $T_{N-2} = \{1, 2\}$ and $T_{N-1} = \{2\}$, and let each of the other sets T_i include three channels. Then, the search tree will explore (almost) all possible $O(3^N)$ assignments while failing to find a connection from node N-1 to node N.

4.   THE ONE-PASS ALGORITHM

The One-Pass Algorithm does not build a search tree. Instead, it looks for the first node, say node m, along the ordered sequence of nodes that has a single channel in the set T_m and assigns the channel in T_m to the link connecting nodes m to node $m+1$. The assigned channel is deleted from set T_{m-1}. The algorithm then proceeds backwards to node m-1 and arbitrarily assigns a channel from set T_{m-1} to the link connecting node m-1 to node m. The algorithm continues in that manner until a channel is assigned to the link connecting node 1 to node 2. Assignment of channels to the links along the path that connects node 1 to node $m+1$ is completed. Note that the backwards assignment of channels to interconnect the subsequence of nodes 1 to $m+1$ is guaranteed to succeed since each of the sets T_i for $i = m$-1, m-2, ..., 1 has at least two channels.

If node $m = N$-1, the algorithm terminates since a path is established from node 1 to node N. Suppose $m < N$-1. The assigned channel on the link into node $m+1$ is deleted from set T_{m+1} and the algorithm searches for the next node in the ordered sequence beyond node m, say node n, that has a single channel in the set T_n. The algorithm then assigns channels to the subsequence of links that connect node n to node $n+1$, node $n-1$ to node n, ..., node $m+1$ to node $m+2$.

The algorithm continues to assign channels to such subsequences until a path that connects node 1 to node N is established or until some updated set, say T_p, is encountered with $T_p = \varnothing$. In the latter case, a communications path can be established only from node 1 to node p.

Note that a subsequence with node N as its last node may have more than one channel in T_{N-1}, in which case the algorithm arbitrarily assigns one of these channels to the link connecting node $N-1$ to node N.

Figure 4 illustrates the One-Pass Algorithm by resolving the example shown in Figure 1.

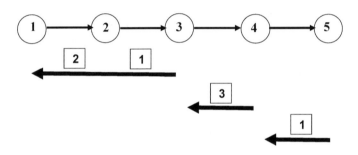

Figure 4. Example of the One-Pass Algorithm

Recall that in Figure 1 $S_1 = \{1, 2\}$, $S_2 = \{1, 2, 4\}$, $S_3 = \{1, 3\}$, $S_4 = \{1, 3, 4\}$, and $S_5 = \{1, 2\}$ resulting in $T_1 = \{1, 2\}$, $T_2 = \{1\}$, $T_3 = \{1, 3\}$, and $T_4 = \{1\}$.

Starting from node 1, set $T_2 = \{1\}$ is the first set with a single channel. Therefore, moving backwards, we select channel 1 on the link from node 2 to node 3, update T_1 by deleting channel 1 from T_1, which results in $T_1 = \{2\}$, and select channel 2 on the link from node 1 to node 2. The selection of channels on this subsequence is depicted in Figure 4 by the arrow pointed backwards from node 3 to node 1. Channel 1 is also deleted from set T_3, leading to $T_3 = \{3\}$.

Next, starting from node 3, $T_3 = \{3\}$ is the first set with a single channel. Therefore, the second subsequence includes only a single link and we select channel 3 on the link from node 3 to node 4. The selection of channels on this subsequence is depicted by the arrow pointed backwards from node 4 to node 3. Since T_4 does not include channel 3, no update is needed.

Finally, starting from node 4, node 5 is reached, and channel 1 is selected from node 4 to node 5.

Note that the One-Pass Algorithm found the same solution provided above by either version of the Depth-First Search Algorithm. However, the One-Pass Algorithm finds an optimal sequence in an effort that is proportional to the number of nodes, i.e., in an effort of $O(N)$ (after computing the sets T_i). The sequence found will generate a communications path from node 1 to node N, or, if not possible, from node 1 to the farthest node possible along the ordered sequence of nodes. Consider again the example with $T_{N-3} = \{1\}$, $T_{N-2} = \{1, 2\}$, $T_{N-1} = \{2\}$, where each of the other sets T_i includes three channels. The One-Pass Algorithm will first find a path from node 1 to node N-2, followed by a path from node N-2 to node N-1 (using channel 2). Finally, it will terminate since the updated set T_{N-1} will be empty. The total effort spent on finding a path from node 1 to node N-1 is $O(N)$. On the other hand, as discussed before, the Depth-First Search Algorithm will terminate after spending an effort of $O(3^N)$.

Let $|T_i|$ denote the number of channels in the set T_i. We conclude this section by presenting the One-Pass Algorithm. Note that in this algorithm we do not realize computational savings by deleting channels from the sets T_i that have more than three channels.

The One-Pass Algorithm

Initialization

$T_i = S_i \cap S_{i+1}$ for $i = 1, 2, \ldots, N$-1.

$N \leftarrow$ minimum[N, smallest i with $T_i = \varnothing$] (a communications path cannot be established from node 1 to a node beyond the revised N).

$MIN = 1$.

End of initialization.

Subsequence Channel Assignments

$MAX = [i:$ Smallest $i \geq MIN$ with $|T_i| = 1]$; if no $|T_i| = 1$ set $MAX = N$-1.

Select some $f_{MAX} \in T_{MAX}$.

$i = MAX$.

While $i > MIN$

$T_{i-1} \leftarrow T_{i-1} - f_i$.

Select some $f_{i-1} \in T_i - 1$.

$i \leftarrow i$-1.

End of while loop.

End of subsequence channel assignments.

Termination Checks

$MIN \leftarrow MAX+1$.

If $MIN = N$, STOP (assigned channels f_1, f_2, ..., f_{N-1} provide a communications path from node 1 to node N).

$T_{MIN} \leftarrow T_{MIN} - f_{MIN-1}$.

If $T_{MIN} = \varnothing$, STOP (assigned channels f_1, f_2, ..., f_{MIN-1} provide a communications path to the farthest node possible, node MIN).

Go to beginning of Subsequence Channel Assignments.

End of termination checks.

End of One-Pass Algorithm.

5. FINAL REMARKS

We presented two algorithms that determine an optimal sequence of channel assignments that establish a communications path from node 1 to the farthest node possible in a specified ordered sequence of nodes, where the sets of available channels S_i may be node-dependent. For given sets T_i, the One-Pass Algorithm assigns channels in a computational effort $O(N)$, whereas the Depth-First Search Algorithm is not polynomial due to possible backtracking. Hence, for the problem of channel assignments for an ordered sequence of nodes, the One-Pass Algorithm is clearly more efficient. Future research may consist of developing algorithms of multiple channel assignments to more complicated problems where, for example, vehicles may be involved in multiple sessions at the same time. Possible extensions of the algorithms presented in this paper to such problems should be explored. It is an open question which of these algorithms could be effectively extended to more complex problems that cannot be modeled as a single ordered sequence of nodes, but would instead be represented by more general network topologies.

ACKNOWLEDGEMENT

This work was supported by Toyota InfoTechnology Center.

REFERENCES

Chen, W., and Cai, S., 2005, Ad hoc peer-to-peer network architecture for vehicle safety communications, *IEEE Communications Magazine*, April, 100-107.

Chen, W., Cai, S., Chennikara-Varghese, J., Hikita, T., and Lee, J., 2006, Dynamic local peer group organizations for vehicle communications, *Proceedings of Vehicle-to-Vehicle Communications Workshop (V2VCOM 2006) co-located with ACM MobiQuitous*, July 21, San Jose, California.

Chisalita, I., and Shahmehri, N., 2002, A peer-to-peer approach to vehicular communication for the support of traffic safety applications, *Proceedings of the 5th IEEE Conference on Intelligent Transportation Systems*, Singapore, September 3-6, 336-341.

Cidon, I., and Sidi, M., 1989, Distributed assignment algorithms for multi-hop packet radio networks, *IEEE Transactions on Computer* **38**: 1353-1361.

Ephremides, A., and Truong, T., 1990, Scheduling broadcasts in multi-hop radio networks, *IEEE Transactions on Communications* **38**: 456-460.

Lin, C. R., and Gerla, M., 1997, Adaptive clustering for mobile wireless networks, *IEEE Journal on Selected Areas in Communication* **15**: 1265-1275.

Lin, C. R., and Liu, M. J. S., 1999, QoS routing in ad hoc wireless networks, *IEEE Journal on Selected Areas in Communications* **17**: 1426-1438.

Lu, L., 1993, Distributed code assignment for CDMA packet radio networks, *IEEE/ACM Transactions on Networking* **1**: 668-677.

McDonald, A. B., and Znati, T. F., 1999, A mobility-based framework for adaptive clustering in wireless ad-hoc networks, *IEEE Journal on Selected Areas in Communications* **17**: 1466-1487.

Xu, C., Liu, K., Yuan, Y., and Liu, G., 2006, A novel multi-channel based framework for wireless IEEE 802.11 ad hoc networks, *Asian Journal of Information Technology* **5**: 44-47.

Chapter 3

THE LABEL-CONSTRAINED MINIMUM SPANNING TREE PROBLEM

Yupei Xiong
Sysmind LLC
38 Washington Road, Princeton Junction, NJ 08550, USA
yupei72@yahoo.com

Bruce Golden
R.H. Smith School of Business, University of Maryland
College Park, MD 20742, USA
bgolden@rhsmith.umd.edu

Edward Wasil
Kogod School of Business, American University
Washington, DC 20016, USA
ewasil@american.edu

Si Chen
College of Business and Public Affairs, Murray State University
Murray, KY 42071, USA
si.chen@murraystate.edu

Abstract   Given a positive integer K and a connected, undirected graph G whose edges are labeled (or colored) and have weights, the label-constrained minimum spanning tree (LCMST) problem seeks a minimum weight spanning tree with at most K distinct labels (or colors). In this paper, we prove that the LCMST problem is NP-complete. Next, we introduce two local search methods to solve the problem. Then, we present a genetic algorithm which gets comparable results, but is much faster. In addition, we present two mixed integer programming formulations for the LCMST problem. We compare these on some small problem instances. Finally, we introduce a dual problem.

Keywords: Local search; genetic algorithm; NP-complete; spanning trees; mixed integer programming.

1.   Introduction

Computing a minimum weight spanning tree (MST) is one of the fundamental and classic problems in graph theory. Given an undirected graph G with a nonnegative weight on each edge, the MST of G is the spanning tree of G with the minimum total edge weight among all possible spanning trees [1]. This problem and many variants such as the k shortest spanning tree problem [3], the problem of updating a minimum spanning tree [7], the minimum diameter spanning tree problem [5], and the most and least uniform spanning trees problem [1, 4] have been studied extensively. Spanning tree problems have applications in many areas, including network design, VLSI, and geometric optimization.

The minimum label spanning tree (MLST) problem was defined in [2]. In the MLST problem, we are given an undirected graph with labeled (or colored) edges as input. Each edge has a single label (or color) and different edges can have the same label (or color). The goal is to find a spanning tree with the minimum number of distinct labels. In other words, in the MLST problem, we seek to construct a spanning tree whose edges are as similar as possible. The MVCA (Maximum Vertex Covering Algorithm) heuristic was developed to solve the MLST problem [6] and its worst-case performance has been examined [6, 8, 10]. In addition, two effective genetic algorithms were used to solve the MLST problem [9, 11].

In communications networks, there may be many types of communications media including fiber optics, cable, microwave, and telephone lines. Communication along each edge requires a pre-specified media type. If we can reduce the number of different media types in the spanning tree, we reduce the complexity of the communications process. On the other hand, there is also a weight (or distance) associated with each edge. In the label-constrained minimum spanning tree (LCMST) problem, we are trying to find a spanning tree that has minimum total weight while using at most K distinct types of communications media. This is somewhat more realistic than the MLST problem, since the LCMST problem considers the total weight as well as the number of labels in the spanning tree. We now formally define the problem.

Definition (LCMST problem). Given an undirected labeled graph $G = (V, E, L)$, where V is the set of nodes, E is the set of edges, and L is the set of labels, a weight function $w(e)$ for all $e \in E$, and a positive integer K, find a spanning tree T of G such that the total weight $W_T = \sum_{e \in T} w(e)$ is minimized and the number of distinct labels of T, denoted by $|L_T|$, is no more than K.

In the next section, we show that the LCMST problem is NP-complete. In Section 3, two local search methods are developed and applied to solve the LCMST problem. In Section 4, a genetic algorithm is proposed. In Section 5, computational results are presented and analyzed. In Section 6, a dual problem is discussed. Concluding observations and remarks are provided in Section 7.

2.   NP-completeness

Theorem 1. The Label-Constrained Minimum Spanning Tree (LCMST) problem is NP-complete.

Proof. We first show that LCMST belongs to NP. Given an instance of the problem, we consider an arbitrary spanning tree T. The verification algorithm checks that T contains at most K labels and that the total cost of T is no more than a given positive number C. This process can certainly be done in polynomial time.

To prove that LCMST is NP-complete, we show that MLST $\leq_P$ LCMST, which means that MLST is polynomial-time reducible to the LCMST problem. The MLST problem is known to be NP-complete [2]. Let $G = (V, E, L)$ be an instance of the MLST problem. It has a minimum label spanning tree T with K labels. We construct an instance of the LCMST problem as follows. We extend G to the complete graph $G' = (V, E', L')$, where E' contains E and L' contains L. For each $e \in E$, we define its weight $w(e)$ to be 0. For each $e \notin E$, we define its weight $w(e)$ to be 1. For each $e \notin E$, we also define its label to be different from all other labels in G'.

We now show that graph G has a minimum label spanning tree with K labels if and only if graph G' has a minimum weight spanning tree with K labels. Suppose that graph G has a minimum label spanning tree T with K labels. Then, each edge in T has weight 0 in G'. Thus, T has total weight of 0. This tree T is the minimum weight spanning tree in G'. Conversely, suppose that graph G' has a minimum weight spanning tree T with K labels and total weight 0, then all the edges in T are contained in E. Thus, T is also a spanning tree in G with K labels.

Therefore, LCMST is NP-complete.   ∎

3.   Local Search Methods

In this section, two local search methods are introduced. Given a labeled graph G with a weight for each edge, G has a minimum label spanning tree T_1 and a minimum weight spanning tree T_2. Suppose T_1 has n_1 distinct labels and T_2 has n_2 distinct labels. In the LCMST problem, a positive number K is given. If $K < n_1$, then the LCMST problem has no solution. If $K > n_2$, then the optimal solution to the LCMST problem is T_2, which can be obtained in polynomial time. So, in this paper, we will assume that $n_1 \leq K \leq n_2$.

3.1   Encoding

The solution to the LCMST problem is a spanning tree. Each spanning tree has a label set. Conversely, given any label set $A \in 2^L$, we can obtain a subgraph G_A of G induced by A. If the subgraph G_A is connected and spans all the nodes in V, a minimum weight spanning tree can be found by Prim's algorithm in polynomial time. From this, we can determine the total weight of the spanning tree. In the subgraph G_A, the minimum weight spanning tree may not be unique, but the total weight is unique. Thus, we can build a map $f : 2^L \rightarrow \mathbb{R}$ as follows. For any $A \in 2^L$, if G_A is connected and spans V, then $f(A)$ is the total weight of a minimum weight spanning tree of G_A; otherwise, $f(A) = \infty$. In Figure 3.1, an example which illustrates how the function f works for different label sets in 2^L is presented. In particular, an input graph and three label sets with their corresponding f values are shown. Let $L_K \subset 2^L$ represent the collection of all label sets with K labels. We restrict f to L_K. Then the goal of the LCMST problem is to find $A^* \in L_K$, such that $f(A^*) = \min_{A \in L_K} f(A)$. By this well-defined map f, it is sufficient to consider a label set $A \in L_K$ as a solution to the LCMST problem.

3.2   Local Search 1 (LS1)

In local search 1 (LS1), we begin with an arbitrary label set $A \in L_K$. Suppose $A = \{a_1, a_2, \ldots, a_K\}$. Then, we start a replacement loop as follows. We first replace a_1 by some label $b_1 \in L - A$. To do this, we check each label in $L - A$. If we can make an improvement, then we find b_1 such that $f(A - \{a_1\} + \{b_1\}) = \min_{b \in L-A} f(A - \{a_1\} + \{b\})$. Then, we set $A = A - \{a_1\} + \{b_1\}$. Otherwise, we set $b_1 = a_1$. Next, we seek to replace a_2 by some label $b_2 \in L - A$. To do this, we check each label in $L - A$ and, if we can make an improvement, we obtain $f(A - \{a_2\} + \{b_2\}) = \min_{b \in L-A} f(A - \{a_2\} + \{b\})$. Then, we set $A = A - \{a_2\} + \{b_2\}$. Otherwise, we set $b_2 = a_2$. We continue with this replacement routine until we replace a_K by some suitable b_K (possibly, $b_K = a_K$). After one replacement loop, we improve the label set to $A = \{b_1, b_2, \ldots, b_K\}$. We repeat until no improvement can be made between two consecutive replacement loops.

3.3   Local Search 2 (LS2)

In local search 2 (LS2), we begin with an arbitrary label set $A \in L_K$. Suppose $A = \{a_1, a_2, \ldots, a_K\}$. Then, we start a replacement loop as follows.

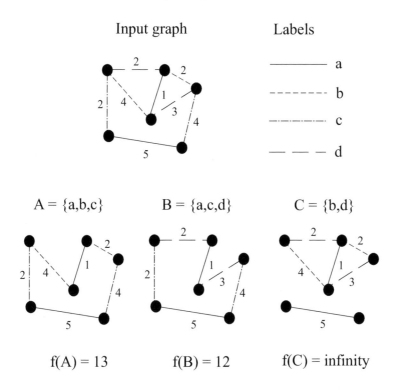

Figure 3.1. An example of encoding

For each $b \in L - A$, we first set $A = A + \{b\}$ and let $a_{K+1} = b$. So, A now has $K + 1$ labels. To maintain K labels, we have to remove one label from A. We check all the labels a_i for $1 \leq i \leq K + 1$ and find a_j such that $f(A - \{a_j\}) = \min_{1 \leq i \leq K+1} f(A - \{a_i\})$. Then, we set $A = A - \{a_j\}$. After one replacement loop, we observe, hopefully, some improvement in the label set A. We repeat until no improvement can be made between two consecutive replacement loops.

If we compare the two methods of local search, we obtain the following result.

Theorem 2. A label set A cannot be improved by LS1 if and only if A cannot be improved by LS2.

Proof. Suppose a label set A cannot be improved by LS1. Then, for any label $a \in A$ and $b \notin A$, we know $f(A - \{a\} + \{b\}) \geq f(A)$. If we apply LS2 to the label set A, we first add a label $b \notin A$, and then remove some label $a \in A$. We obtain the label set $A + \{b\} - \{a\} = A - \{a\} + \{b\}$. We still have $f(A + \{b\} - \{a\}) = f(A - \{a\} + \{b\}) \geq f(A)$. So, the label A cannot be improved by LS2. Conversely, if a label set A cannot be improved by LS2, from the above logic, since $A + \{b\} - \{a\} = A - \{a\} + \{b\}$, we also know that A cannot be improved by LS1.   ∎

3.4   Running Time Analysis

In the LCMST problem, we are given a labeled graph $G = (V, E, L)$ and a positive integer K. Let $|V| = n$, $|E| = m$, and $|L| = \ell$. We consider only complete graphs here. So, $m = O(n^2)$. For each $A \in 2^L$, we use Prim's algorithm to find a minimum weight spanning tree in the subgraph G_A. Prim's algorithm requires $O(m + n \lg n) = O(n^2)$ running time. So, $f(A)$ requires $O(n^2)$ running time. Both LS1 and LS2 run $f(A)$ at most $K|L| = K\ell$ times in each replacement loop. Thus, the running time of each replacement loop in LS1 and LS2 is $O(K\ell n^2)$.

4.   Genetic Algorithm

Given previous success in applying genetic algorithms to the MLST problem [9, 11], we thought a genetic algorithm might also work well for the LCMST problem. In this section, we introduce a genetic algorithm (GA) to solve the LCMST problem. The encoding of the GA is the same as that in local search. Each chromosome is a label set in L_K. Each label is a gene.

4.1   Crossover

Given two parent chromosomes P and Q, one child C is created by the crossover operation. First, we set $R = P \bigcup Q$ and we get a subgraph G_R induced by R. We also set $C = \phi$. Second, we apply Prim's algorithm to the subgraph G_R. In Prim's algorithm, we begin with a random node $v \in V$. Then, we grow a tree by adding the least-weight edge, one at a time, until the tree spans all the nodes in G_R. Each time we add edge e, e has a label c. If $c \notin C$, we set $C = C \bigcup \{c\}$. So, as the tree is growing, so is the label set C. Once $|C|$ reaches K, the label set is restricted to C and Prim's algorithm is applied over the induced subgraph G_C. Finally, we obtain the output, child C, and the minimum weight spanning tree in the subgraph G_C. Of course, C may not be a feasible solution. If an infeasible solution is obtained, we select another start node and run Prim's algorithm again to find another child. If each start node results in infeasibility, $f(C) = \infty$. If K is large, the child C is more likely to be feasible. Crossover is illustrated in Figure 3.2. In this figure, the two parents are $P = \{a, b, c\}$ and $Q = \{a, d, e\}$ and $K = 3$. Note that $f(P) = 23$, $f(Q) = 21$. The union of the two parents is $R = \{a, b, c, d, e\}$. In Figure 3.3, Prim's algorithm starts at the right-most node. The output child is a feasible solution $C = \{b, c, e\}$ and $f(C) = 17$. In Figure 3.4, Prim's algorithm starts

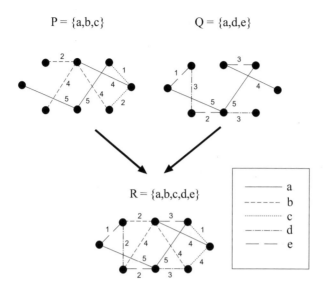

Figure 3.2. An example of crossover: $f(P) = 23$, $f(Q) = 21$.

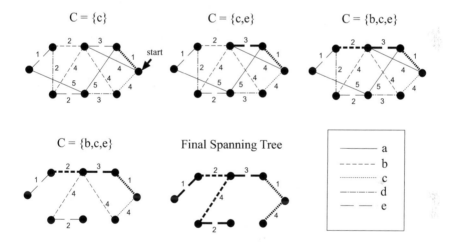

Figure 3.3. Prim's algorithm to get a feasible solution C and $f(C) = 17$, where $K = 3$.

at the left-most node. The output child is an infeasible solution $C = \{b, d, e\}$ and $f(C) = \infty$. The crossover operation is very fast with a running time that is the same as that of Prim's algorithm.

To make the procedure more efficient, we implement the queen-bee crossover in our GA. In each generation, we find the best chromosome QB and designate it the queen-bee chromosome. Then, we only allow crossover between QB and other chromosomes.

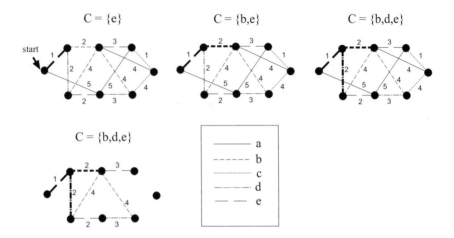

Figure 3.4.   Prim's algorithm to get an infeasible solution C and $f(C) = \infty$, where $K = 3$.

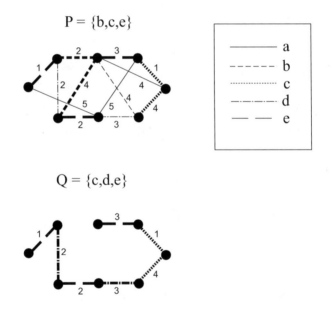

Figure 3.5.   An example of mutation: $f(Q) = 16$.

4.2   Mutation

Given one chromosome P, the mutation operation creates a new chromosome Q. Suppose $P = \{p_1, p_2, \ldots, p_K\}$. First, we randomly select $b \in L - P$. Second, we check each p_i for $1 \le i \le K$ to see if the replacement of p_i by b obtains a better solution. If it does for some p_i, then we set $Q = P - \{p_i\} + \{b\}$.

If it does not, then we set $Q = P$. We take the child from Figure 3.3 and denote it as the input P in Figure 3.5. We note that $f(P) = 17$. In Figure 3.5, we illustrate mutation. Here, label b is replaced by label d and we obtain an improved solution $Q = \{c, d, e\}$ with $f(Q) = 16$. The mutation operation requires that Prim's algorithm is run at most K times. It is, therefore, slower than the crossover operation.

4.3 Building Each Generation

Suppose the population size is p (we set $p = 20$ in our computational tests). It is easy to randomly generate p chromosomes as the initial generation. To be more specific, we randomly generate K labels and check to see if the induced subgraph is connected and spans V. If it is, then we have a feasible chromosome. If it is not, then we try again. This process continues until we obtain p feasible chromosomes. (Randomness seems to ensure a sufficient level of diversity in the starting population.) To build the next generation, we find the queen-bee chromosome in the current generation. Then, we perform crossover between QB and the $p - 1$ other chromosomes. The crossover of QB and another chromosome P outputs a solution Q. This solution may be infeasible since Prim's algorithm may select the "wrong" labels. For example, in Figure 3.4, labels e, b, and then d are chosen in Prim's algorithm. Since the induced subgraph G_C where $C = \{b, d, e\}$ does not span V, $f(C) = \infty$. The better solution of P and Q becomes the child, which is feasible. Then, we perform mutation for each of the children and obtain $p - 1$ "mutated" children. These children, along with QB, comprise the p chromosomes for the next generation. We stop building generations if the queen-bee chromosome of three consecutive generations does not change. After the last generation, we make a final improvement. We find the queen-bee chromosome QB and execute one replacement loop of LS1 on QB. From the above discussion, we observe that the population size p is the only parameter of GA.

5. Computational Results

5.1 Small Cases

In this section, we report on computational results for small problem instances. For each of these instances, we solve a Mixed Integer Program (MIP) to obtain the optimal solution. This MIP is presented in detail in Appendix A. The computational results for $n = 20, 30, 40$, and 50 are presented in Tables 3.1 to 3.4. The coordinates of the nodes and the label matrix for the instance examined in Table 3.1 are provided in Appendix B.

Table 3.1.   Computational results for a graph with $n = \ell = 20$

K	MIP Value	MIP Time(sec)	LS1 Gap(%)	LS2 Gap(%)	GA Gap(%)
2	6491.35	3.30	0.00	0.00	0.00
3	5013.51	7.70	0.00	0.00	0.00
4	4534.67	81.20	0.00	0.00	0.00
5	4142.57	277.56	0.00	0.00	0.00
6	3846.50	216.00	0.00	0.00	0.00
7	3598.05	97.97	0.00	0.00	0.00
8	3436.57	65.56	0.00	0.00	0.00
9	3281.05	74.36	0.00	0.00	0.00
10	3152.05	30.34	0.00	0.00	0.00
11	3034.01	9.77	0.00	0.00	0.00

LS1, LS2, and GA are implemented on a Pentium 4 PC at 1.80 GHz with 256 MB RAM. The MIP formulation is implemented using OPL Studio 3.7 on a Pentium 3 PC at 993 MHz with 512 MB RAM.

For each instance, we test all possible K values. For each combination of instance and K value, we report the MIP (optimal) solution value and the percent gap (i.e., percent above optimality) for LS1, LS2, and GA. We point out that the gap tends to be larger when K is small. This is because there are a relatively small number of feasible solutions for small K. For larger K, all three heuristics work very well. They obtain the optimal solution or the gap is about 1%. For each input, we run LS1 five times and output the best result. The same is true for LS2. Both LS1 and LS2 are very fast on small instances. They each require about one second, on average, for each input (i.e., five runs). The GA is faster; it requires less than half a second for each input (i.e., a single run). The MIP running times are provided in Tables 3.1 to 3.4. When $n = \ell = 50$ (in Table 3.4), these running times are already quite large (we stopped at $K = 8$ because for $K > 8$ the MIP could not find the optimal solutions within 72 hours). We are unable to solve the MIP for instances with more than 50 nodes.

5.2   Large Cases

In this section, we report on computational results for large problem instances ($n \geq 100$). We consider at most two values of K for each combination of n and ℓ. In particular, we use $K = 20$ and $K = 40$. For each instance, we run LS1 and LS2 five times and output the best result. The results are presented in Table 3.5. The GA gap is the percent above the better of LS1 and LS2 for each problem. Running times are presented in Table 3.6. From these two tables, we observe that GA is much faster than LS1 and LS2. Although the solution quality of GA is not as high as that of LS1 and LS2, the gap is, typically, under 1%.

Table 3.2.   Computational results for a graph with $n = \ell = 30$

K	MIP Value	MIP Time(sec)	LS1 Gap(%)	LS2 Gap(%)	GA Gap(%)
3	7901.81	20.83	0.00	0.00	0.00
4	6431.58	38.89	0.00	0.00	0.00
5	5597.36	30.47	0.00	0.00	0.00
6	5106.94	174.20	0.00	0.00	0.00
7	4751.00	464.30	0.00	0.46	0.00
8	4473.11	1229.48	0.00	0.00	0.00
9	4196.71	579.63	0.00	0.00	0.00
10	3980.99	931.83	0.52	0.52	0.00
11	3827.23	279.73	0.00	0.00	1.41
12	3702.08	297.36	0.00	0.23	0.00
13	3585.42	90.78	0.00	0.00	0.00

Table 3.3.   Computational results for a graph with $n = \ell = 40$

K	MIP Value	MIP Time(sec)	LS1 Gap(%)	LS2 Gap(%)	GA Gap(%)
3	11578.61	9651	0.00	0.00	0.00
4	9265.42	5305	1.72	2.56	1.72
5	8091.45	5841	0.00	0.00	0.75
6	7167.27	1844	0.00	0.00	2.53
7	6653.23	2904	0.13	0.00	0.13
8	6221.63	10744	0.00	0.00	0.00
9	5833.39	16487	0.00	0.00	0.48
10	5547.08	8830	0.00	0.00	0.00
11	5315.92	13641	0.00	0.00	0.00
12	5164.14	109284	0.00	0.00	0.00

Table 3.4.   Computational results for a graph with $n = \ell = 50$

K	MIP Value	MIP Time(sec)	LS1 Gap(%)	LS2 Gap(%)	GA Gap(%)
3	14857.09	3285	0.00	0.00	3.08
4	12040.89	5894	0.00	0.00	0.00
5	10183.95	2750	0.00	0.00	0.00
6	9343.69	11820	0.00	0.00	0.00
7	8594.36	74138	0.00	0.00	1.51
8	7965.52	303389	0.00	0.00	0.00

Table 3.5.   Computational results for large cases (best solutions in bold)

Cases	LS1	LS2	GA	GA Gap(%)
$n = 100, \ell = 50, K = 20$	**8308.68**	**8308.68**	8335.75	0.33
$n = 100, \ell = 100, K = 20$	**10055.85**	**10055.85**	10138.27	0.82
$n = 100, \ell = 100, K = 40$	7344.72	**7335.61**	**7335.61**	0.00
$n = 150, \ell = 75, K = 20$	11882.62	**11846.80**	11854.17	0.06
$n = 150, \ell = 75, K = 40$	**9046.71**	**9046.71**	9047.22	0.01
$n = 150, \ell = 150, K = 20$	15427.54	**15398.42**	15688.78	1.89
$n = 150, \ell = 150, K = 40$	**10618.58**	10627.36	10728.93	1.04
$n = 200, \ell = 100, K = 20$	**14365.95**	**14365.95**	14382.65	0.12
$n = 200, \ell = 100, K = 40$	**10970.94**	**10970.94**	**10970.94**	0.00
$n = 200, \ell = 200, K = 20$	18951.05	18959.37	**18900.25**	-0.27
$n = 200, \ell = 200, K = 40$	**12931.46**	12941.85	12987.29	0.43
$n = 500, \ell = 500, K = 40$	34320.00	**34138.61**	35117.61	2.87

Table 3.6.   Running times for large cases (in seconds)

Cases	LS1	LS2	GA
$n = 100, \ell = 50, K = 20$	8	8	7
$n = 100, \ell = 100, K = 20$	13	16	3
$n = 100, \ell = 100, K = 40$	24	26	5
$n = 150, \ell = 75, K = 20$	30	37	12
$n = 150, \ell = 75, K = 40$	52	57	41
$n = 150, \ell = 150, K = 20$	65	56	7
$n = 150, \ell = 150, K = 40$	140	145	13
$n = 200, \ell = 100, K = 20$	72	63	30
$n = 200, \ell = 100, K = 40$	176	222	35
$n = 200, \ell = 200, K = 20$	125	166	29
$n = 200, \ell = 200, K = 40$	342	333	35
$n = 500, \ell = 500, K = 40$	9063	7440	672

In one case, GA outperforms both LS1 and LS2. The largest instance studied has $n = \ell = 500$ and $K = 40$. In this case, the GA solution is 2.87%
higher than the LS2 solution. However, LS1 and LS2 require more than 10
times as much running time as GA. We point out that if LS1 and LS2 were run
a single time (rather than five), then they would underperform GA in the vast
majority of cases. This point is illustrated in Table 3.7.

Additional computational results are presented in Appendix C. These tests
also demonstrate the ability of LS1, LS2, and GA to obtain optimal or near-
optimal solutions to large problem instances of the LCMST problem.

6.   A Related Problem

In the LCMST problem, the primary concern is with the total cost and there
is an upper bound on the number of labels. In a related problem, the primary

Table 3.7. Computational results for a graph with $n = \ell = 30$, with a single run of LS1 and LS2

K	MIP	Time(sec)	LS1 Gap(%)	LS2 Gap(%)	GA Gap(%)
3	7901.81	20.83	7.42	0.67	0.00
8	4473.11	1229.48	0.03	0.03	0.00
10	3980.99	931.83	1.61	0.52	0.00
12	3702.08	297.36	0.23	0.23	0.00

concern is with the number of labels and there is an upper bound on the total cost. We refer to this problem as the cost-constrained minimum label spanning tree (CCMLST) problem. Given a labeled graph $G = (V, E, L)$ and a positive number C, the goal of the CCMLST problem is to find a spanning tree with the smallest number of labels and a total cost of no more than C.

There is an easy way to obtain good solutions to the CCMLST problem by using algorithms to solve the LCMST problem. Let ALG represent an algorithm (e.g., LS1, LS2, or GA) to solve the LCMST problem. The input for ALG is a labeled graph G and a positive integer K and the output is a label set X. Let k represent the number of labels in a minimum weight spanning tree of G. Then, we can use a bisection search method to find the solution to the CCMLST problem. To begin, the lower bound is $lower = 1$ and the upper bound is $upper = k$. We run ALG for $mid = \frac{lower + upper}{2}$ labels. If the solution has a cost greater than C, we need more labels and we set $lower = mid$. If the solution has a cost less than C, then we need fewer labels and we set $upper = mid$. A detailed description of the method is shown next.

Input: A labeled graph G and a positive number C.

CCMLST(G,C)

1 Set $lower = 1$ and $upper = k$

2 *if* $(upper - lower) \geq 1$ *do*

3      $mid = \frac{lower + upper}{2}$

4      $X = \text{ALG}(G, mid)$

5   *if* $f(X) > C$ *do lower* $= mid$

6   *else do upper* $= mid$

7 *end do*

8 Output X

7.   Conclusions

In this paper, we introduced and motivated the LCMST problem. We proved that the LCMST problem is NP-complete. Next, we proposed three heuristics (two local search methods and a genetic algorithm) to solve the LCMST problem and we formulated the problem as a MIP. Extensive computational experiments were performed. In all of these tests, the three heuristics generated high-quality solutions. Finally, a related problem was introduced and a solution approach was presented.

References

[1] P.M. Camerini, F. Maffinoli, S. Martello, and P. Toth. Most and least uniform spanning tree. *Discrete Appl. Math*, 15:181–197, 1986.

[2] R.-S. Chang and S.-J. Leu. The minimum labeling spanning trees. *Inform. Process. Lett.*, 63(5):277–282, 1997.

[3] D. Eppstein. Finding the k smallest spanning trees. *BIT*, 32:237–248, 1992.

[4] Z. Galil and B. Schieber. On finding most uniform spanning trees. *Discrete Appl. Math.*, 20:173–175, 1988.

[5] J.-H. Ho, D.T. Lee, C.-H. Chang, and C.K. Wong. Minimum diameter spanning trees and related problems. *SIAM J. Comput.*, 20:987–997, 1991.

[6] S.O. Krumke and H.-C. Wirth. On the minimum label spanning tree problem. *Inform. Process. Lett.*, 66(2):81–85, 1998.

[7] X. Shen and W. Liang. A parallel algorithm for multiple edge updates of minimum spanning trees. *Proc. 7th Internet. Parallel Processing Symp.*, pages 310–317, 1993.

[8] Y. Wan, G. Chen, and Y. Xu. A note on the minimum label spanning tree. *Inform. Process. Lett.*, 84:99–101, 2002.

[9] Y. Xiong, B. Golden, and E. Wasil. A one-parameter genetic algorithm for the minimum labeling spanning tree problem. *IEEE Transactions on Evolutionary Computation*, 9(1):55–60, 2005.

[10] Y. Xiong, B. Golden, and E. Wasil. Worst-case behavior of the MVCA heuristic for the minimum labeling spanning tree problem. *Operations Research Lett.*, 33(1):77–80, 2005.

[11] Y. Xiong, B. Golden, and E. Wasil. Improved heuristics for the minimum label spanning tree problem. *IEEE Transactions on Evolutionary Computation*, 10(6):700–703, 2006.

Appendix: A: MIP Formulations for the LCMST Problem

In this section, we provide two mixed integer programming formulations for the LCMST problem and compare their performances. The first one uses the single-commodity flow model while the second uses the multi-commodity flow model. For small instances of the LCMST problem, we are able to obtain optimal solutions from both formulations. This enables us to compare solution values found using LS1, LS2, and GA with optimal solution values.

Notation and Variables

In the LCMST problem, we assume that L is the set of all labels, E is the set of all edges, $V = \{1, 2, \cdots, n\}$ is the set of all nodes, $|V| = n$ is the total number of nodes, and K is the maximum number of labels allowed in a solution. Let E_k be the set of all the edges with color k. Additionally, let A be the set of all arcs. In particular, for every edge (i, j) in E, there are two corresponding arcs $< i, j >$ and $< j, i >$ in A. For any $1 \leq i, j \leq n$ and $i \neq j$, we define c_{ij} to be the cost or weight of edge (i, j). We define the variables e_{ij}, x_{ij}, and y_k as follows:

$$e_{ij} = \begin{cases} 1 & \text{if edge } (i, j) \text{ is used} \\ 0 & \text{otherwise} \end{cases}$$

$$x_{ij} = \begin{cases} 1 & \text{if arc } < i, j > \text{ is used} \\ 0 & \text{otherwise} \end{cases}$$

$$y_k = \begin{cases} 1 & \text{if label } k \text{ is selected} \\ 0 & \text{otherwise.} \end{cases}$$

MIP Formulation using the Single-Commodity Flow Model (F1)

In this subsection, we formulate the LCMST problem as a single-commodity flow problem.

$$\min \sum_{(i,j) \in E} c_{ij} e_{ij} \tag{3.A.1}$$

$$\text{subject to} \sum_{(i,j) \in E} e_{ij} = n - 1 \tag{3.A.2}$$

$$\sum_{i:(i,j) \in A} f_{ij} - \sum_{l:(j,l) \in A} f_{jl} = 1 \quad \forall j \in V - \{1\} \tag{3.A.3}$$

$$\sum_{i:(i,1) \in A} f_{i1} - \sum_{l:(1,l) \in A} f_{1l} = -(n - 1) \tag{3.A.4}$$

$$f_{ij} + f_{ji} \leq (n - 1) \cdot e_{ij} \quad \forall (i, j) \in E \tag{3.A.5}$$

$$\sum_{(i,j) \in E_k} e_{ij} \leq (n - 1) \cdot y_k \quad \forall k \in L \tag{3.A.6}$$

$$\sum_{k \in L} y_k \leq K \tag{3.A.7}$$

$$e_{ij}, y_k \in \{0, 1\} \quad \forall (i, j) \in E \quad \forall k \in L \tag{3.A.8}$$

$$f_{ij} \geq 0 \quad \forall (i, j) \in A. \tag{3.A.9}$$

The objective function (3.A.1) seeks to minimize the total cost or weight of the spanning tree. Constraint (3.A.2) ensures that the tree contains $n - 1$ edges. The flow variables f_{ij} are included to guarantee connectivity. They work as follows: select one node (say, node 1) out of the set V and think of it as the root node. Create a supply of $n - 1$ units of flow at this node. For all other nodes, create a demand of one unit of flow. Send one unit of flow from the root node to all other nodes in order to satisfy their demands. The above notion of connectivity is represented by the flow balance constraints (3.A.3) and (3.A.4). Constraints (3.A.5) ensure that if flow is sent along an edge, then that edge must be in the tree. Constraints (3.A.6) ensure that if an edge with label k is used, then this label must be counted. Finally, an upper bound on the number of labels is imposed in constraint (3.A.7).

Suppose we want to formulate the CCMLST as an MIP. The objective function would become

$$\min \sum_{k \in L} y_k$$

and the constraints would include (3.A.2) to (3.A.6), (3.A.8), (3.A.9), and the new constraint

$$\sum_{(i,j) \in E} c_{ij} e_{ij} \leq C. \tag{3.A.7'}$$

MIP Formulation using the Multi-Commodity Flow Model (F2)

Alternatively, we can formulate the LCMST problem as a multi-commodity flow problem as follows.

$$\min \sum_{(i,j) \in E} c_{ij} e_{ij} \tag{3.A.10}$$

$$\text{subject to } \sum_{(i,j) \in E} e_{ij} = n - 1 \tag{3.A.11}$$

$$\sum_{i:(i,h) \in A} f_{ih}^h - \sum_{l:(h,l) \in A} f_{hl}^h = 1 \quad \forall h \in V - \{1\} \tag{3.A.12}$$

$$\sum_{i:(i,1) \in A} f_{i1}^h - \sum_{l:(1,l) \in A} f_{1l}^h = -1 \quad \forall h \in V - \{1\} \tag{3.A.13}$$

$$\sum_{i:(i,j) \in A} f_{ij}^h - \sum_{l:(j,l) \in A} f_{jl}^h = 0 \quad \forall h \in V - \{1\}, \forall j \neq h \tag{3.A.14}$$

$$f_{ij}^h \leq x_{ij} \quad \forall (i,j) \in A, \forall h \in V - \{1\} \tag{3.A.15}$$

$$x_{ij} + x_{ji} \leq e_{ij} \quad \forall (i,j) \in E \tag{3.A.16}$$

$$\sum_{(i,j) \in E_k} e_{ij} \leq (n-1) \cdot y_k \quad \forall k \in L \tag{3.A.17}$$

$$\sum_{k \in L} y_k \leq K \tag{3.A.18}$$

$$e_{ij}, \; y_k \in \{0,1\} \quad \forall (i,j) \in E \quad \forall k \in L \tag{3.A.19}$$

$$x_{ij} \in \{0,1\} \quad \forall (i,j) \in A \tag{3.A.20}$$

$$f_{ij}^h \geq 0 \quad \forall (i,j) \in A, \forall h \in V - \{1\}. \tag{3.A.21}$$

The objective function is the same as in (3.A.1). Constraint (3.A.11) ensures that the tree contains $n - 1$ edges. The flow variables f_{ij}^h are included to guarantee connectivity. They work as follows: select one node (say, node 1) out of the set V and think of it as the root node. Create a supply of 1 unit of flow h for every node h ($h \in V - \{1\}$) at node 1. For every node h, create a demand of one unit of flow h. Send one unit of flow h from the root node to every h node in order to satisfy their demands. The above notion of connectivity is represented by the flow balance constraints (3.A.12), (3.A.13), and (3.A.14). Constraints (3.A.15) and (3.A.16) ensure that if flow is sent along an edge, then that edge must be selected in the tree. Constraints (3.A.17) ensure that if an edge with label k is used, then this label must be counted. Finally, an upper bound on the number of labels is imposed in constraint (3.A.18).

Suppose we want to formulate the cost-constrained minimum label spanning tree (CCMLST) as an MIP. The objective function would become

$$\min \sum_{k \in L} y_k$$

and the constraints would include (3.A.9) to (3.A.17), (3.A.19) to (3.A.21), and the new constraint

$$\sum_{(i,j) \in E} c_{ij} e_{ij} \leq C. \tag{3.A.18$'$}$$

Table 3.A.1. Comparison of two MIP formulations based on a graph with $n = \ell = 50$

K	F1 Time (sec)	F2 Time (sec)
4	12040.89	NA
5	10183.95	67473.37
6	9343.69	186148.83
7	8594.36	59783.95
8	7965.52	15869.49
9	NA	6380.30
10	NA	3418.46
11	NA	5133.17
12	NA	20199.94

Table 3.B.1. Coordinates of nodes for the graph with $n = \ell = 20$

node	1	2	3	4	5	6	7	8	9	10
x	41	334	169	478	962	705	281	961	995	827
y	467	500	724	358	464	145	827	491	942	436
node	11	12	13	14	15	16	17	18	19	20
x	391	902	292	421	718	447	771	869	667	35
y	604	153	382	716	895	726	538	912	299	894

Comparison of MIP Models

We compare the performance of F1 and F2 based on a graph with 50 nodes. The formulations are implemented using OPL Studio 3.7 on a Pentium III PC with 993MHz and 512MB RAM. The results are shown in Table 3.A.1, where the time to reach optimality is recorded for each model. NA indicates no optimal solution can be found after 72 hours. As we can see, F2 seems to work better for $K > 8$, while F1 does better for $K \leq 8$. We also conduct experiments on larger examples (graphs with 100 nodes) using F2. However, it fails to find solutions due to a lack of memory.

We point out that constraints (3.A.6) and (3.A.17) can be written in disaggregate form. This increases the number of constraints. In our experiments, the disaggregated formulations did not solve as quickly as F1 and F2.

Appendix: B: A Small Sample Graph for the LCMST Problem

We give a small instance of the LCMST problem. This instance is a complete graph of 20 nodes and 20 labels, where $V = \{1, 2, \ldots, 19, 20\}$ and $L = \{1, 2, \ldots, 19, 20\}$. For each node, its (x, y) coordinates are randomly selected integers from $[0, 999]$. The label matrix of the graph is symmetric. Each entry is randomly selected from L. Computational results for this problem are shown in Table 3.1. In Table 3.B.1, the (x, y) coordinates are provided and the label matrix is given in Table 3.B.2.

Appendix: C: A Special Family of Graphs

We construct a special family of graphs for which we know a reasonably good solution to the LCMST problem. When we run LS1, LS2, and GA on these graphs, we can then compare the solution values to the reasonably good (known) solution values.

Table 3.B.2.   The label matrix for the graph with $n = \ell = 20$

10	7	4	7	16	8	7	18	17	19	4	17	19	10	4	4	19	1	17	—
2	11	7	14	17	12	3	5	1	20	9	10	17	10	14	15	1	19	—	17
4	11	20	7	2	8	9	20	15	14	14	15	20	5	6	8	9	—	19	1
20	10	5	18	11	11	2	11	17	15	7	14	10	9	16	4	—	9	1	19
18	11	9	11	7	7	19	16	12	2	8	18	1	5	3	—	4	8	15	4
18	6	12	5	13	5	10	3	11	5	8	11	12	4	—	3	16	6	14	4
3	7	17	19	18	2	10	12	3	9	9	2	16	—	4	5	9	5	10	10
5	9	7	20	14	11	6	1	2	20	1	8	—	16	12	1	10	20	17	19
8	5	1	16	18	11	4	9	16	9	19	—	8	2	11	18	14	15	10	17
9	3	17	14	10	13	14	14	4	2	—	19	1	9	8	8	9	14	9	4
14	1	15	2	11	12	8	11	9	—	2	9	20	9	5	2	15	14	20	19
12	7	5	10	13	15	18	7	—	9	4	16	2	3	11	12	17	15	1	17
2	9	4	3	5	16	18	—	7	11	14	9	1	12	3	16	11	20	5	18
5	3	10	19	6	8	—	18	18	8	14	4	6	10	10	19	2	9	3	7
14	11	9	19	2	—	8	16	15	12	13	11	11	2	5	7	11	8	12	8
14	16	14	18	—	2	6	5	13	11	10	18	14	18	13	7	11	2	17	16
3	17	2	—	18	19	19	3	10	2	14	16	20	19	5	11	18	7	14	7
12	19	—	2	14	9	10	4	5	15	17	1	7	17	12	9	5	20	7	4
4	—	19	17	16	11	3	9	7	1	3	5	9	7	6	11	10	11	11	7
—	4	12	3	14	14	5	2	12	14	9	8	5	3	18	18	20	4	2	10

Table 3.C.1. Computational results for a special family of graphs with $r = 80\%$ (best solutions in bold)

Cases	T	LS1	LS2	GA	GA Gap(%)
$n = \ell = 100, K = 40$	8433.69	7418.82	**7418.37**	7418.82	0.01
$n = \ell = 120, K = 40$	9545.52	**8424.78**	**8424.78**	8449.90	0.30
$n = \ell = 150, K = 40$	10120.65	**9682.18**	**9682.18**	**9682.18**	0.00
$n = \ell = 180, K = 40$	10910.71	**10539.14**	10599.39	10549.64	0.10
$n = \ell = 200, K = 40$	11453.89	**11298.40**	**11298.40**	11339.51	0.36

Table 3.C.2. Computational results for a special family of graphs with $r = 50\%$ (best solutions in bold)

Cases	T	LS1	LS2	GA	GA Gap (%)
$n = \ell = 100, K = 40$	7784.84	**7234.45**	**7234.45**	7244.37	0.14
$n = \ell = 120, K = 40$	8846.22	**8253.57**	**8253.57**	**8253.57**	0.00
$n = \ell = 150, K = 40$	9300.71	9037.11	**9032.54**	9045.35	0.14
$n = \ell = 180, K = 40$	10177.16	10131.91	**10127.83**	10150.17	0.22
$n = \ell = 200, K = 40$	10541.98	**10463.57**	**10463.57**	**10463.57**	0.00

Table 3.C.3. Computational results for a special family of graphs with $r = 0\%$ (best solutions in bold)

Cases	T	LS1	LS2	GA	GA Gap(%)
$n = \ell = 100, K = 40$	6870.59	**6870.59**	**6870.59**	**6870.59**	0.00
$n = \ell = 120, K = 40$	7528.71	**7528.71**	**7528.71**	**7528.71**	0.00
$n = \ell = 150, K = 40$	8343.89	**8343.89**	**8343.89**	**8343.89**	0.00
$n = \ell = 180, K = 40$	9006.14	**9006.14**	**9006.14**	**9006.14**	0.00
$n = \ell = 200, K = 40$	9336.30	**9336.30**	**9336.30**	**9336.30**	0.00

We construct a complete graph G as follows. First, we randomly generate n nodes in the square $[0, 999] \times [0, 999]$. The cost of each edge (i, j) is the Euclidean distance between i and j. Then, we sort all the edges by cost, from lowest to highest. A spanning tree requires $n - 1$ edges. We know that Kruskal's algorithm obtains a minimum weight spanning tree by selecting the $n - 1$ shortest edges, without forming a cycle. In order to find a reasonably good solution T to the LCMST problem, we set a parameter r with $0 \leq r < 1$. Next, we select $r(n - 1)$ edges randomly from the $2n$ shortest edges, without forming a cycle. Then, we select the other $(1 - r)(n - 1)$ edges by applying Kruskal's algorithm to the complete graph. Thus, we have tree T. Next, we need to assign a label to each edge. To do this, we randomly select K distinct labels from L and call this label subset L_1. Let $L_2 = L - L_1$. For each edge in T, we assign it a label from L_1, at random; for each edge not in T, we assign it a label in L_2, at random. As a result, we obtain a labeled graph G with a reasonably good spanning tree T which has K distinct labels.

Computational results for $r = 80\%$, $r = 50\%$, and $r = 0\%$ are presented in Tables 3.C.1, 3.C.2 and 3.C.3, respectively. The GA gap is the percentage gap between the GA solution value and the better solution value of LS1 and LS2. From the three tables, we observe that all three heuristics obtain a solution that is no worse than T. In most cases, they are better than T. The

GA gap is always less than 0.4%. Table 3.C.3 gives the computational results for $r = 0\%$. In this case, T is the minimum weight spanning tree. This is because T is generated entirely from Kruskal's algorithm. We observe that all three heuristics obtain the optimal solution. In fact, given the increasing reliance on Kruskal's algorithm as we move from Table 3.C.1 to Table 3.C.2 to Table 3.C.3, we expect T to be a very good solution in Table 3.C.2 and a good solution in Table 3.C.1. Tables 3.C.1, 3.C.2 and 3.C.3 reinforce the conclusion that the three heuristics obtain very high-quality solutions to the LCMST problem.

Chapter 4

EX-POST INTERNET CHARGING

Joseph P. Bailey

The Robert H. Smith School of Business, University of Maryland, College Park, MD 20742
jbailey@rhsmith.umd.edu

Jose Nagel

UUNet Technologies, Inc., 22001 Loudon County Parkway, Ashburn, VA 20147
jnagel@uu.net

S. Raghavan

The Robert H. Smith School of Business and Institute for Systems Research
University of Maryland, College Park, MD 20742
raghavan@umd.edu

Abstract   Pricing Internet bandwidth is of growing importance as the Internet grows and matures. While many residential consumers have "flat rate" Internet pricing, the pricing policies facing campus, regional, and metropolitan-area networks are becoming more complex. While it may be possible to price every bit or packet of data, this pricing policy requires significantly additional accounting and billing overhead to make it practical. Instead, many Internet Service Providers (ISPs) are using a form of aggregate statistics to determine prices. This class of pricing policies—wherein the pricing algorithm is determined ex-ante but the charge is calculated after the fact—we call "ex-post" because the charges are determined after the traffic has been sent.

In this paper, we construct a framework that identifies the mechanisms and goals of Internet pricing. We use this framework to argue that charging models that have better user accountability and are likely to be implemented could achieve these goals through better network management.

Expanding on the potential for ex-post charging, we construct a general form of an ex-post charging model. This model determines prices using metrics describing both the utilization and burstiness of network traffic. We then provide examples of the general form of the ex-post pricing model using three different ways of characterizing utilization and burstiness: 1) effective bandwidth, 2) token buckets, and 3) using first and second moments of the traffic distribution and the moving average of the traffic distribution.

Finally, we discuss the implications of ex-post Internet charging. We discuss the granularity or sampling rate that is reasonable given the cost of collecting traffic data and the need for accurate representation of the traffic using aggregate statistics. We also explore the possibility of new business opportunities for ISPs to use ex-post Internet pricing to better manage their Internet Protocol (IP) networks and compete in the market.

Keywords: Internet charging; effective bandwidth; Internet economics.

1.   Introduction

Part of the Internet's success comes from the simplicity of its technical and economic model. Technically, the Internet is a best-effort network where packets are transported across heterogeneous, interoperable networks. Economically, the Internet marketplace is dominated by a simple pricing policy where prices are based on a user's connection bandwidth rather than on the characteristics of the traffic that is actually being sent. Although this minimalist model is an important reason why the Internet has grown to its current size, the model does have some limitations that must be addressed for the Internet to fully exploit its potential.

The limitations to this minimalist model are both technical and economic. The technical limitations include the inability of the best effort model to allow for differentiated services. In other words, when all traffic is treated equally, as it is under best effort service, all applications experience the same network response even though some traffic is more time sensitive than other traffic. The economic limitations include the inability for capacity-based pricing to give proper incentives for efficient development and use of Internet resources. For example, all users pay one price for the same connection even though the utilization of the network may be very different. In this way, heavy users (as measured by utilization and/or burstiness of the traffic they send) are subsidized by light users and some light users might find the connection price too high relative to the traffic they wish to send. Therefore, there may be deadweight loss, an undesirable economic outcome, associated with this market.

This paper makes several contributions to Internet charging by introducing an ex-post model and detailing the benefits of such a model. The first contribution is the development of a model, which is an alternative mechanism to Internet charging. Unlike prior Internet charging models, this model examines network usage both in terms of the volume of traffic, but the burstiness of that traffic as well. The second contribution is the application of the ex-post charging models in the Internet charging context. This paper describes where it makes sense to apply the ex-post charging model and how it will be consistent with the overall network management policies of the Internet. The final contribution of the paper is an analysis of the benefits that may follow from the application of new ex-post charging models. Specifically, how ex-post charging may increase social welfare derived from the Internet.

The remainder of the paper is structured as follows. First, the paper proposes an Internet Pricing Framework that details how new charging mechanisms hope to accomplish some of the goals for improvement in the Internet infrastructure. Next, the paper describes the general form of an ex-post charging model that, if implemented, may start the transition to an improved Internet infrastructure. Then the paper describes specific analytical models that fit within the general ex-post charging model. Finally, the paper provides suggestions for future research.

2.   An Internet Pricing Framework

To develop a model that goes beyond the minimalist model, we propose that technology and economic approaches to a new model must be developed simultaneously while being paired complementary. This goal is consistent with the proposal of [9] who propose bridging the technical and economic communities to further Internet development.

Some of the goals of an Internet pricing framework include:

- **Quality of Service**. The implementation of a new pricing policy should allow for some Internet traffic to receive a quality of service (QoS) so that applications that require better quality may request it. Furthermore, prices should be higher for higher priority traffic relative to best effort traffic. Management of congestion through economic as well as technical solutions should be supported. Instead of only using the flow control mechanism built into the transmission control protocol (TCP), other economic means can be used to shape traffic. One benefit of an economic approach may be the reduction in the TCP slow start problem where it takes applications some time to reach its "optimal" statistically shared bit rate. Pricing the network may be an alternative to TCP flow control because users have an incentive to shape their outgoing traffic, thereby acting as a congestion control mechanism.

- **Extensibility**. The Internet should allow for the creation and diffusion of new software applications. Such applications are being developed constantly and many impose an increasing load on portions of the Internet. A special class of applications–applications that require differentiated service, such as video or audio traffic–is of particular importance because the best effort Internet cannot fully support this class of applications.

- **Scalability**. The new model should encourage increased bandwidth connections to the Internet. This is especially important in the local loop where xDSL, cable modems, and direct satellite access will allow residential users to become potential massive traffic sources. Currently, there is little incentive for these new users to shape or limit their traffic because the pricing policies have not been developed.

- **Security**. A pricing model should encourage better security management. Many security risks still exist for the Internet including denial of service attacks and invasion of privacy. The goal of the proposed pricing model should be at an aggregate level sufficient enough to not invade privacy. Furthermore, the collection of data should help, not hinder, the detection of security risks such as a denial of service attack.

We argue that the first necessary step to accomplish these goals is for network administrators to adopt better network management practices. By encouraging users to manage their network resources more effectively, they may accomplish all four of the stated goals. Constant and consistent monitoring of the network status can give network managers timely and detailed information about network congestion. This may certainly enable short-term solutions to problems that arise. However, potentially a more significant benefit is the long-term implications for network design. As network managers have more information about the sources of network congestion, they can do a better job allocating and increasing the availability of resources.

Since network management is optional, not mandatory, outside interested parties (such as network managers from other interconnected networks) must provide incentives for network management.[1] We believe that this can best be accomplished by rewarding users for better network management by reducing the charge for Internet interconnection. We propose a charging model that gives users an incentive to manage their network resources. This charging model has two key elements:

- **Accountability**. New pricing policies should enable better cost recovery. This ensures that investors in the Internet infrastructure can recover their investments. Furthermore, prices can better reflect the actual usage costs that are required to maintain Internet growth.

- **Implementation**. Allowing more demanding users the ability to decide how they would like their traffic to be handled by the Internet. This must be done in conjunction with pricing to ensure that users have an incentive to send lower priority service and avoid a "tragedy of the commons."

---

[1] In this regard, we recognize that network management has an inherent network externality.

For a charging model to have these two elements, we propose a pragmatic approach to the charging model employing two fundamental principles: the model should be simple, and traffic metering should be done in a Bayesian fashion. Because this charging model must be understood by salespeople who are negotiating service level agreements with customers and implemented by the network engineers, the charging model must be understood by all three parties. If any one group does not understand the algorithm being used to calculate the charge, the business model is fundamentally flawed. Secondly, by metering network traffic in a Bayesian fashion, the entire trace of network traffic does not need to be stored for analysis. Since many charging cycles are 30 days or longer, Bayesian updating will eliminate the need to store terabytes of data. Furthermore, not storing this data eliminates the potential security risk of a third-party gaining access to trace data.

The overall framework proposes a charging model to accomplish some of the goals of Internet pricing by providing incentives for network management. The implementation of a charging algorithm gives network managers aggregate statistics regarding the use of their network. Network managers then have an incentive to lower these metrics, to reduce the cost of their ISP service and provide better allocation of network resources. If a user is charged for the speed of their network connection, they may have some incentive to manage their network traffic. However, the ex-post charging model provides a greater incentive for network management because the user can make real-time admissions policies to packets based upon the packet's effect on the ex-post charge. If the charge was only assessed ex-ante based upon the connection speed, then the user has only a performance incentive to shape traffic. With an ex-post charge, they have both a performance and cost benefit of shaping their traffic. The relationship between the charging model, network management, and the goals of Internet pricing are detailed in Figure 4.1.

After some first steps in developing a new charging model, users may realize some of their goals through network management but it does not stop there. Rather, the framework has a feedback loop from the goals to the charging model. As users implement charging and monitor their network performance, they may be able to quantify some of the goals of Internet pricing. For example, as a user manages their network, they may be able to quantify the reduction in jitter. The collection and interest in these new metrics then enable new charging mechanisms that include the goals of Internet pricing.

Furthermore, the benefits to network management have an inherent network externality. As user i adopts better network management practices, it helps user j in managing their network resources as well. Because user i can only manage traffic on their network but traffic performance on their network depends on the full end-to-end performance of the network, as user j better manages its network, user i benefits.

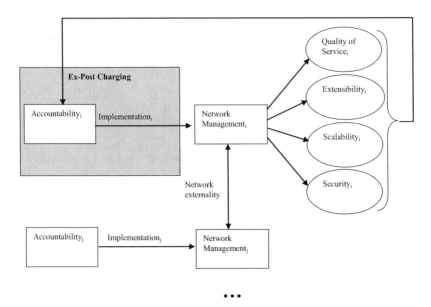

Figure 4.1.   Internet Pricing Framework

The diffusion of the charging model in the market will likely occur in the following stages (consistent with [10]):

- user i, a light user of Internet resources, who currently subsidizes some of the heavier users, switches from an ex-ante charging model to an ex-post charging model to lower their costs.

- user j, a medium user of Internet resources, is now faced with larger costs because they are no longer subsidized by user i, chooses to manage their network better and adopt an ex-post charging model.

- user k, a heavy user of Internet resources, is now faced with larger costs because they are no longer subsidized by users i and j, so they switch to an ex-post charging model.

As more users switch to an ex-post charging model and manage their network resources better, they create positive network externalities so that all users benefit.

3.   General Form of the Ex-Post Charging Model

The ex-post charging model is one that is built on the pragmatic approach to Internet pricing. Therefore, the model is fairly simple to understand by the ISP who sets the pricing policy and the consumer who accepts the pricing policy. In this way, the ex-post charge may be calculated after use of network resources, but it should not be a surprise to users who continually monitor their traffic patterns. There is an important timing issue, the duration over which to collect traffic statistics (and the granularity of collection) and settle on the ex-post charge, that must be determined in the marketplace. We believe that this cycle should be consistent with the billing cycle so that the complete traffic trace that corresponds to the billing period can be analyzed to set the price accurately.

We further argue that charging only using the ex-post approach may not be acceptable in the marketplace. If there was only an ex-post charge, then a user could have numerous, costly connections to the Internet and not pay anything to those networks that are never used. An ISP may have fixed costs of installing a connection but no mechanism to recover those costs when it relies solely on ex-post charges. Therefore, we view ex-post charges to fit in with equation 1 where the overall price is calculated as the sum of the ex-ante and ex-post charge:

$$P = P_{\text{ex-ante}} + P_{\text{ex-post}} \tag{1}$$

In this way, the ex-post pricing model will consist of a basic fixed fee that is proportional to the maximum bandwidth being contracted, plus a penalization amount that will provide the right incentives to shape and limit the traffic. Since it is the ex-post charge that this paper concentrates on, we will not go into detail about the ex-ante portion. However we believe that the ex-ante charge should be a function of the bandwidth and/or the technology of the Internet connection:

$$P_{\text{ex-ante}} = f(bandwidth, technology) \tag{2}$$

The ex-post charge should be related to the actual usage of the network. Similar to the model described by [2], the ex-post charge should account for the traffic sent and/or received by a user. This leads to the first assumption:

- **Assumption 1:** There is a monotonically increasing function that relates the total amount of network traffic sent and/or received (i.e. utilization) and the ex-post charge.

This may seem like a trivial assumption, but it is important to be clear as to the form of the model. We also believe that the model described by [2] is limited because it only discusses traffic sent and received and does not discuss the shape of that traffic. Burstiness of traffic represents, in some sense, the burden the traffic places on the network. Therefore, we believe that the burstiness of the traffic should have an impact on price as stated in the second assumption:

- **Assumption 2:** There is a monotonically increasing function that relates burstiness and ex-post charge.

The specific functions that relate ex-post charge to utilization and burstiness can be of many different forms. Since very bursty behavior of the traffic can have a very detrimental effect on the aggregate traffic patterns, we propose bursty traffic be assessed a higher charge as the burstiness increases. In this way, users are penalized more when traffic is burstier. Therefore, the ex-post charge vs. burstiness function is likely to be convex. Utilization is different than burstiness because there may be economies of scale with utilization just as there are economies of scale with capacity prices. Therefore, the ex-post charge as a function of utilization should be a concave function.

The selection of an appropriate traffic measurement metric to capture utilization and burstiness is critical to the design of an ex-post pricing policy. Two important aspects of measurement include metrics and granularity. Metrics should be chosen so that they can accurately represent the actual volume and burstiness usage characteristics of a wide range of customers. Further, in order for an ex-post charging mechanism to be commercially viable and acceptable the data collection burden should be minimal. Thus, the metrics chosen should be such that it is unnecessary to store a traffic trace of the billing cycle (akin to how electricity meters function). Ideally, the price should be updated in a Bayesian fashion. Secondly, the selection of the optimal traffic sampling granularity is important so that bursty events are recorded with minimum overhead. We elaborate on granularity later in this Section.

Examples of utilization metrics that can be used in ex-post schemes include average bit rate and total volume sent. Burstiness metrics examples include peak-average distance measurements, the moments of moving averages of the traffic, or the depth of a fitted leaky token bucket. There are also approaches that combine both volume and burstiness in a single calculation that results in a number that is proportional to the net resource utilization, this is the case for the effective bandwidth method. As important as the selection of an appropriate traffic measurement method is the selection of an appropriate function that relates these measurements with the price to charge for the service.

The next section describes some specific examples of the general form of ex-post charging. While this is not an exhaustive list of the possible ex-post charging models possible, they do illustrate different approaches within the umbrella of ex-post charging as we described earlier. Furthermore, these models are consistent with the basic elements of ex-post charging.

4.   Examples of the Ex-Post Charging Model

To illustrate the ex-post charging model, we present three models in this paper. All models use trace data to suggest well-defined metrics to measure traffic volume and burstiness. Once this data is collected, an ex-post charging model can calculate the overall charge consistent with the general model described above.

In this section we present three examples of ex-post charging models. Our first model, the effective bandwidth model uses the concept of effective bandwidth to determine the ex-post charge. The second model fits the traffic to the parameters of a token bucket to determine the ex-post charge. The first two models may be slightly technical for a manager without an engineering background. Consequently, we describe a third model, which may be more easily understood by managers, that is based on the first and second moments of the traffic and the moving average of the traffic.

4.1 Effective Bandwidth Model

Effective bandwidth is a scalar that summarizes resource usage of a shared multiplexed traffic medium. It depends upon the statistical properties and quality of service requirements of the various sources of traffic. Effective bandwidth is usually derived by means of asymptotic analysis. There are two types of asymptotic analysis in the literature: the many sources asymptotic (see [5] or [6]) and the large buffer asymptotic (see [4]). The many sources asymptotic model provides an accurate characterization of the effective bandwidth. However, the many sources asymptotic model calculation of effective bandwidth depends upon the other sources of traffic in the shared multiplexed transport medium. Consequently, it is impractical as a measure in the ex-post charging model we envision. An ex-post scheme following this model would base a users charge on the other users traffic. Thus a user will not be able to calculate his/her charge unless he also knows the other users traffic.

Because the many sources asymptotic model is problematic, we use the large buffer asymptotic instead. This model is much simpler and provides an upper bound on the effective bandwidth. Here, effectively one assumes that there is only a single source of traffic into the transport medium, and wish to determine the resource usage for that single traffic stream. Because we use these calculations for charging, as long as the bandwidth obtained by the large buffer asymptotic is more or less consistent (in terms of relative proportions) with the many sources asymptotic, it is adequate for our needs. In the effective bandwidth model for a single source, we are interested in determining the smallest value C of capacity, that for a given Buffer size (B) provides a buffer overflow probability of less than ε. This value C is referred to as the effective bandwidth of the source.

Following [4], using a two state Markov chain to represent the traffic source, the effective bandwidth may be approximated as

$$C = \frac{\alpha b(1-\rho)R_p - B + \sqrt{(\alpha b(1-\rho)R_p - B)^2 + 4B\alpha b\rho(1-\rho)R_P}}{2\alpha b(1-\rho)} \qquad (3)$$

Here, the Markov source is fully characterized by its peak rate (R_p), utilization[2] (ρ) and mean burst period (b). The buffer size is represented by B, and $\alpha = ln(1/\varepsilon)$ where ε is the buffer overflow probability. This model can actually be used for traffic sources with non-exponential burst and idle periods. However, for simplicity we do not discuss these extensions here.

There are two ways in which effective bandwidth can be used for ex-post pricing. By using the same buffer size B for all users with the same connection speed (for example, using the same buffer size B for all users with a 45 Mb/s DS-3 connection), the effective bandwidth provides a measure of resource usage and burstiness of the traffic. In this case,

$$P_{\text{ex-post}} = a * C \qquad (4)$$

where a is a scaling constant.

Another option is to create a market for buffers and allow users to select buffer sizes for their traffic (which will be placed at the ISP). In this case, the ISP will charge for both the buffer and effective bandwidth. Selecting a higher buffer size will reduce the effective bandwidth, and a lower buffer size results in a higher effective bandwidth. The pricing model should tradeoff buffer size and effective bandwidth in such a way that users with bursty traffic have incentives to choose higher buffer sizes, and users with well-behaved traffic have incentives to choose lower buffer sizes. We suggest the following ex-post charging model.

$$P_{\text{ex-post}} = a * (C + \Delta B) \qquad (5)$$

Where, a is a scaling constant, Δ is a scalar used to appropriately weight the effective bandwidth against buffer size in the pricing formula, B is the predefined buffer size selected by the user for the effective bandwidth calculations, and C is the effective bandwidth.

Observe that the constant a can be used to reflect the congestion that may exist in the network during certain periods of the day. To illustrate, during the hour with the highest expected congestion (busy hour), the value of a could be increased to reflect the high demand. In this paper, the appropriate values of a

---

[2]This measurement of utilization is the volume of traffic divided by the speed of the connection times the duration.

are not analyzed. Nevertheless, one must recognize the importance of selecting appropriate values for a.

The scalar Δ is used to appropriately weight the trade-offs in buffer size and effective bandwidth.[3] One simple way to set Δ could be to evaluate the effective bandwidths (C_{Bmin} and C_{Bmax}) for two pre-determined buffer sizes, a minimum and a maximum value corresponding to the range of possible buffer sizes that a user might contract for. For example, the amount of buffer space installed in the router. Thus one could set $\Delta = |\frac{C_{Bmax} - C_{Bmin}}{B_{max} - B_{min}}|$. In our research we are continuing to experiment with variations of this model (basically in the way Δ is set). At present, the simple method suggested above appears to perform well.

Finally, we note that the calculations for the effective bandwidth can be updated in a Bayesian fashion, as all of the parameters within are either constant or can be updated in a Bayesian fashion. Thus no cumbersome requirement to store the traces is necessary in order to calculate the ex-post charge.

4.2 Token Bucket Model[4]

Token bucket models have been quite effective for traffic shaping ([1, p. 511]). In this model, we examine setting the ex-post price by fitting a leaky token bucket to the traffic sent with a given depth (d) and the rate (r). Unlike the proposal from [3] where the leaky token bucket was an allocation control parameter, the dimensions of the leaky token bucket are descriptive instead of prescriptive. This model, shown in equation 6, uses the product of a logarithmic function (a concave function with base b, a constant) of the utilization, and an exponential function (a convex function with base c, a constant) for the depth.

$$P_{\text{ex-post}} = a(log_b r)c^d \qquad (6)$$

The price in the fitted leaky token bucket model, a, may change based on the bandwidth of the connection or other differentiated characteristics of the service. It is important to note that the depth and rate parameters of a fitted leaky token bucket are not unique. Rather, there are many different rates and depths that could be used to describe the same network trace.

Another option is to fit a token bucket to the trace repeatedly throughout the contract period. If we compute only one set of bucket parameters for the whole

---

[3]The appropriate value for Δ may depend upon the context. Specific issues that may influence Δ include the link capacity, current level of congestion in the network, or the cost of additional buffers and bandwidth.
[4]We would like to thank Michel Mandjes, Debasis Mitra, and Iraj Saniee at Bell Laboratories for pointing out this approach.

trace, we are, in essence, taking the worst case and charging for that. However, if we break up the entire trace into equal time segments, we can then separate bursty anomalies from repeated bursty behavior. For example, we can pick a 60-minute time interval of computing bucket parameters and then average (or take the 95th percentile) of those values over the entire contract period.

If the ISP or the user wants to set rate *and* depth ex-post, they must capture the entire trace during the billing cycle. Because there is an inherent trade-off between rate and depth, a user could pick many different combinations of the rate (r) and depth (d) parameters for the same traffic. If a user wants to minimize their charge, picking the rate and depth combination ex-post ensures the lowest charge. However, as discussed previously in this chapter, capturing the entire trace has security and overhead cost drawbacks. Alternatively, the charging model could be used in a Bayesian updating fashion if either the rate or the depth of the bucket is set ex-ante. Because we propose Bayesian up-dating is an important element to ex-post charging, we envision the customer selecting the rate ex-ante and the ISP will compute the depth in real-time. In this way, the ISP does not need to store the entire trace.

4.3   Moment-Based Model

In the hope that an ex-post charging methodology could be simplified from the effective bandwidth model, we propose a charging algorithm solely using simple time series statistics to capture utilization and burstiness. Given a time series $x_1, x_2, x_3, \ldots, x_t, x_{t+1}, \ldots$, the first moment of the first $t + 1$ points, $E[X_{t+1}]$, can be recursively expressed as:

$$E[X_{t+1}] = \frac{t}{t+1} E[X_t] + \frac{X_{t+1}}{t+1} \qquad (7)$$

The second moment of the first $t + 1$ points, $E[X_{t+1}^2]$, can be expressed as:

$$E[X_{t+1}^2] = \frac{t}{t+1} E[X_t^2] + \frac{X_{t+1}^2}{t+1} \qquad (8)$$

We use the first moment to describe the utilization of the link. To scale the utilization parameter between 0 and 1, we take the first moment of the trace and divide it by the bandwidth of the link:

$$\rho = \frac{E[x]}{B} \qquad (9)$$

Using variance as a measure of burstiness is fraught with problems since it is tied to the mean. The second moment alleviates this problem by removing the dependence on the mean. However, the second moment does not capture

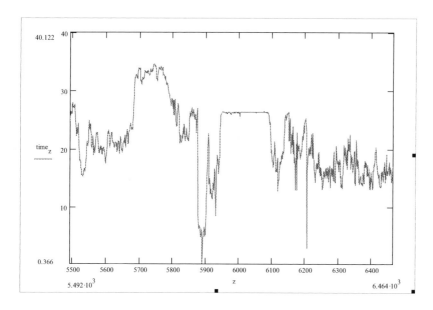

Figure 4.2. Length and Intensity of the Burst

within it any notion of the length of the burst. As Figure 4.2 shows, each burst not only has intensity, but it also has a duration or length of burst. To determine the overall burstiness of the trace, we introduce a notion of vertical and horizontal burstiness and bring them together for the ex-post charging function.

The vertical burstiness, r, is measured from the second moment of the trace. It is represented as follows:

$$r = \frac{\sqrt{E[x^2]}}{B} \qquad (10)$$

A smoothed trace, created by taking the moving average of the original trace, provides the foundation for horizontal burstiness. By using a smoothed trace, short bursts in the original trace will have little effect on the smoothed trace while large bursts that come all at once for a long duration constitute a larger horizontal burstiness, and is represented as a higher rate in the smoothed trace. Quantitatively, the smoothed trace is the moving average of the of the original trace and is computed using:

$$y_i = \frac{1}{w} \sum_{k=i}^{w+i-1} x_k \; for \; i = 0..n - w - 1 \; and \; k = 0..n \qquad (11)$$

Figure 4.3 shows the relationship between the smoothed trace and the original trace from Figure 4.2.

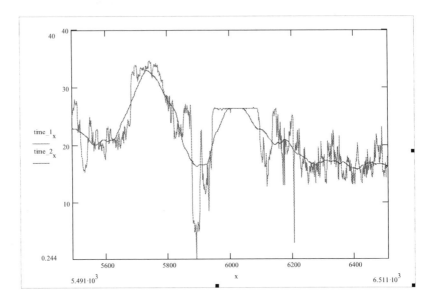

Figure 4.3.   Smoothing a Trace

The horizontal burstiness, l, can be computed by using the second moment of the smoothed trace and normalizing this value using the bandwidth capacity of the link as shown below:

$$l = \frac{\sqrt{E[y^2]}}{B} \tag{12}$$

Finally, we combine the burstiness properties of the trace by considering the vertical and horizontal burstiness as orthogonal components of burstiness and compute the vector length as shown in Figure 4.4.

Using the moments of the original and smoothed traces, we suggest the following moment based ex-post charging formula:

$$P_{\text{ex-post}} = aLn(b\rho + 1)(e^{c\sqrt{r^2 + l^2}} - 1) \tag{13}$$

Here a, b and c are shaping scalars.

Notice that the charging function can be modified for a smaller or larger moving average window by changing the value w. The length of the window represents the impact of the horizontal burstiness of the trace. Therefore, the ISP should select the window size to represent the point where the length of a burst starts to impose a congestion cost on its network.

The main benefit of the moment-based model is that it uses simple statistical concepts: the first and second moment, and the moving average. Therefore, all

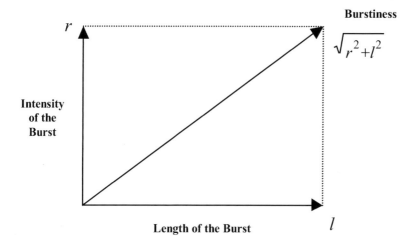

Figure 4.4. Combining Horizontal and Vertical Burstiness

communities who use the charging model (e.g. users, ISP salespeople, and network managers) are likely to understand the model and use it appropriately. This meets one criterion of a charging model as described in section 2.

5. Implementation

Developing a charging formula that meets the criterion of better account-ability achieves only half of what this paper hopes to accomplish. The charging model must be more than just a theoretical contribution to Internet pricing. Rather, the charging model must also be implementable so that it can make a difference in the marketplace. To this end, we describe three aspects of ex-post charging that are critical to implementation: traffic measurement, quality of service, and business implications.

5.1 Traffic Measurement

A necessary component to the success of an ex-post charging mechanism is accurate traffic measurement at the packet level. Packet measurement is done with a combination of hardware and software. For an appropriate charge to be assessed for a traffic flow, both the hardware and software tools must have accuracy that is at least as accurate as the granularity of the ex-post charging model.[5] In our research, we have millisecond accuracy since we use a

---

[5]Measurement accuracy is often less accurate than the number of digits given by a packet's timestamp. The timestamps correspond to the time that the kernel (of the operating system of the computer on which the

3Com 10BaseT network card and tcpdump software that each have millisecond accuracy.[6] Higher precision can be obtained by hardware and software improvements. However, this could be costly. An ISP implementing ex-post charging, needs to weigh the tradeoffs between granularity and the cost of the traffic measurement system.

For the effective bandwidth model, the traffic source is assumed to be an on-off source, transmitting at the speed of the link when it is on. Let us assume the granularity of the data collection is at the seconds level. Thus, when a trace is captured, all packets within a second are assumed to be transmitted at the same time and are aggregated together. This implies, that as the precision increases, the traffic is less bursty. And so the ex-post charge is reduced. This is consistent with the fact that higher precision measurement places a greater cost on the ISP. Consequently, an ISP could set a charge for the granularity of traffic measurement. Thus a higher precision results in a higher charge for the measurement of traffic, but a lower ex-post charge. This allows the ISP to share the cost of traffic measurement with the end user.

For the moment-based model, the traffic is assumed to be transmitted at the same constant speed, and not the speed of the link, over the duration of the second (assuming the precision is at the seconds level). Thus, as the precision increases, the burstiness is more accurately captured, and so the ex-post charge increases.

As one might conclude from the preceding discussion, traffic measurement is a very important issue for ex-post charging (or for any mechanism that charges based on traffic). As usage based pricing methods are implemented and accepted in the marketplace, we see a need for standards for traffic measurement in the marketplace, and for equipment that is consistent with the standards of the industry.

5.2   Quality of Service

We now describe how to extend the previous models by introducing traffic differentiation. This may be simply done by separating the metrics for the different classes of traffic, and calculating the ex-post price as the sum of the ex-post price for each of the classes of traffic. The benefit of separating the different classes of traffic is that prices can be set differently for the different classes. This is very important if the network is designed to support differenti-

---

software runs) sees the packet. Thus the granularity of the timestamp on the packets reflects the precision to which the kernel can measure time. This depends on a multitude of factors, such as the operating system, software (which is usually tcpdump) and the processor speed of the computer. Actually, tcpdump reports timestamps at the microsecond level. However, it is generally accepted that the precision of the timestamps, for traces available within the research community, is usually at the millisecond level (see Internet Traffic Archive mailing list at http://ita.ee.lbl.gov/html/mailing.html).

[6]The tcpdump software that captures traces relies on the BSD Packet Filter (BPF) (see [8]).

ated services. To expand on how priority models can be used, we discuss two examples: TCP/UDP charging and user-defined priority charging.

One example of QoS pricing is metering and charging at a layer above the IP layer. For example, a network decides to provide a better quality of service for user datagram protocol (UDP) traffic over transmission control protocol (TCP) traffic and sets ex-post prices higher for the UDP traffic. An ISP may want to do this because many of the real-time Internet traffic flows that would benefit from differentiated service currently use UDP because the traffic flow is actually hurt by the TCP flow control. If the ISP gives better service to UDP traffic, perhaps by queuing UDP traffic ahead of TCP, then the ISP will likely want to charge UDP traffic more. Therefore, the ISP collects data at the TCP/UDP level and not the IP level so that there are two utilization and burstiness measurements for each billing cycle. This might also make sense because a burst from UDP may be more costly on the network than a similar sized burst from TCP because the UDP traffic will not "back off" since UDP has no flow control mechanism. The following equation shows how the effective bandwidth charging model is modified to charge at the TCP/UDP layer.

$$P_{\text{ex-post}} = a_{\text{UDP}} * (C_{\text{UDP}} + \Delta_{\text{UDP}} B_{\text{UDP}}) + a_{\text{TCP}} * (C_{\text{TCP}} + \Delta_{\text{TCP}} B_{\text{TCP}}) \quad (14)$$

In this second example, a user sends two classes of traffic to the ISP and the ISP gives one class of traffic, differentiated service. The ISP only needs to measure the utilization and burstiness of the traffic of each of the two classes to determine prices (with $a_1 > a_2$). The user may choose to allocate priority using a token bucket similar to the proposal by [3]. However, since the end user does not have to purchase the token bucket ex-ante, they can actually change their leaky token buckets many times during a billing cycle. For example, a user may choose to reduce the number of packets that receive a higher priority when the network is lightly loaded so they may have a lower charge. The charging formula for this example using the effective bandwidth model is shown in equation 115.

$$P_{\text{ex-post}} = a_1 * (C_1 + \Delta_1 B_1) + a_2 * (C_2 + \Delta_2 B_2) \quad (15)$$

5.3   Business Implications

The ex-post charging model benefits we describe above focus on the demand side of the marketplace, i.e. an individual user. However, there are benefits to the supply side of the market (i.e. the ISP) as well. In this section we describe some of these benefits and explain why an ISP may choose to implement ex-post charging.

As ISPs implement this system, they may sustain a competitive advantage in winning business from the early adopters. As described in section 2, the initial users who adopt ex-post charging are users with lightly loaded networks. They are currently subsidizing the more demanding users. It is this group of customers that ISPs with ex-post charging can target as their initial set of customers.

As ISPs start to implement ex-post charging mechanisms, the diffusion of new Internet pricing models is likely to accelerate. When an ISP negotiates with a user to provide Internet connectivity, users are increasingly demanding more complex service level agreements because of their dependence on reliable Internet connectivity to their business models. This has become apparent recently as Internet retailer's web sites "go down" because of denial of service attacks or routing errors. An ISP with ex-post charging gives users a greater guarantee that they will monitor network traffic in a timely and accurate manner because it is necessary to assess a charge. Therefore, ISPs who implement ex-post charging will have better (or at least more quantifiable and predictable) QoS and security that could help them construct more competitive service level agreements (SLAs).

Consumers who use an ex-post charging mechanism may build in network management safeguards to control for budgeting uncertainty. Since the amount of traffic that a consumer sends during a business cycle is uncertain, they will likely face different charges for different billing periods. Since most consumers will want some amount of ex-ante budgeting information on how much the charges will be for multiple billing periods, ISPs may find it important that they give consumers an estimate of the ex-post charges at the beginning of a billing cycle. They may be able to do this by capturing some traffic measurements for a past billing cycle and then formulate the estimate based upon past behavior. However, a better way to reduce the uncertainty in the ex-post charge may be for the ISP to give its users the tools to do better network management and control the upper bound of the ex-post charge.

Finally, ISPs use of ex-post charging helps them design and allocate network resources. As an ISP collects metrics on the utilization and burstiness of its customers' traffic, it can forecast the demand for network resources more accurately. In the short term, this helps the ISP define allocation policies for routing and buffering policies.[7] In the long term, the ISP can get clear signals on where to expand network resources. Overall, we see this benefit of ex-post charging to help with the scalability and extensibility goals of Internet pricing.

---

[7] In some cases where an ISP may cache content on its network, the caching policies may also be affected by ex-post charging in the short run.

6. Conclusions

This paper presents the benefits and drawbacks of ex-post Internet charging. We believe that the general approach of ex-post charging has some definite advantages to other approaches especially when supporting differentiated services. Specifically, the ex-post charging approach works with aggregate statistics of utilization and burstiness so the administrative overhead is quite small relative to dynamic pricing. Furthermore, since the user knows the charging model before they send the traffic, users can more easily budget their costs (unlike dynamic pricing) and independently decide if and how they want to shape their traffic to reduce their costs. Finally, charging different prices for different service qualities ensures that customers will have better incentives to use higher service qualities when the higher price can be justified unlike ex-ante pricing.

The increased availability of bandwidth does not detract from some of the benefits of ex-post charging. Although greater bandwidth may eliminate some causes for congestion, it may never alleviate the problem of burstiness that we identify in the paper. Even if bandwidth availability approaches infinity, there will still be a chance for Internet traffic to collide before it ever reaches the "fat pipes" of the network. More importantly, the increased demand of bandwidth to support real-time applications-including video and voice-may increase the likelihood of bursty traffic thereby making ex-post charging even more attractive.

Further exploration of ex-post charging models is required. In particular, there are two specific areas where the models have room for further investigation. The first involves the best granularity for data collection. Finer granularity gives more precise measurement of utilization and burstiness and, therefore, the ex-post charge. However, finer granularity imposes an overhead cost of data collection. The second area that deserves more attention is the formulae themselves. While we understand the general shape of the relationships between burstiness, utilization, and price, it is important to determine how to set the values of the constants in the functions. We need to do further empirical research to understand how an ISP should set these constants. Perhaps simulation using traffic sources along with market modeling similar to [7] can help in this setting. Finally, the question of overall network utilization needs to be considered. While this paper argues that network traffic should be better behaved (i.e. less bursty), it is unknown whether or not network utilization may go up or down. On one hand, network utilization may go down because the network administrator tries to reduce their charge and starts preventing some types of traffic to be sent. On the other hand, network utilization may increase because a more well-behaved network may open up the possibility for new types of real-time applications such as real-time. Perhaps through an implementation of these charges, one could investigate the overall impact on network utilization.

Perhaps the most significant benefit of ex-post charging is that it may become the first step in creating an improved Internet infrastructure. As ISPs and Internet users adopt an ex-post charging mechanism, both may benefit in the long run. ISPs can now set prices to give an incentive for users to manage their networks. This can be accomplished without the billing and computation overhead that is necessary for dynamic pricing models. As a result of better network management, the infrastructure may have increased quality of service, better security, and enhanced scalability and extensibility. These are the goals for Internet pricing as outlined by this paper. Perhaps, because of the positive attributes of ex-post charging, future high bandwidth applications, such as Internet telephony or video on demand, may hold greater promise.

Acknowledgments

The authors wish to thank Ioannis Gamvros, Carlos Hernandez, Cesar Lapuerta and Joab Noda for their contributions to this work. The authors are solely responsible for any errors. Dr. Bailey and Dr. Raghavan's research has been supported in part by contract # MDA 90499C2521 from the National Security Agency. Mr. Nagel's work has been supported in part by the Center for Satellite and Hybrid Communication Networks at the University of Maryland. This paper was first presented at the MIT Workshop on Internet Service Quality Economics, December 2-3, 1999. We thank the workshop participants for their feedback.

References

[1] D. Bertsekas and R. Gallager. *Data Networks*. Prentice Hall, New Jersey, second edition, 1992.

[2] N. Brownlee. *Internet Economics*, chapter Internet Pricing in Practice, pages 77–90. MIT Press, Cambridge, MA, 1997.

[3] David B. Clark. *Internet Economics*, chapter Internet Cost Allocation and Pricing, pages 215–252. MIT Press, Cambridge, MA, 1997.

[4] R. Guérin, H. Ahmadi, and M. Naghshineh. Equivalent capacity and its application to bandwidth allocation in high-speed networks. *IEEE J Sel. Areas in Commun.*, 9(7):968–981, 1991.

[5] J. Hui. Resource allocation for broadband networks. *IEEE J Sel. Areas in Commun.*, 6(9):1598–1608, 1988.

[6] F. P. Kelly. Effective bandwidths at multi-class queues. *Queueing Systems*, 9:5–16, 1991.

[7] M. Mandjes and N. van Foreest. Aspects of pricing in an integrated services network. Working paper, Bell Labs, Lucent Technologies, 1999.

[8] Steven McCanne and V. Jacobson. The bsd packet filter: A new architecture for user-level packet capture. In *USENIX Technical Conference Proceedings*, pages 259–269, San Diego, Winter 1993. USENIX.

[9] Lee W. McKnight and Joseph P Bailey. *Internet Economics*. MIT Press, Cambridge, MA, 1997.

[10] V. Siris, D. J. Songhurst, G. D. Stamoulis, and M. Stoer. Usage-based charging using effect bandwidth: Studies and reality. Technical Report 243, ICS-FORTH, January 1999.

Chapter 5

ERROR BOUNDS
FOR HIERARCHICAL ROUTING

Eric Rosenberg

AT&T Labs
Middletown, NJ 07748
U.S.A.
ericr@att.com

Abstract   We present a general model of hierarchical routing, with multiple levels of hierarchy, which introduces the concept of a cluster estimator to approximate the distance from a border node of a cluster to any node in the cluster. We characterize the hierarchical path length c_E^H and prove that the average error is minimized using the overall best routing cluster estimator. We present the first worst case upper bound on the error $c_E^H - c^\star$ in hierarchical routing that is valid for any cluster estimator, and show the bound is sharp for two-level networks.

Keywords: Network; hierarchical routing; shortest path; telecommunications.

1.   Introduction

In hierarchical routing schemes, nodes are grouped into clusters at multiple levels, and a given node sees only a summarized view of the entire network. Hierarchical routing is needed, for example, when the number of nodes or links becomes larger than can be supported by a flat (non-hierarchical) routing method, or for administrative/organizational reasons (e.g., Autonomous Systems in the Internet). Hierarchical routing reduces the memory and processing required at each node, and reduces the time required to compute each node's routing table. The routing table for node n specifies, for each destination t, a cost to reach t and the next node to visit on the best path to t. Two categories of hierarchical methods are (*i*) link-state methods, based on the classic Dijkstra label-setting method [1], in which each node stores a view of the network topology, and (*ii*) distance-vector methods, based on the classic Bellman-

Ford label-correcting method [1], in which nodes exchange and update routing tables until convergence has occurred. In telecommunications, the hierarchical routing protocols PNNI [14] and OSPF [12] are link-state methods, while the inter-domain routing protocol BGP4 [18] and the Kleinrock-Kamoun method [7] are distance-vector methods. The first link-state hierarchical routing method not requiring complete topology information at each level is [4].

In Section 2 we present a general method of hierarchical routing, based on the new concept of a cluster estimator. In Section 3 we show that this method (which is not limited to telecommunications applications) encompasses BGP (under appropriate configuration), and the Kleinrock-Kamoun method. Since a hierarchical routing method uses a summarized view of the network, it yields a route that may be worse than the route obtained using a flat routing method. In Section 4 we study the error in hierarchical routing. Let $c_E^H(s, t)$ be the cost of the path from s to t obtained by a hierarchical routing scheme, and let $c^\star(s, t)$ be the cost of the shortest path obtained using flat routing. Previous work [7] provided a worst case (over all s, t) upper bound on $c_E^H(s, t) - c^\star(s, t)$ only for the particular case of the "closest entry routing" cluster estimator, which models the destination cluster as a single logical point. Here we present a worst case upper bound on $c_E^H(s, t) - c^\star(s, t)$ that is valid for any cluster estimator. The bound is tight for a two-level network. We also consider the average error with hierarchical routing and show that the "overall best routing" cluster estimator yields a smaller average error than any other cluster estimator. This extends previous work [7] showing only that the "overall best routing" cluster estimator has lower average error than the "closest entry routing" cluster estimator.

2.   Hierarchical Routing

Consider the undirected network $(\mathcal{N}, \mathcal{A})$ with node set $\mathcal{N}$ and arc set $\mathcal{A}$. In telecommunication applications, a node is a physical piece of equipment that receives and forwards data (e.g., Internet Protocol (IP) packets), based on the destination address and the information in the local routing table, to the next node in the best path towards the destination node. Two nodes are *adjacent* if there is an arc connecting them. A network is *connected* if there is a path between any two nodes. Let c_{ij} be the non-negative cost of the arc connecting adjacent nodes i and j. The *path length* of a path is the sum of the arc costs over all the arcs in the path. The terms "cost" and "length," and "path" and "route," are used interchangeably.

A hierarchical routing method groups nodes into H levels of hierarchy. When $H = 1$, there is no hierarchy, and the network is said to be "flat." For $H > 1$, a network with H levels of hierarchy contains, for $h = 1, 2, \cdots, H-1$,

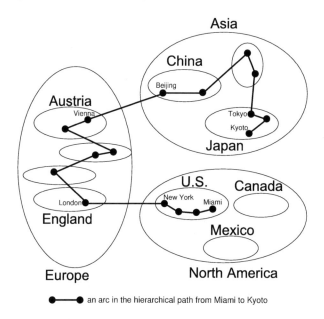

Figure 5.1. Routing in a 3-level hierarchy.

one or more level-h clusters, where a level-h cluster $\mathcal{C}_h$ is a collection of one or more level-$(h-1)$ clusters $\mathcal{C}_{h-1}$, together with the arcs connecting the level-$(h-1)$ clusters, such that each node in a given level-h cluster has the same view of the hierarchical network topology. A level-0 cluster is a node. We define the single level-H cluster $\mathcal{C}_H$ to be the entire network. For example, Figure 1 shows a three-level ($H = 3$) node/country/continent world hierarchy, where each country (e.g., England or China) is a level-1 cluster, each continent (e.g., Europe or Asia) is a level-2 cluster, and the entire network is the single level-3 cluster. (All future hierarchy examples will refer to this three-level hierarchy.) The number of nodes in the cluster $\mathcal{C}$ is denoted by $|\mathcal{C}|$.

Assumption 1. In a network with H levels of hierarchy, for each node n and for $h = 1, 2, \cdots, H - 1$, there is a level-h cluster containing n.

Two clusters are *peers* if they have the same parent cluster in the hierarchy tree (e.g., Mexico and Canada are peers). The topology of each $\mathcal{C}_h$, for $h \geq 2$, might, but need not, be designed by hierarchical methods (e.g., [17]). In the PNNI protocol, which supports up to 104 levels of hierarchy ($H = 104$), clusters are called "peer groups." In OSPF, which supports only two levels of hierarchy ($H = 2$), clusters are called "OSPF areas." In BGP, which natively supports only two levels of hierarchy, clusters are called "autonomous systems" (ASs).

A level-h cluster is visible only to the nodes in the parent level-$(h+1)$ cluster. For example, Japan is visible only to the nodes in Asia but not to the nodes in any other continent. The *scope* of a node $n \in \mathcal{N}$, denoted by $scope(n)$, is the set of clusters for which n has a routing table entry. For example, if $n =$ Paris, then $scope(n)$ contains all nodes in France (including Paris itself), all countries in Europe (including France), and all continents (including Europe). Let $\mathcal{C}_h(n)$ denote the unique level-h cluster containing n. We can determine $scope(n)$ as follows.

---

procedure $scope(n)$
1   **initialize**: $scope(n) = \emptyset$;
2   **for** $(h = 0, 1, 2, \cdots, H - 1)$ {
3   **for** (each level- h cluster $\mathcal{C}$ in $\mathcal{C}_{h+1}(n)$) {
5            $scope(n) = scope(n) \bigcup \mathcal{C}$;
6   }
7   }
8   **return** $scope(n)$;

Let $\mathcal{C}_h$ be a level-h cluster. A level-h border node of $\mathcal{C}_h$ is a node of $\mathcal{C}_h$ adjacent to some node in some other level-h cluster $\tilde{\mathcal{C}}_h$, such that $\mathcal{C}_h$ and $\tilde{\mathcal{C}}_h$ belong to the same parent level-$(h + 1)$ cluster. The level-0 border nodes of England are those nodes in England adjacent to some other node in England. The level-1 border nodes of England are those nodes in England adjacent to some node in some other country in Europe. A node in England adjacent to a node in some other continent (e.g., adjacent to a Miami, Florida node), but not to a node in some other country in Europe, is a level-2 border node of Europe but not a level-1 border node. A node can be a level-h border node for multiple values of h. Let $\mathcal{B}_h$ denote the set of level-h border nodes of a given level-h cluster $\mathcal{C}_h$, and let $\mathcal{B}_h(n)$ be the set of level-h border nodes of $\mathcal{C}_h(n)$. Note that for $\mathcal{C}_H$, the entire network, we have $\mathcal{B}_H = \emptyset$.

For $s \in \mathcal{N}$ and $t \in \mathcal{N}$, define $h(s,t) = \min\{h \mid s \in \mathcal{C}_h(t)\}$. Note that $h(s,t) = h(t,s)$ and $\mathcal{C}_{h(s,t)}$ is the smallest cluster containing both s and t. If $s \neq t$, then $1 \leq h(s,t) \leq H$, and $\mathcal{C}_{h(s,t)-1}(t)$ is the unique cluster at level $h(s,t) - 1$ which contains t but does not contain s. Define $\mathcal{H} = \{1, 2, 3, \cdots, H\}$ and $\mathcal{H}_0 = \{0, 1, 2, \cdots, H\}$. Any routing method applied to a flat network is said to be a "flat" routing method.

Assumption 2. For $h \in \mathcal{H}$, each level-h cluster is connected.

Pick $s \in \mathcal{N}$ and $t \in \mathcal{N}$. We consider two path costs:
(i) $c^*(s,t)$: the minimum path length in $(\mathcal{N}, \mathcal{A})$ from s to t, using flat routing,
(ii) $c^R(s,t)$: the minimum path length from s to t, using flat routing, and where the path is restricted to lie in $\mathcal{C}_{h(s,t)}$.

2.1 Cluster Estimator

A cluster estimator is a function that returns a number representing the cost from a border node of a cluster to *any* node of the cluster. Formally, we say that the function $c^E(\cdot,\cdot)$ is a *cluster estimator* if for each $h \in \mathcal{H}_0$, each level-h cluster $\mathcal{C}_h$, and each $b \in \mathcal{B}_h$ we have (*i*) $c^E(b,\mathcal{C}_h) \geq 0$ and (*ii*) if $\mathcal{C}_0 = \{b\}$ then $c^E(b,\mathcal{C}_0) = 0$. This definition generalizes previously published schemes we will consider below. In hierarchical routing schemes, the estimate $c^E(b,\mathcal{C}_h)$, where $b \in \mathcal{B}_h$, is advertised to each node in $\mathcal{C}_{h+1} - \mathcal{C}_h$, where $\mathcal{C}_{h+1}$ is the parent cluster of $\mathcal{C}_h$.

2.1.1 Closest Entry Routing. The Closest Entry Routing (CER) scheme [7] models the cluster $\mathcal{C}_h$ by assuming that all arcs inside the cluster have zero cost. (This is the "simple node representation" scheme of PNNI [14].) The CER estimator $c_{cer}^E(\cdot,\cdot)$ is defined by

$$c_{cer}^E(b,\mathcal{C}_h) = 0 \quad \text{for each } \mathcal{C}_h, \ h \in \mathcal{H}_0, \text{ and } b \in \mathcal{B}_h . \tag{1}$$

We can now present a generic hierarchical routing method and convergence proof. If $\mathcal{R}_1$ is a path from u to v, and $\mathcal{R}_2$ is a path from v to w, then by $\mathcal{R}_1 \bigcup \mathcal{R}_2$ we mean the concatenated path from u to w. Let $\mathcal{R}^R(s,t)$ denote any path in $\mathcal{C}_{h(s,t)}$ from s to t with cost $c^R(s,t)$. Let $\emptyset$ be the null route (whose cost is 0), and define $\emptyset \bigcup \mathcal{R} = \mathcal{R}$. We say that $y \in \text{argmin}\{f(x) \mid x \in \mathcal{X}\}$ if $y \in \mathcal{X}$ and $f(y) = \min\{f(x) \mid x \in \mathcal{X}\}$.

```
procedure  HierarchicalRoute(s, t)
data:   source s, destination t,
   cluster estimator c^E(·, ·);
1   initialize:  R = ∅  and  h = h(s, t);
2   while (h > 0) {
3       let b⁰ ∈ argmin{c^R(s, b) + c^E(b, C_{h-1}(t)) | b ∈ B_{h-1}(t)};
4       R = R⋃R^R(s, b⁰);
5       s = b⁰  and  h = h − 1;
6   }
7   return R;
```

We call the path $\mathcal{R}$ returned by this procedure a "hierarchical path."

Theorem 1. Under Assumptions 1 and 2, for each $s \in \mathcal{N}$ and $t \in \mathcal{N}$, the procedure $HierarchicalRoute(s,t)$ returns a path from s to t in $h(s,t)$ iterations of the **while** loop.

Proof. Pick $s \in \mathcal{N}$ and $t \in \mathcal{N}$. If $h(s,t) = 0$ then $s = t$ and the procedure returns $\mathcal{R} = \emptyset$, so assume $h(s,t) > 0$. By Assumption 2 there is a path $\mathcal{R}$

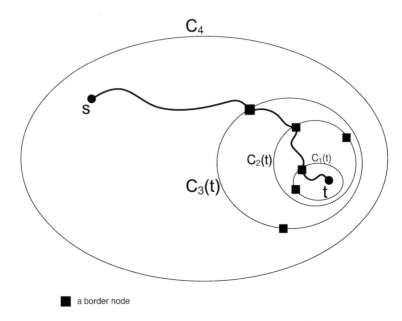

Figure 5.2.   Hierarchical routing using CER ($H = 4$).

from s to t contained in $\mathcal{C}_{h(s,t)}$. Suppose first $h(s,t) = 1$. Then s and t lie in the same level-1 cluster. Thus in Step 3 we have $b^0 = t$ and we return $\mathcal{R}$ after 1 iteration. Now suppose the result holds for $h(s,t) = 2, 3, \cdots, k-1$, where $k - 1 < H$, and now suppose $h(s,t) = k$. By Assumption 1, s and t lie in different level-$(k-1)$ clusters, so $\mathcal{R}$ must contain some arc (n, b^0), where $b^0 \in \mathcal{C}_{k-1}(t)$ and $n \notin \mathcal{C}_{k-1}(t)$. By Assumption 1, n is contained in some level-$(k-1)$ cluster (which could be $\mathcal{C}_{k-1}(s)$). Hence, by definition, $b^0 \in \mathcal{B}_{k-1}(t)$, so $\mathcal{B}_{k-1}(t) \neq \emptyset$, and Step 3 can be executed. Since b^0 and t are both in $\mathcal{C}_{k-1}(t)$, by the induction hypothesis the procedure will compute a path from b^0 to t in $k - 1$ iterations.   ∎

Figure 2 illustrates hierarchical routing with CER when $H = 4$ and $|\mathcal{B}_h(t)|$ $= 2$ for $h = 1, 2, 3$. We can now define a third path cost: let $c_E^H(s,t)$ be the total path length for the route $\mathcal{R}$ obtained from $Hierarchical Route(s,t)$ with the cluster estimator $c^E(\cdot, \cdot)$. We call $c_E^H(s,t)$ the "hierarchical path length." Thus, e.g., $c_{cer}^H(s,t)$ is the hierarchical path length using the CER cluster estimator, and $c_{obr}^H(s,t)$ is the hierarchical path length using the OBR cluster estimator, which we now consider.

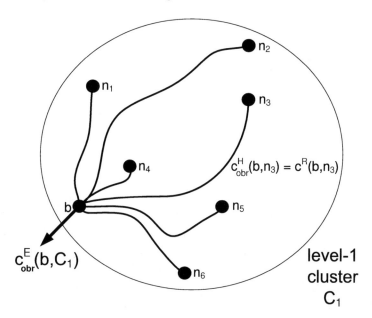

Figure 5.3. OBR cluster estimator ($h = 1$).

2.1.2 Overall Best Routing.

The Overall Best Routing (OBR) cluster estimator $c_{obr}^E(\cdot, \cdot)$ is defined in [7] by

$$c_{obr}^E(b, \mathcal{C}_h) = \frac{1}{|\mathcal{C}_h|} \sum_{n \in \mathcal{C}_h} c_{obr}^H(b, n) \text{ for } \mathcal{C}_h, \ h \in \mathcal{H}_0, \text{ and } b \in \mathcal{B}_h. \quad (2)$$

Pick $b \in \mathcal{B}_h$. If $h = 0$, then $c_{obr}^E(b, \mathcal{C}_0) = c_{obr}^H(b, b) = c^R(b, b) = 0$. If $h = 1$, then $b \in \mathcal{B}_1$ and $n \in \mathcal{C}_1$ lie in the same level-1 cluster, so $c_{obr}^H(b, n) = c^R(b, n)$. Since $scope(b)$ includes all nodes in $\mathcal{C}_1$, then b has all the data needed to compute $c_{obr}^E(b, \mathcal{C}_1)$ using (2). This is illustrated in Figure 3. We defer the discussion of how to recursively compute $c_{obr}^E(b, \mathcal{C}_h)$ for $h > 1$.

Another cluster estimator is $c_{max}^E(b, \mathcal{C}_h) = \max\{c_{max}^H(b, n) \mid n \in \mathcal{C}_h\}$. Note that for a level-1 cluster $\mathcal{C}_1$ we have $c_{max}^E(b, \mathcal{C}_1) = \max\{c^R(b, n) \mid n \in \mathcal{C}_1\}$. This is the estimator recommended by Moy [12] for OSPF.

2.2 Hierarchical Path Length

We now begin our study of the path length of a route returned by *HierarchicalRoute*(s, t). The following fundamental result extends [7], Proposition 8, which considers only the CER and OBR estimators and the Kleinrock-Kamoun method to be described below.

Theorem 2. Let Assumptions 1 and 2 hold, let $c^E(\cdot, \cdot)$ be a cluster estimator, let $s \in \mathcal{N}$ and $t \in \mathcal{N}$, and set $h = h(s, t)$. Then the total path length $c_E^H(s, t)$ from s to t, using *HierarchicalRoute*(s, t) satisfies the recursion

$$c_E^H(s, t) = c^R(s, b^0) + c_E^H(b^0, t), \qquad (3)$$

where

$$b^0 \in \operatorname{argmin}\{c^R(s, b) + c^E(b, \mathcal{C}_{h-1}(t)) \mid b \in \mathcal{B}_{h-1}(t)\}.$$

Proof. Let $c^E(\cdot, \cdot)$ be a cluster estimator, pick $s \in \mathcal{N}$ and $t \in \mathcal{N}$, and set $h = h(s, t)$. The proof proceeds by induction on h. If $h = 0$ then $s = t$ and the result holds, so assume $s \neq t$. Suppose $h = 1$. Then s and t belong to the same level-1 cluster, so $\mathcal{C}_0(t) = \mathcal{B}_0(t) = \{t\}$. Then $b^0 = t$, which implies $c^E(b^0, \mathcal{C}_0(t)) = 0$ and $c_E^H(b^0, t) = 0$, which establishes (3) when $h = 1$.

Suppose the theorem is true for $h = 2, 3, \cdots, k - 1$, where $k - 1 < H$, and now suppose $h = k$. Let $b^0 \in \mathcal{B}_{k-1}(t)$ be the border node selected in Step 3 of *HierarchicalRoute*(s, t). Then the hierarchical path from s to t will follow the shortest path in $\mathcal{C}_k(t)$ to b^0, and the length of this path is $c^R(s, b^0)$. At b^0, procedure *HierarchicalRoute*(b^0, t) calculates a hierarchical path in $\mathcal{C}_{k-1}(t)$ from b^0 to t, and the cost of this path is, by definition, $c_E^H(b^0, t)$. Hence the total path length from s to t, using hierarchical routing, is given by (3). ∎

3.   Two Hierarchical Routing Schemes

To implement *HierarchicalRoute*(s, t) we must be able to execute Step 3 of that procedure. We now show how this is accomplished in the Kleinrock-Kamoun method [7] and in BGP. Step 3 can also be executed for PNNI routing, but that discussion is omitted for brevity.

3.1   Kleinrock-Kamoun Method

Pick $t \in \mathcal{N}$, define $\mathcal{C}_h = \mathcal{C}_h(t)$, and let $\mathcal{C}_{h+1}$ be the parent cluster of $\mathcal{C}_h$. Let i and j be adjacent nodes such that $i \in \mathcal{C}_{h+1} - \mathcal{C}_h$ and $j \in (\mathcal{C}_{h+1} - \mathcal{C}_h) \cup \mathcal{B}_h$. Let $c^E(\cdot, \cdot)$ be a cluster estimator. Previously we defined $c^E(b, \mathcal{C}_h)$ only for $b \in \mathcal{B}_h$. We now compute $c^E(i, \mathcal{C}_h)$ for $i \in \mathcal{C}_{h+1} - \mathcal{C}_h$ using a Bellman-Ford type scheme. Let $NextNode(i, \mathcal{C}_h)$ denote the successor node to i on any path $\mathcal{R}$ returned by *HierarchicalRoute*(s, t) (note that $NextNode(i, \mathcal{C}_h)$ is independent of where in $\mathcal{C}_h$ the destination lies).

Update Rule Initialization. For $h = 1, 2, \cdots, H - 1$, (i) set $c^E(i, \mathcal{C}_h) = +\infty$ for $i \in \mathcal{C}_{h+1} - \mathcal{C}_h$, and (ii) compute $c^E(b, \mathcal{C}_h)$ for $b \in \mathcal{B}_h$.

Update Rule. If $i \in \mathcal{C}_{h+1} - \mathcal{C}_h$ receives from $j \in (\mathcal{C}_{h+1} - \mathcal{C}_h) \bigcup \mathcal{B}_h$ the value $c^E(j, \mathcal{C}_h)$, and if $c_{ij} + c^E(j, \mathcal{C}_h) < c^E(i, \mathcal{C}_h)$, then we set $c^E(i, \mathcal{C}_h) = c_{ij} + c^E(j, \mathcal{C}_h)$ and $NextNode(i, \mathcal{C}_h) = j$.

We showed above that $b \in \mathcal{B}_1$ has all the data required to compute $c^E_{obr}(b, \mathcal{C}_1)$ for the OBR estimate (2). Now we prove that, for $h = 2, 3, \cdots, H - 1$, node $b \in \mathcal{B}_h$ has all the data required to compute $c^E_{obr}(b, \mathcal{C}_h)$, so that part (*ii*) of the Update Rule Initialization can be performed. This result is not provided in [7].

Assumption 3. For $h = 1, 2, \cdots, H - 2$, and for each level-h cluster $\mathcal{C}_h$, the values $|\mathcal{C}_h|$ and $c^E_{obr}(b, \mathcal{C}_h)$, $b \in \mathcal{B}_h$ are advertised to all nodes in the parent cluster of $\mathcal{C}_h$.

Theorem 3. Under Assumptions 1, 2, and 3, for $h = 1, 2, \cdots, H - 1$ and $b \in \mathcal{B}_h$, node b has all the data required to compute the OBR estimate $c^E_{obr}(b, \mathcal{C}_h)$ in the Kleinrock-Kamoun method.

Proof. The proof is by induction on h. For $h = 1$, we showed above that each $b \in \mathcal{B}_1$ stores the data required to compute $c^E_{obr}(b, \mathcal{C}_1)$. Suppose the result holds for $h = 2, 3, \cdots, k$, where $k < H - 1$, and now suppose $h = k + 1$. Let $\mathcal{C}_{k+1}$ be a level-$(k + 1)$ cluster, pick $b \in \mathcal{B}_{k+1}$, and consider the computation of $c^E_{obr}(b, \mathcal{C}_{k+1})$.

The set of nodes in cluster $\mathcal{C}_{k+1}$ is the union of the nodes in all level-k child clusters of $\mathcal{C}_{k+1}$. Suppose there are J child clusters. Define $\mathcal{J} = \{1, 2, \cdots, J\}$ and denote the J child clusters by $\{\mathcal{C}_k^j \mid j \in \mathcal{J}\}$. By the induction hypothesis, for each $j \in \mathcal{J}$ and each $d \in \mathcal{B}_k^j$, node d has the data required to compute $c^E_{obr}(d, \mathcal{C}_k^j)$. For $j \in \mathcal{J}$, let

$$d_j^0 \in \operatorname{argmin}\{c^R(b, d) + c^E_{obr}(d, \mathcal{C}_k^j) \mid d \in \mathcal{B}_k^j\} .$$

By Theorem 2, for each $n \in \mathcal{C}_k^j$ we have $c^H_{obr}(b, n) = c^R(b, d_j^0) + c^H_{obr}(d_j^0, n)$. Thus

$$\sum_{n \in \mathcal{C}_k^j} c^H_{obr}(b, n) = \sum_{n \in \mathcal{C}_k^j} \{c^R(b, d_j^0) + c^H_{obr}(d_j^0, n)\}$$

$$= |\mathcal{C}_k^j| c^R(b, d_j^0) + \sum_{n \in \mathcal{C}_k^j} c^H_{obr}(d_j^0, n)$$

$$= |\mathcal{C}_k^j| c^R(b, d_j^0) + |\mathcal{C}_k^j| c^E_{obr}(d_j^0, \mathcal{C}_k^j) , \qquad (4)$$

where the final equality follows from (2). By Assumption 3, for $j \in \mathcal{J}$, node $b \in \mathcal{B}_{k+1}$ receives from $d_j^0 \in \mathcal{B}_k^j$ the values $|\mathcal{C}_k^j|$ and $c^E_{obr}(d_j^0, \mathcal{C}_k^j)$. Hence b has the data required to compute $\sum_{n \in \mathcal{C}_k^j} c^H_{obr}(b, n)$ using (4). We have

$$c^E_{obr}(b, \mathcal{C}_{k+1}) = (1/|\mathcal{C}_{k+1}|) \sum_{n \in \mathcal{C}_{k+1}} c^H_{obr}(b, n)$$

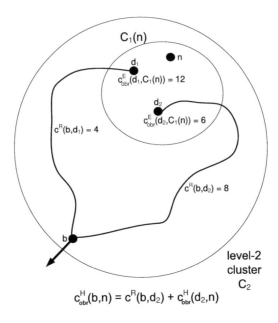

$$c_{obr}^{H}(b,n) = c^{R}(b,d_2) + c_{obr}^{H}(d_2,n)$$

Figure 5.4.　Path length with OBR ($h = 2$).

$$
\begin{aligned}
&= \left(1 / \sum_{j \in \mathcal{J}} |\mathcal{C}_k^j|\right) \sum_{j \in \mathcal{J}} \sum_{n \in \mathcal{C}_k^j} c_{obr}^{H}(b,n) \\
&= \left(1 / \sum_{j \in \mathcal{J}} |\mathcal{C}_k^j|\right) \sum_{j \in \mathcal{J}} \Big\{ |\mathcal{C}_k^j| c^{R}(b, d_j^0) \\
&\quad + |\mathcal{C}_k^j| c_{obr}^{E}(d_j^0, \mathcal{C}_k^j) \Big\},
\end{aligned}
\tag{5}
$$

where the final equality follows from (4). Hence b has the data required to compute $c_{obr}^{E}(b, \mathcal{C}_{k+1})$ using (5). ■

Computation of $c_{obr}^{E}(b, \mathcal{C}_h)$ for $h = 2$ is illustrated in Figure 4, where the two border nodes of $\mathcal{C}_1(n)$ are d_1 and d_2, and $b \in \mathcal{B}_2$. Since $c^{R}(b, d_1) + c_{obr}^{E}(d_1, \mathcal{C}_1(n)) = 4 + 12 > c^{R}(b, d_2) + c_{obr}^{E}(d_2, \mathcal{C}_1(n)) = 8 + 6$, we have $d^0 = d_2$ and $c_{obr}^{H}(b, t) = c^{R}(b, d_2) + c_{obr}^{H}(d_2, t)$ for $t \in \mathcal{C}_1(n)$.

3.2　　BGP

In BGP, which natively models a two-level hierarchy ($H = 2$), level-1 clusters are Autonomous Systems (ASs), and level-1 border nodes are called Autonomous System Boundary Routers (ASBRs). In BGP4 [18], when all local preferences are set to the same value, and when no AS-path padding is used, the BGP path selection method will find a minimum AS path length route to the destination AS, where the AS path length is the number of ASs traversed.

We now show that BGP4 routing, with all local preference values equal and no AS-path padding, is a special case of the Kleinrock-Kamoun method with $H = 2$. First, set $c_{ij} = 0$ for each intra-AS arc (i, j). Second, if adjacent ASBRs i and j are in different ASs, set $c_{ij} = 1$. Third, let the CER estimator (1) be used, so $c_{cer}^E(b, C_1) = 0$ for each ASBR b of the AS C_1. Let C be an AS and let n be an ASBR in AS D, where $D \neq C$. Using the *Update Rule*, upon convergence the value $c_{cer}^E(n, C)$ is the minimum AS path length from n to C. Internal routing protocols such as OSPF are then used to disseminate $c_{cer}^E(n, C)$ to all nodes in D.

4. Hierarchical Routing Error

In this section we derive the first worst case bound on $c_E^H(s, t) - c^\star(s, t)$ that is valid for any cluster estimator, and show that the average error is minimized using the overall best routing cluster estimator. These results are useful when the hierarchy is geographical, e.g., if state-level clusters are combined into country-level clusters. In telecommunications, geographically based clustering is typically utilized in the IP and PNNI networks offered by service providers ([2], [5], [9], [10], [11], [13], [15], [16], [21]).

The *diameter* of a level-h cluster C_h, denoted by $\text{diam}(C_h)$, is defined by $\text{diam}(C_h) = \max\{c^R(s, t) \mid s, t \in C_h\}$. Let $\{\Delta_h \mid h \in \mathcal{H}_0\}$ be $H + 1$ non-negative numbers such that (*i*) $\Delta_0 = 0$ and (*ii*) $\Delta_h = \max\{\text{diam}(C_h) \mid C_h$ is a level-h cluster$\}$ for $h \in \mathcal{H}$. Thus Δ_h is an upper bound on the diameter of any level-h cluster, Δ_H is the diameter of the entire network, the diameter of a single node is $\Delta_0 = 0$, and $\Delta_1 \leq \Delta_2 \leq \cdots \leq \Delta_H$. In practice, typically, $\Delta_1 < \Delta_2 < \cdots < \Delta_H$ (the strict inequality fails to hold, e.g., when each cluster is fully connected, since then each $\Delta_h = 1$). A method for designing a cluster subject to an upper bound on the diameter is given in [17]. The following lemma generalizes [7], Lemma 1 to any cluster estimator.

Lemma 1. Let Assumptions 1 and 2 hold, let $c^E(\cdot, \cdot)$ be a cluster estimator, let $s \in \mathcal{N}$, and let $t \in \mathcal{N}$. Then

$$c_E^H(s, t) \leq \sum_{i=1}^{h(s,t)} \Delta_i . \tag{6}$$

Proof. Let $c^E(\cdot, \cdot)$ be a cluster estimator, pick $s \in \mathcal{N}$ and $t \in \mathcal{N}$, and set $h = h(s, t)$. The proof proceeds by induction on h. If $h = 0$ then $s = t$ and the result holds, so assume $s \neq t$. If $h = 1$, then s and t belong to the same level-1 cluster and $c_E^H(s, t) = c^R(s, t) \leq \Delta_1$, hence the result holds. Suppose the result holds for $h = 2, 3, \cdots, k - 1$, where $k - 1 < H$, and now suppose $h = k$.

By Theorem 2, $c_E^H(s, t) = c^R(s, b^0) + c_E^H(b^0, t)$, where $b^0 \in \mathcal{B}_{k-1}(t)$. Since s and b^0 lie in $\mathcal{C}_k(t)$, we have $c^R(s, b^0) \leq \Delta_k$. Since b^0 and t lie in $\mathcal{C}_{k-1}(t)$, by the induction hypothesis we have $c_E^H(b^0, t) \leq \sum_{i=1}^{k-1} \Delta_i$. Thus $c_E^H(s, t) \leq \sum_{i=1}^{k-1} \Delta_i + \Delta_k$, which proves the result. ∎

4.1   Worst Case Routing Error

Recall that $c^\star(s, t)$ is the minimum path length in $(\mathcal{N}, \mathcal{A})$ from s to t, using flat routing. For a two-level hierarchy, Baratz and Jaffe [3] showed that $c_E^H(s, t)/c^\star(s, t) \leq 3$ for all $s \in \mathcal{N}$ and $t \in \mathcal{N}$, and this worst case bound is sharp (i.e., it is achievable). A general result by Hagouel [6] showed that, for H-level networks, $c_E^H(s, t)/c^\star(s, t) \leq 2^H - 1$ for all $s \in \mathcal{N}$ and $t \in \mathcal{N}$; this bound is also sharp.

In practice, a bound on $c_E^H - c^\star$ is more useful than a bound on $c_E^H/c^\star$. For example, if each arc cost c_{ij} is the latency (delay) on arc (i, j), then a telecommunications service provider and its customers care about the increase in latency $c_E^H - c^\star$, not the ratio $c_E^H/c^\star$. We present the first upper bound on $c_E^H - c^\star$ that is valid for any cluster estimator. Our bound is sharp for a two-level network.

Assumption 4 below, also used in [7], is typically satisfied in practice, and can be enforced by proper selection of arc costs [22]. It says that, for any two nodes in a cluster, there is a shortest path between the nodes that lies entirely within the cluster.

Assumption 4. For $1 \leq h < H$, for each level-h cluster $\mathcal{C}_h$, and for each $s \in \mathcal{C}_h$ and $t \in \mathcal{C}_h$, we have $c^R(s, t) = c^\star(s, t)$.

Figure 5 illustrates a hierarchy for which Assumption 4 fails to hold. There are two level-1 clusters: X, containing s, t, and the arc (s, t) with cost 4, and Y, containing a, b, and the arc (a, b) with cost 1. The inter-cluster arcs (s, a) and (b, t) each have cost 1. We have $c^\star(s, t) = 3$ (for the path $s - a - b - t$), and $c^R(s, t) = 4$ (for the path $s - t$).

Recalling that $h(s, t)$ is the level of the smallest cluster containing both s and t, define

$$\mathcal{E}(h) = \max\{c_E^H(s, t) - c^\star(s, t) \mid s \in \mathcal{N}, t \in \mathcal{N}, h(s, t) = h\}. \quad (7)$$

In [6] it is shown that, for the CER cluster estimator only, $\mathcal{E}(h) \leq \sum_{i=1}^{h-1} \Delta_i$ whenever Assumptions 1, 2, and 4 hold. We now prove a bound valid for any cluster estimator.

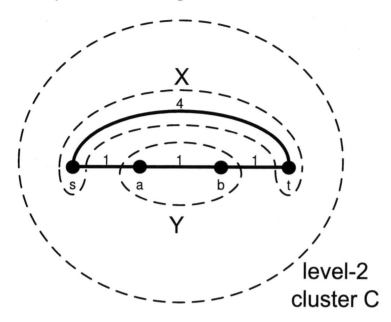

Figure 5.5. Assumption 4 fails to hold.

Theorem 4. Let Assumptions 1, 2, and 4 hold, and let $c^E(\cdot, \cdot)$ be a cluster estimator. Then

$$\mathcal{E}(h) \leq 2\Delta_{h-1} + \sum_{i=1}^{h-2} \Delta_i . \tag{8}$$

Moreover, the bound is sharp for $h = 2$.

Proof. Let $c^E(\cdot, \cdot)$ be a cluster estimator, pick $s \in \mathcal{N}$ and $t \in \mathcal{N}$, and let $h = h(s, t)$. By Assumption 4, there is a path $\mathcal{R}^\star$ from s to t, contained in $\mathcal{C}_h(t)$, whose cost is $c^\star(s, t)$. Following $\mathcal{R}^\star$ from s to t, let $b^\star$ be the first node encountered on this path that is contained in $\mathcal{C}_{h-1}(t)$. Then $c^\star(s, t) = c^\star(s, b^\star) + c^\star(b^\star, t)$. By Theorem 2, $c_E^H(s, t) = c^R(s, b^0) + c_E^H(b^0, t)$ for some $b^0 \in \mathcal{B}_{h-1}(t)$. Since $b^0 \in \mathcal{B}_{h-1}(t)$, by Lemma 1 we have

$$c_E^H(b^0, t) \leq \sum_{i=1}^{h-1} \Delta_i . \tag{9}$$

By Assumption 4, $c^R(s, b^0) = c^\star(s, b^0)$. As $c^\star(s, b^0) \leq c^\star(s, b^\star) + c^\star(b^\star, b^0)$,

$$c^R(s, b^0) \leq c^\star(s, b^\star) + c^\star(b^\star, b^0) . \tag{10}$$

Since both $b^\star$ and b^0 lie in $\mathcal{C}_{h-1}(t)$, we have $c^\star(b^\star, b^0) = c^R(b^\star, b^0) \leq \Delta_{h-1}$. By (10) we have

$$c^R(s, b^0) - c^\star(s, b^\star) \leq c^\star(b^\star, b^0) \leq \Delta_{h-1} . \tag{11}$$

From (11) and (9),

$$
\begin{aligned}
c_E^H(s,t) - c^\star(s,t) &= [c^R(s,b^0) + c_E^H(b^0,t)] - [c^\star(s,b^\star) + c^\star(b^\star,t)] \\
&= [c^R(s,b^0) - c^\star(s,b^\star)] + [c_E^H(b^0,t) - c^\star(b^\star,t)] \\
&\leq \Delta_{h-1} + c_E^H(b^0,t) \\
&\leq \Delta_{h-1} + \sum_{i=1}^{h-1} \Delta_i \\
&= 2\Delta_{h-1} + \sum_{i=1}^{h-2} \Delta_i \ .
\end{aligned}
$$

To show that the bound is sharp for $H = 2$, consider the network of Figure 6, where two level-1 clusters are interconnected by two arcs of length L. We have $\Delta_1 = \Delta$. Let the cluster estimator $c^E(\cdot,\cdot)$ be defined by

$$
c^E(b,\mathcal{C}_1) = (1/|\mathcal{C}_1|) \sum_{n \in \mathcal{C}_1} [c^R(b,n)]^2 \ .
$$

Consider routing from $s = b_1$ to $t = b_3$. Border node b_3 advertises the cost $c^E(b_3,\mathcal{C}_1) = (1/3)(0 + (\Delta - \delta)^2 + \Delta^2)$, and border node b_4 advertises the cost $c^E(b_4,\mathcal{C}_1) = (1/3)(0 + \delta^2 + \Delta^2)$. A little algebra shows that $c^R(s,b_4) + c^E(b_4,\mathcal{C}_1) < c^R(s,b_3) + c^E(b_3,\mathcal{C}_1)$ whenever $2\delta\Delta + 3\Delta < \Delta^2$, which holds for all sufficiently large Δ. Hence, for all sufficiently large Δ, source s chooses the path (s,b_2,b_4,t) with cost $L + 2\Delta$, rather than the shortest path (s,t) with cost L. ∎

It is not known if the bound is sharp for $h(s,t) > 2$. As an application of Theorem 4, consider a two-level network with rectilinear (Manhattan) routing, where each level-1 cluster is a square array of m^2 nodes, and the network is a square array of m^2 level-1 clusters. If each $c_{ij} = 1$ then $\Delta_1 = 2(m-1)$, so $\mathcal{E}(2) = 2\Delta_1 = 4(m-1)$, and $\mathcal{E}(2)/|\mathcal{N}| \approx 4/m^3$.

4.2   Average Routing Error

Let $N = |\mathcal{N}|$ be the number of nodes in the network. Assume that the connection between each of the $N(N-1)$ pairs of nodes is given the same weight, namely $1/(N(N-1))$. Define

$$
\bar{c}^\star = \frac{1}{N(N-1)} \sum_{s \in \mathcal{N}} \sum_{t \in \mathcal{N}} c^\star(s,t) \tag{12}
$$

$$
\bar{c}_E^H = \frac{1}{N(N-1)} \sum_{s \in \mathcal{N}} \sum_{t \in \mathcal{N}} c_E^H(s,t) \ . \tag{13}
$$

Then $\bar{c}^\star$ is the average optimal path length using flat routing, and $\bar{c}_E^H$ is the average hierarchical path length using *HierarchicalRoute*(s,t) and cluster es-

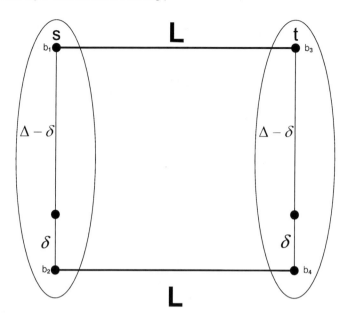

Figure 5.6. Worst case error is achieved.

timator $c^E(\cdot, \cdot)$. Similarly, let $\bar{c}_{obr}^H$ be the average hierarchical path length using *HierarchicalRoute*(s, t) with the OBR cluster estimator $c_{obr}^E(\cdot, \cdot)$.

Assumption 5 below is typically adopted to facilitate the analysis of hierarchical routing, e.g., [8], [19]. In addition, it can be shown that when Assumption 5 holds $\max_{n \in \mathcal{N}}\{|\, scope(n)\,|\}$ (the maximum routing table size) is minimized ([7], [10]).

Assumption 5. For $h \in \mathcal{H}$, each cluster at level h contains the same number x_h of child clusters at level $h - 1$.

For example, $x = (10, 4, 5)$ specifies that each level-1 cluster contains ten nodes, each level-2 cluster contains four level-1 clusters, and the single level-3 cluster contains five level-2 clusters. Under Assumption 5, $\prod_{h=1}^{H} x_h = N$, and for $h \in \mathcal{H}$, the number of nodes in each level-h cluster is $\prod_{i=1}^{h} x_i$. The following result ([7], Proposition 9) bounds the average error for the CER and OBR cluster estimators only.

Theorem 5. Let Assumptions 1, 2, 4, and 5 hold. Then for the CER and OBR cluster estimators we have

$$\bar{c}_E^H - \bar{c}^\star \leq \frac{1}{N-1} \sum_{h=1}^{H-1} \left(N - \prod_{i=1}^{h} x_i \right) \Delta_h . \tag{14}$$

Let $\bar{c}_{cer}^H$ be the average hierarchical path length (13) using procedure *HierarchicalRoute*(s, t) with the CER estimator $c_{cer}^E(\cdot, \cdot)$. In [7] it is shown that

$\bar{c}_{obr}^H \le \bar{c}_{cer}^H$. We now generalize this result by showing that, for *Hierarchical-Route*(s, t), the OBR estimator yields a smaller average error than any other cluster estimator.

Theorem 6. Let Assumptions 1 and 2 hold, and let $c^E(\cdot, \cdot)$ be a cluster estimator. Then $\bar{c}_{obr}^H \le \bar{c}_E^H$.

Proof. Let $c^E(\cdot, \cdot)$ be a cluster estimator. Define $M = 1/(N(N-1))$. Recalling that $C_h(s)$ is the level-h cluster containing s, from (13) we have

$$\bar{c}_E^H - \bar{c}_{obr}^H = M \sum_{s \in \mathcal{N}} \sum_{t \in \mathcal{N}} \left(c_E^H(s, t) - c_{obr}^H(s, t) \right)$$

$$= M \sum_{s \in \mathcal{N}} \sum_{h=2}^{H} \sum_{t \in C_h(s) - C_{h-1}(s)} (c_E^H(s, t) - c_{obr}^H(s, t)) , \quad (15)$$

where $C_h(s) - C_{h-1}(s)$ are those nodes in $C_h(s)$ and not in $C_{h-1}(s)$. The summation over h begins with $h = 2$, since when $h = 1$ the points s and t are in the same level-1 cluster, in which case $c_E^H(s, t) = c_{obr}^H(s, t) = c^R(s, t)$. Note that $C_H(s) - C_{H-1}(s)$ is the set of all nodes in the network except for those nodes in $C_{H-1}(s)$. For $2 \le h \le H$, let J_{h-1} index the set of the level-$(h-1)$ clusters in $C_h(s)$ other than $C_{h-1}(s)$; we denote these clusters by C_{h-1}^j, $j \in J_{h-1}$. (Although J_{h-1} and C_{h-1}^j depend on s, we ignore this for notational simplicity.) Thus

$$\bar{c}_E^H - \bar{c}_{obr}^H = M \sum_{s \in \mathcal{N}} \sum_{h=2}^{H} \sum_{t \in C_h(s) - C_{h-1}(s)} \left(c_E^H(s, t) - c_{obr}^H(s, t) \right)$$

$$= M \sum_{s \in \mathcal{N}} \sum_{h=2}^{H} \sum_{j \in J_{h-1}} \sum_{t \in C_{h-1}^j} \left(c_E^H(s, t) - c_{obr}^H(s, t) \right) . \quad (16)$$

From (16), it suffices to prove the following claim: for $s \in \mathcal{N}$, $2 \le h \le H$, and $j \in J_{h-1}$, we have

$$\sum_{t \in C_{h-1}^j} c_E^H(s, t) \ge \sum_{t \in C_{h-1}^j} c_{obr}^H(s, t) . \quad (17)$$

We will prove this claim by induction on h.

Pick any $s \in \mathcal{N}$ and any h such that $2 \le h \le H$. For $j \in J_{h-1}$, let

$$b_j^E \in \operatorname{argmin}\{ c^R(s, b) + c^E(b, C_{h-1}^j) \mid b \in \mathcal{B}_{h-1}^j \} , \quad (18)$$

and let

$$b_j^0 \in \operatorname{argmin}\{ c^R(s, b) + c_{obr}^E(b, C_{h-1}^j) \mid b \in \mathcal{B}_{h-1}^j \} \quad (19)$$

(although both b_j^E and b_j^0 depend on s and h, we ignore this dependence for notational simplicity).

Suppose first that $h = 2$. Then $b_j^E \in \mathcal{B}_1^j$ and $b_j^0 \in \mathcal{B}_1^j$. For $t \in \mathcal{C}_1^j$ we have $c_E^H(b_j^E, t) = c^R(b_j^E, t) = c_{obr}^H(b_j^E, t)$. By Theorem 2,

$$
\begin{aligned}
\sum_{t \in \mathcal{C}_1^j} c_E^H(s, t) &= \sum_{t \in \mathcal{C}_1^j} \{c^R(s, b_j^E) + c_E^H(b_j^E, t)\} \\
&= |\mathcal{C}_1^j| \, c^R(s, b_j^E) + \sum_{t \in \mathcal{C}_1^j} c^R(b_j^E, t) \\
&= |\mathcal{C}_1^j| \, c^R(s, b_j^E) + |\mathcal{C}_1^j| c_{obr}^E(b_j^E, \mathcal{C}_1^j) \\
&\geq |\mathcal{C}_1^j| \, c^R(s, b_j^0) + |\mathcal{C}_1^j| c_{obr}^E(b_j^0, \mathcal{C}_1^j) \\
&= \sum_{t \in \mathcal{C}_1^j} c^R(s, b_j^0) + \sum_{t \in \mathcal{C}_1^j} c_{obr}^H(b_j^0, t) \\
&= \sum_{t \in \mathcal{C}_1^j} c_{obr}^H(s, t) \,,
\end{aligned}
$$

which establishes the claim for $h = 2$.

Now suppose the claim holds for $3 \leq h \leq k - 1$, where $k - 1 < H$ and suppose $h = k$. From (18) and (19) for $j \in J_{k-1}$ we have $b_j^E \in \mathcal{B}_{k-1}^j$ and $b_j^0 \in \mathcal{B}_{k-1}^j$. Then for $s \in \mathcal{N}$ and $j \in J_{k-1}$ we have

$$
\begin{aligned}
\sum_{t \in \mathcal{C}_{k-1}^j} c_E^H(s, t) &= \sum_{t \in \mathcal{C}_{k-1}^j} \{c^R(s, b_j^E) + c_E^H(b_j^E, t)\} \\
&\geq \sum_{t \in \mathcal{C}_{k-1}^j} \{c^R(s, b_j^E) + c_{obr}^H(b_j^E, t)\} \\
&= |\mathcal{C}_{k-1}^j| \, c^R(s, b_j^E) + |\mathcal{C}_{k-1}^j| c_{obr}^E(b_j^E, \mathcal{C}_{k-1}^j) \\
&\geq |\mathcal{C}_{k-1}^j| \, c^R(s, b_j^0) + |\mathcal{C}_{k-1}^j| c_{obr}^E(b_j^0, \mathcal{C}_{k-1}^j) \\
&= \sum_{t \in \mathcal{C}_{k-1}^j} c^R(s, b_j^0) + \sum_{t \in \mathcal{C}_{k-1}^j} c_{obr}^H(b_j^0, t) \\
&= \sum_{t \in \mathcal{C}_{k-1}^j} c_{obr}^H(s, t) \,,
\end{aligned}
$$

where the first inequality follows from the induction hypothesis and the second inequality follows from the definition of b_j^0. Thus the claim is proven. ∎

5.   Summary

We conclude by summarizing the contributions of this paper. A general scheme for hierarchical routing was proposed, which uses the new concept of a cluster estimator to approximate the cost of routing from a border node of a cluster to any node in the cluster. This general scheme encompasses PNNI, BGP (under appropriate configuration), and the Kleinrock-Kamoun method, but is not limited to telecommunications. We presented a worst case upper bound on $c_E^H(s,t) - c^*(s,t)$ that is valid for any cluster estimator. The bound is tight for a two-level network. We also proved that the "overall best routing" estimator yields a smaller average error than any other cluster estimator.

Acknowledgment: Thanks to Dr. Ron Levine and the anonymous referees for their valuable comments.

References

[1] R.K. Ahuja, T.L. Magnanti, and J.B. Orlin, *Network Flows*, Prentice-Hall, New Jersey, 1993.

[2] J. Ash and G. Choudhury, "PNNI Routing Congestion Control," *IEEE Communications Magazine*, vol. 42, pp. 154-160, 2004.

[3] A.E. Baratz and J.M. Jaffe, "Establishing Virtual Circuits in Large Computer Networks." *Computer Networks and ISDN Systems*, 12 (1986) 27-37.

[4] J. Behrens and J.J. Garcia-Luna-Aceves, "Hierarchical Routing Using Link Vectors," *Proc. IEEE InfoCom '98*, pp. 702-710, 1998.

[5] B.-J. Chang and R.-H. Hwang, "Performance Analysis for Hierarchical Multirate Loss Networks," *IEEE/ACM Transactions on Networking*, vol. 12, pp. 187-199, 2004.

[6] J. Hagouel, "Issues in Routing for Large and Dynamic Networks," Ph.D. Thesis, Columbia University, May 1983.

[7] L. Kleinrock and F. Kamoun, "Hierarchical Routing for Large Networks: Performance Evaluation and Optimization," *Computer Networks*, vol. 1, pp. 155-174, 1977.

[8] L. Kleinrock and F. Kamoun, "Optimal Clustering Structures for Hierarchical Topological Design of Large Computer Networks," *Networks*, vol. 10, pp. 221-248, 1980.

[9] W.S. Lai, E. Rosenberg, L. Amiri, M. Ball, Y. Levy, H. Shulman, H. Tong, and M. Ungar, "Analysis and Design of AT&T's Global PNNI Network," *Proc. IEEE Pacific Rim Conference on Communications, Computers, and Signal Processing* (PacRim 2005), August, 2005, pp. 129-132.

[10] W.S. Lai, L. Amiri, M. Ball, E. Rosenberg, and H. Tong, "The Scalable Growth of AT&T's Global PNNI Network," *Proc. 2006 Symposium on Performance Evaluation of Computer and Telecommunication Systems* (SPECTS 2006), Calgary, Alberta, Canada, July 31 - August 2, 2006, pp. 363-370.

[11] X. Masip-Bruin, S. Sánchez-López, J. Solé-Pareta, J. Domingo-Pascual, and E. Marin-Tordera, "Hierarchical Routing with QoS Constraints in Optical Transport Networks," *Lecture Notes in Computer Science*, Springer-Verlag, Heidelberg, vol. 3042, pp. 662-674, 2004.

[12] J.T. Moy, *OSPF: Anatomy of an Internet Routing Protocol*, Addison-Wesley, Reading, MA, 1998.

[13] A. Orda and A. Sprintson, "Precomputation Schemes for QoS Routing," *IEEE/ACM Transactions on Networking*, vol. 11, pp. 578-591, 2003.

[14] Private Network-Network Interface Specification Version 1.1, The ATM Forum Technical Committee, af-pnni-0055.002, April, 2002.

[15] E. Rosenberg, "The Expected Length of a Random Line Segment in a Rectangle," *Operations Research Letters*, vol. 32, pp. 99-102, 2004.

[16] E. Rosenberg, "Hierarchical PNNI Addressing by Recursive Partitioning," *Proc. IEEE Pacific Rim Conference on Communications, Computers, and Signal Processing* (PacRim 2005), August, 2005, pp. 133-136.

[17] E. Rosenberg, "Hierarchical Topological Network Design," *IEEE/ACM Transactions on Networking* vol. 13, pp. 1402-1409, 2005.

[18] J.W. Stewart, *BGP4: Inter-Domain Routing in the Internet*, Addison-Wesley, Reading, MA, 1999.

[19] P. Van Mieghem, "Estimation of an Optimal PNNI Topology," in *Proc. IEEE ATM'97 Workshop*, Lisbon, Portugal, May 26-28, 1997.

[20] W.T. Tsai, C.V. Ramamoorthy, W.K. Tsai, and O. Nishiguchi, "An Adaptive Hierarchical Routing Protocol," *IEEE Trans. on Computers*, vol. 38, pp. 1059-1075, 1989.

[21] A. Vasilakos, M.P. Saltouros, A. F. Atlassis, and W. Pedrycz, "Optimizing QoS Routing in Hierarchical ATM Networks Using Computation Intelligence Techniques," *IEEE Transactions on Systems, Man, and Cybernetics - Part C*, vol. 33, pp. 297-312, 2003.

[22] E.W. Zegura, K.L. Calvert, and M.J. Donahoo, "A Quantitative Comparison of Graph-Based Models for Internet Topology," *IEEE/ACM Transactions on Networking* vol. 5, pp. 770-783, 1997.

Chapter 6

AN ENTROPY BASED METHOD TO DETECT SPOOFED DENIAL OF SERVICE (DOS) ATTACKS

Willa K. Ehrlich, Kenichi Futamura and Danielle Liu

AT&T Labs, 200 Laurel Avenue, Middletown, NJ 07748, {wehrlich, futamura, dliu}@att.com

Abstract: A Spoofed Denial of Service (DoS) System is described that analyzes a level of entropy in distributions of source and destination IP address aggregate flow share, for IP traffic traversing one or more links. A source IP address aggregate entropy time series and a destination IP address aggregate entropy time series are derived and then adaptive thresholding is applied to each time series to identify upper and lower entropy thresholds for current measurements. Given current traffic traversing the set of monitored links, current source and destination entropy values are computed on a near real-time basis. If the entropy of the current distribution of destination IP address aggregates flow share falls below the destination entropy time series' identified lower entropy threshold, a possible Denial of Service attack may be declared. If, in addition, the decline in entropy in the destination entropy time series is accompanied by a rise in the entropy of the current distribution of source IP address aggregates flow share and the current source entropy is greater than the source entropy time series' identified upper entropy threshold, a Spoofed Denial of Service attack may be declared. We document an application of this approach to identifying Spoofed Denial of Service attacks on Peering Links monitored by the AT&T Common IP Backbone Tier 1 ISP.

Keywords: Adaptive thresholding; DoS attacks; entropy; source address spoofing.

1. INTRODUCTION

Denial of Service (DoS) attacks deny users of system services that a system usually provides. In a DoS attack, requests arrive at a host machine's Web Server or at a Router or at a Firewall at such a high rate of occurrence that the system is unavailable to legitimate users. In a spoofed DoS attack, the perpetrators employ spoofing to misrepresent the source IP address of

DoS packets, thereby obscuring the identity of the physical source. Differentiating a DoS attack from an unusually high or sustained burst of legitimate connections and connection attempts is difficult. Furthermore, in the case of a spoofed DoS attack, approaches are needed that do not require the use of performance-impacting Router functions (e.g., Unicast Reverse Path Forwarding; Access Control Lists, etc.) or protocol-specific authentication techniques (e.g., SYNs, SYN ACKs, FINs for TCP packets) in order to detect source spoofing.

In this paper, we describe a Spoofed Denial of Service Detection System that efficiently analyzes flow level traffic traversing one or more links within and/or between networks to detect the occurrence of spoofed DoS attacks, where spoofed addresses are randomly generated across a wide variety of IP addresses. We assume that any link or network has a characteristic distribution of IP addresses for initiators of IP traffic and another probability distribution for IP addresses that are the recipients of network traffic. An important network event, such as a DoS attack, source spoofing, or worm propagation, should modify these distributions of source and destination IP addresses in terms of new IP addresses entering the system or certain IP addresses becoming more dominant. Consequently, by monitoring address structure (i.e., the arrangement of active addresses in the IPv4 address space), we may be able to detect significant network events in near real-time. Specifically, we use Shannon's mathematical definition of entropy as a measure of uncertainty in a distribution to quantify source IP and destination IP address structure.

The remainder of this paper is organized into 6 sections. In Section 2, we briefly describe related work on source spoofing and spoofed DoS detection and indicate the contributions of the current work. In Section 3, we describe our theoretical framework with respect to the Shannon entropy measure together with the use of adaptive thresholding to adjust for cyclical effects and/or to react to changes in trend with respect to the entropy metric. A description of a Spoofed Denial of Service System that uses both entropy and adaptive thresholding is presented in Section 4. An application of this approach to detecting Spoofed DoS events based on flow data collected on several Peering Links monitored by the AT&T Common IP Backbone is given in Section 5. In Section 6, we contrast the sensitivity of an entropy-based approach with a purely volumetric-based approach for detecting spoofed DoS event occurrence under lower rates of anomalous traffic. Finally, implications of this work for network management are discussed in Section 7.

2. RELATED WORK

Prior IP address-based approaches to spoofed DoS events have addressed proactive prevention of spoofed IP packets from reaching destination hosts and reactive source identification of spoofed IP packets.

With respect to the prevention of spoofed DoS attacks, several variants of packet filtering have been proposed for restricting transit traffic originating from a downstream network to a set of advertised address prefixes, in order to prevent spoofed IP packets from reaching their destination. In egress or outbound filtering, traffic filters are placed on ingress (input) links of a Router providing Internet connectivity to an internal network via a Provider Autonomous System (AS), so that traffic originating from the internal network is restricted to certain source IP address ranges (Ferguson and Senie, 1998). In the case of a Cisco Express Forwarding (CEF) Router with Unicast Reverse Path Forwarding (RPF) enabled on an interface, the Router examines all packets received as input on the interface to confirm that one of the best reverse paths for the source address matches the input port. If there is a matching path, the packet is forwarded; else, the packet is dropped. Finally, it has been suggested that due to the power law structure of Internet AS connectivity, distributed packet filtering based on source IP address can prevent spoofed IP flows from reaching their intended destination and drastically decrease the number of AS sites from which attacks can be launched when such filters are deployed at a relatively small proportion of AS sites (Park and Lee, 2001). Note, however, that a proactive approach to identifying spoofed IP packets may require special hardware; create (negative) performance implications for Router or Firewall devices or require an assumption in inter-domain routing that is not justified given the current BGP protocol.[1]

Several techniques have been described for the reactive identification of spoofed IP packets. In link testing, starting from the Router closest to the victim node, an input debugging filter is applied to the victim's upstream egress port to uncover the associated input port and hence the upstream Router that originated the traffic. This procedure is then applied recursively to upstream Routers to test upstream links until the originating node is identified (Burch and Cheswick, 2000; Savage et al., 2000). Another technique consists of marking packets, either probabilistically or deterministically, with the addresses of the Routers they traverse. The victim attempts to reconstruct the attack path using only the information in the marked packets (Savage et al., 2000). Note that these techniques attempt to identify the physical hosts serving as the generators of the spoofed IP

---

[1] IP routing is destination-based so that routing table update messages relate only to destination reach ability and not necessarily to source reach ability.

packets (i.e., the source of the attack) as opposed to the controllers of these generators (the source of the attackers).

In contrast to proactively preventing spoofed IP packets from reaching their destination or resolving the identity of the attack location, another approach is simply to detect the occurrence of a spoofed DoS in near real-time. Although DoS attack occurrence is easily discernible upon performance degradation of the victim host, DoS detection during the early stages of an attack is especially challenging in that attack traffic can be made arbitrarily similar to legitimate traffic in order to avoid anomaly detection. Thus, a DoS attack does not require malformed packets (e.g., TCP packets with abnormal flags) or specific packet sequences to exploit software bugs or protocol vulnerabilities (Peng, Leckie and Rammamohanarao, 2007) but instead only requires a sufficient volume of traffic. However, if a DoS event were to be detected quickly, prior to performance degradation of the target host, then attack mitigation can help protect legitimate users. In the case of a spoofed DoS event, an operator can notify the Peer Autonomous Systems (ASes) submitting the offending traffic to apply ingress and egress[2] filters to prevent attack traffic from entering and leaving the Peer Networks. (The rationale for ingress filtering is that if random or invalid source addresses can be prevented from entering (and therefore departing) a network, source spoofed traffic can be suppressed and spoofing traced back to source networks.)[3] The target AS, in turn, could apply a filter to drop those packets: a) whose source IP addresses were inconsistent with the Peering Link traversed and b) whose destination IP address matched the destination IP address (aggregate) under attack, while forwarding other packets to customer ASes,

Rate-based approaches to DoS event detection employ traffic volume thresholds by traffic type (e.g., spoofed, malformed, legitimate, NULL content) for specific destination IP addresses. These thresholds are cumbersome to maintain since changing network conditions may cause address (aggregates) to rise or fall in popularity over time, requiring modifications to these thresholds. An alternative approach is to detect the occurrence of a spoofed DoS event in near real-time based *on some change in IP address structure* as opposed to a *network traffic overload condition* event occurrence. An application of this approach, based on the distribution of port features in flow traces, has been applied to worm propagations. For example, in the case of worm propagations, Kohler et al. (2002)

---

[2] Filtering is called ingress filtering if it applies to traffic coming into a network and is called egress filtering if it is applied to traffic departing a network.

[3] Ingress filtering can be implemented via Ingress Access Lists, Strict Reverse Path Forwarding, Feasible Path Reverse Path Forwarding, and Loose Reverse Path Forwarding (Baker and Savola, 2004).

demonstrated that during the Code Red 1 and 2 worm occurrences, the destination IP address structure shifted in that a much broader range of destination IP address aggregates were contacted as compared to pre-Code Red time periods. Using the Kolmogorov Complexity measure of information complexity, Wagner and Plattner (2005) demonstrated that during the Blaster (TCP) and Witty (UDP) worm propagations, source IP addresses became more predictable (attributed to a smaller number of (scanning) hosts generating more flows) with destination IP addresses becoming more random (resulting from the random scanning algorithm sending packets to many more destination IP addresses than usual). An application of Kolmogorov Complexity to DoS detection was presented by Kulkarni, Bush and Evans (2001). In a DoS attack, there are large numbers of packets originating from different locations but intended for the same destination that are similar with respect to their protocol type, size, etc. In contrast, in the case of a network traffic overload only condition, the traffic flows are not highly correlated and appear to be random. To determine the extent to which traffic flows are correlated during a DoS event, Kulkarni et al. used the compressibility of packets accumulated over a given time interval as a measure of the packets' complexity differential.[4] If the complexity differential exceeded some threshold, then a DoS was declared. However, they demonstrated this approach by using data from only a simple test bed as opposed to an actual network event. Finally, Lakhina, Crovella and Diot, 2005 applied the entropy measure of information complexity to a variety of traffic anomalies, including both single-source and multi-source DoS attacks against single target destinations, and demonstrated that these DoS events are characterized by a concentrated set of destination IP addresses. However, they did not address spoofed DoS events nor how to alarm given an entropy metric under changing traffic conditions.

---

[4]Complexity differential is defined as the difference between the cumulative complexities of individual packets/flows and the total complexity when these packets/flows are concatenated to form a single packet/flow. If packets/flows x_1, x_2, ..., x_n have complexities $K(x_1)$, $K(x_2)$, ..., $K(x_n)$, then complexity differential is computed as: $[K(x_1) + K(x_2) + ... + K(x_n)] - K(x_1 x_2 ... x_n)$, where: $[K(x_1) + K(x_2) + ... + K(x_n)]$ is the sum of the individual packet/flow complexities (i.e., their cumulative complexity) and where $K(x_1 x_2 ... x_n)$ is the complexity of the packets/flows concatenated together. If packets/flows x_1, x_2, ..., x_n are completely random, then $K(x_1 x_2 ... x_n)$ will be equal to the sum of the individual complexities and the complexity differential will therefore be 0. However, if the packets/flows are highly correlated, then its complexity $K(x_1 x_2 ... x_n)$ will be much smaller than the cumulative complexity (Kulkarni, Bush and Evans, 2001).

2.1   Current Contribution

The current approach is based on a similar   observation made by Kulkarni et al. and Lakhina et al. that during a DoS attack, a single destination IP address (or alternatively, a very, very few number of unique destination IP addresses) receives many more flows than other normal conditions. If, in addition, source address spoofing is involved in the DoS attack, then the distribution of the source IP addresses will tend to be more uniform or spread out than under normal conditions.

A time series of the entropy of the distribution of traffic share among source IP address aggregates and a corresponding time series of the entropy of the distribution of traffic share among destination IP address aggregates are calculated for a set of links based on historical data. For each time series, upper and lower entropy thresholds are identified to be applied to current measurements.   Once such thresholds are identified, the entropy of the current distribution of source IP address aggregates traffic share and the entropy of the current distribution of destination IP address aggregates traffic share can be analyzed in a near real-time basis. Current entropy values are subsequently used to update the entropy time series thresholds adaptively so as to account for seasonality effects and/or trend effects in entropy values. Such effects occur in Internet traffic-- we have observed instances of a sudden drop in a Source IP Address entropy time series as a result of the retirement of certain IP addresses within Customer Autonomous Systems. An adaptive algorithm would alarm on the mean shift but then, within a week, adjust to the new baseline (i.e., stop alarming), and then subsequently alarm on new anomalies. In contrast, given the mean shift, a non-adaptive threshold could alarm longer or perhaps for the duration of the time series.

In summary, the novel aspect of our work is jointly analyzing entropy time series based on source IP address and destination IP address traffic share and identifying a spoofed DoS attack when there is both a statistically significant decrease in destination IP address entropy and a statistically significant increase in source IP address entropy.

3. THEORETICAL FRAMEWORK

3.1 Entropy Approach

3.1.1 Overview of Entropy Approach

Let X be a finite or countable set and let X be a random variable that takes values in X with distribution $P(X=x)=p_x$. Then the Shannon entropy of a random variable X is given by:

$$H(X) = -\sum_{x \in N} p_x \log p_x \qquad (1)$$

If $X=\{1,...,N\}$, then we can write $H(X)=H(p)=H(p_1, p_2, ..., p_N)$ where p_i stands for the probability of i.   The function H maps the probability distribution on X to real numbers.   The function H has the following properties: a) $H(p_1, p_2, ..., p_N)$ is a concave function of the p_i; b) For each N, H achieves its unique maximum for the uniform distribution, $p_i=1/N$, equal to $\log(N)$ and c) $H(p_1, p_2, ..., p_N)$ is 0 iff one of the p_i has a value of 1 (Grunwald and Vitanyi, 2004).

3.1.2 Rationale for Entropy Approach

Given that the IPv4 address space has over 4 billion IP addresses, it is prudent to group IP addresses into mutually exclusive and exhaustive address aggregates for scalability reasons.

Depending on how the IP address aggregation (i.e., IP address partitioning) is performed (Kim, Reddy and Vannucci, 2004), each IP address aggregate may contain a different number of IP addresses. For example, one approach to defining IP address aggregates is to specify an IP address prefix length. The prefix length determines the resolution to which a flow traversing a given monitored link is monitored. If an IP address prefix length of 16 is specified, then all flow IP addresses that share a common initial 16 bits, are treated as a single IP address aggregate for the purpose of monitoring and analyzing flow traffic. In this case, the entire IPv4 IP address space will be partitioned into 2**16 or 65356 IP address aggregates, where each IP address aggregate represents 65356 unique IP addresses.

However, IP address aggregation may be performed in any manner such as by using a defined IP address prefix of any length, selecting specific IP addresses based upon an assessment of prior traffic volume, or by random sampling of IP addresses for inclusion in an IP address aggregate. *However the partitioning of the IP address space is achieved (i.e., by whatever procedure)* the result is that there will be N mutually exclusive and exhaustive groups of IP addresses. The distribution of traffic share associated with such a set of source address aggregates and the corresponding traffic share distribution associated with such a set of destination address aggregates represent probability distributions. It is intuitive to ask 'how much information is gained on the average' when an address aggregate is 'made available.' Under a spoofed DoS attack, given that the traffic distribution of destination address aggregates becomes more concentrated, more information will be gained when a destination aggregation is selected. In contrast, given that the traffic distribution of source address aggregates becomes more depressed, less information will be gained when a source address aggregate is selected from a network traffic stream. Shannon entropy captures a distribution's concentration/dispersal and it is also a simple metric to apply. Hence, Shannon entropy is a reasonable metric to apply for the purpose of detecting changes in IP address structure.

3.2   Anomaly Detection[5]

3.2.1   Basic Overview of Adaptive Thresholding

For illustrative purposes, we present an overview using an hourly interval and a daily cycle. The actual interval and cycle length that is used in the implementation of the spoofed DoS detection system differs from these settings and may not be shared for proprietary reasons.

Let μ represent the current estimate of the overall mean. Let S_i represent the current estimate of the seasonality factor for time interval i, that is, the mean of a particular interval in relation to the overall mean. For example, if the daily mean traffic volume is 50GB/hour, but the mean traffic volume at 2:00pm is 75GB/hour, the seasonality factor $S_{2:00pm} = 75/50 = 1.5$ (assuming a daily cycle). Let *Var* represent the current estimate of the overall normalized variance (in other words, the variance if there were no seasonality effects). Since the variables in question are non-negative, it is unrealistic to assume that the variance is fixed. Instead, the variance is assumed to be approximately proportional to the seasonality factor or, equivalently, the mean – that is, we expect the variance to be larger if the mean is higher. Examination of historical data showed that this is a reasonable approximation for the data sets analyzed. (A consequence is that compared to a threshold that assumes a fixed variance, the threshold range will be wider during peak intervals and narrower during non-peak intervals.)

---

[5] Patents have been filed at the USPTO for various components of these Anomaly Detection Methods and Systems.

Therefore, an estimate of the variance for a given time interval i would be $S_i Var$.

Given a new data point, X, which, in the current context, represents measured or observed entropy, we calculate new estimates for these parameters using the following equations:

$$\text{New } \mu = \alpha\theta\tfrac{X}{S_i} + (1-\alpha\theta)\mu$$
$$\text{New } S_i = \beta\theta\tfrac{X}{\mu} + (1-\beta\theta)S_i \tag{2}$$
$$\text{New } Var = \max(\gamma\theta S_i(\tfrac{X}{S_i}-\mu)^2 + (1-\gamma\theta)Var, MinSD^2)$$
$$i = \text{interval of cycle}$$
$$0 < \alpha,\beta,\gamma < \tfrac{1}{\theta}, MinSD > 0 \,(\text{minimum SD})$$

Furthermore, we put bounds on the magnitude of the change (upwards for mean and variance; upwards and downwards for seasonality) to reduce the effect of outliers. For example, New μ is upper bounded by $\mu+(\alpha\theta$ sqrt(Var)).

During the ramp-up phase, where estimates are unknown or unstable, we set the ramp-up factor $\theta > 1$ in order to speed up convergence. During the ramp-up phase, no alarms are generated. The estimated baseline for period i would be $S_i\mu$ with an estimated variance of $S_i Var$. These parameters are calculated for both the Source IP (i.e., SIP) Entropy and Destination IP (i.e., DIP) Entropy time series. Given these estimates, we check for the appropriate anomalies in both the Source IP entropy data stream and the Destination IP entropy data stream to indicate a spoofed DoS attack.

$$D(SIP) = \frac{X(SIP) - S_i(SIP)\mu(SIP)}{\sqrt{S_i(SIP)Var(SIP)}}$$
$$D(DIP) = \frac{X(DIP) - S_i(DIP)\mu(DIP)}{\sqrt{S_i(DIP)Var(DIP)}} \tag{3}$$
$$\text{Generate alarm if } D(SIP) > L \text{ and } D(DIP) < -L.$$
$$i = \text{interval of cycle}, \; L = \text{alarm level}$$

D represents a measure of the deviation of X from the estimated baseline. This value has been normalized for mean, seasonality, and variance. L is the level at which an alarm is generated.

After the check for anomalies is complete, the parameters are updated for both data streams:

$$\mu := \text{New } \mu, \; S_i := \text{New } S_i, \; Var := \text{New } Var \tag{4}$$

In the case of missing data, the parameters (μ, S_i, *Var*) do not change. Of course, no alarms are generated (except perhaps to indicate that data was missing).

For numerical stability, the baseline variables are renormalized periodically as follows:

$$S = \frac{\sum_{i=1}^{N} S_i}{N}$$

$$S_i := \frac{S_i}{S}, \quad i = 1,..., N$$

$$\mu := S\mu$$

$$Var := \max(SVar, MinSD^2)$$

(5)

3.2.2   Rationale for Adaptive Approach

By adaptive thresholding, we mean that the threshold is updated regularly. Many detection tools use a fixed threshold to alarm on anomalous traffic. If the background traffic changes, these thresholds may become meaningless and need to be changed. This method makes sense for some applications. For example, in control systems, there may be a certain tolerance level for products to be considered "acceptable." If this tolerance level is exceeded, then the product is considered "bad." But for network traffic monitoring, the background is continually changing. Therefore, in this application, it is critical to update these estimates adaptively. Since this adaptive approach continually updates the mean, variance and seasonality factors, the model adjusts to reflect changes in background traffic. By adjusting α, β and γ, the baseline estimates can adjust more or less quickly to changes in the background.

Furthermore, approaches that involve calculations (e.g., mean, variance) over large intervals of data require significant data storage, manual analysis, and/or fixed thresholds. For example, recalculating the mean and variance each period requires storing sufficient history to make this calculation stable. If, on the other hand, this calculation is done periodically, then the thresholds would be fixed between calculations and would still require significant data storage and possibly manual intervention. In addition, these methods generally require significantly more processing power. Because of these drawbacks, these methods may not be feasible for monitoring data streams in a large network, where calculations may be applied to many individual circuits or data types.

The method we used for identification of anomalies was a variation on the Holt-Winter's three-parameter exponential smoothing model (Barford et al., 2002; Lakhina, Crovella and Diot, 2004). The Holt-Winter's model assumes that a time series can be decomposed into the three components: an overall mean; a linear trend and a seasonal trend. Alarming assumes a Gaussian distribution and is based on the predicted value and calculated standard deviation. Our goal was to minimize the amount of manual intervention required for detecting anomalies and resetting the parameters after anomaly-detection, while also reducing the amount of data storage and processing required to produce the baseline and alarms. Therefore, an exponential smoothing technique was used. Unlike the Holt-Winter's three-parameter model, the trend component was removed and a multiplicative seasonality factor was used. Furthermore, the seasonality estimates as well as a variance estimate (required for anomaly determination) were updated via exponential smoothing.

4.   SPOOFED DOS DETECTION SYSTEM[6]

Given that we have defined the IP address aggregates of interest, the set of links to be monitored (Figure 1) and time interval, t, traffic monitoring occurs for subinterval j. Upon completion of the jth subinterval, we compute the distribution of the flow share (i.e., a probability distribution) over the source and destination IP aggregates and then calculate the entropy value H_j for the monitoring subinterval j using Eq. (1).

If the entropy of the current distribution of destination IP address aggregates traffic share falls below the destination entropy time series' identified lower entropy threshold, a possible Denial of Service attack may be declared, If, in addition, the decline in entropy in the destination entropy time series is accompanied by a rise in the entropy of the current distribution of source IP address aggregates traffic share and the current source entropy is greater than the source entropy time series' identified upper entropy threshold, a Spoofed Denial of Service attack may be declared. The source and destination entropy time series are augmented with the current j subinterval entropy values and the source and destination entropy thresholds are re-calculated based on Eq. (4) (see last step of Figure 1). Hence, with our Spoofed DoS Detection System, we are able to automatically alarm on current destination entropy dips and current source entropy spikes suggestive of a spoofed DoS event.

---

[6] A patent has been filed at the USPTO for various components of the AT&T Common IP Backbone Spoofed DoS Detection System.

5.   EXAMPLE ENTROPY AND ADAPTIVE THRESHOLDING EMPRICAL RESULTS

In this Section, we document an application of the entropy and adaptive thresholding approach to spoofed DoS events for traffic traversing a given link into the AT&T Common Back Bone from a Peer ISP. Parameter settings corresponding to a time (sub) interval of one hour and an IP address prefix length of 16 were used for the entropy measurements, while the alarm level, L, was set to 3 standard deviations for the adaptive thresholding component. We emphasize that a shorter time (sub) interval (e.g., 5 minutes) (resulting in greater variation in the measured entropy values) and/or a more fine-grained address aggregation (e.g., prefix length of 24) could also have been applied. In the current context, these specific entropy-related parameter values were utilized because these data were most easily accessible.

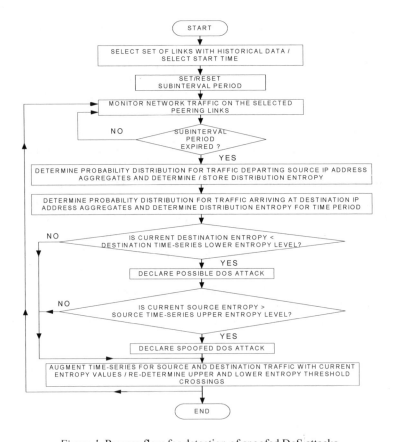

Figure 1. Process flow for detection of spoofed DoS attacks

5.1 Applying Entropy Analysis and Adaptive Thresholding to Detect Spoofed DoS Events

5.1.1 Entropy Time Series

Figure 2 presents a time series of the entropy values calculated on hourly distributions of flow share for source IP address aggregates of prefix length 16 (top panel) and a corresponding time series of the entropy values calculated on hourly distributions of flow share for destination IP address aggregates of prefix length 16 (bottom panel). These time series are based on IP flows traversing a specific Peering Link that was monitored by the AT&T Common IP Backbone ISP, over an observation interval corresponding to approximately 800 hours. Note that each data point represents an entropy value calculated on the Peering Link's hourly distribution of 256**2=65536 IP address aggregates' flow share.

5.1.2 Alarming on Entropy Time Series Using Adaptive Thresholding

The adaptive thresholding algorithm indicated that *both* an increase in source entropy *and* a decrease in destination entropy occurred within a 22-hour interval starting on April 15 at 17:00 (UTC time) and terminating on April 16 at 14:00 since it alarmed throughout this time interval. Consequently, our Spoofed DoS Detection System would have declared a spoofed DoS attack for this Peering Link during the time interval of April 15, 17:00 to April 16, 14:00.

Preliminary analysis indicated that for each hour within this interval, there existed a single destination address aggregate of prefix length 16 (Destination IP block) that consistently received an unusually large proportion of flows in contrast to a non-DoS hour. Figure 3 presents the change in the number of flows to each Destination IP block between a normal hour (April 8, 23:00) and a representative hour within the DoS event time interval (April 15, 23:00). Note that the existence of a single popular Destination IP address block is consistent with the drop in destination address entropy depicted in Figure 2.

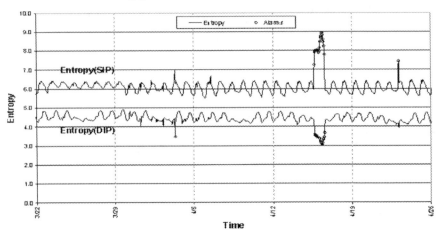

Figure 2. Entropy time series calculated for hourly distributions of source and destination address aggregates flow share given a single Peering Link

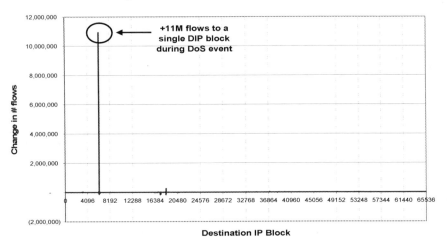

Figure 3. Change in number of flows to each Destination IP block (normal vs. spoofed DoS event hour). Activity to a single Destination IP block increased by 11M flows

Furthermore, looking at the distribution of Source IP blocks by the number of flows originating from it, there is a significant shift in the activity from a normal hour to a spoofed DoS event hour (Figure 4). The solid line in Figure 4 represents the distribution of Source IP Block number of flows during a normal hour (April 8, 23:00) while the dashed line represents the distribution of Source IP Block number of flows during a spoofed DoS event hour (April 15, 23:00). During the normal hour, 95% of the Source IP Blocks have 0 flows, implying that only 5% of the Source IP blocks are typically active. In contrast, during the spoofed DoS event hour, 38% of the Source IP Blocks have 0 flows, with the 62% remaining blocks tending to demonstrate significant activity (with 250-300 flows originating from most of these now active blocks). Thus, Figure 4 is consistent with the increase in source address entropy depicted in Figure 2.

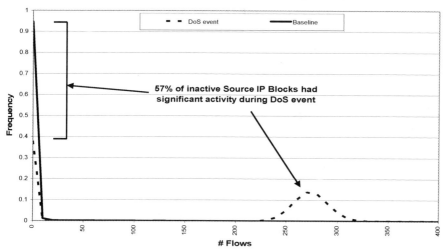

Figure 4. Distribution of Source IP Block by # flows (normal vs. spoofed DoS event hour). During spoofed DoS event hour 62% of Source IP blocks have significant activity, compared to 5% during normal hour

5.2 Validation of Spoofed DoS Event

5.2.1 DoS Characterization

Analysis of flows to the single destination address aggregate receiving the largest flow share during the alleged spoofed DoS event indicated that over 90% of the flows were destined for the same single destination IP address. Given flows destined for the single destination IP address over this time interval, virtually 100% of these flows were single packet TCP flows containing only a SYN flag, with a Bytes per Packet Ratio of 40. In contrast, given this same time interval, for flows destined for all other destination IP addresses, the proportion of single packet TCP flows with only a SYN flag set and a Bytes per Packet Ratio of 40 was always $\leq 0.4\%$ Consequently, the DoS event detected by our entropy analysis and adaptive thresholding algorithms corresponded to a TCP SYN flood attack directed at a single host. The rate of arrival of these DoS attack flows (i.e., flows with this DoS signature) was 196,683 attack flows per minute (i.e., 3,278 attack flows per second).

With respect to source and destination port usage, we were further able to characterize the DoS signature as one in which source and destination ports were selected with equal probability. Thus, given single packet TCP flows containing only a SYN flag and with a Bytes per Packet Ratio of 40, destined for the destination IP address under attack, TCP source and TCP destination ports were selected uniformly for the DoS attack.

5.2.2   Source Spoofing Characterization

Our analysis of the traffic characteristics of the attack flows indicates that they are synthetic flows. Consequently, we would expect that their source addresses are also synthetic in the sense that they demonstrate some type of pattern in the IP address structure.

Analysis of attack vs. non-attack flows failed to reveal SIP addresses allocated or assigned directly by IANA for global or specialized purposes or allocated for private internets (i.e., IP addresses not allocated for public Internet use)[7] (IANA, 2002). Despite the absence of such SIP addresses, we were able to detect a pattern in the SIP addresses associated with attack flows. This is indicated by a second analysis, presented in Figure 5 which contrasts the number of unique IP addresses by source address aggregate for attacks flows (i.e., single packet TCP flows with only a SYN flag set and a Bytes per Packet Ratio of 40 destined for the single destination IP address under attack—left panel) vs. non-attack flows (right panel) for a representative hour (i.e., hour 2300).

Figure 5 indicates that, for the attack flows, the number of unique SIP addresses per source address aggregate is approximately constant for 3 contiguous IP address regions in the IP address space. In contrast, for the non-attack flows, there is more variation in the number of unique SIP

---

[7]These IP addresses include: a) 10.0.0.0- 10.255.255.255 (reserved for intranet local networks); b) 127.0.0.0-127.255.255.255 (reserved for local loop on each computer); c) 172.16.0.0 – 172.31.255.255 (reserved for intranet local networks); d) 192.168.0.0-192.168.255.255 (reserved for intranet local networks); e) 224.0.0.0-239.255.255.255 (used for multicast routing)

addresses for a source address aggregate within an IP address region. This suggests that for the attack flows, the SIP addresses were synthetically generated.

A third analysis was performed to determine the extent to which the source IP address of an attack flow is consistent with its BGP routing path. Thus, for a representative spoofed DoS event hour, we randomly sampled 1500 flows from the set of attack flows (i.e., flows exhibiting the DoS attack signature) and then randomly sampled 1500 flows from the set of non-attack flows. For each such sampled flow, we determined the originating Autonomous System Number (ASN) associated with the source IP address and then used the AT&T Common IP Backbone (BGP) Routing Table to derive the set of AS paths associated with the originating ASN. Table 1 summarizes the results of BGP path analysis. For the 1500 flows exhibiting the DoS attack signature, 89% of the flows exhibited either a route anomaly (i.e., the flow's originating ASN was inconsistent with an arrival on the inbound link to ASN7018) or else the source IP address could not be associated with an originating ASN. In contrast, for the flows not exhibiting the DoS attack signature, only 3% of the flows exhibited a route anomaly. Hence, the BGP routing results are consistent with the attack flows' SIP addresses being synthetically generated.

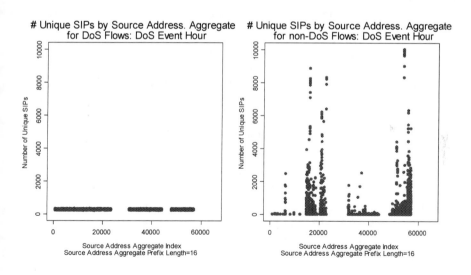

Figure 5. SIP addresses by source address aggregate for DoS attack flows (left panel) vs. non-attack flows (right panel) for a representative hour within the attack interval (i.e., 2300)

Table 1: Number of flows by category for sampled DoS attack flows vs. sampled non-attack flows

Sampled DoS Attack Flows			Sampled non-Attack Flows		
Orig. ASN Not Found	Orig. ASN In-Consistent with Link Traversal	No Route Anomaly Detected	Orig. ASN Not Found	Orig. ASN In-Consistent with Link Traversal	No Route Anomaly Detected
637	700	163	0	44	1456

6.   SENSITIVITY OF ENTROPY TO ATTACK TRAFFIC VOLUME

To document the sensitivity of the entropy-based approach to spoofed DoS event detection to anomalous traffic volume, the number of attack flows within each hour of the 22-hour attack interval (corresponding to April 15, 17:00 to April 16, 14:00) was systematically reduced by a given factor (e.g., 50%) and then the measured source and destination entropies were re-computed within the attack interval. The adaptive thresholding algorithm (using the same alarm level, L, of 3 standard deviations) was then applied to the new source entropy and destination entropy time series and the number of source entropy and destination entropy alarms were computed during the 22-hour attack interval. The adaptive thresholding algorithm (again, with an alarm level, L, of 3 standard deviations) was also applied to the resulting flow volumetric time series to generate a set of purely volumetric-based alarms. Various sampling rates ranging from 0.1% to 50% were applied and compared.

For example, in the case of a "retain" attack flow probability of 0.50, if a flow were determined to be an attack flow, then the attack flow would be randomly "tossed" 50% of the time (whereas the non-attack flows would be retained 100% of the time). The actual time series and actual alarms, together with the simulated time series and simulated alarms, for both the entropy and flow volumetric time series, for this "retain" attack flow probability setting are given in Figure 6. The top panel presents the actual (i.e., when 100% of the attack flows were retained) vs. simulated source and destination entropy time series and the actual (i.e., when 100% of the attack flows were retained) vs. simulated alarms for the retain probabilities of 1.0 and 0.50. The bottom panel presents the actual vs. simulated flow volumetric time series and the actual vs. simulated alarms, again for retain probabilities of 1.0 and 0.50.

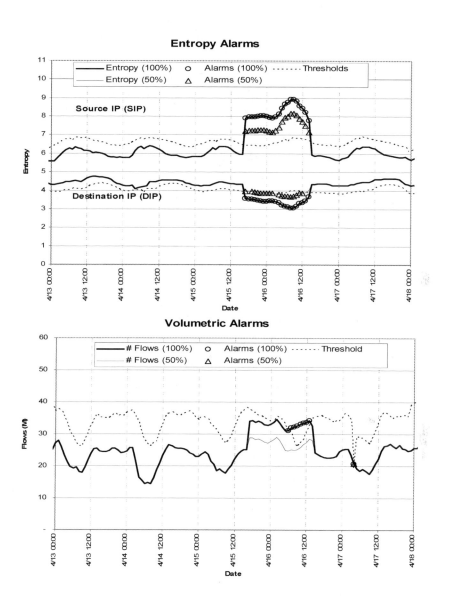

Figure 6. Entropy and volumetric time series and alarms

Applying the adaptive thresholding alarm to the volumetric time series, only 8 of the 22 attack hours triggered an alarm, with the first alarm occurring 13 hours after the start of the attack. Furthermore, for retain probabilities that are ≤0.50, the volumetric time series fails to alarm at all. In contrast, for the source entropy and destination entropy time series the adaptive thresholding alarms on all 22 hours for both entropy time series. For a retain attack flow probability of 0.50, the dynamic thresholding alarms on all 22 hours for the simulated source entropy time series and alarms on 18 hours for the simulated destination entropy time series. For a retain attack flow probability of 0.25, the dynamic thresholding alarms on 22 hours for the simulated source entropy time series, but does not alarm for any hour within the attack time period for the simulated destination entropy time series. For retain attack flow probabilities ≤0.10, the dynamic thresholding does not generate any alarms for both the simulated source and simulated destination entropy time series. Thus, the entropy approach has a higher detection rate when attack flows occupy a smaller fraction of overall traffic flow.

7.   CONCLUSIONS AND IMPLICATIONS

A spoofed DoS detection system is described that provides network administrators with the ability to analyze traffic between networks in near real-time to determine whether a spoofed DoS is in progress, while assuring that network throughput is not adversely affected. By monitoring source and destination address structure of flows arriving at a network with respect to a specific interface, this approach is able to differentiate a DoS event from an unusually high or sustained traffic level that, nonetheless, is legitimate. Furthermore, by using adaptive thresholding for alarming, we are able to account for seasonality and trend effects in changes in source address and/or destination address structure over time.

The spoofed DoS detection system can be configured in various ways, depending on the particular goals of the network and/or on customer needs. Thus, the number of links to be monitored simultaneously with subsequent flow data aggregation, can be varied, as can the manner in which IP addresses are aggregated for IP address space partitioning. For example, the IP address aggregate prefix length may be increased for some networks while decreased for others. Thus, the prefix length of 16 and single link used in the current analysis are only examples of possible system configurations that can be employed.

With respect to the spoofed DoS detection system performance and scalability, at the Router level, dedicated hardware/software for generating meta-data from (possibly) sampled raw peering traffic would be co-located at Internet Service Provider (ISP) Border Router(s) at a given Peering Link. Rule sets could be applied to perform IP address aggregation by IP address/prefix length (or by Autonomous System Number) and flow counts subsequently generated for each address aggregate for a given fixed time interval (e.g., 5 minutes to 1 hour). (See Narus Anomaly Detection Guide for example rule sets for aggregating flows into groups (Narus, 2005).) Upon termination of this interval, the processors would then transfer the meta-data records associated with a given Peering Link to a set of Application Servers.

At an application level, it would seem reasonable to implement one or more processes to perform IP address aggregation (if this were not already done), entropy calculation and adaptive thresholding, where each process would analyze meta-data associated with a single Peering Link or a set of links associated with the same Peer Autonomous System of the ISP . The process associated with each Peer Autonomous System would execute in parallel to process meta-data on all Peer Autonomous Systems associated with the ISP. Both the entropy calculation and the dynamic thresholding are computationally negligible and so the frequency with which they are performed would have minimal performance implications. Assuming that IP address aggregation were to occur at the application level, then the IP address aggregation applied to individual flows would appear to be more CPU intensive and hence a trade-off may be required between the granularity of the IP address aggregation and the speed of the analysis. Alternatively, a Tier 1 ISP may already perform such aggregation on their flow data at the application level for the purpose of summarizing data currently being collected so that the entropy calculation and adaptive thresholding could be directly applied to these IP flow counts. In summary, the spoofed DoS detection system appears to be both an efficient and effective approach for detecting spoofed DoS events that can augment purely volumetric-based approaches.

ACKNOWLEDGMENTS

We would like to thank John H. Hemenway for his discussions on implementations of a detection system. We would also like to acknowledge the contributions of Dave Hoeflin and Brett Smith for their discussions on entropy and IP address aggregation.

REFERENCES

1. Baker, F. and Savola, P., 2004, Ingress filtering for multihomed networks, *RFC 3704*.
2. Barford, P., Kline, J., Plonka, D., and Ron, A., 2002, A signal analysis of network traffic anomalies, *Proceedings of 2nd ACM SIGCOMM Workshop on Internet Measurement*: 71-82.
3. Bursch, H. and Cheswick, B., 2000, Tracing anonymous packets to their approximate source, *Proceedings of the 14th USENIX Systems Administration Conference (LISA 2000)*:319-327.
4. Cisco, Unicast reverse path forwarding,Cisco IOS Release 11.1(17)CC, www.cisco.com/univercd/cc/td/ doc/product/software/ios111/cc111/uni_rpf.pdf
5. Ferguson, P. and Senie, D., 1998, Network ingress filtering: defeating denial of service attacks which may employ IP source address spoofing, *RFC 2827*.
6. Grunswald, P. and Vitany, P., 2004, Shannon information and Kolmogorov complexity, Submitted to *IEEE Trans Information Theory*.
7. Internet Assigned Numbers Authority (IANA), 2002, Special-use IPv4 addresses, *RFC 3330*.
8. Kim, S.S., Reddy, A.L.N., and Vannucci, M., 2004, Detecting traffic anomalies at the source through aggregate analysis of packet header data, in: *NETWORKING 2004*, Springer, Berlin, pp. 1047-1059.
9. Kohler,E., Li,J., Paxson, V., and Shenker, S., 2002, Observed structure of addresses in IP traffic, *Proceedings of ACM SIGCOMM Workshop on Internet Measurement:*253-266.
10. Kulkarni, A.B., Bush, S.F., and, Evans, S.C., 2001, Detecting distributed denial of service attacks using Kolmogorov complexity metrics, GE Research & Development Center, Report Number 2001CRD176.
11. Lakhina, A., Crovella, M., and Diot, C., 2004, Diagnosing network-wide traffic anomalies, *SIGCOMM'04* **34**(4): 219-230.
12. Lakhina, A., Crovella, M., and Diot, C., 2005, Mining anomalies using traffic feature distributions, *SIGCOMM'05*: 217-228.
13. Narus, Narus anomaly detection user guide, 2005, Release 1.1, Document Number 031-05-1.1.
14. Park, K. and Lee, H., 2001, On the effectiveness of route-based packet filtering for distributed DoS attack prevention in power-law Internets, *SIGCOMM'01* **31**(4): 15-26.
15. Peng,T., Leckie, C., and Ramamohanarao, K., 2007, Survey of network-based defense mechanisms countering the DoS and DDoS problems, *ACM Computing Surveys* **39** (1).
16. Savage, S., Wetherall, D., Karlin, A., and Anderson, T, 2000, Practical network support for IP traceback, *SIGCOMM'00,* **30**(4): 295-306.
17. Wagner, A. and Plattner, B., 2005, Entropy based worm and anomaly detection in fast IP networks, *14th IEEE International Workshops on Enabling Technologies Infrastructures for Collaborative Enterprise (WET ICE 2005)*: 172-177.

Chapter 7

MOBILE NETWORKS COMPETITION AND ASYMMETRIC REGULATION OF TERMINATION CHARGES

Livio Cricelli[1], Francesca Di Pillo[2], Massimo Gastaldi[3] and Nathan Levialdi Ghiron[4]

[1]*Department of Mechanics, Structures, the Environment and Land Management, , University of Cassino, Italy, e-mail: cricelli@unicas.it;* [2,4]*Department of Enterprise Engineering, University of Rome "Tor Vergata", Italy, e-mail: {dipillo, levialdi@disp.uniroma2.it};* [3]*Department of Electrical and Information Engineering, University of L'Aquila, Italy, e-mail: gastaldi@ing.univaq.it*

Abstract: This paper is aimed to verify the effectiveness of the asymmetric regulation of mobile termination charges, under the assumption of discriminatory retail pricing. In the mobile competition, the networks revenue depends on two factors: the retail price and the termination charge. If the retail prices are different between calls that terminate on the same network (on net) and calls that terminate on the rival network (off net), the competition is more complex, involving positive networks externalities for the incumbent operator.[1]

Keywords: Brand loyalty; interconnected asymmetric networks; discriminatory retail prices; non reciprocal termination charges.

1.   INTRODUCTION

The liberalization process of the network industries and the technological progress have increased the complexity of the interconnection problem. In fact, the access to the essential facility and the interconnection among different networks have become very important for protection and development of the competition.

Interconnection battles have arisen regularly over the past century in the telephone, the railroad, the airline and the computer industries, among others

[1] This paper has been supported by MIUR funds PRIN 2005 (n.2005098172).

(Shapiro and Varian, 1999). However, it is useful conceptually to divide networks industries into two classes corresponding to the access modality needed by firms in the industry: one-way access and two-way interconnection. The case of one-way access refers to a setting where a firm monopolizes an input which is needed by all firms in order to provide their own service to the end users.

An example of one-way access is represented by the supply of internet services, where the different services providers must interconnect with the telephony network in order to provide their services to the final users. Other industries that are characterized for the modality of one-way access are the ones of gas supply, electricity supply and rail services.

A characteristic of one-way access situations is that, for important inputs at least, regulation of the terms of access is likely to be required to ensure socially desirable outcomes in competitive sectors, since the monopolist will choose to set too high access charge if free to do so (Armstrong, 1998).

The two-way access (or network interconnection) refers to a situation where firms, each with their own network, need to purchase the access from each other in order to provide the service to the end users. The two-way access situations can be divided into two classes: those with and those without competition for consumers. The latter case is exemplified by international telecommunications, where an operator in Italy must pay an operator in the United States to delivery its calls, but the two operators do not actually compete in the same market for the same consumers. The case of two-way interconnection with competition is represented by the local telecommunications, such as mobile and fixed.

A crucial difference between one-way access and two-way interconnection is the access (or interconnection) charge. In the one-way case, the access charge is the price fixed by the monopolist firm to allow the use of the vital input (essential facility) to the other competing firms. Therefore, the price competition among firms is focalized only on the price to the end users and not on the access charge that is fixed exclusively by the monopolist. In the two-way case, the interconnection charge (or termination charge) is the price paid by each operator for terminating the call on the rival network. At the same time, the interconnection charge represents the price collected from each operator for terminating the rival's call on its own network. Therefore, in this case, the price competition among firms is based on two key elements: the interconnection charge and the price to the end users.

This paper is focalized on mobile telecommunications market that represents an interesting case of two-way interconnection.

The interconnection in the mobile telecommunications industry requires cooperation between rival operators that must agree on their price, in order to provide the service to all users (Laffont, Rey and Tirole, 1998b). Unluckily, without an intervention of regulation authority and when networks are of unequal size (asymmetry in market shares), the incumbent operator could use the termination charge as an instrument of market foreclosure.

This threat becomes more feasible in the case of price discrimination strategy. Under such a strategy, networks can set different prices depending on the termination of call: on net price (if the call terminates on the same network) and off net price (if the call terminates on the rival network). The competitive problem of market foreclosure realized by the incumbent through the termination charge has been summarized by the European Regulators Group (ERG) of National Regulatory Authorities, in its "Common Position on the Approach to Appropriate Remedies in the New Regulatory Framework". The ERG (2006) shows that price discrimination can involve tariff mediated network externalities when the incumbent network fixes low on net and high off net prices, putting networks with a small consumer base at a disadvantage. In fact, setting a higher termination charge than the cost for terminating the call on own network involves that the off net calls are more expensive than the on net ones. Since the incumbent has a large consumer base, it is more probable that the consumers of the incumbent make more on net calls than the consumers of the smaller network. Therefore, the consumers of the smaller network must pay a higher average price of calls. Moreover, the higher price paid could represent the reason to change network for the smaller network consumers.

Hence, the price discrimination strategy could represent a competitive advantage for the incumbent operator for a double kind of reasons:
1. the large consumer base of the incumbent represents an incentive for the rival's consumers to change network;
2. The large consumer base of the incumbent allows to bear a lower cost of termination (the on net termination is cheaper than the off net termination).

The main aim of this paper is to verify if an intervention of regulation authority based on non reciprocal termination charge could alleviate the competitive problem of the price discrimination strategy. In fact, in Italy, the Italian Communication Authority (AGCOM, 2006), following the ERG position, has imposed the asymmetric regulation: the termination charge fixed by the incumbent operators is lower than that of the follower operators.

The need of regulating the Italian market of mobile-to-mobile termination is due to the asymmetric dimensions of operators and the consequent not balanced traffic between networks.

Besides, the AGCOM resolution of non reciprocal termination charges is based on the particular context of the Italian market. In fact, historically in

Italy the relative dimension of the operators has affected the market power in the negotiation of the interconnection agreements, favoring the incumbent operators.

Also the Antitrust Authority (2006) has underlined that the termination charge is fundamental to ensure the competition in the market of mobile telecommunication. Besides, by analyzing the networks agreements of the M2M termination, the Antitrust Authority has considered fundamental the elimination of the reciprocity principle in negotiating the interconnection charges.

Recently, the Italian Communication Authority (2007) has begun a market analysis in order to define the market of "Voice call termination on individual mobile networks" and to designate the operators having significant market power. This new market analysis is based on the consideration that a rapid technological and market change occurs in the Italian mobile telecommunications industry, deriving from the following factors:

- the development of the wireless technologies and the growing fixed to mobile convergence;
- the entry in the retail market of the operators that offer mobile services without being owners of infrastructures: the MVNO (Mobile Virtual Network Operator) and the ESP (Enhanced Service Provider).

Despite these changes, the Italian mobile market is still characterized by the presence of only four operators with own infrastructures and with largely diversified market shares. In fact, as we can observe in table 1, in the Italian mobile market the asymmetry among the operators' market shares is still strong, mainly in terms of revenues.

It is important to underline that the Italian delay in the competition process and the consequent necessity of an asymmetric regulation is motivated from the modality of market opening in consequence of the industry liberalization. In fact, contrarily of the American market where the process of competition has already reached a mature phase, the opening of the Italian market has been slow and gradual, characterized by a sequential entry by the competitors. Such type of entry is still evident in the subdivision of the market (see table 1): the first entered operators have held the greatest market shares.

In the Italian debate about the regulation of termination, there were many critics of the reciprocity principle. These criticisms were based on the possibility that the asymmetric regulation could protect the follower instead of promote the competition. Actually, it is important to underline that also the Italian Communication Authority (2006) limits the asymmetric regulation, imposing two restrictions:

1. The increase of the follower termination charge follower is bounded (price cap regulation). Currently, the Italian follower can fix a maximum interconnection charge of 12,9 eurocent/minute, while the maximum termination charge of the incumbent is 11,9 eurocent/minute. In other European countries, such as Hungary and Germany, the asymmetric regulation is much more amplified since the follower has the possibility to fix a mark up of 40% with respect to the termination charge of the incumbent.

2. Time limits: this type of regulation is applied for three years (2006-2008).

When this regulation period will expire, the authority will have to analyse again the market and to evaluate if a suitable level of competition has been attained. In this last case, the authority can decide to adopt reciprocal termination charges.

Table 1. Market shares of the Italian mobile networks

	Revenues (%)	Active lines (%)
TIM	42,4	40,0
VODAFONE	35,7	33,1
WIND	15,2	19,1
H3G	6,7	7,8
Total	100,0	100,0

Source: AGCOM - Annual Report on activities carried out and work program

In this paper, we extend the model of discriminatory retail pricing of Laffont, Rey and Tirole (1998b), by introducing the assumption of non reciprocal termination charges and by taking into account the parameters that affect the competition, as the brand loyalty and the degree of substitutability between the offered services (Carter and Wright, 1999). The brand loyalty represents an important strategic variable for competing with rival operators. In fact, the mobile telecommunications market of many European countries and, more specifically, the Italian one, is characterized by the presence of incumbents (former monopolists) that have a dominant position just due to the high brand loyalty of their consumers.

This paper is organized as follows. Section 2 provides a review of the most important literature on the topic of the two-way interconnection. Section 3 introduces the model of competition between two mobile phone networks. Section 4 describes the networks pricing strategies. Section 5 provides some simulations in order to verify the effectiveness of the regulatory remedy based on non reciprocal termination charges. Section 6 provides other simulations in order to test the model with respect to the demand function. In Section 7 some conclusions are drawn.

2.   LITERATURE REVIEW

There is a considerable academic literature on the topic of two-way interconnection (Armstrong, 1998; Laffont and Tirole, 1994, 1996, 1997; Cricelli, Gastaldi and Levialdi, 1999). This access modality is verified when each firm in the market must negotiate with each other to gain access to each other's subscribers (Armstrong, 2002). In the two-way interconnection, in absence of regulation, the operators compete deciding on two strategic leverages: the termination charge and the final price.

The two-way interconnection can be among firms that are not rivals, such as in the international telecommunications market (Cricelli, Di Pillo, Gastaldi, Levialdi, 2005), or among competitor firms, like the mobile operators. In this last case, the termination charge represents an important strategic variable that could be used as an instrument of collusion or to foreclose the market.

Armstrong (1998) and Laffont, Rey and Tirole (1998a) analyse the use of the termination charge as an instrument of collusion, under the following hypotheses: a) symmetric unregulated networks, b) homogeneous demand, c) linear retail prices, d) reciprocal termination charges and e) non discriminatory retail prices. These authors show that, when the offered services are sufficiently diversified, networks can fix a high reciprocal termination charge, so that even if they choose retail prices independently, they can get the monopoly outcome. The collusion is stable only if the offered services are sufficiently diversified. In fact, in this case, the choice of a high termination charge discourages networks to unilaterally decrease the retail price and to deviate from the collusive agreement.

In the following, we analyse the main theories on interconnection issue based on overcoming the starting assumptions of Armstrong and Laffont, Rey and Tirole.

As concerns the hypothesis of symmetric networks, Armstrong (1998) himself has relaxed this assumption. This author shows that the termination charge could be used as an instrument of market foreclose when the rival operators are of unequal size (market asymmetry) (Armstrong, 1998). Actually, in absence of regulation, if the operators that compete in the market are different in terms of dimensions (incumbent and follower) there is the possibility that the incumbent choose a very high termination charge, with the consequent increase of the follower cost for the calls termination (the quantity of off net calls of the follower is much more higher than that of the incumbent). Alternatively, the incumbent could choose a low level of the final price, getting, in the same way, the follower exit from the market. Such considerations underline the necessity to regulate an asymmetric market.

The hypothesis of symmetric networks has been relaxed also by Carter and Wright (1999, 2003) by analysing the interconnection in a deregulated network where the participants compete in the final retail market. Carter and Wright individualize, as differentiation factors between networks, the brand loyalty and the switching cost. The brand loyalty allows the incumbent network to get a greater market share, even if its price is equal to that of the follower operator. The authors show that, in absence of regulation, network externalities allow the incumbent to use the terms of interconnection to maintain its dominant position.

The hypothesis of homogeneous demand has been overcome by Armstrong (2004). This author considers asymmetric networks under the hypothesis of heterogeneous consumers in their demand for call. In particular, Armstrong individualizes two groups of consumers: the first one is characterized by a low volume of calls and the second with a high volume of traffic.

Under these hypotheses, the retail price varies according to the termination charge. More in detail, the increase in the incumbent termination charge causes entrants to raise their prices to all subscribers. On the contrary, the increase in the entrants' termination charges implies their lower retail prices. In fact, in this case, because of the higher cost for terminating the calls, it is more profitable for the entrants to attract further subscribers, and so competition is intensified. Finally, the increase in both reciprocal termination charges causes entrants to lower their price to low-volume users and to raise their price to high-volume users. This result is due to the increase in both termination charges, implying a high convenience for the entrants to attract a subscriber with a net inflow of calls (a subscriber who receives more calls than he makes).

The hypothesis of non linear retail pricing has been analysed by Dessein (2003) and Hahn (2003), getting similar results. Both these authors are focalized on the impact of the termination charge on the equilibrium prices, under the hypotheses of symmetric networks and reciprocal termination charges. Particularly, Dessein shows that, when the termination charges are non linear, these cannot be employed as an instrument of collusion. Moreover, Dessein (2004) shows, under the hypothesis of heterogeneous customers how the impact of the termination charge on profits crucially depends on how customers differ in the way they perceive the substitutability of competing networks.

Laffont, Rey and Tirole (1996) analyse the hypothesis of non linear pricing without discriminatory retail pricing. In this case, the authors show an effect of profit neutrality of the termination charges.

The hypothesis of non reciprocal termination charges has been analysed by Carter and Wright (1999), by considering asymmetric networks and non discriminatory retail prices. The main result of this analysis is that the threat of collusion still holds when non reciprocal termination charges are set above costs. Carter and Wright (2003) consider also reciprocal termination charges, showing that, if the market asymmetry is wide, both networks (incumbent and follower) prefer termination charges equal to the marginal costs.

The hypothesis of discriminatory retail pricing has been analysed by Laffont, Rey and Tirole (1998b), by considering reciprocal termination charges and symmetric networks. Laffont, Rey and Tirole show that if the two networks are poor substitutes and if there is a mark up on access, social welfare is higher under price discrimination than under uniform pricing. Moreover, Laffont, Rey and Tirole relax the hypothesis of symmetric networks, considering the service coverage as the reason of the asymmetry. Particularly, the incumbent has full coverage, whereas the entrant chooses its coverage and incurs an investment cost. Under these hypotheses, the price discrimination represents a threat for the small-scale entrant. In fact, the full-coverage incumbent can squeeze the entrant by fixing a high termination charge: this strategic behavior can represent a serious anticompetitive problem.

3.   THE MODEL

Starting from the model of Laffont, Rey and Tirole (1998b), we consider the following extended hypotheses:

1. the asymmetry between the operators is based on the brand loyalty of the incumbent (Carter and Wright, 1999) and not on the possibility of the service coverage;
2. non reciprocal termination charges.

The asymmetry between networks based on the possibility of the service coverage is a feature of the first step of liberalization when an entrant operator incurs an investment cost to entry in the market and gets its coverage. In this paper, we consider the case of a mature industry where operators have full coverage but have different market shares depending on consumers brand loyalty. For example, in Italy, the asymmetry among networks is not due to the service coverage but to the historical presence of incumbent networks in the market. In fact, the first operators entered in the market (TIM and Vodafone) have captured the whole market and the brand loyalty of their customers. In spite of the price undercutting and the innovative offered services, the last entrant operators (Wind and H3G) didn't get reasonable market shares. So, the Italian competitive situation shows the existence of incumbent market power and brand loyalty.

The second hypothesis is based on the regulatory remedy introduced by the Italian Communications Authority (2006) that fixes a price cap on mobile termination. Such deliberation provides for non reciprocal termination charges: the follower operator can fix a higher termination charge than that of the incumbent operator.

The main aim of this paper is to verify if non reciprocal termination charge could allow the follower operators to get a competitive benefit in spite of the price discrimination strategy of the incumbent.

In this work we consider a mobile telecommunications market where two networks compete, respectively network 1 and 2, both providing full coverage and serving all consumers (Laffont, Rey and Tirole, 1998b). We consider that networks consumers can make calls to subscribers belonging to the same network (on net calls) or to the rival network (off net calls). We analyse only the mobile traffic, since this work is aimed at verifying the impact of non reciprocal termination charge between mobile networks.

We assume that networks charge different prices to on net and off net calls. Therefore, we consider that p_1 is the price paid by a consumer of network 1 to make an on net call and $\hat{p}_1$ is the price paid by a consumer of network 1 to terminate its call on network 2. We assume analogous prices definition ($p_2, \hat{p}_2$) for network 2. Under the hypothesis of retail price discrimination, the net surplus of consumers of network 1 depends on prices of on net and off net calls and is given by:

$$w_1\left(p_1, \hat{p}_1\right) = S_1 V\left(p_1\right) + S_2 V\left(\hat{p}_1\right) \tag{1}$$

where S_1 and S_2 are the market shares of networks 1 and 2, $V(p_1)$ is the net surplus for on net calls, and $V(\hat{p}_1)$ is the net surplus for off net calls. The net surplus $V(p_1)$, $V(\hat{p}_1)$ are given by:

$$V\left(p_1\right) = \frac{p_1^{1-\eta}}{\eta - 1} \text{ and } V\left(\hat{p}_1\right) = \frac{\hat{p}_1^{1-\eta}}{\eta - 1} \tag{2}$$

where η is the demand elasticity. We assume that $\eta > 1$.

Analogous expressions of net surplus are valid for network 2. As concerns S_1 and S_2, the market shares are given by (Carter and Wright, 1999):

$$S_1 = \frac{1+\beta}{2} + \sigma\left[w_1\left(p_1, \hat{p}_1\right) - w_2\left(p_2, \hat{p}_2\right)\right] \tag{3a}$$

$$S_2 = 1 - S_1 \tag{3b}$$

where β represents the brand loyalty and σ the degree of substitutability between the offered services. By analysing the networks market shares expressions, we can make some considerations about the parameters β and σ. Both parameters determine the switching cost. In particular, the aim of the parameter σ is to gauge the relative importance of price competition. As concerns the parameter β, following Carter and Wright (1999), it is introduced in order to amplify the asymmetry between the incumbent and the follower. Indeed, the parameter β can be considered as a competitive advantage obtained by the incumbent and deriving from its historical presence in the market. Therefore, it represents the extra benefits which an entrant must offer to persuade consumers to switch from the incumbent.

For low values of the degree of substitutability σ, a network can price higher than its rival, without loosing its market share. Moreover, for low values of σ, the brand loyalty (parameter β) plays a relevant role in the determination of market share. Vice-versa, from Eq. (3) it follows that when σ tends to infinity only price differentials matter. Moreover, even if the incumbent brand loyalty is high, the reduction in follower prices allows it to capture the whole market.

The parameter β can take values between 0 and 1. When $\beta=0$, networks are symmetric. In this case, networks market shares are determined only by the price differentials. When $\beta>0$ we refer to network 1 as the incumbent and network 2 as the follower.

Substituting Eq. (1) in Eq. (3a), we obtain the following market share of network 1:

$$S_1 = \frac{1+\beta}{2} + \sigma \left[S_1 V(p_1) + S_2 V(\hat{p}_1) - S_2 V(p_2) - S_1 V(\hat{p}_2) \right]$$

Solving with respect to S_1:

$$S_1 = \frac{\frac{1+\beta}{2} + \sigma \left[V(\hat{p}_1) - V(p_2) \right]}{1 - \sigma \left[V(p_1) - V(\hat{p}_1) + V(p_2) - V(\hat{p}_2) \right]} \tag{4}$$

The demand functions q_1, $\hat{q}_1$ for on net and off net calls of network 1 are given by:

$$q_1 = \frac{A}{p_1^{\eta}} \quad \text{and} \quad \hat{q}_1 = \frac{A}{\hat{p}_1^{\eta}} \tag{5}$$

where A is a constant multiplicative factor of quantity.

Analogous expressions of quantity are valid for network 2. The profit π_1 of network 1 is given by:

$$\pi_1 = S_1 \{ S_1 (p_1 - 2c_1) q_1 + S_2 (\hat{p}_1 - c_1 - t_2) \hat{q}_1 + S_2 (t_1 - c_1) \hat{q}_2 \} \tag{6}$$

where:

- c_1 is the cost of network 1 at the originating ends (equal to the cost of on net calls at the terminating ends);
- t_1 is the termination charge fixed by network 1;
- t_2 is the termination charge fixed by network 2.

The first term of Eq. (6) represents profit from on-net calls. The second term represents profit from off-net traffic and the last term is the profit deriving from the incoming traffic.

There are four types of pairs of users $(1, 1)$, $(1, 2)$, $(2, 1)$, $(2, 2)$, representing the four possibilities of call. The fraction of pairs of each type $(S_1 S_1, \ S_1 S_2, \ S_2 S_1, \ S_2 S_2)$, which sums to one, represents the four probability of types of calls.

Analogous profit expression is valid for network 2.

Here we assume that the two networks have the same cost structure $(c_1 = c_2)$.

In this paper, we start from the model of discriminatory retail pricing of Laffont, Rey and Tirole and we extend it by assuming the hypothesis of asymmetric regulation. Moreover, we assume that the asymmetry between networks is due to the brand loyalty and not to the service coverage.

4.   NETWORKS STRATEGY

The networks strategy consists in the choice of optimal prices, starting from given market shares ($\overline{S}_1, \overline{S}_2$). In doing so, networks must offer a constant average net surplus to its consumers (Laffont, Rey and Tirole, 1998b). We start from given market shares, without using Eq. (4), since we want to find optimal prices under the hypotheses of asymmetric networks ($\overline{S}_1 \succ \overline{S}_2$). This paper is aimed at analysing the competition between asymmetric networks, therefore we impose the asymmetry in market shares as input datum and we find optimal prices according to asymmetric market shares.

We maximize the networks profit with respect to the prices and considering non reciprocal termination charges. For network 1 we solve:

$$\max_{p_1,\hat{p}_1}\left\{\overline{S}_1(p_1-2c_1)q_1+\overline{S}_2(\hat{p}_1-c_1-t_2)\hat{q}_1\ \middle|\ \overline{S}_1 V(p_1)+\overline{S}_2 V(\hat{p}_1)=\overline{w}_1\right\}$$

By substituting the demand function and the net surplus for on and off net calls, we can write the maximization problem as follows:

$$\max_{p1,\hat{p}1}\left\{\begin{array}{l}A\left[\overline{S}_1 p_1^{1-\eta}-2\overline{S}_1 c_1 p_1^{-\eta}+\overline{S}_2\hat{p}_1^{1-\eta}-\overline{S}_2(c_1+t_2)\hat{p}_1^{-\eta}\right]\\ \left[\overline{S}_1 p_1^{1-\eta}+\overline{S}_2\hat{p}_1^{1-\eta}=\overline{w}_1(\eta-1)\right.\end{array}\right\}\tag{7}$$

and by solving Eq. (7), we obtain the following optimal prices of network 1:

$$p_1=\left[\frac{\overline{w}_1(\eta-1)}{\left(\dfrac{2c_1}{c_1+t_2}\right)^{\eta-1}\overline{S}_2+\overline{S}_1}\right]^{\frac{1}{1-\eta}}\quad\text{and}\quad\hat{p}_1=\frac{c_1+t_2}{2c_1}p_1\tag{8}$$

Analogous expressions of optimal prices are valid for network 2.

From Eq. (8) we observe that the networks optimal prices depend on: the cost structure c_1 and c_2, the demand elasticity η, the consumers net surplus w_1 and w_2, the market shares S_1 and S_2, and the termination charges fixed by the rival operator t_1 and t_2.

Since the aim of this paper is the analysis of the asymmetric termination price regulation, it is of interest to examine the trend of optimal prices of network 1 due to the increase in termination charge of network 2. As already said, we consider network 1 as the incumbent and network 2 as the follower.

In order to assign starting values for the net surplus and market shares, we resort to the actual price plans fixed by mobile telephone Italian networks: the small operator offers both prices lower than those of the incumbent operator. Therefore, by using the actual Italian networks price plans and for an elastic demand (for ex. $\eta=1.4$), we have the following starting surplus and market shares: $w_1=0.8$, $w_2=0.9$, $S_1=60\%$, $S_2=40\%$. It is interesting to observe that, for these values, in spite of the greater incumbent brand loyalty, the low level of prices allows the follower consumers to get a higher net surplus.

By fixing an unitary value of cost c_1, we can study the trend of incumbent optimal prices deriving from a variation of the termination charge t_2 fixed by follower 2.

In figure 1 we can see that as t_2 increases, the network 1 off net price also increases. This result is due to the mark up relative to termination cost. In the limit, as t_2 tends to infinity the incumbent off net price tends to infinity, nullifying the outgoing calls of incumbent and the ingoing traffic profit of follower. In the simulations of the following section, we consider a limited increase in the follower termination charge, not greater than 40% of the incumbent termination charge.

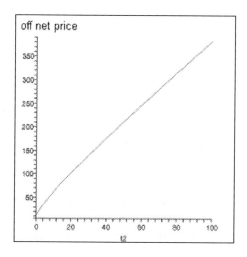

Figure 1. Trend of off net optimal price of network 1 due to the increase in the termination charge fixed by network 2

It is more interesting to observe the trend of incumbent on net price due to the increase in the termination price charged by network 2 (figure 2). As t_2 increases, the incumbent on net price decreases. The reduction of on net price involves two effects. The first one is immediate: the growth of the on net calls. The second effect is shown after a time period during which consumers observe new prices: the growth of the incumbent market share. In fact, the follower consumers switch network because of the higher probability to call on net at a cut price.

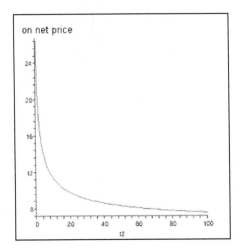

Figure 2. Trend of on net optimal price of network 1 due to the increase in the termination charge fixed by network 2

5.   SIMULATIONS

In this section, we consider two kinds of simulations. In the first one, we assume constant market shares, cost structure, demand elasticity, and consumers' net surplus: only the follower termination charge varies. We suppose that the increase in the follower termination charge varies between 0% (reciprocal termination charges) and 40% of the incumbent termination charge. Starting from these values we obtain the networks optimal prices. We consider that these optimal prices modify the quantity of calls and profits.

In the second simulation, we assume that the optimal prices modify not only the quantities and the profits, but also the market shares. This hypothesis is based on a fictitious time process: consumers observe optimal prices at time t-1 and than, at time t, they choose to change operator, determining the variation of the market shares and the profits. Given these optimal prices, we calculate market shares and profits with respect to every level of the brand loyalty and the degree of substitutability between the offered services.

5.1   Constant Market Shares

In this simulation we calculate optimal prices by using Eq. (8). This first simulation concerns a short time period: we assume that optimal prices do not modify the market shares but only the quantity of calls and the profits.

Therefore, starting from optimal prices obtained from Eq. (8) we calculate the new profits using Eq. (6). We assume constant market shares ($S_1 = 60\%$, $S_2 = 40\%$).

We start the analysis by considering the values of the preceding section: $c_1 = c_2 = 1$, $w_1 = 0.8$, $w_2 = 0.9$, $\eta=1.4$.

Since the main aim of the proposed model is to verify the validity of the regulatory remedy of asymmetric termination charges, in all simulations we consider both the case of reciprocal termination charge and the case of non reciprocal termination charge. For reciprocal termination charges we consider: $t_1 = t_2 = 1.2$, for non reciprocal termination charges we assume an increase in t_2 of 10%, 20%, 30%, 40% with respect to t_1.

It is interesting to analyse the incumbent optimal prices level with respect to the case of reciprocal termination charges. Obviously, the follower optimal prices do not vary as a consequence of the variation of its termination charge, since they only depend on the incumbent termination charge.

We can see in figures 3 and 4 the percentage variation in incumbent optimal prices with respect to the hypothesis of reciprocal access charges. The incumbent prices trend due to the increase in the follower access charge is reverse. In fact, while off net price increases, on net price decreases. More specifically, the percentage variation in the off net price is greater than that in the on net price.

In figures 5 and 6, we can analyse the profit trends of networks.

It is interesting to examine the networks profit variations due to the increase in the follower termination charge. As follower termination price increases, the incumbent profits decrease, whereas the follower profits increase. The networks profits variations are reasonable. In fact, the incumbent bears a higher termination cost, but this loss is compensated by the greater revenues of outgoing calls, due to the increase in the off net price. The increase of the follower profit is reasonable as a result of the reduction in the quantity of incoming calls.

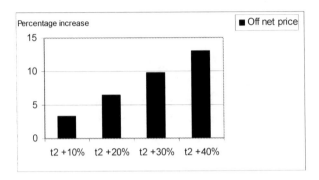

Figure 3. Percentage variations of incumbent off net price due to the increase of the follower termination charge

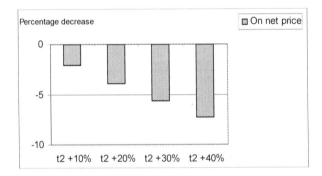

Figure 4. Percentage variations of incumbent on net price due to the increase of the follower termination charge

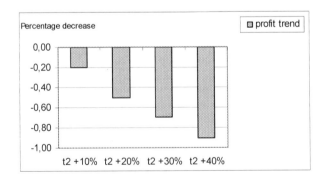

Figure 5. Percentage variation of incumbent profits due to the increase of the follower termination charge

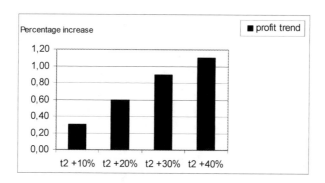

Figure 6. Percentage variation of follower profits due to the increase of the follower termination charge

5.2 Variable Market Shares

We start the analysis by considering the same values of the previous section: $c_1 = c_2 = 1$, $w_1 = 0.8$, $w_2 = 0.9$, $\eta=1.4$. Also in this case, in all simulations we compare the case of reciprocal termination charge with the case of non reciprocal termination charge. As before, for reciprocal termination charges we consider: $t_1 = t_2 = 1.2$, for non reciprocal termination charge we assume an increase in t_2 of 10%, 20%, 30%, 40% with respect to t_1.

In this simulation, we assume given asymmetric market shares ($S_1 = 60\%$, $S_2 = 40\%$) in calculating optimal prices. We consider that, after a period of time, the optimal prices modify networks market shares. Therefore, we calculate through Eq. (4) the new networks market share, for each level of incumbent brand loyalty (parameter β) and degree of substitutability between the offered services (parameter σ).

In particular, we want to study the effect deriving exclusively from the increase of the brand loyalty and that deriving exclusively from the degree of substitutability between the offered services. Since these two parameters, at the same time, influence market shares, in order to isolate the effect deriving from one variable, in the following simulations we keep constant the value of the other variable. In particular, we set the other variable at a low level so that it does not imply adverse effects in calculating the market shares.

The parameter β, as already said, represents the competitive advantage of the incumbent deriving from its historical presence in the market. Therefore, as β grows, the incumbent market share increases.

For the simulations we consider a range of variation of β between 0.2 and 0.8. We have chosen this range because it represents an asymmetric market. In fact, if β were equal to 0, the operators would be almost symmetric, if β were equal to 1 the market would be characterized by the only presence of the monopolist.

The parameter σ plays a relevant role in the determination of market shares since it represents the importance of price in the choice of consumers. Therefore, as σ grows, the importance of price in the consumers choice increases and the determinants regarding the extra benefits and brand loyalty decrease. Therefore, if σ increases the two services are more substitutable since the only differentiating factor is the price. Since in the following simulations the follower optimal prices are always lower than those of the incumbent, when β is constant, as σ grows the follower market share increases.

In particular, from the following simulation we show that for $\sigma>1.6$ the follower becomes the incumbent. Therefore, the maximum value chosen for σ in the simulations is 1.6. The minimum value is 0.6. In fact, from the simulations, for $\sigma=0.6$ the importance of price in the consumers choice is low and the services are not very substitutable.

Therefore, as β grows the market asymmetry and the incumbent market share increase. As σ grows the asymmetry between operators decreases and, as a consequence, the follower market share increases.

Given the new market shares we calculate the new profits through Eq. (6).

The trend of incumbent optimal prices due to the increase in the follower termination charge is the same observed in the previous section. Therefore, as follower termination charge grows, off net price increases, whereas on net price decreases.

5.2.1   Simulation on the Brand Loyalty

Given optimal prices, we calculate through Eq. (4) the new market shares. Since we want to isolate the effect deriving from the variation in the incumbent brand loyalty, we keep constant and at a low level the degree of substitutability between the offered services ($\sigma=0.6$). We consider that the incumbent brand loyalty varies between 0.2 and 0.8. From the new market shares we find the new profits through Eq. (6).

As the incumbent brand loyalty increases, the follower market share obviously decreases, whereas the incumbent market share grows (see figures 7 and 8).

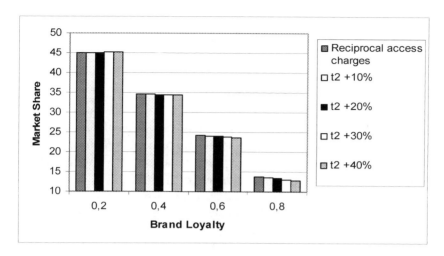

Figure 7. Trend of follower market share due to the increase of the follower termination charge for each level of the incumbent brand loyalty

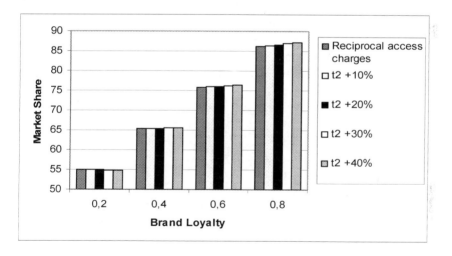

Figure 8. Trend of incumbent market share due to the increase of the follower termination charge for each level of the incumbent brand loyalty

It is interesting to underline that, for a low brand loyalty ($\beta=0.2$), networks market shares are almost constant with respect to the increase in the follower termination charge. This result is due to the balance between the increase in the incumbent off net price and the reduction in the incumbent on net price.

When the brand loyalty is medium-high (β=0.4, 0.6, 0.8), the reduction in the on net price involves an increase in the incumbent market share. In fact, when networks are more asymmetric, the reduction in the on net price motivates follower consumers to switch network. Indeed, by switching operator, follower consumers could have a higher probability to call on net at a lower price.

In figures 9 and 10 we show the percentage variations of networks profits compared with the case of reciprocal termination charges. We show only the percentage variations and not the absolute values since we want underline the impact of asymmetric regulation on networks profits.

With regard to the increase in follower termination charge, we observe that for a medium-low brand loyalty (β=0.2, 0.4), the regulatory remedy based on non reciprocal termination charge is effective, allowing the follower to get a higher profit than that obtained under the hypothesis of reciprocal termination charges. On the contrary, for a high brand loyalty (β=0.6, 0.8), the increase in follower termination charge involves an elevated growth in the incumbent market share as a result of the reduction in its on net price. For instance, when there is a high brand loyalty (β=0.8), the asymmetric regulation fails: as the follower termination charge increases, the incumbent on net price decreases and the positive network externality rises. In this case, the follower suffers the highest profit loss. Therefore, when networks are widely asymmetric, the regulatory remedy based on non reciprocal termination charges is not sufficient. In this case, a regulation also on retail prices is necessary.

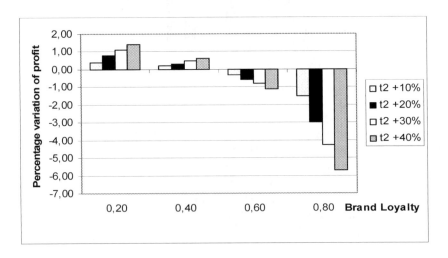

Figure 9. Percentage variation of follower profits due to increase of the follower termination charge for each level of the incumbent brand loyalty

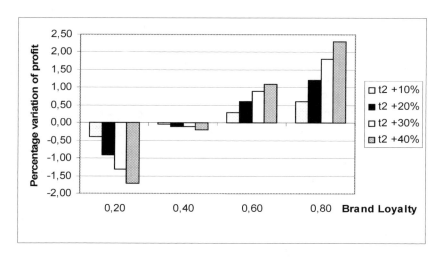

Figure 10. Percentage variation of incumbent profits due to increase of the follower termination charge for each level of the incumbent brand loyalty

5.2.2 Simulation on the Degree of Substitutability Between the Offered Services

Given optimal prices, we calculate the new market shares through Eq. (4). Since we want to isolate the effect deriving from the variation in the degree of substitutability, we keep constant and at a low level the incumbent brand loyalty (β=0.3). We consider that the degree of substitutability has the following values: 0.6, 1.0 and 1.6. We have chosen this range because σ =1.6 represents the threshold value from which network 1 becomes the follower and network 2 the incumbent. The minimum value σ =0.6 has been chosen since it represents the value where the importance of price in the consumers choice is low and the variations of prices do not cause a significant variation of market shares.

Then, from the new market shares we calculate the new networks profits using Eq. (6).

When the degree of substitutability grows, the competition focalizes on prices and the follower gets an increase in its market share. This result follows from the profit maximization: both optimal prices of the follower are lower than those of the incumbent, and, for a low brand loyalty, the incumbent consumers prefer change operator because they are interested to call at a lower prices.

As we can observe in figures 11 and 12, the increase in the degree of substitutability involves the growth in the follower market share and the decrease in the incumbent market share.

When the degree of substitutability is low ($\sigma=0.6$), as the follower termination charge increases, the incumbent market share grows as a result of the reduction in the incumbent on net price.

For a medium-high level of σ ($\sigma=1.0$, 1.6), the importance of price in the choice of network grows.

Therefore, the low level of prices causes a considerable increase in the follower market share. Moreover, the growth in the follower market share makes more important the incumbent off net price. In fact, as the follower market share increases, the quantity of the incumbent outgoing calls rises. As t_2 increases, the incumbent optimal off net price grows. Consequently, such increase motivates incumbent consumers to switch operator.

As the degree of substitutability increases, the follower profits grow and the incumbent profits decrease (see figures 13 and 14), as a result of the raise in the follower market share.

For each levels of the degree of substitutability, the asymmetric termination charges regulation is effective, allowing the follower to get a higher profit than that obtained through reciprocal termination charges. Also in the case of $\sigma=0.6$, the elevated revenue of the incoming calls allows the follower to get an higher profit than that obtained through reciprocal termination charges, in spite of the slight reduction in its market share.

When the degree of substitutability is high and the incumbent brand loyalty is low, the asymmetry between networks is reduced so that the regulatory remedy based on non reciprocal termination charges is not necessary. In fact, for $\sigma=1.6$, as the follower termination charge increases, the incumbent suffers a considerable profit and market share decrease. When $\sigma=1.6$, by increasing the gap between networks termination charges, operator 1 becomes the follower and operator 2 the incumbent. Hence, in this case, the asymmetric regulation could be harmful to the incumbent.

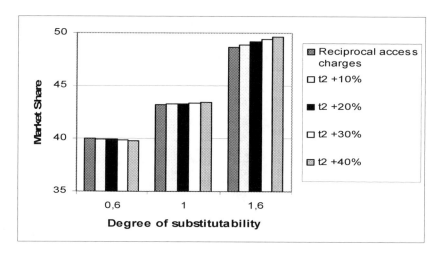

Figure 11. Trend of follower market share due to the increase of the follower termination charge for each level of the degree of substitutability

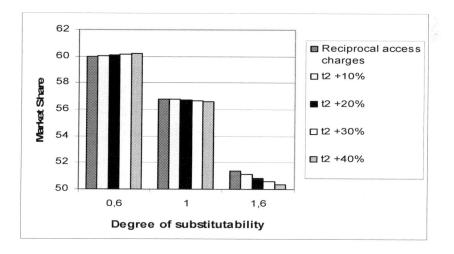

Figure 12. Trend of incumbent market share due to the increase of the follower termination charge for each level of the degree of substitutability

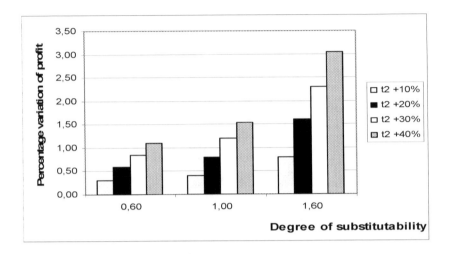

Figure 13. Percentage variation of follower profits due to increase of the follower termination charge for each level of the degree of substitutability

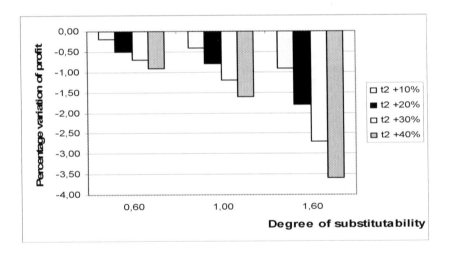

Figure 14. Percentage variation of follower profits due to increase of the follower termination charge for each level of the degree of substitutability

5.2.3   Comparative Analysis of the Impact on Networks Profit

In figures 15 and 16 it is possible to compare the percentage increases of follower profits with respect to the different hypotheses of simulation. For the comparison, we take into consideration the case of both constant market share and the variable one. In this last case, we consider the highest profit increase of follower with respect to the simulations on β and on σ.

The results of the simulation on β show that the highest follower profit increase is obtained when β is low, whereas through the simulation on σ the highest increase is attained when σ is high. This result is due to the variation of follower market share. In fact, as β grows the incumbent market share increases, while as σ grows the asymmetry between operators decreases and, as a consequence, the follower market share increases. Therefore, the follower obtains its highest profit when it has the greater market shares.

By comparing the three cases of simulation, from figure 15 we can illustrate that the follower gets the highest profit when σ is high and β is low. Obviously, under this hypothesis the incumbent suffers the highest profit loss (see figure 16). In this limit case, since the degree of substitutability is high and the incumbent brand loyalty is low, the asymmetry between networks is reduced and the asymmetric regulation could be not necessary anymore. This is an example of failure of the asymmetric regulation that causes adverse effects on competition.

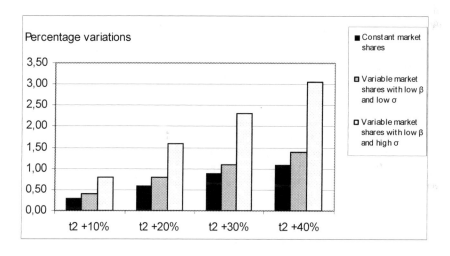

Figure 15. Percentage variation of follower profits due to increase of the follower termination charge for each hypothesis of simulation

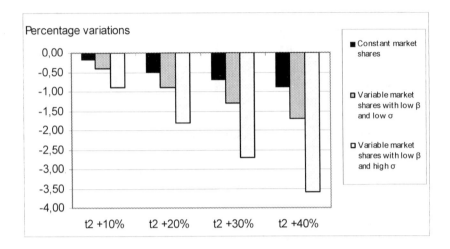

Figure 16. Percentage variation of incumbent profits due to increase of the follower termination charge for each hypothesis of simulation

6.　COMPARATIVE DEMAND MODEL

In the present paper we have assumed the hypothesis of a demand function with constant elasticity, largely used in the literature (Laffont, Rey and Tirole, 1998a, 1998b; Dessein, 2004).

In this section we study the effect of asymmetric termination charge under the hypothesis of a linear demand function in order to test the validity of the model.

Also in this case, we calculate optimal prices by solving the maximization problem Eq. (7) and by considering the following demand functions respectively for on net and off net calls:

$$q_1 = a - bp_1 \quad \text{and} \quad \hat{q}_1 = a - b\hat{p}_1$$

Analogous expressions of quantities are valid for operator 2.

We carry out the same simulations and we consider the same starting values of the case of the demand function with constant elasticity.

From the maximization process we get similar results with respect to the previous case regarding the trend of the incumbent prices. In fact, while off net price increases, on net price decreases (see figure 17). Also in this case, the percentage variation in the off net price is greater than that in the on net price. The only difference between the two cases is that, under the hypothesis of linear demand, price variations are much slighter than the case of demand with constant elasticity (see figures 3 and 4).

This result is due to the greater elasticity that is attained under the hypothesis of linear demand. In fact, for each level of optimal price, the demand elasticity is greater than that of the case of the demand function with constant elasticity.

The greater elasticity implies that a smaller variation of prices provokes a larger variation in quantity. Therefore, the variation of optimal prices is smaller because it is balanced by the greater variation in quantities.

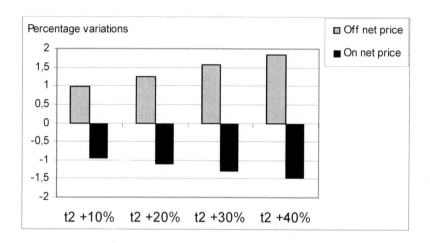

Figure 17. Percentage variations of incumbent on net and off net price due to the increase of the follower termination charge

As concerns the simulations on profit variations under the hypothesis of constant market share, we get results similar to that obtained under the assumption of demand with constant elasticity. In fact, as follower termination price increases, the incumbent profits decrease, whereas the follower profits increase. Also in this case, the networks profit variations are small.

As concerns the simulations under the hypothesis of variable market share, like under the hypothesis of demand with constant elasticity, we get the same optimal price variations with respect to the case of constant market share. Since, as already said, these price variations are slight, the effect on market share deriving from the increase of t_2 is smaller than in the case of demand with constant elasticity.

As concerns the effect on networks profits and the efficacy of asymmetric regulation we get analogous results with respect to the case of constant elasticity model, even if the impact on market share is small.

In concluding, the use of a linear demand model causes an attenuated effect on prices and on market shares but does not modify the policy implications about the regulation of termination.

7.   CONCLUSIONS

The main economic literature and the Italian Communications Authority have identified, as competitive problem, the positive network externality of the incumbent, due to the strategy of price discrimination between on net and off net calls. In fact, the incumbent operator with a greater brand loyalty and a large consumer base, can use the discriminatory retail pricing as an anticompetitive instrument. In the mobile telecommunications market, the cost of the off net termination is greater than that of the on net termination.

Since the incumbent has the greatest market share, its consumers make more on net calls than the off net ones. Therefore, the incumbent bears a smaller cost of termination than that of the follower. Moreover, the retail price discrimination can be an incentive for the follower consumers to change operator, since they are attracted by the greater probability of making more on net calls at a lower price.

The Italian Communications Authority has identified non reciprocal termination charge as a possible regulatory remedy. Starting from a previous research (Cricelli, Di Pillo, Gastaldi and Levialdi 2007), the present work is aimed at verifying the validity of this remedy.

We have assumed an asymmetric market, where two networks operate: an incumbent and a follower. We have considered that networks choose their own prices through a simultaneous maximization of the profits.

In the first simulation, we have assumed that the variation of optimal prices does not change the networks market shares. This hypothesis could be realistic during short-term. Under this hypothesis, as the follower termination charge grows, its profits increase.

In the second simulation, we have assumed that prices deriving form the profit maximization modify networks market shares. We have considered that networks market shares depend on brand loyalty and degree of substitutability between the offered services. Under these hypotheses, the trend of follower profits depends on the brand loyalty and the degree of substitutability.

For a low degree of substitutability, when the brand loyalty is low ($\beta=0.2$, 0.4), the asymmetric termination charges regulation is effective since the follower profits increase and its market share is almost constant. On the contrary, when the brand loyalty is high, as the follower termination charge increases, the incumbent market share grows and, consequently, the follower market share and profit decrease.

For a low brand loyalty and for a medium-high level of the degree of substitutability between the offered services ($\sigma=1.0$, 1.6), as the follower termination charge increases, its market share and profit rise. In fact, for a high level of σ, the importance of price in the choice of network grows. Therefore, the increase in the incumbent off net price causes a considerable raise in the follower market share. Such increase involves a relevant growth in the follower profit and an incumbent profit loss. In this case, the asymmetric regulation could be harmful to the incumbent.

In conclusion, whereas in the short term the regulatory remedy based on non reciprocal termination charges is always effective, we have obtained a different result for the long term. In fact, by considering that optimal prices modify networks market shares, the asymmetric termination charges regulation is effective only if the incumbent brand loyalty and degree of substitutability between the offered services are low.

Actually, if the degree of substitutability between the offered services is high, the asymmetric regulation could be too much penalizing for the incumbent. Vice-versa, if the incumbent brand loyalty is high, the regulatory remedy based on non reciprocal termination charges does not involve a competitive benefit for the follower. Therefore, when the incumbent brand loyalty is high, the asymmetric termination charges regulation is not sufficient to restore the equality in the market: a simultaneous regulation on retail prices is necessary.

ACKNOWLEDGEMENTS

We would like to thank the two anonymous referees for their comments and suggestions to improve the quality of this paper.

References

AGCM, 2006, Mercato della terminazione di chiamate vocali su singole reti mobili, *Segnalazione n. 28/12/05*, Bollettino n.3/2006, available: http://www.agcm.it/.

AGCOM, 2006, Mercato della terminazione di chiamate vocali su singole reti mobili: identificazione ed analisi del mercato, valutazione di sussistenza di imprese con significativo potere di mercato ed individuazione degli obblighi regolamentari, *Delibera n. 3/06/CONS*, Gazzetta Ufficiale della Repubblica Italiana n. 32 del 08/02/06, available: http://www.agcom.it/.

AGCOM, 2007, Mercato della terminazione di chiamate vocali su singole reti mobili: definizione del mercato rilevante, identificazione delle imprese aventi significativo potere di mercato ed eventuale imposizione di obblighi regolamentari, *Delibera n. 342/07/CONS*, available: http://www.agcom.it/.

Armstrong, M., 1998, Network interconnection in telecommunications, *The Economic Journal*, **108**: pp.545-564.

Armstrong, M., 2002, The theory of access pricing and interconnection in: *Handbook of Telecommunications Economics, Structure, Regulation and Competition*, M. E. Cave et al, eds., Elsevier Science Publishers, Amsterdam, pp. 320-350.

Armstrong. M., 2004, Network interconnection with asymmetric networks and heterogeneous calling patterns, *Information Economics and Policy*, **16**: pp.375-390.

Carter, M. and Wright, J., 1999, Interconnection in network industries, *Review of Industrial Organization*, **14**: pp.1-25.

Carter, M. and Wright, J., 2003, Asymmetric network interconnection, *Review of Industrial Organization*, **22**: pp.27-46.

Cricelli, L., Gastaldi, M. and Levialdi, N., 1999, Vertical integration in international telecommunications systems", *Review of Industrial Organization*, **14**: pp.337-353.

Cricelli, L., Di Pillo, F., Gastaldi, M. and Levialdi, N., 2005, The wholesale competition in the international telecommunications system, *Network and Spatial Economics*, **5**: pp.261-277.

Cricelli, L, Di Pillo, F., Gastaldi, M. and Levialdi, N., June 2007, Could asymmetric regulation of access charges improve the competition between mobile networks, in: *IEEE electronic proceedings of the 6th Conference on Telecommunication Techno-Economics*, Helsinki, Finland.

Dessein, W., 2003, Network competition in non linear pricing, *Rand Journal of Economics*, **34**: pp.1-19.

Dessein, W., 2004, Network Competition with Heterogeneous Customers and Calling Patterns, *Information Economics and Policy*, **16**: pp.323-345.

ERG, 2006, Revised ERG common position on the approach to appropriate remedies in the new regulatory framework, available: http://erg.eu.int/.

Hahn, J-H., 2003, Non linear pricing of telecommunications with call and network externalities, *International Journal of Industrial Organization*, **21**: pp. 949-967.

Laffont, J-J. and Tirole, J., 1994, Access pricing and competition, *European Economic Review*, **38**: pp. 1673-1710.

Laffont, J-J. and Tirole, J., 1996, Creating competition through interconnection: theory and practice, *Journal of Regulatory Economics*, **10**: pp.227-256,.

Laffont, J-J., Rey, P. and Tirole, J., 1997, Competition between telecommunications operators, *European Economic Review*, **41**: pp.701-711.

Laffont, J-J., Rey, P. and Tirole, J., 1998a, Network competition: I. Overview and nondiscriminatory pricing, *Rand Journal of Economics*, **29**: pp.1-37.

Laffont, J-J., Rey, P. and Tirole, J., 1998b, Network competition: II. Discriminatory pricing, *Rand Journal of Economics*, **29**: pp.38-56.

Shapiro, C. and Varian, H. R., 1999, *Information Rules a Strategic Guide to the Network Economy*, Harvard Business School Press Boston, Massachusetts, pp. 173-227.

Chapter 8

A PACKAGE BIDDING TOOL FOR THE FCC'S SPECTRUM AUCTIONS, AND ITS EFFECT ON AUCTION OUTCOMES

Karla Hoffman[1], Dinesh Menon[2], and Susara A. van den Heever[3]
[1]Dept. of Systems Engineering and Operations Research, George Mason University, Fairfax, VA; [2]Optimization Solutions Division, Decisive Analytics, Arlington VA 22202; [3]ILOG SA, Nice, France;

Abstract: We present a bidder aid tool that allows bidders to more effectively participate in combinatorial FCC spectrum auctions by enabling concise expression of preferences. In addition to logical relationships between items, bidders may express spectrum-specific preferences such as those related to minimum population coverage, bandwidth, and budget. The tool can be used to simultaneously generate and evaluate a set of most profitable biddable packages, both at the start of the auction and dynamically before each round. We also explore the effect of creating "best-fit" packages at each round. Our preliminary results show that the use of this tool may significantly simplify bidders' efforts in generating packages of interest and lead to efficient auction outcomes.[1]

Keywords: Combinatorial auctions; bidder aid tool; bidding; combinatorial optimization; telecommunications modeling.

1. INTRODUCTION

In combinatorial auctions, bidders face the daunting task of generating the optimal set of biddable packages, often requiring the enumeration of a vast number of alternatives. In this paper, we propose a Bidder Aid Tool

---

[1] This research was funded by the Federal Communications Commission under a contract to Computech Inc. All views presented in this research are those of the authors and do not necessarily reflect the views of the Federal Communications Commission or any of its staff.

(BAT) that will allow bidders to concisely express their preferences. This tool interprets bidder preferences to simultaneously generate and evaluate a set of package bids at each round of the auction. Our design is intended for the Federal Communications Commission's (FCC) spectrum auctions, and is based on ideas from Cramton (2002a, 2003) and Ausubel (2002), as well as interviews with several participants in past spectrum auctions (*e.g.* Wilkie (2002) and Tarnutzer (2002)).

The FCC has been auctioning spectrum to companies providing wireless services since 1994 (McMillan, 1994). Over the past decade, thousands of spectrum licenses have been auctioned to hundreds of companies. Before auctions, the FCC initially used comparative hearings and later, lotteries. Comparative hearings were too slow in allocating spectrum, while neither method raised any revenues - billions of dollars worth of spectrum licenses were given away for free. In addition, licenses often did not end up with the companies that valued them the most. Auctions are not only better at achieving timely allocation of licenses to the parties that value them the most, but also raise substantial revenues for the US Treasury. In addition, auctions encourage innovation and competition, while benefiting all parties involved from consumers to wireless service providers (Cramton, 2002b). Spectrum auctions have been used across the globe, with the FCC considered the leader in this area worldwide.

Efficiency, meaning allocating the spectrum to those who value it the most, is often the primary goal of government spectrum auctions, in general. Revenue is usually a secondary goal, although not often emphasized. In determining their initial auction mechanism, the FCC considered several designs and gathered input from both industry and academia. This process has been continuing with the FCC's auction designs evolving as new economic theories come to light and bidder behavior and auction outcomes are better understood. For an excellent review on the history of the FCC spectrum auctions, as well as auction theory in general, see Milgrom (2004).

The majority of FCC auctions to date have been Simultaneous Multiple Round (SMR) auctions (see Milgrom (1998)). In these auctions, bidders bid on individual licenses, and can bid on multiple licenses during each round. At the end of each round, each license's price increases with a percentage increment as long as bids are being placed on that license. The auction stops when there are no new bids on any licenses, at which time the licenses are allocated to the bidders with the highest bids. SMR auctions have worked well, but do not allow bidders to express synergies among licenses without running the risk of winning only a subset of the items they desire, and possibly paying more than their value for this subset (Bykowsky et al. (2000)). Such risk is known as the "exposure problem". Many authors, for example Ausubel et al. (1997) and Cramton (1995), have cited examples of geographic synergies with the FCC spectrum auctions.

Recently, the FCC implemented a combinatorial auction design that allows the placing of bids on combinations or packages of items, referred to as Simultaneous Multiple Round with Package Bidding (SMRPB). This design mitigates some of the problems associated with single item bidding, such as the exposure problem, and allows bidders to express their valuations on items that are substitutes (where bidders will accept a greater number of items, but at a decreasing price) and complements (where bidders value the combination of items more than the sum of the individual item values).

Even though combinatorial bidding alleviates some problems associated with single-item bidding, it introduces the difficulty of generating packages of items that fully express the bidders' preferences. Several bidding languages have been suggested to help bidders in this task, for example OR, XOR, OR-of-XOR, XOR-of-OR and OR* languages. Nisan (2000) gives a thorough analysis of these bidding languages and determines that the OR* language (OR-bids with phantom items) is both completely expressive and the most compact of the bidding languages listed. While these languages are very expressive, they are not the most natural way for bidders in a spectrum auction to frame their business plans. Such plans are generally budget constrained and require a minimum amount of bandwidth and population coverage in specific geographic regions. Bidders need to translate these high-level preferences into logic that explicitly refers to the individual items being auctioned in order to use existing bidding languages.

The bidding language currently used by the FCC is the XOR language, implying that a bidder may win at most one of its bids. Without price information to direct package composition, a bidder must enumerate and evaluate all possible combinations of items it is interested in winning. Linear pricing mechanisms, where bidders are given information on item prices that can be summed up to determine package prices, help with the task of package creation because bidders can use the current pricing information to find packages that are both affordable and profitable. However, bidders still have the problem of finding the selection of packages that satisfy non-price package criteria, such as bandwidth and population requirements, and that fit well with other bidders' packages in order to have a greater probability of winning. In addition, the auctioneer may limit the total number of package bids a given bidder may bid on. This limitation may be implemented for a number of reasons, for example to limit gaming (parking or saturating the system so as to sabotage the auction) or to limit the computational complexity of the auctioneer's winner determination problem. Having a limited number of bids available forces the bidder to guess which of the packages it values have the greatest potential to win – a computationally difficult task. Our goal is to simplify the task of generating and valuating packages by providing bidders with a tool that allows concise expression of their preferences and values, and responds with suggested packages that meet bidders' preferences.

Specifically, the tool will translate the bidder's preferences, as expressed in "bidder's language", into a set of bids expressed in the XOR bidding language. To do this translation, a set of constraints are derived from the bidder's preference inputs. These constraints form the basis of an optimization model that is used to generate packages that satisfy a specific objective, such as maximizing the bidder's profit. The proposed tool is designed to allow bidders to more effectively participate in ascending combinatorial FCC spectrum auctions, by enabling quicker bid generation and valuation, both at the start of the auction and before each round, based on the current prices set by the auctioneer. Confidentiality of all the private information required by the BAT can be ensured by using local versions of the tool that reside on the bidders' computers.

In order to test our proposed design, we simulated bidders that express their preferences using the rules and options available in the BAT. The simulation was done using BidBots - a simulation tool used at the FCC for research purposes that is capable of simulating a variety of auction mechanisms, bidder types and bidding strategies. An earlier version of BidBots is discussed in Dunford et al. (2004). Our goal was to test the feasibility of the BAT in terms of package creation time and flexibility, and to test its impact on the allocative efficiency and the auction revenue. To simulate the preferences of different types of bidders, we created four distinct bidder types, namely Cherry Pickers, Regional-, National-, and Global bidders. In addition, we simulated three bidding strategies that can be used by any of the bidder types, namely a Myopic Best Response (MBR) strategy, a Myopic Best Response within Profitability Range (MBRPR) strategy, and a Fit strategy (FIT). Please refer to Section 6 for more detail on the bidder types and strategies.

In the next section, we describe related work. In Section 3, we give an overview of the requirements and conceptual design of our proposed Bidder Aid Tool (BAT). We describe the preference elicitation steps in Section 4 and the derived optimization model in Section 5. Section 6 provides some preliminary results, together with a brief description of our experimental setup. Conclusions and directions for future work are presented in Section 7.

2. RELATED WORK

Several approaches have been proposed to deal with the difficult task associated with combinatorial auctions of generating and valuating all packages of interest while avoiding complete enumeration. An ascending mechanism such as the one used at the FCC alleviates the problem by allowing bidders to only submit those packages that are of the greatest interest given the current round's prices and the bidders' bidding strategies (see e.g. Banks et al. (1989), DeMartini et al. (1998), Kwon et al. (2005), Parkes (1999), and Wurman and Wellman (2000)). Some ascending mechanisms apply proxy bidding, where the human bidders supply their valuation functions to automated proxy agents, and the proxies then make the bidding decisions on their behalf (e.g. Ausubel and Milgrom (2002), Parkes and Ungar (2000)). Another approach is to elicit bidders' preferences through queries (e.g. Conen and Sandholm, (2002), Hudson and Sandholm (2002)). In this approach, an auctioneer agent asks bidders questions regarding package preference, package valuations, and/or package ranking, starting with all the bidders' packages, but only asking questions about those the agent deems potentially desirable according to the problem's inherent structure.

Even with improved auction mechanisms such as those mentioned in the previous paragraph, bidders often need to enumerate and evaluate a very large number of packages to be able to make good bidding decisions at each round, or in the case of a proxy, to supply the proxy with sufficient information. Rothkopf et al. (1998) proposed limiting the allowable combinations of items and showed that for certain allowable combinations the computational complexity of the revenue problem becomes polynomial. However, the limitations proposed in their work are not practical for most of the FCC's spectrum auctions. Other researchers have proposed expressing bidder preferences in terms of constraints, as opposed to explicitly listing packages, in order to avoid enumeration of all combinations of interest. Most often, the constraints are converted to package bids by solving an optimization problem that maximizes the bidder's profit, and the bids are then submitted to an auction designed for package bidding. For example, An et al. (2005) present a model for package creation and valuation for sealed-bid auctions in the transportation industry. Their valuation model requires only item values and pair-wise synergies, thereby eliminating the need to enumerate and evaluate all possible combinations. One result from their work is that educating bidders in making better packaging decisions benefits both bidders and the auctioneer more than simply increasing the number of package bids allowed. This result is an important motivation for the development of tools that aid bidders in package creation and valuation, especially when the number of allowable package bids is limited, as is often the case.

Some researchers have taken the concept of constraint-based bids a step further, by proposing that such bids be submitted directly to the winner determination problem, thus eliminating the need for package creation entirely (see e.g. Boutilier and Hoos (2001), Boutilier (2002), Jones and Koehler (2002), and Parkes et al. (2005)). Although we successfully used this approach to determine the efficient auction outcome in our simulations, its use is not realistic for the FCC auctions, because bidders have indicated their unwillingness to reveal the required information to the auctioneer. Bidders mentioned concerns that their private information might be disclosed to other bidders at some future time.

The first work we found in the literature that specifically addresses package valuation and creation for the FCC spectrum auctions, albeit for test data generation, was presented by Leyton-Brown et al. (2000) as part of their Combinatorial Auction Test Suite (CATS). This is a suite of distributions for modeling realistic bidding behavior in varying market environments, for the study of algorithm performance. Their method considers bidder's item values, geographical synergies, minimum package requirements and budgets. While it was at the time the most realistic published version of a package creation and valuation tool for spectrum auctions, the authors stated that "clearly the problem of realistic test data for spectrum auctions remains an area for future work". Günlük et al. (2002) derive problem instances from an actual FCC auction for testing their branch-and-price algorithm to be used with the XOR-of-OR bidding language that was at the time considered by the FCC (the FCC currently uses the XOR bidding language). They present an algorithm for bid generation and valuation, intended for the creation of test data, as well as an optimization model to find the optimal package to bid based on the current price estimates at each round.

The first description in the literature of a bidder aid tool for the FCC's spectrum auctions was presented by Csirik et al. (2001). They developed a simulation environment for studying automated agent bidding strategies specifically for the FCC's non-package SMR auctions, and state that their work was originally motivated by a desire to create a tool to aid auction participants. Their simulation environment is similar to BidBots, in that it simulates the exact rules of the FCC auction system, and allows simulation of various bidder types and bidding strategies. Csirik et al.'s work was extended by Reitsma et al. (2002), who proposed a Punishing Randomized Strategic Demand Reduction (PRSDR) strategy that enables tacit collusion among the largest bidders and is also intended for use in the FCC's non-package SMR auctions. This strategy requires estimates of other bidders' values, as well as knowledge of all bids and associated bidder identities.

They assume that no synergies between markets exist, mainly due to the complexity of expressing such synergies. According to this strategy, bids are constructed in such a manner that the strategic bidders effectively partition the licenses in a mutually beneficial way and punish any strategic bidders that deviate from this behavior. The authors point out that the collusion their proposed strategy encourages would be hard to prove, but that the occurrence of such collusion can be reduced if the FCC initiated bidding with higher opening bids, thus reducing the available time for tacit collusion, or restricted the information revealed to bidders. Their work underscores the need for a bidder aid tool for the FCC auctions that can be made available to all bidders and that can effectively capture the relevant bidder preferences, including synergies.

The work presented in this paper is, to the best of our knowledge, the first to address the need for a package valuation and/or generation tool for the FCC's combinatorial spectrum auctions, and is the most comprehensive in the range of preferences that can be expressed. Our tool allows not only logical constraints, but also other constraints tailored to spectrum auctions and the way spectrum bidders think. A major change in the way package bidding for the FCC auctions has been thought of in the past, is that bidders need not refer to each package of interest, or even to each license of interest. Instead, the BAT takes the bidders' preferences expressed in terms of constraints, and translates them into the best choice of packages at each round, based on the current prices. This translation is done through an optimization model, thus enabling goal-oriented bidding strategies such as best response or best competitive bid. Note that even though this tool is proposed in the context of the FCC's combinatorial auctions, it can also be used to aid decision-making in SMR-, proxy-, or clock auctions[2]. In addition, the proposed design may impact combinatorial spectrum auctions across the globe, seeing that the FCC is considered to be on the forefront with research in this area and other countries often model their spectrum auctions after the FCC's. Finally, our research on the proposed tool helps address the lack of a robust method to generate test data for spectrum auctions, by introducing a simulation of the BAT that produces both realistic and mathematically challenging problem instances.

---

[2] In the clock auction mechanism all items are bid on simultaneously, similar to the SMR auctions, and prices rise monotonically according to a clock for each item as long as excess demand exists. The assignment of frequency is done by the auctioneer at the end of the auction. See e.g. Porter et al. (2003) or Ausubel and Cramton (2004) for more details.

3.   REQUIREMENTS OVERVIEW

To be useful to bidders participating in the FCC spectrum auctions, the bidder aid tool should enable bidders to express complex business plans in terms of logical relationships between items and other preferences such as minimum population coverage, bandwidth requirements, and budget. From information gathered during interviews conducted with previous auction participants, we concluded that bidders tend to group markets into sets of equivalent markets with associated unit values expressed in dollar per MHz-Pop (a product of bandwidth and population coverage). We refer to these sets as "sub-classes" and are synonymous to the "equivalence classes" terminology used by Ausubel (2003) and Cramton (2002, 2003). Sub-classes may be characterized as (a) primary, consisting of markets that are core to the bidder's business plan, (b) secondary, consisting of markets that may provide added value but are not essential, such as markets adjacent to the primary markets, or (c) tertiary, consisting of markets that are not of much interest, but that the bidder may still accept at a sufficiently low price. For each of these sub-classes, bidders may wish to define the minimum population coverage, minimum and maximum bandwidth requirements, a maximum unit price, and a budget. Bidders may also wish to specify different unit prices based on the quantity of bandwidth acquired. This will enable them to express their marginal preferences. In addition, bidders may wish to express synergies for markets that are complementary due to reasons such as geographical adjacency. They may also wish to express logical relationships among markets, for example that markets from a secondary sub-class are only of interest if all or a subset of the markets from the corresponding primary sub-class is acquired.

The FCC currently auctions bandwidth in the form of licenses, with each license consisting of a fixed amount of bandwidth in a specific market area (geographic region). When dividing the spectrum into alternative bands, some licenses may be treated as substitutes (that is they are completely comparable or "fungible") while other bandwidths may be considered by some bidders to have more value than others in the same region. One reason for bands to not be substitutable is that there may be some restrictions on the use of parts of the band in order to limit interference, there may some encumbrances, or because the Federal Government has military facilities that have priority over use. The bidder aid tool should be able to function regardless of whether bandwidth is considered fungible or non-fungible. In the case where bandwidth is not considered fungible, the bidder may also need to express preferences regarding the frequency bands being auctioned. It may, for example, require bandwidth to be on the same frequency for all its markets, or may prefer one band to another if it already owns that band in an adjacent market. Finally, bidders should be able to update their preferences as the auction progresses, keep track of existing packages, and keep private information hidden from the auctioneer.

The proposed design assumes that information on bids by other bidders is not used. Therefore, the tool does not specifically enable bidders to compose packages that are intended to form coalitions with other bidder's bids. Such a capability may be desired by smaller bidders to overcome the "threshold problem" (the problem of determining how much each of a collection of smaller bidders must pay to overcome the total price of a larger package). As a preliminary investigation into this issue, we include in this paper the FIT strategy that creates packages to best fit with coalitions of other bidders' packages so as to increase the auctioneer's revenue. This is however not proposed as part of the Bidder Aid Tool at this time, seeing that more research is required to investigate the effect on the auction outcomes of encouraging such coalitions.

4. PREFERENCE ELICITATION STEPS

The preference elicitation with the proposed tool has two main parts. The first part collects information regarding the bidder's values and preferences related to markets and bandwidth assuming fungible bandwidth, while the second optional part collects information regarding the bidder's additional value for specific frequency bands, to be used in the case where bandwidth is not fungible and specific licenses are auctioned for each band. Each part consists of a number of steps the bidder should go through to input data in a concise and structured manner. This input is then used to derive the optimization model shown in Section 5. For those interested in the Graphical User Interface that surrounds this elicitation and further examples of its application, see [ ].

4.1 Markets and Bandwidth

Step 1.1: *Input the bidder's overall budget, a limit on the number of packages to be generated, and a lower bound on the profit required.*

The limit on the number of packages generated can be defined as either (a) a fixed number of packages, (b) the set of most profitable packages (with equal profitability), or (c) the set of packages with profit within x% of the profit of the most profitable package, with a y% profit gap between packages. The lower bound on the profit required may be the bidder's existing profit in the case where it is a provisional winner from the previous round, or any other number.

Step 1.2: *Group markets of interest into classes and sub-classes within a class and then input the minimum population required, minimum and maximum bandwidth required, unit price (based on the minimum bandwidth), and budget associated with each market in a sub-class.*

Each class may contain up to three sub-classes, namely primary, secondary, and tertiary. The number of classes will depend on the type of bidder. For example, a bidder who wants nationwide coverage will likely have only one class, while a regional bidder may have several classes, each focusing on a number of related markets. Primary markets are those forming the core of the package. Secondary markets are contingent on choosing at least one of the primary markets in the same group, while tertiary markets are contingent on choosing at least one of the secondary markets in the same class. Each market may be present in at most one class. Bidders may also specify budgets and minimum population coverage for all primary markets, all secondary markets, and all tertiary markets. If a bidder wishes to obtain a market of secondary importance without also obtaining one of primary importance, he can simply put these markets in a separate primary class. Note that the "Price" is the bidder's maximum unit bid price based on its value, in other words, the maximum price it is willing to pay for one unit of bandwidth and one unit of population, assuming it wins the minimum specified amount of bandwidth.

Step 1.3: *Input any market-specific exceptions to the data input in Step 1.2.*

The markets for which one might wish to specify an exception are those already specified in Step 1.2. For any such market, the user can override the minimum and maximum bandwidth required, unit price or budget.

Step 1.4: *For each sub-class, input price increments based on different quantities of bandwidth.*

The bidder can specify any size of increment and number of increments, and the quantity of bandwidth is then defined within the bounds of the increments. The prices are in units of $/MHzPop, and not cumulative. For example, a bidder can specify that it is willing to pay 0.2 $/MHzPop for 20MHz, and 0.18 $/MHzPop for any amount of bandwidth between 21 and 30 MHz for any market in sub-class P1. Thus, if it wins 20 MHz, it pays $(20*0.2) = 4$ $/pop, while if it wins 23 MHz it pays $(23*0.18) = 4.14$ $/pop.

Step 1.5: *For each exception in Step 1.3, input price increments based on the amount of bandwidth. Add any additional market specific exceptions to Step 1.4.*

Step 1.6: *Supply synergy information to reflect complements that result from regional adjacency.*

The extent to which regional adjacency can be enforced will depend on the size of the auction. Here we assume that a bidder may choose to either (a) enforce that each market is adjacent to at least N other markets, (b) not enforce adjacency but give a preference to adjacent markets in terms of an additional price it is willing to pay due to the synergy, or (c) not enforce or encourage adjacency in any way. Thus, as an example, a bidder who is willing to pay an additional 0.01 $/MHzPop for adjacent markets within P1 can specify this. It can also specify that there is no added synergy for adjacency within S1.

Step 1.7: *Supply information regarding any remaining logical relationships between sub-classes or markets that have not been covered in previous steps.*

The bidder may state whether all classes are mutually exclusive in the sense that each package may only contain markets from one class. Bidders may indicate additional logical relationships between classes and markets. This step is intended to cover any remaining logic that could not be captured in Steps 1.1 through 1.6 and is not intended to be an exhaustive listing of all possible relationships. For example, a bidder might wish to indicate that it was interested in S1 or S2 but not both.

Step 1.8: *If bandwidth is considered fungible, trigger the model generation, solution, and report, else continue to Part 2.*

4.2   Band Selection (Optional)

Step 2.1: *Supply "same band" requirements.*

The bidder may indicate whether it requires adjacent markets in a package to be on the same frequency band.

Step 2.2: *Supply band preferences.*

Indicate any additional frequency band preferences for bands that are not required, but considered more valuable. For example, let p be the dollar per MHzPop price prior to any changes resulting from band preferences. Then a bidder can indicate (a) that it prefers frequencies B and D for NY, (b) that it prefers to have a package containing all of the P2 markets and is therefore willing to pay an additional 0.025 $/MHzPop if it is able to win this band, and/or (c) that the bidder is uninterested in band E for the S1 markets.

Step 2.3: *Trigger the model generation, solution, and report.*

5.   MODEL

The model presented here is derived from the bidder input in Section 4, and can be solved repeatedly to simultaneously generate and evaluate a number of packages up to the limit stated in Step 1.1. A cut is added after each solution to ensure that the same package is not generated more than once in the same round. A detailed discussion of the constraints is provided below. We indicate the relationship between each constraint and the elicitation process that required the constraint. The names in italics represent variables, while the fixed parameters are shown in bold print. Please refer to the nomenclature list at the end of the paper.

We present the model with an additional index, a, to indicate bidding agent a as used in our simulation. For any one bidder this index would be redundant, but we include it to reflect its use in the efficiency model (see Appendix B). The additional constraints that apply to the FIT strategy are presented in Appendix C. The objective (1) is to maximize the profit, where profit is defined as the difference between the package value and the cost of the package at the current price (Constraint (2)):

$$\max profit^a \tag{1}$$

$$profit^a = value^a - cost^a \tag{2}$$

For a package to be accepted, its profit should be greater than the minimum profit from Step 1.1, as stated in Constraint (3).

$$profit^a \geq \mathbf{minProfit}^a \tag{3}$$

The total cost for the package equals the sum of the costs over sub-classes (Constraint (4)), where the cost of an sub-class is defined as the sum of the minimum acceptable bid prices for one MHz of bandwidth of each of the markets in that sub-class (from Steps 1.2 through 1.5), multiplied by the amount of bandwidth included in that package for that market (Constraint (5)).

$$cost^a = \sum_{c \in \mathbf{C_A}(a)} classCost_c^a \tag{4}$$

$$classCost_c^a = \sum_{r\in R_C(c)} unitMAB_r bandwidth_r^a$$

$$\forall c \in C_A(a) \tag{5}$$

The value of a package equals the sum of the values of all the sub-classes in the package (Constraint (6)), with the value of an equivalence class being the sum of the values of all markets in that sub-class plus any additional value derived from synergies with adjacent markets (Constraint (7)). For each market, the value is calculated in Constraint (8) as the population of the market, multiplied by the product of the bandwidth and the price in the price increment the bandwidth falls into (from Steps 1.2 through 1.5). The synergy value for each market is calculated in Constraint (9) as the population of that market, multiplied by the product of the shared quantity of bandwidth with each adjacent market and the additional price the bidder is willing to pay for this synergy (from Steps 1.2 and 1.6).

$$value^a = \sum_{c\in C_A(a)} classValue_c^a \tag{6}$$

$$classValue_c^a = \sum_{r\in R_A(c)} (marketValue_r^a + synergyValue_r^a) \quad \forall c \in C_A(a) \tag{7}$$

$$marketValue_r^a = (\sum_{i\in I(a,r)} price_{i,r}^a incrBandwidth_{i,r}^a)pops_r \quad \forall r \in R_A(a) \tag{8}$$

$$bandwidth_r^a \le bandwidth_{r'}^a + \mathbf{bwUB}_{r,r'}^a(1-y\_minBandwidth_{r,r'}^a) \quad \forall r,r'\in R_A(a), r'\in \mathbf{ADJ_R}(r) \tag{9}$$

The bandwidth for each market falls into at most one price increment, as shown in Constraint (10), where the Boolean variable $x\_market_r^a$ takes a value of 1 if market r is included in the package, and 0 otherwise, and the Boolean variable $y\_bandwidth_{ir}^a$ takes a value of 1 of the bandwidth for market r falls in increment i and 0 otherwise.

$$\sum_{i\in I(a,r)} y\_bandwidth_{i,r}^a = x\_market_r^a \qquad \forall r \in R_A(a) \tag{10}$$

Constraints (11) and (12) state that for the bandwidth to fall into a certain increment, it should be less than the upper bound and greater than the lower bound of bandwidth associated with that increment as defined in Steps 1.2 through 1.5. The bandwidth associated with a market is the sum of the bandwidths of all that market's increments, as shown in Constraint (13), where at most one of the increment bandwidths will have a positive value as enforced by Constraint (10). Constraint (14) states that for a market to be chosen, its associated bandwidth has to be at least the minimum unit of bandwidth to be auctioned as specified by the auctioneer.

$$incrBandwidth_{i,r}^a \leq \text{maxBandwidth}_{i,r}^a y\_bandwidth_{i,r}^a$$
$$\forall r \in R_A(a), i \in I(a,r)$$

(11)

$$incrBandwidth_{i,r}^a \geq \text{minBandwidth}_{i,r}^a y\_bandwidth_{i,r}^a$$
$$\forall r \in R_A(a), i \in I(a,r)$$

(12)

$$bandwidth_r^a = \sum_{i \in I(a,r)} incrBandwidth_{i,r}^a$$
$$\forall r \in R_A(a)$$

(13)

$$bandwidth_r^a \geq \text{minUnitBandwidth}x\_market_r^a$$
$$\forall r \in R_A(a)$$

(14)

The synergistic bandwidth is the amount of bandwidth shared between two adjacent markets, and is determined by Constraints (15) through (20). These inequalities result in the choice of a synergistic bandwidth equaling the lesser of the bandwidths of the two adjacent markets. Constraints (15) through (18) are sufficient for ensuring that the synergistic bandwidth is the minimum of the bandwidth in the two adjacent regions. However, Constraints (19) and (20), that explicitly determine which of the two adjacent markets have the lesser bandwidth, are added to the model seeing that they seem to speed up the solution. The parameter $bwUB_{r,r'}$ represents the upper bound on the bandwidth that can be shared by markets r and r', namely the minimum of their respective available bandwidths, based on the licenses agent a is eligible for.

$$synBandwidth_{r,r'}^{a} \leq bandwidth_{r}^{a}$$
$$\forall r, r' \in R_{A}(a), r' \in ADJ_{R}(r) \tag{15}$$

$$synBandwidth_{r,r'}^{a} \leq bandwidth_{r'}^{a}$$
$$\forall r, r' \in R_{A}(a), r' \in ADJ_{R}(r) \tag{16}$$

$$synBandwidth_{r,r'}^{a} \geq bandwidth_{r}^{a} - bwUB_{r,r'}^{a}(1 - y\_minBandwidth_{r,r'}^{a})$$
$$\forall r, r' \in R_{A}(a), r' \in ADJ_{R}(r) \tag{17}$$

$$synBandwidth_{r,r'}^{a} \geq bandwidth_{r'}^{a} - bwUB_{r,r'}^{a} y\_minBandwidth_{r,r'}^{a}$$
$$\forall r, r' \in R_{A}(a), r' \in ADJ_{R}(r) \tag{18}$$

$$bandwidth_{r}^{a} \leq bandwidth_{r'}^{a} + bwUB_{r,r'}^{a}(1 - y\_minBandwidth_{r,r'}^{a})$$
$$\forall r, r' \in R_{A}(a), r' \in ADJ_{R}(r) \tag{19}$$

$$bandwidth_{r'}^{a} \leq bandwidth_{r}^{a} + bwUB_{r,r'}^{a} y\_minBandwidth_{r,r'}^{a}$$
$$\forall r, r' \in R_{A}(a), r' \in ADJ_{R}(r) \tag{20}$$

Constraints (21) through (25) represent the various budget constraints, namely the overall budget, budget for each class, and budgets over all primary classes, all secondary classes, and all tertiary classes, as defined in Steps 1.1 and 1.2.

$$cost^{a} \leq overallBudget^{a} \tag{21}$$

$$classCost_{c}^{a} \leq budget_{c}^{a} \qquad \forall c \in C_{A}(a) \tag{22}$$

$$\sum_{c \in \mathbf{CPrim}(a)} classCost_{c}^{a} \leq \mathbf{primBudget}^{a} \tag{23}$$

$$\sum_{c \in \textbf{CSec}(a)} classCost_c^a \leq \textbf{secBudget}^a \tag{24}$$

$$\sum_{c \in \textbf{CTert}(a)} classCost_c^a \leq \textbf{tertBudget}^a \tag{25}$$

Value limiting constraints (not shown here) similar to these budget constraints may be included in the case where the bidder does not want to create a package that it values higher than its budget. This may not always be the case, seeing that a bidder may want to submit packages with values higher than its budget in the hope of winning such a package at a low price.

For each class, the total population of all markets chosen in that class has to be greater than the minimum population required for that class (from Step 1.2), as shown in Constraint (26), where the Boolean variable x_class_c takes a value of 1 if class c is included in the package, and 0 otherwise. Constraint (27) states that the class has to be chosen for any of its markets to be chosen. Constraints (28) through (30) enforce the minimum population requirements for all primary markets, all secondary markets, and all tertiary markets.

$$\sum_{r \in R_C(c)} \text{pops}_r x\_market_r^a \geq minPops_c^a x\_class_c^a \tag{26}$$
$$\forall c \in C_A(a)$$

$$\sum_{r \in R_C(c)} x\_market_r^a \leq |R_C(c)| x\_class_c^a \tag{27}$$
$$\forall c \in C_A(a)$$

$$\sum_{r \in R_C(c | c \in \textbf{CPrim}(a))} \textbf{pops}_r x\_market_r^a \geq \textbf{primMinPops}^a \tag{28}$$

$$\sum_{r \in R_C(c | c \in \textbf{CSec}(a))} \textbf{pops}_r x\_market_r^a \geq \textbf{secMinPops}^a \tag{29}$$

$$\sum_{r \in R_C(c | c \in \textbf{CTert}(a))} \textbf{pops}_r x\_market_r^a \geq \textbf{tertMinPops}^a \tag{30}$$

Constraint (31) states that secondary markets can only be chosen if at least one primary market in the same class is chosen. Similarly, Constraint (32) states that tertiary markets can only be chosen if at least one secondary market in the same class is chosen. These constraints use the class information from Step 1.2.

$$\sum_{r \in RSec(g)} x\_market_r^a \leq |RSec(g)| \sum_{r \in RPrim(g)} x\_market_r^a$$
$$\forall g \in G(a) \tag{31}$$

$$\sum_{r \in RTert(g)} x\_market_r^a \leq |RTert(g)| \sum_{r \in RSec(g)} x\_market_r^a$$
$$\forall g \in G(a) \tag{32}$$

Constraints (33) and (34) are optional constraints to be applied if the bidder requires all classes to be mutually exclusive, as specified in Step 1.7.

$$\sum_{c \in C_G(g)} x\_class_c^a \leq |C_G(g)| x\_group_g^a$$
$$\forall g \in G(a) \tag{33}$$

$$\sum_{g \in G(a)} x\_group_g^a \leq 1 \tag{34}$$

Any remaining logical constraints from Step 1.7 representing conditional choices between classes, sub-classes or markets are represented by Constraint (35). These will be additional *logical* constraints that may require new integer variables to transform into a linear form for the optimizer.

$$\Omega^a(x\_class_c^a, x\_market_r^a) = true \tag{35}$$

A bidder may require all the markets in the package to be adjacent, or only that groups of adjacent markets exist in the package. We consider only partial adjacency from Step 1.6, which can be achieved by applying the optional Constraint (36). This constraint states that a market may only be chosen if at least N_{adj}^a of its adjacent markets are chosen, i.e. the package will consist of groups of N_{adj}^a or more adjacent markets. Care should be taken, however, that N^a_{adj} is not too high, seeing that a market may have a limited number of directly adjacent markets.

$$x\_market^a_r \le \frac{1}{N^a_{adj}} \sum_{r' \in ADJ_R(r)} x\_market^a_{r'}$$

$$\forall r \in R_A(a)$$

(36)

In the case where fungible quantities of bandwidth are auctioned, Constraint (37) will be used to prevent the same combination of bandwidth increments and markets to be chosen if that combination has already been chosen for a previously created package, p.

$$\sum_{(i,r) \in IR_1(a,p)} y\_bandwidth_{i,r} - \sum_{(i,r) \in IR_0(a,p)} y\_bandwidth_{i,r} \le |IR_1(a,p)| - 1$$

$$\forall p \in P(a)$$

(37)

In the case where bandwidth is not considered fungible, and a set of licenses are auctioned instead of flexible quantities of bandwidth, the package creation tool will include optional Constraints (38) through (44) , as well as variations on Constraints (5) and (31), to facilitate the choice of specific licenses based on the frequency band preferences. The bandwidth for each market equals the sum of bandwidths of all licenses chosen in that market, as shown in Constraint (38), where the Boolean variable $x\_license^a_l$ takes a value of 1 if license l is included in the package, and 0 otherwise. Constraint (5alt) shows an alternative cost calculation for the case where specific licenses are auctioned instead fungible bandwidth. In this case, the cost of a sub-class equals the sum of the minimum acceptable bids of all chosen licenses in that sub-class.

$$bandwidth^a_r = \sum_{l \in L_R(r)} bandwidth_l x\_license^a_l$$

$$\forall r \in R_A(a)$$

(38)

$$classCost^a_c = \sum_{l \in L_C(c)} licenseMAB_l x\_license^a_l$$

$$\forall c \in C_A(a)$$

(5alt)

A bidder may specify in Step 2.1 that licenses in adjacent markets should be on the same band. This requirement can be enforced by applying the optional Constraints (39) through (42). Constraint (39) states that any shared bandwidth between two adjacent markets ($synBandwidth^a_{r,r'}$) has to be on the same bands, while Constraints (40) through (42) force the Boolean variable $x\_adj^a_{l,l'}$ to take a value of 1 if two adjacent licenses l and l' are chosen, and 0 otherwise.

$$synBandwidth^a_{r,r'} = \sum_{(b,l,l')|l\in L_R(r),l'\in L_R(r'),l,l'\in L_B(b)} bandwidth_b x\_adj^a_{l,l'}$$

$$\forall r,r'\in R_A(a), r'\in ADJ_R(r) \tag{39}$$

$$x\_adj^a_{l,l'} \geq x\_license^a_l + x\_license^a_{l'} - 1$$

$$\forall l,l'\in L_A(a), l'\in ADJ_L(l) \tag{40}$$

$$x\_adj^a_{l,l'} \leq x\_license^a_l$$

$$\forall l,l'\in L_A(a), l'\in ADJ_L(l) \tag{41}$$

$$x\_adj^a_{l,l'} \leq x\_license^a_{l'}$$

$$\forall l,l'\in L_A(a), l'\in ADJ_L(l,l') \tag{42}$$

A bidder may also specify in Step 2.1 that all licenses should be from at most one band, and this requirement can be enforced by Constraints (43) and (44).

$$\sum_{l\in L} x\_license^a_l \leq |L_B(b)| x\_band^a_b$$

$$\forall b \in B \tag{43}$$

$$\sum_{b\in B} x\_band^a_b \leq 1 \tag{44}$$

Any additional band preferences indicated in Step 2.2 are dealt with by excluding any license with zero value from the set of licenses, and by adding the following term to the objective function (1):

$$+ \sum_{(l,b)|b\in B, l\in(L_B(b)\cap L_A(a))} \text{preference Price}\,_b^a x\_license\,_l^a$$

In the case where licenses are auctioned, Constraint (31alt) will be used to prevent a combination of licenses to be chosen when that combination had already been chosen for a previously created package.

$$\sum_{l\in L_1(a,p)} x\_license_l^a - \sum_{l\in L_0(a,p)} x\_license_l^a \le |L_1(a,p)| - 1 \tag{31alt}$$

$$\forall p \in P(a)$$

Finally, optional constraints on eligibility and activity requirements may be added to the model if such rules have been specified by the auctioneer. These are shown here for the non-fungible case (Constraints (45) and (46)), where the sum of the bidding units of the chosen licenses has to be less than the bidder's eligibility, and greater than the bidder's activity requirement.

$$\sum_{l\in L_A(a)} \text{biddingUnits}_l\, x\_license_l^a \le \text{eligibility}^a \tag{45}$$

$$\sum_{l\in L_A(a)} \textbf{biddingUnits}_l\, x\_license_l^a \ge \textbf{activityRequirement}^a \tag{46}$$

Flexibility is achieved by allowing only the relevant subset of constraints to be triggered depending on the bidder's input into the user interface. Additional constraints may be added to this interface, and the decision to include these in the model will be in the bidder's hands.

6.   PRELIMINARY RESULTS

In this section, we briefly describe the FCC's package auction mechanism and then present the experimental setup, followed by our preliminary results. We considered four bidder types using three strategies, and simulated six auctions of varying sizes. We discuss the solution time required for the optimization model, the number of bids created by the BAT, the auction revenues and the auction efficiencies.

6.1   The FCC's Package Auction Mechanism

In the ascending combinatorial auction mechanism used at the FCC, bids may be placed on collections of items. All highest bids of each bidder are considered throughout the auction and are mutually exclusive, i.e. each bidder can win at most one of its bids. Winning bids are determined after each round by maximizing the total revenue based on all bids placed throughout the auction, and ties are broken randomly. Each bidder's initial payment determines its initial eligibility in terms of bidding units. In order to maintain eligibility, each bidder's bidding activity must meet a bidder specific activity requirement in each round. Eligibility is reduced if a bidder does not meet its activity requirement and does not have any activity waivers remaining. The Minimum Acceptable Bid (MAB) at the start of each round equals the maximum of the FCC's reserve price and the price estimate plus the bidding increment, where the bidding increment is determined by the amount of activity on the item. There are limits on the number of packages each bidder may bid on per round and for the duration of the auction. After each round, all bids, provisionally winning bids, price estimates, new MABs, updated eligibility, and bidder identities are revealed to all bidders. The auction closes after two consecutive rounds with no new bids. For a more detailed description of the FCC's XOR package auction mechanism, please see Goeree and Holt (2005). For information on how the price estimates are calculated, see Dunford *et al.* (2004).

6.2   Experimental Setup

6.2.1   Bidder Types

To simulate the preferences of different types of bidders, we created the following four distinct bidder types:

1. **Cherry Pickers:** These bidders are eligible for 5-15% of the available licenses, and are interested in any combination of items that maximize their profit.
2. **Regional Bidders:** These bidders are eligible for 15-50% of the available licenses, and are interested in multiple markets clustered around home markets, with a preference for geographical adjacency.
3. **National Bidders:** These bidders are eligible for 50-100% of the available licenses, and are interested in as much as possible geographical coverage, with a preference for geographical adjacency.

4. **Global Bidders:** These bidders are eligible for 100% of the available licenses, and only interested in packages that cover the entire geographical map.

6.2.2   Bidding Strategies

We simulated the following bidding strategies that can be used by any of the bidder types:

1. **Myopic Best Response (MBR):** This strategy uses the BAT to create and bid on the profit maximizing package(s) at each round.
2. **Myopic Best Response within Profit Range (MBRPR):** This strategy is based on the MBR strategy, with the major difference being that packages within a specified profitability range are created at each round, as opposed to only the packages with highest profit. The MBRPR strategy creates and bids on up to fifteen different packages during each round, with varying levels of profitability. To be exact, the bidder starts with the most profitable package, and then also creates the package with at least 1% lower profit, and so forth, until 15% lower profit is reached. Our goal with this strategy is to increase the variety of packages submitted, thus increasing competition as well as fit with other bidders' bids, without significantly sacrificing profitability.
3. **Fit (FIT):** This strategy creates and bids on the most profitable package that best fits with other bidders' existing bids at each round, so as to create more competitive bids. At most one package is submitted per bidder per round when using this strategy. The objective function of this strategy is the same as for the other strategies, namely to maximize the bidder's profit. However, constraints are added to the model to force the bidder's package, in combination with other bidders' bids and estimated bid amounts, to increase the auctioneer's revenue above the level from the preceding round (see Appendix C). This requirement for an increase in revenue is added to increase the bidder's chances of being included in the efficient allocation. For our simulations, we assume that non-winning bids placed by other bidders in the preceding two rounds are increased to the current round's minimum acceptable bid amount, so as to contribute to an increase in the auctioneer's revenue.

6.2.3   Efficiency Calculation

In order to calculate the efficient allocation for each auction profile, we solved an optimization model that maximizes the value of the allocation subject to all bidders' constraints, based on their input into the BAT. The optimization model used to determine the efficient allocation is shown in Appendix B. The auction efficiency was then calculated after each round by dividing the value of the winning allocation by the value of the efficient allocation. This calculation allows a comparison between the different strategies, seeing that the efficient allocation is not merely based on the created packages, but instead on all bidders' constraints, thus on all possible packages.

6.2.4 General Setup

Our results were generated using the six auction profiles listed in Table 1. Each profile was run with all bidders alternatively using each of the three strategies. All simulations were done on an HP Proliant DL380 G3 workstation, with 2 processors, 3.06 GHz, and 6GB of memory. All optimization models were solved using CPLEX 9.0.

Table 1: Auction Profiles

Profile	Markets	# of Bands	Licenses	Number of bidders			
				Global	National	Regional	Cherry picker
1	51	1	51	2	20	20	18
2	51	1	51	0	10	10	10
3	51	2	102	2	20	20	18
4	51	2	102	0	6	20	18
5	175	1	175	0	2	30	28
6	175	1	175	0	6	6	40

6.3 Results

The main goal of the experiments presented in this paper is to determine the feasibility and usability of the proposed tool, in terms of flexibility in expressing preferences for different bidder types and in terms of the required solution time for the optimization model. Secondary goals include studying the impact of the tool on the number of considered bids, the auction revenue and the allocative efficiency. Our results are preliminary and should not be considered to be conclusive. As can be seen in the following sections, our results thus far indicate that the proposed tool is promising and worthy of further research. Future work will include more extensive testing using the tool with a greater variety of auction settings and profiles.

Number of rounds considered in this testing:

- All the simulations were stopped at 100 rounds if bids were still being placed. We feel this stopping rule is acceptable for the purpose of this study, seeing that the revenue had in most cases leveled off by this point with no significant increase in several rounds, as shown in Section 6.2.3.
- For Profile 2 the MBRPR strategy was stopped before 100 rounds were reached due to a particularly complex winner determination problem. An efficiency of 98% had been achieved at this point (see Section 6.2.4) and we therefore do not consider this interruption to significantly impact the quality of the results. We are evaluating alternative strategies for solving this complex winner determination.
- For Profiles 3, 5 and 6, the FIT strategy was interrupted before 100 rounds was reached due to the complexity associated with solving the FIT modified optimization model (see Appendix B). Solution times for the FIT model are not discussed here, but it suffices to say that the computation required several minutes to an hour when more than 100 items were involved, due to the fact that all bids by all bidders are included in the model. Future work will address the solution complexity of the FIT model. Although the FIT model may therefore not be a practical option for generating several packages in a short time, it shows promise due to the high efficiencies achieved with only a small number of packages as discussed in Section 6.2.4. In addition, it may be a practical option if large time intervals, such as a few hours, exist between auction rounds.
- All models were solved with the default CPLEX options and improvements may be possible with some tuning.

6.3.1   BAT Solution Time

Figure 1 shows solution times required by the BAT optimization model used by the MBR and MBRPR strategies for the different bidder types and profiles. These values represent a sampling of the times required to create fifteen different packages for each bidder type. The high, low and average values are depicted in the graph. Results for the Global bidders are not shown for Profiles 1, 2, 5, and 6, because only one band is involved in these profiles and the Global bidder therefore has a trivial decision problem. For Profiles 1, 2, 5, and 6 the average time required to create a package was below 0.12 seconds for all bidder types. For Profiles 3 and 4, the average time required to create a packages was below 6 seconds for all bidder types, with the longest time being 14 seconds for one of the National bidders.

These results indicate that the BAT can be used to quickly generate a large number of highly profitable packages.

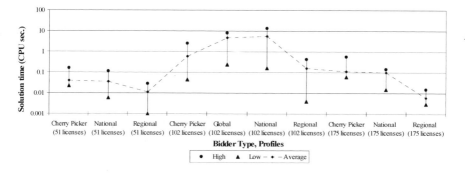

Figure 1: Sample BAT Solution Times

6.3.2   Number of Bids Generated

Table 2 shows the possible combinations of licenses for each profile compared to the total number of packages created by all bidders during the auction. In general, these results indicate that the BAT significantly reduces the number of packages that a bidder needs to consider in a combinatorial auction. For example, in the case of Profile 6, the MBR strategy created only 7949 packages, the MBRPR strategy only 39781 packages, and the FIT strategy only 3042 packages, among all bidders, of the possible $9.58*10^{52}$ packages. The relationship between the number of bids generated and the efficiencies achieved is explored further in Section 6.2.4.

The number of variables and constraints differed significantly among rounds and among bidders.   In the simulations described, the most complex profile, Profile 3, generated the greatest number of variables and that for the National Bidder.   In this case, the code generated over 30,000 variables and close to 20,000 constraints.

Table 2: Possible Number of Packages vs. Created Packages

Profile	Number of possible packages	Number of created packages		
		MBR	MBRPR	FIT
1	$2.25*10^{15}$	4146	10876	2808
2	$2.25*10^{15}$	1768	5693	885
3	$5.07*10^{30}$	5218	16093	2405
4	$5.07*10^{30}$	3654	5287	1883
5	$9.58*10^{52}$	5406	26564	2205
6	$9.58*10^{52}$	7949	39781	3042

6.3.3   Auction Revenue

Figures 2 through 7 show the revenue per round for each of the profiles and strategies. The MBR strategy achieved significantly lower revenue levels than the other two strategies. This can be explained by the reduced competition compared to the other two strategies, because the MBR strategy submits only one or two most profitable packages per round and does not consider other bidders' bids. The MBRPR strategy achieved higher revenue levels earlier than the FIT strategy. This early revenue climb by the MBRPR strategy can be explained by the greater number of packages submitted compared to the FIT strategy (see Table 2), thus creating more competition that increased the prices early on. The FIT and MBRPR strategies achieved similar revenue levels by the end of the simulations. Note that the higher revenues achieved by the FIT and MBRPR strategies compared to the MBR strategy do not necessarily imply lower bidder profits. For example, for Profile 3 the winning bidders achieved a profit of only 7.2% with the MBR strategy compared to 10.3% for the MBRPR strategy and 14.5% for the FIT strategy, even though the MBRPR and FIT strategies achieved much higher revenues.

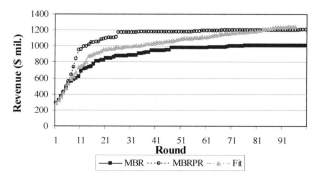

Figure 2: Revenue per round for Profile 1.

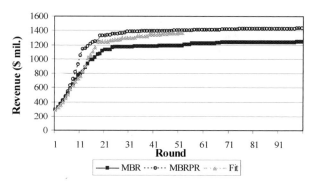

Figure 3: Revenue per round for Profile 2.

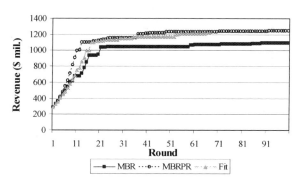

Figure 4: Revenue per round for Profile 3.

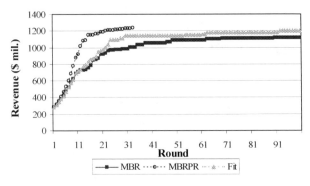

Figure 5: Revenue per round for Profile 4.

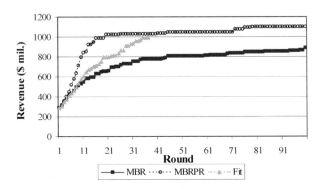

Figure 6: Revenue per round for Profile 5.

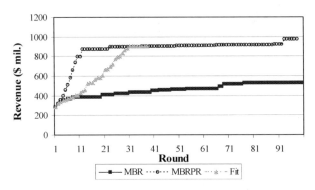

Figure 7: Revenue per round for Profile 6.

6.3.4   Auction Efficiency

Table 3 shows the highest efficiencies (%) achieved by round 25 and round 100, for each profile and each strategy. The asterisks indicate which profiles were interrupted before 100 rounds were reached, for the reasons stated at the start of this section. In general, both the FIT and MBRPR strategies achieved higher efficiencies much earlier than the MBR strategy. For example, both the MBRPR and the FIT strategies achieved the round 100 efficiency of 98% and 96%, respectively, by round 25 for Profile 2, while the MBR strategy had only achieved 89% efficiency by round 25 compared to its round 100 efficiency of 96%. This result suggests that a bidder aid tool that creates a number of highly profitable and/or competitive packages will lead to higher efficiencies earlier in the auction than simply concentrating on the profit maximizing package at each round, assuming that the bidders bid on the packages recommended by the BAT. In the case of the MBRPR strategy, the higher efficiencies can be explained by the fact that a larger number of highly profitable packages are submitted per round, thus increasing the probability of fitting with other bidders' bids. In the case of the FIT strategy higher efficiencies are achieved than the MBR strategy, even though only one package is submitted per bidder per round, due to better fit with other bidders' bids.

When considering the efficiencies achieved by round 100, the FIT and MBRPR strategies usually outperformed the MBR strategy, due to improved fit with other bidders' bids. For example, the FIT strategy achieved 100% efficiency for two profiles, while the MBRPR strategy achieved 100% efficiency for one profile, and the MBR strategy never achieved 100% efficiency for any of the profiles.

Table 3: Highest efficiencies (%) achieved by rounds 25 and 100, for each profile and strategy

Profile	MBR		MBRPR		FIT	
	Round 25	Round 100	Round 25	Round 100	Round 25	Round 100
1	90.1	96.6	98	98.1	96.6	100
2	89.4	96.2	98.2	98.3	96.1	96.1
3	86.0	97.3	98.7	100	95.0	100*
4	77.8	86.8	88.8	88.8*	90.5	94.1
5	80.7	83.7	83.3	86.3	86.9	86.9*
6	79.9	79.9	88.1	89.7	92.5	93.2*

In all cases, high efficiencies were achieved with a very small fraction of the possible packages (see also Table 2). For example, the three strategies achieved efficiencies of 97.3% (MBR), and 100% (MPRPR and FIT) for Profile 3, by creating only 5218, 16093, and 2405 of the possible $5.07*10^{30}$ packages, respectively. It can be seen that the FIT strategy achieved efficiencies comparable to the MBRPR strategy, even though far fewer packages were created. For example, both strategies achieved 100% efficiency for Profile 3 where the FIT strategy created only 2405 packages compared to the 16093 created by the MBRPR strategy. This can be explained by the fact that the FIT strategy considers other bidders' bids as opposed to only focusing on maximizing profit.

7.   CONCLUSIONS AND FUTURE DIRECTIONS

The ideas presented in this paper are not only new to spectrum auctions in general, but also applicable to other combinatorial auction mechanisms. The FCC has been on the forefront of government auction design, with many of the resulting concepts being applied to auctions across the globe. Our proposed tool illustrates how the need for software that aids bidders in expressing bids in terms of their business plans, as opposed to expecting bidders to perform the translation from business plans into combinatorial bids themselves, can be met. We believe that tools such as the one proposed in this paper will encourage auction participation by reducing the cost of package creation and valuation, and therefore likely leading to more efficient auction outcomes.

Our proposed bidder aid tool allows bidders to more effectively participate in combinatorial FCC spectrum auctions by enabling concise expression of preferences. In addition, it enables bidders to express complex business plans involving logical relationships between items, as well as population coverage, bandwidth, and budget constraints. The bidder aid tool allows bidders to update their preferences and reevaluate their bid composition dynamically before each round based on the latest price information. The bidder preferences input through the user interface are converted into a well-defined optimization model. This model is solved iteratively to simultaneously generate and evaluate a set of packages with decreasing profitability based on the latest price information at the start of each round.

Our preliminary results show that the use of the proposed tool in each round enables bidders to relatively quickly generate and evaluate the most profitable package or a set of highly profitable packages, and leads to high allocative efficiencies with a relatively small number of package bids. In terms of revenue, when the BAT generated a greater number of highly profitable bids (MBRPR) or a small number of highly competitive bids (FIT), higher revenues were achieved earlier in the auction than when only the most profitable bids were generated at each round. All instances of the BAT model could be solved within a few seconds. The variation of the model that considers other bidders' bids and the auctioneer's revenue (FIT), in addition to profitability, cannot yet be solved in reasonable time, although it shows promise in achieving higher efficiencies with fewer bids compared to the purely profit driven approach (MBR and MBRPR).

Future work includes a thorough testing of this tool and addressing the computational issues in solving the optimization models. We also intend to test the use of the tool by agents using different strategies within the same profile, or possibly switching among strategies during the auction. Refinements to the bidder aid tool will be made as required after we have had the opportunity to evaluate the tool further by using it within mock auctions and getting feedback from prospective users.

REFERENCES

An, N. Elmaghraby, W. and Keskinocak,P, Bidding Strategies and their Impact on Revenues in Combinatorial Auctions, *Journal of Revenue & Pricing Management* **3**, 337–357 (2005).

Ausubel, L, E-mail communication (2002).

Ausubel, L.M., and Cramton, P., Demand Reduction and Inefficiency in Multi-Unit Auctions, Working paper, Department of Economics, University of Maryland. (1998).

Ausubel, L.M. and Cramton, P., Auctioning Many Divisible Goods *Journal of the European Economic Association*, **2**, 480-493 (2004).

Ausubel, L.M. and Milgrom, P. Ascending Auctions with Package Bidding, *Frontiers of Theoretical Economics*, **1**, 1-45 (2002).

Banks, J.S., Ledyard, J.O., and Porter, D., Allocating Uncertain and Unresponsive Resources: An Experimental Approach, *The Rand Journal of Economics*, **20**(1), 1- 25 (1989).

Boutilier, C., Solving Concisely Expressed Combinatorial Auction Problems, *Proceedings of the 18th National Conference on Artificial Intelligence (AAAI-02)*, pp. 359-366 (2002).

Boutilier, C., and Hoos, H.,H., Bidding Languages for Combinatorial Auctions, *Proceedings of the 7th International Joint Conference on Artificial Intelligence*, pp. 1211-1217, (2001).

Bykowsky, M.M., Cull, R.J., and Ledyard, J.O., Mutually Destructive Bidding: The FCC Auction Design Problem, *Journal of Regulatory Economics*, **17**(3), 205-228 (2000).

Conen, W., and Sandholm, T, Minimal Preference Elicitation in Combinatorial Auctions, *Proceedings of the Seventeenth International Joint Conference on Artificial Intelligence*, Workshop on Economic Agents, Models, and Mechanisms, 71-80, (2001).

Cramton, P., Money Out of Thin Air: The Nationwide Narrowband PCS Auction, *Journal of Economics and Management Strategy*, **4**, 267-343 (1995).

Cramton, P., The FCC Spectrum Auctions: An Early Assessment, *Journal of Economics and Management Strategy,*.**6**(3), 431-495, (1997).

Cramton, P., Interview at the University of Maryland, 2002a.

Cramton, P., Spectrum Auctions, in *Handbook of Telecommunications Economics*, Cave. M., Majumdar, S., and Vogelsang, I., Eds., Amsterdam: Elsevier Science B.V., Chapter 14, 605-639 (2002b).

Cramton, P., E-mail communication, 2003.

Cramton, P., Shoham, Y., and Steinberg, R., Introduction to Combinatorial Auctions, in *Combinatorial Auctions*, edited by Peter Cramton, Yoav Shoham, and Richard Steinberg , MIT Press (2005).

Csirik, J.A., Littman, M.L., Singh, S., and Stone, P., FAucS: An FCC Spectrum Auction Simulator for Autonomous Bidding Agents, In *Electronic Commerce: Proceedings of the*

Second International Workshop edited by Fiege, L., Mühl, G., and Wilhelm, U, 139-151, Springer Verlag, Heidelberg, Germany, (2001).

DeMartini, C., Kwasnica, A.M., Ledyard, J.O., and Porter, D., A New and Improved Design for Multi-Object Iterative Auctions, Technical report, California Institute of Technology, (1998).

Dunford, M., Hoffman, K., Menon, D., Sultana, R., and Wilson, T., Testing Linear Pricing Algorithms for use in Ascending Combinatorial Auctions, working paper, George Mason University, Department of Systems Engineering and Operations Research, (2004).

FCC Public Notice, DA 03-1994, Auction of Regional Narrowband PCS Licenses Scheduled for September 24, 2003; Notice and Filing Requirements, Minimum Opening Bids, Upfront Payments, Package Bidding and Other Auction Procedures,"http://wireless.fcc.gov/auctions/default.htm?job=release&id=53&y=2 003, (2003).

Goeree, J.K., and Holt, C.A., Comparing the FCC's Combinatorial and Non-Combinatorial Simultaneous Multiple Round Auctions: Experimental Design Report, http://hraunfoss.fcc.gov/edocs_public/attachmatch/DA-05-1267A2.pdf, (2005).

Günlük, O., Ladányi, L., and De Vries, S., A Branch-and-Price Algorithm and New Test Problems for Spectrum Auctions, *Management Science 51(3) 391-406 (2005)*

Hudson, B., and Sandholm, T. Effectiveness of Preference Elicitation in Combinatorial Auctions, *AAMAS-02 Workshop on Agent-Mediated Electronic Commerce (AMEC)*, Italy, (2002).

Jones, J.L., and Koehler, G.J., Combinatorial Auctions using Rule-based Bids, *Decision Support Systems*, Vol. **34**(1), pp. 59-74, (2002).

Kwon, R.H., Anandalingam, G., and Ungar, L.H., Iterative Combinatorial Auctions with Bidder-Determined Combinations,"\ *Management Science*, **51**(3), 407-418, (2005).

Leyton-Brown, K., Pearson, M., and Shoham, Y., Towards a Universal Test Suite for Combinatorial Auction Algorithms, *Proceedings of the ACM Conference on Electronic Commerce (EC-00)*, 66-76, (2000).

McMillan, J., Selling Spectrum Rights, *Journal of Economic Perspectives*, **8**, pp. 145-162, (1994).

Nisan, N., Bidding and Allocation in Combinatorial Auctions, presented at the *ACM Conference on Electronic Commerce*, (2000).

Parkes, D.C., *i*Bundle: An Efficient Ascending Price Bundle Auction, *Proceedings of the ACM Conference on Electronic Commerce (EC-99)*, (1999).

Parkes, D.C., Cavallo, R., Elprin, N., Juda, A., Lahaie, S., Lubin, B., Michael, L., Shneidman, J., and Sultan, H., "ICE" An Iterative Combinatorial Exchange, *Proceedings of the 6th ACM conference on Electronic Commerce*, 249 – 258, (2005).

Parkes, D.C., and Ungar, L. H., Preventing Strategic Manipulation in Iterative Auctions: Proxy Agents and Price-Adjustment, *Proceedings of the 17th National Conference on Artificial Intelligence (AAAI-00)*, 82-89, (2000).

Porter, D., Rassenti, S., and Smith, V., Combinatorial Auction Design, *Proceedings of the National Academy of Sciences*, **100**(19) 11153-11157, (2003).

Reitsma, P.S.A., Stone, P., Csirik, J.A., and Littman, M.L., Self-enforcing Strategic Demand Reduction, *Agent Mediated Electronic Commerce IV: Designing Mechanisms and Systems*, Lecture Notes in Artificial Intelligence, 289–306, Springer Verlag, (2002).

Rothkopf, M.H., Pekeč, A., and Harstad, R.M., Computationally Manageable Combinational Auctions, *Management Science*, **44**(8), 1131-1147, (1998).

Tarnutzer, B., Interview at the Federal Communications Commission, 2002.

Wilkie, S., Interview at the Federal Communications Commission, 2002.

Wurman, P.R., and Wellman, M.P., A*k*BA: A Progressive, Anonymous-Price Combinatorial Auction, In *Proceedings of the ACM Conference on Electronic Commerce (ACM-EC)*, 21-29, (2000).

APPENDIX A: NOMENCLATURE

Sets

A - All agents *a*, including the auctioneer.

ADJ$_R$(*r*) - Markets adjacent to market *r*.

ADJ$_L$(*l*) - Licenses adjacent to license *l*, with adjacency implying regional adjacency on the same band.

B - Set of bands.

BID$_A$(*a*) - Set of bids placed by agent *a*.

BID$_L$(*l*) - Set of bids that include license *l*.

C$_A$(*a*) – sub-classes associated with agent *a*.

C$_G$(*g*) - sub-classes associated with group *g*.

CPrim(*a*) - Agent *a*'s primary sub-classes.

CSec(*a*) - Agent *a*'s secondary sub-classes.

CTert(*a*) - Agent *a*'s tertiary sub-classes.

G(*a*) - Agent *a*'s classes. **I**(*a,r*) - Agent *a*'s price increments associated with market *r*.

I(*a,r*) – Bandwidth increment associated with agent *a* and market *r*.

IR$_1$(*a,p*) - The set of Boolean variables, *y_bandwidth$_{i,r}$*, that took a value of 1 for package *p*, agent *a*.

IR$_0$(*a,p*) - The set of Boolean variables, *y_bandwidth$_{i,r}$*, that took a value of 0 for package *p*, agent *a*.

L - Licenses being auctioned.

IR$_1$(*a,p*) - The set of Boolean variables, *y_bandwidth$_{i,r}$*, that took a value of 1 for package *p*, agent *a*.

IR$_0$(*a,p*) - The set of Boolean variables, *y_bandwidth$_{i,r}$*, that took a value of 0 for package *p*, agent *a*.

L - Licenses being auctioned.

L$_A$(*a*) - Licenses valued by agent *a*.

L$_B$(*b*) - Licenses associated with frequency band *b*.

L$_C$(*c*) - Licenses associated with sub-class *c*.

L$_1$(*a,p*) - The set of Boolean variables, *x_license^a_l*, that took a value of 1 for package *p*, agent *a*.

L$_0$(*a,p*) - The set of Boolean variables, *x_license^a_l*, that took a value of 0 for package *p*, agent *a*.

L$_R$(*r*) - Licenses associated with market *r*.

P(a) - Package created by agent *a*.

R - Markets.

R$_A$(*a*) - Markets associated with agent *a*.

R$_C$(*c*) - Markets associated with class *c*.

RPrim(*g*) – Primary markets associated with group g.

RSec(*g*) – Secondary markets assoc. with group g.

RTert(*g*) – Tertiary markets assoc. with group g.

Indices

a - Bidder $a \in \mathbf{A}$

b - Frequency band $b \in \mathbf{B}$.

bid - Bid $bid \in \mathbf{BID}_{(.)}$.

c - Class $c \in \mathbf{C}_{(.)}$.

g - Group $g \in \mathbf{G}$.

i - Increment $i \in \mathbf{I}$.

l - License $l \in \mathbf{L}_{(.)}$.

p - Package $p \in \mathbf{P}$

r - Market $r \in \mathbf{R}_{(.)}$.

Parameters

activityRequirement^a - Required bidding activity for **agent** *a* (bidding units).

bandwidth$_b$ - Bandwidth for band *b* (MHz).

bandwidth$_l$ - Bandwidth for license *l* (MHz).

biddingUnits$_l$ - Bidding units required for license *l*.

budget^a_c – Agent *a*'s budget for class *c* ($).

bwUB$^a_{r,r'}$ – Upper bound on synergistic bandwidth between markets *r* and *r'* for agent *a*, namely the minimum of their respective available bandwidths based on the licenses *a* is eligible for (MHz).

currentRevenue – Actual current auction revenue.

eligibility^a - The number of bidding units agent *a* is eligible to bid on.

licenseMAB$_l$ - Min. acceptable bid for license *l* ($).

maxBandwidth$^a_{i,r}$ - Max. bandwidth required by agent *a* for market *r* in increment *i* (MHz).

minBandwidth$^a_{i,r}$ - Min. bandwidth required by agent *a* for market *r* in increment *i* (MHz).

minPops^a_c - Min. pops required by agent *a* for class *c*.

minProfit^a – Min. profit required by agent a ($).

minUnitBandwidth - Min. amount of bandwidth that can be bid on (MHz).

N$^a_{adj}$ - Number of adjacent markets required by agent a for a market to be chosen.

overallBudget^a – Agent a's overall budget ($).

pops$_r$ - Population of market r (pop).

preferencePrice^a_b – Additional price agent a will pay for bandwidth on band b ($/MHzPop).

prevBidAmount$_{bid}$ – Previous bid amount for bid bid

primBudget^a – Agent a's budget for all primary markets ($).

primMinPops^a - Minimum pops for all agent a's primary markets.

price$^a_{i,r}$ – Price agent a is willing to pay for bandwidth in market r falling in increment i ($/MHzPop).

reservePrice$_l$ – The auctioneer's reserve price for license l ($).

secBudget^a – Agent a's budget for all secondary markets ($).

secMinPops^a - Minimum pops for all agent a's secondary markets.

synergyPrice$^a_{r,r'}$ - Additional price agent a will pay if adjacent markets r and r' are chosen ($/MHzPop).

tertBudget^a – Agent a's budget for all tertiary markets ($).

tertMinPops^a - Minimum pops for all agent a's tertiary markets.

unitMAB$_r$ - Minimum acceptable bid for one MHz of bandwidth in market r ($).

Continuous Variables

bandwidth^a_r - Bandwidth in market r associated with agent a (MHz).

incrBandwidth$^a_{i,r}$ – Bandwidth associated with agent a, falling in increment i for market r (MHz).

bidAmount$_{bid}$ – Bid amount for bid bid.

cost^a –Agent a's total cost ($).

classCost^a_c - Cost assoc. with agent a's sub-class c ($).

profit^a – Agent a's profit based on the current prices ($).

revenue – Total estimated auction revenue.

synBandwidth$^a_{r,r'}$ – Bandwidth, associated with agent, a shared between market r and adjacent market r' (MHz).

synergyValue^a_r – Agent a's value contributed by market r's adjacency to other chosen markets ($).

totalProfit – Total profit achieved due to all bidders in the auction, including the auctioneer.

value^a – Agent a's total value ($).

classValue^a_c – Agent a's value assoc. with class c ($).

marketValue^a_r – Agent a's value associated with market r

Discrete Variables

$x\_adj^a_{l,l'}$ - 1 if adjacent licenses l and l' are chosen by agent a, 0 otherwise.

$x\_band^a_b$ - 1 if band b is chosen by agent a, 0 otherwise.

x_bid_{bid} - 1 if bid bid is included in the winning allocation, 0 otherwise.

$x\_class^a_c$ - 1 if class c is chosen by agent a, 0 otherwise.

$x\_group^a_g$ - 1 if group g is chosen by agent a, 0 otherwise.

$x\_license^a_l$ - 1 if license l is chosen by agent a, 0 otherwise.

$x\_market^a_r$ - 1 if market r is chosen by agent a, 0 otherwise.

$y\_bandwidth^a_{i,r}$ - 1 if the bandwidth associated with agent a in market r falls in increment i, 0 otherwise.

$y\_minBandwidth^a_{r,r'}$ - 1 if the bandwidth in market r is less or equal than the bandwidth in market r' for agent a, 0 otherwise.

z_agent^a - 1 if agent a is part of the winning allocation, 0 otherwise.

$z\_license_l$ - 1 if license l gets sold in the efficient allocation, 0 otherwise

APPENDIX B: EFFICIENCY OPTIMIZER

The optimization model to determine the efficient auction outcome based on the bidders' preferences includes the constraints from each bidder, the auctioneer's bids at the reserve prices, as well as some additional variables and constraints to ensure that each item is won by at most one bidder. The model is shown below for the non-fungible case, where the bidders' preference constraints as stated in the BAT decision model are referred to by number to avoid repetition. We present the model in disjunctive form for compactness. Note that we converted the model to mixed-integer form before solving it with CPLEX, and we ask that readers interested in seeing the written out mixed-integer formulation to contact the authors.

The objective (B.1) is to maximize the profit, which is defined as the sum of the values of all the bidders plus the reserve prices of any unsold items. The Boolean variable $z\_license_l$ takes a value of 1 if license l is sold in the auction, and 0 otherwise.

$$\max totalProfit$$

$$\textbf{totalProfit} = \sum_{a \in A} value^a + \sum_{l \in \textbf{L}} \textbf{reservePrice}_l (1 - z\_license_l) \qquad (B.1)$$

The following disjunction indicates that each bidder's preferences, as defined in the model in Section 4, get enforced if that bidder is part of the efficient winning coalition ($z\_agent^a = 1$), and ignored otherwise ($z\_agent^a = 0$). Constraints (B.2) though (B.6) replace Constraints (21) through (25) to ensure that a bidder's value does not exceed its budget. Constraint (B.7) states that at least one license should be chosen if that bidder is included in the efficient allocation. Note that if agent a is not part of the efficient allocation ($z\_agent^a = 0$), all the variables related to that agent are set to zero as indicated by Constraints (B.8) through (B.13).

$$
\begin{bmatrix}
z\_agent^a \\
(1.6) - (1.20), (1.26) - (1.36), (1.38) - (1.45) \\
value^a \le \textbf{overallBudget}^a \qquad (B.2) \\
classValue_c^a \le \textbf{budget}_c^a \quad \forall c \in \textbf{C}_\textbf{A}(a) \qquad (B.3) \\
\sum_{c \in \textbf{CPrim}(a)} classValue_c^a \le \textbf{primaryBudget}^a \qquad (B.4) \\
\sum_{c \in \textbf{CSec}(a)} classValue_c^a \le \textbf{secondaryBudget}^a \qquad (B.5) \\
\sum_{c \in \textbf{Ctert}(a)} classValue_c^a \le \textbf{tertiaryBudget}^a \qquad (B.6) \\
\sum_{l \in \textbf{L}_\textbf{A}(a)} x\_license_l^a \ge 1 \qquad (B.7)
\end{bmatrix}
\vee
\begin{bmatrix}
\neg z\_agent^a \\
x\_band_b^a = 0 \quad \forall b \in \textbf{B} \qquad (B.8) \\
x\_class_c^a = 0 \quad \forall c \in \textbf{C}_\textbf{A}(a) \qquad (B.9) \\
x\_group_g^a = 0 \quad \forall g \in \textbf{G}(a) \qquad (B.10) \\
x\_license_l^a = 0 \quad \forall l \in \textbf{L}_\textbf{A}(a) \qquad (B.11) \\
x\_market_r^a = 0 \quad \forall r \in \textbf{R}_\textbf{A}(a) \qquad (B.12) \\
y\_minBandwidth_{r,r'}^a = 0 \\
\forall r, r' \in \textbf{R}_\textbf{A}(a), r' \in \textbf{ADJ}_\textbf{R}(r) (B.13)
\end{bmatrix}
\forall a \in \textbf{A}
$$

Constraints (B.14) and (B.15) tie the bidder-specific variables to the auction variables. Constraint (B.14) states that, for each market, the quantity of bandwidth won by all bidders must equal the sum of the bandwidths of all licenses sold in that market. Constraint (B.15) states that each license is one by at most one bidder.

$$\sum_{a \in A} bandwidth_r^a = \sum_{l \in \textbf{L}_\textbf{R}(r)} bandwidth_l z\_license_l$$

$$\forall r \in R \qquad (B.14)$$

$$z\_license_l = \sum_{a \in A} x\_license_l^a$$

(B.15)

$$\forall l \in L$$

APPENDIX C: FIT MODEL

The BAT decision model given in Section 5 and used for the MBR and MBRPR strategies considers only the bidder's own preferences in generating the profit maximizing bid. The model used for the FIT strategy considers all other bidders' bids as well, in order to generate the profit maximizing bid that fits with other bids in a manner that increases the auctioneer's revenue. The requirement of increasing the auctioneer's revenue is included to ensure that the bidder has a chance at being part of the winning allocation. This model is exactly the same as the one presented in Section 5, with the same objective function, and the only difference being that additional constraints are added as described next (please refer to the Appendix A for the nomenclature list).

Constraints (C.1) and (C.2) ensure a coalition that "fits" with bidder a's package. Constraint (C.1) exists for each other bidder, a', not including bidder a solving the model, and states that each bidder can win at most one of the bids from its set of bids $BID_A(a')$. The variable x_bid_{bid} takes a value of 1 if bid bid is included in the coalition with bidder a's package, and 0 otherwise. Constraint (C.2) states that each license, l, is won exactly once by either the bidder solving the model, as indicated by the variable $x\_license_l^a$, or by one of the other bids that include that license as indicated by the set of bids $BID_L(l)$. Note that the set of bids includes the FCC's reserve bids on each license.

$$\sum_{bid \in BID_A(a')} x\_bid_{bid} = z\_agent^{a'}$$

(C.1)

$$\forall a' \in A \setminus a$$

$$\sum_{bid \in BID_L(l)} x\_bid_{bid} + x\_license_l^a = 1$$

(C.2)

$$\forall l \in L$$

Constraints (C.3) and (C.4) enforce the requirement that the estimated combined revenue of the bidder's package in combination with other bids must be greater than the auctioneer's current revenue. Constraint (C.3) specifies that the estimated revenue achieved in combination with other bids equals the revenue achieved by bidder a's choice of licenses plus the revenue achieved by the other bids. For simulation purposes, we estimated the bid amounts on other bids to equal the previous bid amounts on those packages if the bids were part of the winning allocation in the preceding round, or if the bids were bid on more than two rounds in the past. If the bids were not part of the winning allocation in the preceding round, and were placed in the previous two rounds, we assume that the bid amounts will equal the minimum acceptable bid amounts for the current round. These assumed bid amounts can be adjusted to any amount a user chooses, depending on its knowledge of the other bidders' preferences. The requirement that the estimated revenue be greater than the actual current revenue is given in Constraint (C.4).

$$
revenue = \sum_{l \in L_A(a)} \text{licenseMAB}_l x\_license_l^a
$$
$$
+ \sum_{bid \in BID_A(A \backslash a)} \text{bidAmount}_{bid} x\_bid_{bid}
\tag{C.3}
$$

$$
revenue \geq \textbf{currentRevenue} \tag{C.4}
$$

Finally, note that the Boolean variables, x_bid_{bid} are relaxed to take any value between 0 and 1 in order to speed up the solution. We found that, in all tested solution, these relaxed variables took integer values.

Chapter 9

COMPARISON OF HEURISTICS FOR SOLVING THE GMLST PROBLEM

Yiwei Chen[†], Namrata Cornick[‡], Andrew O. Hall[§], Ritvik Shajpal[#], John Silberholz[§], Inbal Yahav[§], Bruce L. Golden[§]

[†] *Department of Electrical Engineering, Stanford University, Stanford, CA, 94305*

[‡] *Department of Applied Mathematics, University of Maryland, College Park, MD, 20742*

[§] *R. H. Smith School of Business, University of Maryland, College Park, MD, 20742*

[#] *Department of Geography, University of Maryland, College Park, MD, 20742*

Abstract   Given a graph G whose edges are labeled with one or more labels, the General-ized Minimum Label Spanning Tree problem seeks the spanning tree over this graph that uses the least number of labels. We provide a mathematical model for this problem and propose effective greedy heuristics and metaheuristics. We finally compare the results of these algorithms with benchmark heuristics for the related Minimum Label Spanning Tree problem.

Keywords: Combinatorial optimization; computational comparison; genetic algorithm; gre-edy heuristic; metaheuristic; minimum label spanning tree.

1.   Introduction

The Generalized Minimum Label Spanning Tree (GMLST) problem is a variant of the Minimum Label Spanning Tree (MLST) problem. The problem takes as input an undirected graph $G = (V, E, L)$, where G is defined to have V as the node set, E as the edge set, and L as the label set, with $n = |V|$ and $m = |L|$. While in the MLST problem, each edge is colored by exactly one label from the set L, in the GMLST problem, each edge has an associated label set, which is a subset of L. In this manner, edge $e \in E$ has an associated label set $l(e) \subset L$. The optimal solution to the GMLST problem is a minimum label

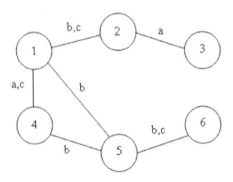

Figure 9.1.   Sample GMLST problem graph

spanning tree, T, such that each edge $e \in T$ has been colored by a label in $l(e)$ and T uses the smallest number of distinct labels.

Consider the sample graph found in Figure 9.1. One feasible spanning tree connects nodes 2 and 3 with label a, nodes 1 and 2 with label c, nodes 1 and 4 with label c, nodes 4 and 5 with label b, and nodes 5 and 6 with label c. As labels a, b, and c are used in the solution, this solution uses 3 total labels. Another spanning tree connects nodes 2 and 3 with label a, nodes 1 and 2 with label b, nodes 1 and 5 with label b, nodes 4 and 5 with label b, and nodes 5 and 6 with label b. As this spanning tree uses only two labels, a and b, it is a superior solution to the first.

The MLST problem was motivated by problems in computer network design. Different types of media are available for computer network construction. It is often considered optimal to minimize the different types of media used within the network. In a typical residential community today, it is common to find cable, optic fiber, and telephone line all connecting computer users to the Internet. Such diversity may not be optimal in planning a computer or telecommunications network, as shown by Patterson and Rolland, 2002. In this example, each type of medium would be represented with a different label, and the MLST would be a spanning tree that uses the minimum number of different medium types. Since it is reasonable that more than one type of medium could connect the same two locations, meaning this network could not be modeled as a MLST problem instance, the GMLST problem also has applications in computer network design. The MLST problem has been shown to be NP-hard by Chang and Leu, 1997, making this problem difficult to solve to optimality in reasonable runtimes for larger datasets.

We will explore several new algorithms for finding good GMLST problem solutions for several classes of graphs and compare these algorithms with Chang and Leu's maximum vertex covering algorithm (MVCA), a benchmark heuristic, and with the modified genetic algorithm (MGA) due to Xiong et al., 2005a; Xiong et al., 2006, an effective metaheuristic for the MLST problem. In Section 2, we further describe the GMLST problem and its general solution strategies. In Section 3, we provide the details of existing MLST problem heuristics and the new algorithms we developed. In Section 4, we describe the results from each of the algorithms solving a series of test problems. Section 5 provides conclusions and directions for future research.

2. The GMLST Problem

2.1 Comparing the MLST and the GMLST Problems

For graph $G = (V, E, L)$, where V is the set of nodes, E is the set of edges, and L is the set of labels, the subgraph induced by the label set $C \subset L$ is $G' = (V, E', C)$, with $E' = \{e \in E | l(e) \cap C \neq \emptyset\}$, where $l(e)$ is the label set associated with edge e.

Both the MLST and the GMLST problems require the search for a minimum-label set for which the induced subgraph is connected. The potential solutions for the MLST and GMLST problems can be represented by similar data structures. The structure of the problem motivates the decomposition of the problem into storing label sets as potential solutions and determining the feasibility of those solutions by checking if the subgraphs induced by the label sets on the graph considered are connected and span all nodes in V. The optimal solution would be represented by the minimum-cardinality feasible label set.

2.2 Optimal Solutions

The GMLST problem can be modeled as a mixed integer program and results can be obtained in reasonable runtimes for small graphs.[1] The integer formulation seeks to minimize the total number of labels needed subject to constraints of having a connected directed graph. Formally, let e_{ijk} be an indicator of the existence of an edge of label k between nodes i and j. Since the graphs we consider are undirected, $e_{ijk} = e_{jik}$. Let M be a very large number (for our purposes: $M = |E|$). We define x_{ijk} as a boolean number that determines whether there is a directed connection from node i to node j with label k in the solution. We use the boolean variable l_k to denote whether label k is in the solution. Finally, we obtain connectivity by defining y_i as a dummy variable associated with the node i. The GMLST problem is formulated as follows.

---

[1] Up to 50 nodes when using ILOG CPLEX 3.6.1

$$\min \sum_{k \in L} l_k$$

s.t.

$Connectivity:$ $\forall i \in V, \quad \sum_{j \in V, k \in L} x_{ijk} \geq 1$ (1)

$$\forall i \in V \setminus \{1\}, j \in V : y_i - y_j + n \sum_{k \in L} x_{ijk} \leq n - 1$$

$Feasibility:$ $\forall i, j \in V, k \in L : x_{ijk} \leq e_{ijk}$ (2)

$Labels:$ $\forall k \in L : \sum_{i,j \in V} x_{ijk} \leq M * l_k$ (3)

$Variables:$ $\forall i, j \in V, k \in L : x_{ijk} \in \{0, 1\}$ (4)

$\forall k \in L : l_k \in \{0, 1\}$ (5)

2.3   Heuristic Algorithms

Ideally, an exact method like solving the model provided with integer programming software would be desired for solving this combinatorial optimization problem because this method can return the optimal solution to any problem instance. However, exact solutions often require a prohibitively long runtime, making them impractical approaches for solving large problem instances of NP-complete problems. For instance, the backtrack search mentioned in Xiong et al., 2005a, which is an exact algorithm, could not be used to analyze datasets containing more than 50 nodes and 50 labels due to its exponential runtime. This shortcoming demonstrates the need for heuristics that return approximate results in much quicker runtimes. Examples of some heuristics for the MLST problem include the genetic algorithm due to Nummela and Julstrom, 2006, the genetic algorithm due to Xiong et al., 2005a, and the tabu search procedure due to Cerulli et al., 2005.

In this paper, we present two greedy heuristics for the GMLST problem. The first heuristic, the maximum vertex covering algorithm (MVCA) first posed in Chang and Leu, 1997, is a benchmark heuristic for the MLST problem. We show the MVCA can be used without modification on the GMLST problem in Section 3. In addition to this benchmark heuristic, we propose a new heuristic algorithm, the rarest insertion (RI) heuristic.

In addition to the greedy heuristics, we present a number of metaheuristics. These metaheuristics allow for randomness. This allows these algorithms to search more of the solution space. We present the Modified Genetic Algorithm (MGA), a heuristic proposed in Xiong et al., 2005a. We also propose two new heuristics: the Increasing Diverse Population Genetic Algorithm (IDP) and the Iterative Perturbation and Correction Heuristic (IPC). Each algorithm is detailed in full in Section 3.

3. Algorithms for the GMLST Problem

3.1 MVCA

An effective heuristic for the MLST problem, the MVCA was proposed in Chang and Leu, 1997. Bruggemann et al., 2003 proved that the MVCA can be used to provide approximate solutions to the MLST problem in polynomial time. Xiong et al., 2005b, using the harmonic numbers $H_b = \sum_{i=1}^{b} \frac{1}{i}$, where b is the maximum frequency of any label in the graph, showed that the number of labels in the MVCA heuristic solution is no worse than H_b times optimal and demonstrated that this bound is tight.

Though the MVCA was developed for the MLST problem, it can be used without modification for the GMLST problem because its data representation is a label set. The MVCA begins with an empty label set. Hence, in this initial state, the subgraph induced by the label set on a graph G has n components. Each of them is composed of a single vertex. At each stage, the MVCA chooses labels to add to the partial label set such that the number of components in the subgraph induced by the new label set is minimum. Pseudocode for the algorithm is shown below.

0 Input: A graph $G = (V, E, L)$, where V is the set of nodes, E is the set of edges, and L is the set of labels.

1 Let $C \leftarrow \{\}$ be the set of added labels.

2 Do while the subgraph induced by C on G has more than one component

  (a) *minnumcomp*← min(the number of components of $C \cup \{k\}$ induced on G) for any $k \in L \setminus C$

  (b) *possiblelbls*← $\{k \in L \setminus C$: the number of components of $C \cup \{k\}$ induced on $G = minnumcomp\}$

  (c) Randomly select label f from *possiblelbls*

  (d) $C \leftarrow C \cup \{f\}$

3 Report C

3.2 Rarest Insertion

We developed the Rarest Insertion (RI) algorithm to decrease the number of labels considered for removal by the MVCA. The RI heuristic maintains the components of the subgraph induced by the current label set on the graph considered. Each iteration, the algorithm selects the component that has the fewest number of labels linking its member nodes to any other node in the graph. From that set of labels, the RI heuristic selects the label that, when added to the current label set, results in the label set whose induced subgraph on the

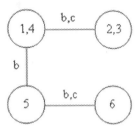

Figure 9.2.   Sample graph after one iteration of the RI algorithm

graph considered has the least number of components. That label is added to the heuristic solution's label set and the components are recalculated. The RI algorithm continues adding labels in this manner until the induced subgraph is connected and spans all nodes in V.

To illustrate this procedure, consider the RI algorithm performed on the graph shown in Figure 9.1. As no labels have been selected yet, each node is its own component. Next, the rarest component (node) must be found. Node 1 is connected to other nodes by all 3 labels, node 2 is connected to other nodes by all 3 labels, node 3 is connected to other nodes by only 1 label (a), node 4 is connected to other nodes by all 3 labels, node 5 is connected to other nodes by 2 labels (b and c), and node 6 is connected to other nodes by 2 labels (b and c). Hence, the component containing node 3 is selected as the rarest component, and label a is added to the solution set. After recomputing the components, the result is the graph shown in Figure 9.2. Now, the rarest component is again selected. Each of the four components pictured is connected to other components by all 2 remaining labels (b and c), so the rarest component is selected randomly from these choices. Suppose the component containing only node 5 is selected. As it is connected to other components by both labels b and c, a decision must be made about which of these labels to use. Since adding b would result in 1 remaining component (containing a feasible spanning tree) but adding c would result in 2 remaining components (one containing nodes 1, 2, 3, and 4 and the other containing nodes 5 and 6), b is added and the procedure terminates, having found the solution set $\{a, b\}$.

Pseudocode for this algorithm is shown next.

0 Input: A graph $G = (V, E, L)$, where V is the set of nodes, E is the set of edges, and L is the set of labels.

1 $C \leftarrow \{\}$, the set of added labels.

2 $N \leftarrow \{\{1\}, \{2\}, ..., \{n\}\}$, the components of the subgraph induced by C on G

3 Do while $|N| > 1$

    (a) *minnumlbl*$\leftarrow$ $\min(|\bigcup_{a \in P, b \in V \setminus P} l(\overline{ab})|)$ for any $P \in N$, where $l(\overline{ab})$ is the label set of the arc between node a and node b

    (b) *possiblecomp*$\leftarrow$ $\{P \in N : |\bigcup_{a \in P, b \in V \setminus P} l(\overline{ab})| = minnumlbl\}$

    (c) Randomly select S from *possiblecomp*

    (d) $T \leftarrow \bigcup_{a \in S, b \in V \setminus S} l(\overline{ab})$, the set of labels connected to the selected component S

    (e) *minnumcomp*$\leftarrow$ $\min($ the number of components of the subgraph induced by $C \cup \{k\}$ on G) for any $k \in T$

    (f) *possiblelblset* $\leftarrow$ $\{k \in T :$ the number of components of the subgraph induced by $C \cup \{k\}$ on $G = minnumcomp\}$

    (g) Randomly select f from *possiblelblset*, the selected label to be added

    (h) $C \leftarrow C \cup \{f\}$

    (i) Do while $\exists J, K \in N, J \neq K$ s.t. $\exists j \in J, k \in K$ s.t. $\{f\} \subset l(\overline{jk})$

       i $N \leftarrow N \setminus \{J, K\} \cup \{J \cup K\}$ /* $|N| \leftarrow |N| - 1$ */

  4 Report C

3.3   Iterative Perturbation and Correction Heuristic

The Iterative Perturbation and Correction (IPC) heuristic is an algorithm aimed at overcoming the drawbacks of hill climbing methods. Hill climbing methods perform a local search for increases in fitness. However, they often get trapped at local optimal solutions, rarely discovering a solution near the global optimal solution. The IPC allows deteriorating moves along with iterative improvement to broaden the search space and to provide better future solutions. The final IPC solution is less dependant upon the starting point than the hill climbing final solution, making the initial solution a less important consideration in the IPC. Parameters for this metaheuristic are found in Section 4.

Algorithm Structure.   To generate the initial feasible solution used in our IPC heuristic, we start with an empty label set. We then add a label using the weighted selection technique described later in this section. We keep adding unadded labels in this manner until the subgraph induced by the label set on the graph considered is connected and spans all nodes in V, meaning the solution is feasible. If this initial label set has cardinality one, we return it as the final solution. If not, one at a time we remove all labels from the label set that are not needed to maintain the connectivity of the label set induced on the graph and then add a label using the weighted selection technique described below.

The algorithm continues until the best solution found has not improved for T iterations. Pseudocode for the algorithm is found below.

0 Input: A graph $G = (V, E, L)$, where V is the set of nodes, E is the set of edges, and L is the set of labels; a set f of the frequencies of each label in the graph, where f_l is the frequency of label l; a value F that is the maximum frequency of any label in the graph; and parameters T and λ.

1 $C \leftarrow \{\}$, the set of used labels.

2 Do while the subgraph induced by C on G has more than one component

   (a) $C \leftarrow C \cup \{$ a randomly selected $l \in L \setminus C\}$, with the probability of selecting l as $\dfrac{e^{-\lambda(\frac{F-f_l}{F})}}{\sum_{k \in L \setminus C} e^{-\lambda(\frac{F-f_k}{F})}}$ for any $l \in L \setminus C$.

3 If $|C| = 1$ then return final solution C and terminate

4 *numstagnant* $\leftarrow 0$, the number of iterations with no improvement in the best solution

5 Do while *numstagnant* $< T$

   (a) *possibleremove* $\leftarrow \{l \in C :$ the subgraph induced by $C \setminus \{l\}$ on G is connected and spans all nodes in $V\}$ /* the set of all labels we can remove while maintaining a feasible solution */

   (b) Do while $|$*textitpossibleremove*$| > 0$

      i Let *rem* be the label in *possibleremove* added to C the longest time ago

      ii $C \leftarrow C \setminus \{rem\}$ /* $|C| \leftarrow |C| - 1$ */

      iii *possibleremove* $\leftarrow \{l \in C :$ the subgraph induced by $C \setminus \{l\}$ on G is connected and spans all nodes in $V\}$ /* As the cardinality of C decreases, the cardinality of *possibleremove* will approach 0 */

   (c) If $|C|$ is the smallest yet encountered by the heuristic, then *numstagnant* $\leftarrow 0$

   (d) $C \leftarrow C \cup \{$a randomly selected $l \in L \setminus C\}$, with the probability of selecting l as $\dfrac{e^{-\lambda(\frac{F-f_l}{F})}}{\sum_{k \in L \setminus C} e^{-\lambda(\frac{F-f_k}{F})}}$ for any $l \in L \setminus C$

   (e) *numstagnant* $\leftarrow$ *numstagnant* $+1$

6 Report the lowest-cardinality C ever encountered

Exponentially Weighted Selection. Selections of labels are made based on an exponential distribution, where labels with a higher frequency in the graph are given preference. A parameter λ is used to govern how strongly more frequent labels are favored. The preference given to a label $l \in L \setminus C$ is modeled by $e^{-\lambda(\frac{F-f_l}{F})}$, where f_l is the number of times a label l is present in the graph, F is the maximum frequency of any label in the graph, L is the set of all labels, and C is the current label set. The probability of a label $l \in L \setminus C$ being selected in the weighted selection is given by that label's selection preference divided by the sum of the selection preferences of all labels not in C, or $\dfrac{e^{-\lambda(\frac{F-f_l}{F})}}{\sum_{k \in L \setminus C} e^{-\lambda(\frac{F-f_k}{F})}}$. Clearly, if λ is set to a high value, labels with a higher frequency will gain more of an advantage in selection over those with a lower frequency, making the IPC more greedy in nature. From our data, the IPC solution quality decreased when λ was set too high or too low.

3.4 Modified Genetic Algorithm

We implemented the MGA due to Xiong et al., 2005a; Xiong et al., 2006. Though this heuristic was designed for the MLST problem, no modifications to the metaheuristic were necessary, as its data representation is a label list. This genetic algorithm uses a single parameter to set the number of generations equal to the population size. A large parameter value is associated with longer runtimes.

3.5 An Increasing Diverse Population Genetic Algorithm

The MGA sacrifices population diversity for intensive local optimization. Therefore, we were motivated to develop a genetic algorithm that involves less local optimization and a greater focus on population diversity to yield better solutions for datasets. This prompted the creation of the IDP.

The IDP stores candidate solutions in data structures called chromosomes. As suggested in Xiong et al., 2005a, we use a list of the labels to store the candidate solutions. The parameters used for this heuristic in data collection are discussed in Section 4.

Initial Chromosome Generation. The initial chromosome begins as an empty label set. An initial chromosome is generated iteratively by randomly selecting *initlabelselect* labels not in the current label set and adding the one that minimizes the number of components of the graph when all edges containing that label are added, continuing until the subgraph induced on the graph by the label set is connected and spans all nodes in V. Though for large *initlabelselect* this process requires more runtime than the random method of initial chromosome generation used in Xiong et al., 2005a, it results in a fitter initial population. If an element of the initial population has a cardinality of one, the IDP terminates after this stage.

Another initial chromosome generation technique we considered but decided not to use involved using domain-specific knowledge to create an overlap matrix to create initial chromosomes of better fitness than those produced by a fully random procedure like the one used by the MGA. The overlap matrix is a $m \times m$ matrix that stores in each entry the number of edges in the graph whose label sets contain both the label represented by the row and the label represented by the column. An initial chromosome is generated by iteratively adding the label with the least overlap with the labels already selected to be included in the chromosome and breaking ties randomly.

The procedure can be made fast by precomputing the overlap matrix. However, we noted that this method did not produce as fit initial chromosomes as other algorithms. This could be due to the fact that some overlapped edges may be counted multiple times as we build up the chromosome.

Crossover and Mutation.   A key component of any genetic algorithm is the crossover operation, which combines the genetic information from two parents into a child that is similar to both. In this genetic algorithm, the crossover begins by first maintaining all the labels in the label sets of both parents. Next, it adds random unused labels from either of the parents' label sets. The crossover continues this process until the subgraph induced by the label set on the graph is connected and spans all nodes in V. A feasible label set is guaranteed to exist, since both parents are feasible solutions, meaning the union of their label sets would also induce a connected subgraph.

To maintain population diversity, *nummutate* chromosomes in the population are randomly selected each generation. Each of these chromosomes is mutated. The mutation operator is very simple: a label $l \notin C$ is selected at random and added to the label set C of the chromosome.

Local Search.   As discussed in Michalewicz, 1996, genetic algorithms for network problems will often perform poorly without a unary local search procedure to iteratively improve chromosomes in a population. For IDP, a non-intensive local search procedure removes the first label it finds that can be removed from the label set while maintaining that label set's feasibility. The IDP also uses a second type of local search, an intensive local search. The intensive local search iterates through all of the labels in the label set, removing each that is not necessary for the feasibility of the label set. Because the non-intensive local search can only remove one unneeded label while the intensive local search can remove multiple labels, the non-intensive local search allows for quicker runtimes but is a weaker local search operator.

Generation Structure.   Each generation, *numreplace* of the *popsize* chromosomes in a population are selected for replacement by new chromosomes. These chromosomes are selected based on a probability distribution, in which the probability of selecting a chromosome P from the population Q for replacement is $\frac{|P|-|best|+1}{\sum_{A \in Q}|A|-|best|+1}$, where *best* is the fittest chromosome in the population. Therefore, chromosomes with a larger number of associated labels, and hence a worse fitness, are more likely to be replaced, simulating an evolutionary process.

The *popsize* − *numreplace* chromosomes not selected to be replaced are maintained until the next population by replication. Next, the *numreplace* new chromosomes for the next generation are generated by the crossover operator described earlier in this section. The unique parents for each crossover operation are also generated using a probability distribution. For this distribution, the probability of selecting a chromosome P from the population Q is $\frac{|worst|-|P|+1}{\sum_{A \in Q}|worst|-|A|+1}$, where *worst* is the least fit chromosome in the population. The chromosomes with the smaller number of labels, and hence a greater fitness, are more likely to be selected as parents, again simulating an evolutionary process.

The *numreplace* new chromosomes are placed into the population for the next generation. After this replacement, mutation is carried out as described above. Next, *numlocaloptimize* random selections of chromosomes are made. Each time a chromosome is selected, local optimization is applied to it as long as the chromosome has not had exhaustive local search performed on it in previous generations, in which case no action is taken after selection. The type of local search used will be discussed during the explanation of the population structure.

Population Structure.   In an effort to prevent premature population convergence, a check is done for concurrent label sets. Two label sets are defined to be concurrent if one is a subset of the other. If two chromosomes have concurrent label sets, then only one needs to be maintained in the population. If two concurrent label sets are found, then the one with fewer labels, P, is maintained, with ties broken randomly. The other chromosome is mutated *numalterations*(P) times, where *numalterations* is a function found in Section 4. Next, the non-intensive local search is performed until no more improvements can be made, but no more than *numalterations*(P) times.

Finally, to avoid having one population converge to a poor solution, *numisolated* isolated populations are maintained in a structure similar to that used in Silberholz and Golden, 2007. Each population contains *popsize* chromosomes and the populations are maintained until the best chromosome found by any of the populations has not improved for *numgensisolated* generations. To maintain shorter runtimes, the non-intensive local search is used during the local search phase for these isolated populations. After this time of isolated evolution, the isolated populations are combined into a final population of *popsize* chromosomes using a probability distribution identical to the one used for parent selection in the reproduction phase of the genetic algorithm. The single combined population is maintained until the best chromosome produced by the population has not improved for *numgensfinal* generations. The intensive local search procedure is used instead of the non-intensive version for this final single population. Additionally, since the MVCA runs so quickly, MVCA solutions are incorporated into this part of the GA. *numinitmvca* of the chromosomes in the initial combined population are generated by the MVCA heuristic, and each generation, *nummvcaeachgen* of the chromosomes are generated by the MVCA.

4.   Computational Results

4.1   Small-World Dataset Generation

The first type of datafile generation technique that we used is based on the Small-World datafile generator proposed in Watts and Strogatz, 1998. Essentially, the Small-World generator works in two steps as follows: for a selected number of nodes n and density d (where $d = \frac{|E|}{|V|^2}$):

1 Create a regular lattice-like network, i.e., n nodes connected to form a circle, with each node linked to its $\frac{|E|}{|V|}$ neighbors.

2 For each arc, with probability p, rewrite the arc's end node such that the graph remains connected.

3 Repeat the second step for i iterations.

To account for arcs labels, we expanded the Watts and Strogatz algorithm by labeling each arc such that the arc has a maximum of l labels (*LabelsPerArc* $\sim Uniform[0, l]$)

In our generator we set the rewriting probability p to be 0.5, the number of iteration $i = 3$, and the maximum labels per arc $l = 5$.[2]

4.2   TSPLib-Based Dataset Generation

In addition to creating datasets based on the Small-World datafile generator as discussed above, we also generated datasets based on the TSPLib datasets from Reinelt, 1990. In the following sections, we will describe the deterministic algorithms used to generate these datasets so that others may compare

---

[2]The graph generator is available at http://www.rhsmith.umd.edu/faculty/phd/inbal/

results with those presented in this paper by downloading TSPLib datasets from the Internet and implementing our labeling algorithms.[3] Our algorithms for creating GMLST problem graphs from TSPLib datasets were divided into two steps. First, we generated a frequency distribution of the number of labels between every pair of nodes. We then determined which labels would be used for each arc. For each of these steps, we generated two algorithms.

Algorithms for Generating Frequency Distributions. Algorithms for generating frequency distributions were based on three parameters. The first, *maxlabelsperarc*, is the maximum number of labels associated with an individual arc in the graph. This value was set to be 5. The next parameter, *totnumlabels*, is the sum of the number of labels associated with each arc over all arcs in the graph. This parameter was set at $\lfloor \binom{n}{2} * density * maxlabelsperarc \rfloor$, where *density* is a value that varied in experimentation between .005 and .1. The final parameter, m, or the number of labels for the dataset, was determined by the equation $m = \lfloor \frac{n^2}{100} \rfloor$, where n is the number of nodes specified in the TSPLib dataset. Since the values of m and *totnumlabels* both varied with degree 2 in relation to n, the number of labels in datasets with the same density stayed approximately constant regardless of the size of that dataset.

Two algorithms were used for generating the frequency distributions. The first, random frequency, uses the distance matrix of the TSPLib dataset to generate a distribution that is relatively pattern-free. Pseudocode for this algorithm is provided in Appendix A. The other algorithm, length-based frequency, is based on the idea that in many applications of the GMLST problem, most labels will be found on shorter arcs. For instance, in the example of a telecommunications network, it is likely that a provider would connect two distant cities through a series of shorter connections rather than a single direct connection. The algorithm assigns each arc a number of labels proportional to the inverse of the length of that arc. Pseudocode for this algorithm is provided in Appendix A.

Algorithms for Determining Labels for Each Arc. Two algorithms were developed for determining the labels for each arc in the graph, given the number of labels associated with that arc determined by one of the two algorithms presented above. The first, random label selection, again uses the distance matrix of the TSPLib dataset to make label selections that are generally pattern-free. Pseudocode for this algorithm is provided in Appendix A. The other algorithm, clustered label selection, stems from the concept of localization of services in the real-world applications of the GMLST problem. A local company would only provide services to a small geographical range, meaning its

---

[3] At http://www.rhsmith.umd.edu/faculty/bgolden/, the graph generator and problem instances can be found

labels would touch a small number of nodes. This effect is approximated in the clustered labels algorithm by assigning each label a central node. The algorithm then labels arcs based on proximity to node centers, finally evening the distribution so that there is less variation in the frequency of labels in the graph. Pseudocode for this algorithm is provided in Appendix A.

4.3   Parameters for Computational Experiments

Parameters for the IPC heuristic were determined based on preliminary modeling runs and were selected to be values that returned good results. The value 3000 was used for T, the number of iterations without improvement. The value 6 was used for λ, the affinity to add high-frequency labels. Preliminary testing showed that as T increased the solution quality became less sensitive to the λ value.

Parameters for the IDP were also selected based on preliminary modeling runs. Parameters for the structure of the GA were also based on suggested values from Michalewicz, 1996. The number of labels considered before choosing the most advantageous in the initial chromosome creation, *initlabelselect*, was selected to be 10. The number of chromosomes mutated in each population, *nummutate*, was selected to be 7. The size of each population, *popsize*, was set to be 40 chromosomes. The number of chromosomes to be replaced by crossover each generation, *numreplace*, was selected to be 25. The number of chromosomes selected to have local optimization performed each generation, *numlocaloptimize*, was selected to be 40. The number of times a chromosome was mutated and then locally optimized if it was found to have a concurrent label set with another chromosome, *numalterations*(P), was set to be $\lfloor \frac{|P|}{10} \rfloor + 3$, where $|P|$ is the number of labels in the candidate chromosome P. The number of isolated populations maintained at the beginning of the IDP heuristic, *numisolated*, was set to be 6. The number of generations without improvement that isolated populations are maintained, *numgensisolated*, was set to be 7. The number of generations without improvement that the final population is maintained, *numgensfinal*, was set to be 30. The number of MVCA solutions introduced to the population after the initial combination of isolated populations, *numinitmvca*, was set to be 3. Finally, the number of MVCA solutions introduced to the final population each generation, *nummvcaeachgen*, was set to be 1.

4.4   Computational Experiments

Computational experiments were performed on 52 datasets generated using the Small-World generation methods described above. We considered densities of 0.04, 0.06, 0.08, and 0.1 for datafiles with 50, 100, 200, and 400 nodes. For datafiles with 800 nodes, we considered densities of 0.04 and 0.06. For each density used, except 0.06 for 800-node problems, we tested a datafile with 10 labels, a datafile with 55 labels, and a datafile with 100 labels. For the remaining datasets, we used 10 labels only. For each dataset, 5 instances were generated with different random seeds and each of those instances was tested, with the average results reported.

Computational experiments were also performed on 64 datafil-es generated using the TSPLib-based methods described above. We chose 4 TSPLib datafiles, $eil51$, $pr152$, $tsp225$, and $rd400$, for experimentation. Using the formula provided earlier in this section, the datafiles generated had 26, 231, 506, and 1600 labels, respectively. For datafiles generated from $eil51$, densities of 0.025, 0.05, and 0.1 were used. For datafiles generated from $pr152$ and $tsp225$, densities of 0.01, 0.025, 0.05, and 0.1 were used. Finally, for datafiles generated from $rd400$, densities of 0.005, 0.01, 0.025, 0.05, and 0.1 were used. For each density used, we generated a datafile with a length-based frequency distribution and random labeling, a datafile with a length-based frequency distribution and clustered labeling, a datafile with a random frequency distribution and random labeling, and a datafile with a random frequency distribution and clustered labeling.

Computational experiments were performed on a Systemax Venture H524 computer with 512 MB RAM and a 3.06 GHz processor using code programmed in C and C++. Computational experiments considered the MGA, the IDP, and the IPC. Additionally, we tested the repeated MVCA (RMVCA), which is the MVCA repeated 100 times with the best result returned, and the repeated RI (RRI), which is the RI procedure repeated 100 times with the best result returned. For each of the executions of these heuristics, a different random seed was used. Because both the MVCA and RI use random selection to break ties, the solutions returned by these heuristics often varied between executions. For each of the TSPLib-based datasets considered, 5 modeling runs were performed with each heuristic with a different random seed used each time. For each of the Small-World datasets considered, 5 modeling runs were performed with each heuristic on each of the 5 instances for that datafile, resulting in 25 total modeling runs performed by each heuristic for each of those datafiles. Multiple trials are necessary because every heuristic considered is nondeterministic, meaning results will vary between modeling runs. The average solutions and runtimes for the modeling runs are provided in Appendix 9.B.1 so direct runtime comparisons can be made with the results of this paper.

4.5 Results

In our computational experiments, we counted the number of datasets for which each heuristic performed better than each other heuristic. In Table 9.1,

Table 9.1. Comparison over 36 small dataset instances. Entries represent the number of datasets for which the algorithm in the row heading returned fewer labels on average than the algorithm in the column heading.

Heuristic	IDP	RMVCA	RRI	MGA	IPC	Sum
IDP	0	23	18	16	4	61
RMVCA	0	0	5	1	0	6
RRI	0	14	0	2	0	16
MGA	1	22	16	0	1	40
IPC	5	23	17	15	0	60
Sum	6	82	56	34	5	183

Table 9.2. Comparison over 44 medium dataset instances. Entries represent the number of datasets for which the algorithm in the row heading returned fewer labels on average than the algorithm in the column heading.

Heuristic	IDP	RMVCA	RRI	MGA	IPC	Sum
IDP	0	28	29	13	14	84
RMVCA	3	0	10	3	8	24
RRI	4	21	0	1	9	35
MGA	18	30	27	0	20	95
IPC	15	28	24	11	0	78
Sum	40	107	90	28	51	316

Table 9.3. Comparison over 36 large dataset instances. Entries represent the number of datasets for which the algorithm in the row heading returned fewer labels on average than the algorithm in the column heading.

Heuristic	IDP	RMVCA	RRI	MGA	IPC	Sum
IDP	0	17	19	13	17	66
RMVCA	3	0	7	7	12	29
RRI	2	11	0	8	10	31
MGA	10	17	17	0	20	64
IPC	8	14	15	5	0	42
Sum	23	59	58	33	59	232

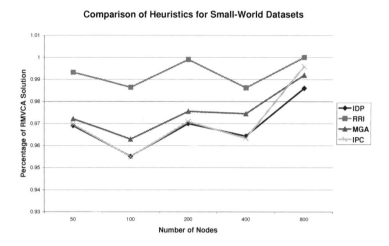

Figure 9.3. Effects of Small-World dataset size on comparative solution qualities of heuristics tested

each heuristic is compared with all of the other heuristics on the smallest datasets, which are all 36 datasets with $n \leq 100$. This includes both Small-World datasets and TSPLib-based datasets. Each entry in the table is the number of datasets considered for which the heuristic in the row label had a lower average number of labels returned than the heuristic in the column label. The column sum shows the number of times the heuristic was outperformed by any other heuristic, and the row sum is the number of times the heuristic outperformed any other heuristic. The row and column sums provide good summary statistics for how well each heuristic performed on the datasets considered. Successful heuristics had high row sums and low column sums. Table 9.2 has the same format, but considers all 44 datasets with $100 < n \leq 225$. Table 9.3 considers all 36 datasets with $n > 225$.

To illustrate the solution quality and runtime trends, we considered the effects of certain datafile attributes of the comparative solutions of the heuristics. In Figures 9.3 and 9.4 we consider how the size of the dataset affects the comparative solution qualities for both Small-World and TSPLib-based datasets. In Figure 9.5, we demonstrate how the density of a TSPLib-based dataset affects comparative solution qualities for the heuristics.

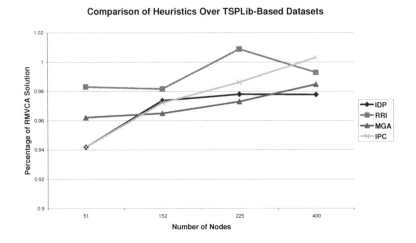

Figure 9.4.   Effects of TSPLib-based dataset size on comparative solution qualities of heuristics tested

The RRI performed better than the RMVCA in modeling runs, averaging 0.79% fewer labels than the benchmark greedy heuristic. Of the 68 datafiles for which the two heuristics did not return the same average solutions, the RRI outperformed the RMVCA in 46 instances. The comparison between the RRI and RMVCA seems to be highly dependent on the particular dataset considered. In TSPLib-based datasets using clustered label selection, the RRI averaged 2.47% fewer labels than the RMVCA, while the heuristic actually performed worse than the RMVCA on TSPLib-based datasets using random label selection, averaging 0.91% more labels than the benchmark. This difference may be due to the fact that the RRI chooses between fewer labels than the RMVCA in an even label distribution like the one found in a dataset generated through clustered label selection, causing the RRI to make more informed label selections that help it perform better than the benchmark. In addition to outperforming the RMVCA in solution quality, the RRI performs faster than the RMVCA, completing all the modeling runs in 56.71% the runtime of the RMVCA.

The IDP and MGA consistently outperformed both of the greedy heuristics, validating both as useful metaheuristics. On average, the IDP returned solutions with 3.16% fewer labels than the RMVCA solution and 2.28% fewer la-

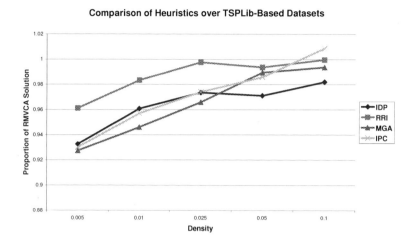

Figure 9.5. Effects of TSPLib-based dataset density on comparative solution qualities of heuristics tested

bels than the RRI solution, while the MGA on average returned solutions with 2.73% fewer labels than the RMVCA solution and 1.84% fewer labels than the RRI solution. The computational results of the two metaheuristics are similar. Over all modeling runs, the IDP outperformed the MGA on 42 datasets and the MGA outperformed the IDP on 29 datasets. On average, the IDP solutions had 0.41% fewer labels than the MGA solutions. Though the IDP performed better than the MGA in solution quality comparisons, this may be due to the parameters for the IDP being set to favor solution quality over runtime. Though the IDP performed in reasonable runtimes, averaging 76.83 seconds per modeling run with the longest average runtime for a datafile slightly more than 15 minutes, the MGA executed all datasets considered in about a third the IDP runtime.

While the RMVCA and RRI solution comparison was most affected by the label selection technique for TSPLib datafiles, the comparison between the IDP and MGA is most affected by a more subtle attribute of datafiles: the cardinality of good solution sets. For this analysis, we introduce b, the best solution encountered by any of the heuristics tested for a given dataset. On datasets with low-cardinality good solutions, specifically those with $b \leq 5$, the IDP averaged solutions with 0.77% fewer labels than the MGA's results. Likewise, on datasets with medium-cardinality good solutions, specifically those with $5 < b \leq 20$, the IDP averaged solutions with 1.12% fewer labels than the MGA's results. However, on the solutions with the high-cardinality good solutions, specifically those with $b > 20$, the MGA averaged solutions with 0.93% fewer labels than the IDP's solutions. Indeed, this trend extends to comparisons with other heuristics. On datasets with medium-cardinality good solutions, the IDP dominates all other heuristics considered, averaging 3.53% fewer labels than the RMVCA, 2.67% fewer labels than the RRI, and 0.87% fewer labels than the IPC. Likewise, on datasets with high-cardinality good solutions, the MGA dominates all other heuristics considered, averaging 3.62% fewer labels than the RMVCA, 2.64% fewer labels than the RRI, and 1.54% fewer labels than the IPC. Though this trend exists based on the cardinality of good solutions for datasets, the trend does not seem to extend to the size of datasets. The IDP actually outperformed the MGA on large datafiles, averaging 0.60% fewer labels than the MGA on 400-node TSPLib-based datasets and 1.10% fewer labels than the MGA on 400-node Small-World datasets.

Over the Small-World datasets, the IPC produced solutions of good quality. Over these datasets, the IPC and the IDP had nearly identical results, with the IPC averaging 0.09% more labels than the IDP, and the IPC outperformed all other heuristics considered in solution quality. Over the Small-World datasets, the IPC averaged 0.61% fewer labels than the MGA, 3.29% fewer labels than the RMVCA, and 2.44% fewer labels than the RRI. In runtime comparisons, the IPC was outperformed by all other heuristics and used 49% more runtime than the IDP, the closest heuristic in runtime, over all problem instances. However, the IPC runtimes were fast; the IPC averaged 8.89 seconds of runtime per Small-World dataset instance and did not average over one minute of runtime for any Small-World dataset.

On TSPLib-based datasets, the IPC performed better on datasets with a low density. With density 0.005, the IPC used 0.30% more labels than the MGA and 6.98% fewer labels than the RMVCA. However, on the highest density TSPLib graphs, with density 0.1, the IPC performed the worst of all the algorithms considered, averaging 1.46% more labels than the MGA and 0.86% more labels than the RMVCA. The IPC results seemed much less affected by the generation technique used for the TSPLib-based dataset considered. In the comparison between the IPC and MGA for different generation techniques, we averaged the number of labels for each heuristic over all datasets of that type and then compared those averages. The MGA averaged 1.5% fewer labels than the IPC on datasets with length-based frequency distribution and clustered label section, 0.8% fewer labels on datasets with length-based frequency distribution and random label selection, 1.05% fewer labels on datasets with random frequency distribution and clustered label selection, and 0.7% fewer labels on datasets with random frequency distribution and random label selection. On TSPLib-based datasets, the IPC performed better on graphs with fewer nodes. The IPC averaged 2.01% fewer labels than the MGA on TSPLib-based datasets with 51 labels, but the MGA outperformed the IPC as the number of nodes increased. For TSPLib-based datasets with 400 nodes, the MGA averaged 1.77% fewer labels than the IPC. For TSPLib-based datasets with 51 nodes, the IPC performed slower than the other heuristics, but for 400-node TSPLib-based graphs the IPC runtime was similar to that of other heuristics except for the IDP, which the IPC outperformed significantly on those datasets in terms of runtime.

From the computational results, the advantages of each type of dataset also became evident. The Small-World datasets are easier to generate, as the procedure for generation is simple compared to that of the TSPLib-based datasets. However, the TSPLib-based datasets seemed to produce more difficult datafiles. The average number of labels returned by any heuristic for the TSPLib-based datasets was 36.67, while that average for the Small-World datasets was only 5.65. Additionally, the average spread between the best and worst heuristic results for the TSPLib-based datafiles was 6.68%, while the average spread for Small-World datafiles was 4.49%. A final consideration should be that the generation of TSPLib-based datafiles requires much less runtime than the generation of a Small-World datafile.

5. Conclusions and Future Research

In this paper we presented the GMLST problem and discussed effective heuristics for generating approximate solutions to the problem. We presented the IDP, a genetic algorithm that performed as well as the MGA, a genetic algorithm in the literature for the MLST problem, and we also proposed the IPC, a fast metaheuristic that performed well in testing runs. The IPC is also a simple concept that is easy to implement, a further benefit of this approach to the GMLST problem. We also developed the RI heuristic, an effective greedy heuristic that produces solutions better than those of the MVCA, a benchmark approach for the MLST problem, in significantly less runtime.

Much can be done to extend the results published in this paper. Though the datafiles considered were interesting from a computation standpoint, creating datasets based on real-world GMLST problems would further strengthen the analysis of the heuristics presented.

Additionally, mathematical analysis of the runtime and solution quality performance of the RI heuristic is needed. For example, it might be possible to derive an upper bound on the solution error.

Finally, we must analyze how the methods we used to solve the GMLST problem perform on similar problems, like the MLST problem. It is likely that some of the methods we developed for the GMLST problem can be applied to other network optimization problems.

References

Bruggemann, Tobia, Monnot, Jerome, and Woeginger, Gerhard J. (2003). Local search for the minimum label spanning tree problem with bounded color classes. *Operations Research Letters*, 31(3):195–201.

Cerulli, Raffaele, Fink, Andreas, Gentili, Monica, and Voss, Stefan (2005). Metaheuristics comparison for the minimum labelling spanning tree problem. In Golden, B, Raghavan, S, and Wasil, E, editors, *The Next Wave in Computing, Optimization, and Decision Technologies*, pages 93–106.

Chang, RS and Leu, Shing-Jiuan (1997). The minimum labeling spanning trees. *Information Processing Letters*, 63(5):277–282.

Michalewicz, Z (1996). *Genetic Algorithms+ Data Structures= Evolution Programs*. Springer.

Nummela, Jeremiah and Julstrom, Bryant A. (2006). An effective genetic algorithm for the minimum-label spanning tree problem. In *GECCO '06: Proceedings of the 8th Annual Conference on Genetic and Evolutionary Computation*, pages 553–558, New York, NY, USA. ACM Press.

Patterson, RA and Rolland, Erik (2002). Hybrid fiber coaxial network design. *Operations Research*, 50(3):538–551.

Reinelt, G (1990). *TSPLIB-A Traveling Salesman Problem Library*. Inst. für Mathematik.

Silberholz, John and Golden, Bruce (2007). The generalized traveling salesman problem: A new genetic algorithm approach. In Baker, E, Joseph, A, Mehrotra, A, and Trick, M, editors, *Extending the Horizons: Advances in Computing, Optimization, and Decision Technology*, pages 165–181.

Watts, Duncan J. and Strogatz, Steven H. (1998). Collective dynamics of 'small-world' networks. *Nature*, 393(6684):409–410.

Xiong, Yupei, Golden, Bruce, and Wasil, Edward (2005a). A one-parameter genetic algorithm for the minimum labeling spanning tree problem. *IEEE Transactions on Evolutionary Computation*, 9(1):55–60.

Xiong, Yupei, Golden, Bruce, and Wasil, Edward (2005b). Worst-case behavior of the mvca heuristic for the minimum labeling spanning tree problem. *Operations Research Letters*, 33(1):77–80.

Xiong, Yupei, Golden, Bruce, and Wasil, Edward (2006). Improved heuristics for the minimum label spanning tree problem. *IEEE Transactions on Evolutionary Computation*, 10(1):700–703.

Appendix: A: Datafile Generation Pseudocodes

1.   Datafile Generation Pseudocodes

As the pseudocode provided in this section is meant to help programmers to reimplement the dataset generation procedures described in this paper, throughout this appendix nodes and labels will be numbered between 0 and $n - 1$ and between 0 and $m - 1$ repectively to emulate common programming techniques.

1.1   Random Frequency Distribution

0 Input: A distance matrix *dist* for TSPLib graph $G = (V, E)$, *totnumlabels*, and *maxlabelsperarc*.

1 *frequencypos* $\leftarrow$ 1

2 for *labeladdcount* = 0 to *totnumlabels* -1

    (a) Add a link between $a = \lfloor \frac{frequencypos}{n} \rfloor$ and $b = frequencypos \bmod n$

    (b) *frequencypos* $\leftarrow$ (*frequencypos* $+ dist_{ab} +$ *labeladdcount*) mod n^2

    (c) While the arc $\overline{ab}$ associated with *frequencypos* as calculated in step 2a already has *maxlabelsperarc* associated with it or both nodes in that arc are the same, *frequencypos* $\leftarrow$ (*frequencypos* $+1$) mod n^2

1.2   Length-Based Frequency Distribution

0 Input: A distance matrix *dist* for TSPLib graph $G = (V, E)$, *totnumlabels*, and *maxlabelsperarc*.

1 *currval*, *currfreq*, *node*$_1$, *node*$_2$ $\leftarrow$ 0

2 for *edgecount* = 0 to $\binom{n}{2} - 1$

    (a) *node*$_2$ $\leftarrow$ *node*$_2 + 1$

    (b) if *node*$_2 = n$ then

        i *node*$_1$ $\leftarrow$ *node*$_1 + 1$

        ii *node*$_2$ $\leftarrow$ *node*$_1 + 1$

    (c) *freqarray*$_{edgecount}$ $\leftarrow$ *currval* $+ \frac{1}{dist_{node_1 node_2} +1}$

    (d) *currval* $\leftarrow$ *freqarray*$_{edgecount}$

3 for *edgecount* = 0 to $\binom{n}{2} - 1$

    (a) Using *node*$_1$, *node*$_2$ associated with *edgecount* as assigned in steps 2a through 2b, assign $\lfloor \frac{freqarray_{edgecount} * totnumlabels}{currval} \rfloor -$ *currfreq* labels to the arc between *node*$_1$ and *node*$_2$

    (b) if more than *maxlabelsperarc* were assigned, assign *maxlabelsperarc* instead

    (c) *currfreq* $\leftarrow$ *currfreq* $+$ the number of labels just added

4 *edgecount* $\leftarrow$ 0

5 do while *currfreq* < *totnumlabels*, meaning not all labels have been distributed

    (a) using *node*$_1$, *node*$_2$ associated with *edgecount* as assigned in steps 2a through 2b, increase the number of labels between *node*$_1$ and *node*$_2$ up to either *maxlabelsperarc* or the *totnumlabels* $-$ *currfreq* $+$ the previous number of labels assigned to the arc, whichever is less

    (b) *currfreq* $\leftarrow$ *currfreq* $+$ the number of labels just added

    (c) *edgecount* $\leftarrow$ *edgecount* $+1$

1.3   Random Label Selection

0 Input: A distance matrix *dist* for TSPLib graph $G = (V, E)$, a matrix *numlabels* of the number of labels for any given arc.

1 for $node_1 = 0$ to $n - 1$, $node_2 = node_1 + 1$ to $n - 1$

    (a) for *labelcount* $= 0$ to $numlabels_{node_1 node_2} - 1$

          i   *currlbl* $\leftarrow$ ($node_1 + node_2 + ($ *labelcount* $+1)*$ $dist_{node_1 node_2})$ mod m

          ii while the label *currlbl* is already used between $node_1$ and $node_2$, *currlbl* $\leftarrow$ (*currlbl* $+1$) mod m

          iii assign *currlbl* to the arc between $node_1$ and $node_2$

1.4   Clustered Label Selection

0 Input: A distance matrix *dist* for TSPLib graph $G = (V, E)$, a matrix *numlabels* of the number of labels for any given arc, *totnumlabels* as provided to earlier algorithms

1 for *ctrcnt*$= 0$ to $m - 1$

    (a) *center$_{ctrcnt}$* $\leftarrow$ *ctrcnt* mod n, the node used as the center of label *ctrcnt*'s cluster

    (b) *labelfreq$_{ctrcnt}$* $\leftarrow 0$, the number of label *ctrcnt* added to the graph

2 for $node_1 = 0$ to $n - 1$, for $node_2 = 0$ to $node_1 - 1$, for *lblcnt*$= 1$ to *numlabels$_{node_1 node_2}$*

    (a) *lblselect* $\leftarrow -1$, the next label selected to be added (-1 means none yet selected)

    (b) for *lbl* $= 0$ to $m - 1$, if *lbl* has not been added to the arc between $node_1$ and $node_2$ then if *lblselect* $= -1$ or $dist_{node_1 center_{lbl}} + dist_{node_2 center_{lbl}} < dist_{node_1 center_{lblselect}} + dist_{node_2 center_{lblselect}}$ then *lblselect* $\leftarrow$ *lbl*

    (c) assign *lblselect* to the arc between $node_1$ and $node_2$

    (d) *labelfreq$_{lblselect}$* $\leftarrow$ *labelfreq$_{lblselect}$* $+ 1$

3 *minlbl* $\leftarrow \lfloor \frac{totnumlabels}{m} \rfloor$, the minimum number of arcs to be assigned to any label

4 for $node_1 = 0$ to $n - 1$, $node_2 = 0$ to $node_1 - 1$, *lbl* $= 0$ to $m - 1$

    (a) if *lbl* is assigned to the arc between $node_1$ and $node_2$ and either *labelfreq$_{lbl}$* $> minlbl +1$ or (*labelfreq$_{lbl}$* $= minlbl +1$ and $\exists l, 0 \leq l \leq m - 1$, s.t. *labelfreq$_l$* $< minlbl$) then

          i   *bestreplace* $\leftarrow -1$, the label to replace *lbl* on the arc (-1 means none found)

          ii for $lbl_2 = 0$ to $m - 1$, if lbl_2 is not on the arc between $node_1$ and $node_2$ and (either *labelfreq$_{lbl_2}$* $< minlbl$ or (*labelfreq$_{lbl_2}$* $= minlbl$ and $\forall l, 0 \leq l \leq m-1$, *labelfreq$_l$* $\geq minlbl$)) and (*bestreplace*$= -1$ or $dist_{node_1 center_{lbl_2}} + dist_{node_2 center_{lbl_2}} < dist_{node_1 center_{bestreplace}} + dist_{node_2 center_{bestreplace}}$) then *bestreplace* $\leftarrow lbl_2$

          iii if *bestreplace* $\neq -1$ then

              A *labelfreq$_{lbl}$* $\leftarrow$ *labelfreq$_{lbl}$* $- 1$

              B *labelfreq$_{bestreplace}$* $\leftarrow$ *labelfreq$_{bestreplace}$* $+ 1$

              C remove *lbl* from the arc between $node_1$ and $node_2$ and add *bestreplace* to the arc

Appendix: B: Detailed Computational Results

1. Detailed Computational Results

In this section, we provide the average results of each heuristic tested over all of the datasets to provide a basis for comparison with the results presented in this paper. In each of the tables, n is the number of nodes in a dataset, m is the number of labels, d is the density, and $type$ describes the type of dataset. For TSPLib-based datasets, LC implies the length-based frequency distribution was used with clustered label selection, LR means the length-based frequency distribution was used with random label selection, RC means the random frequency distribution was used with clustered label selection, and RR means the random frequency distribution was used with random label selection. A $type$ of SW means a Small-World dataset was used. Beneath each heuristic name, lbl is the average number of labels returned over the modeling runs for each dataset and sec is the average runtime in seconds for the modeling runs. Bolded entries indicate the best solution for a given dataset.

Table 9.B.1 displays the results of the heuristics (IDP, RMVCA, RRI, MGA, and IPC) on TSPLib-based datasets, and Table 9.B.2 displays the results of the heuristics on Small-World datasets.

Table 9.B.1.   Heuristic results on TSPLib-based datasets. n is the number of nodes, m is the number of labels, d is the density, *lbl* is the average number of labels returned by a heuristic, *bst* is the best number of labels returned by a heuristic over the 5 modeling runs, and *sec* is the average runtime in seconds of a heuristic.

d	n	m	type	IDP lbl	IDP sec	RMVCA lbl	RMVCA sec	RRI lbl	RRI sec	MGA lbl	MGA sec	IPC lbl	IPC sec
0.025	51	26	LC	**10**	0.85	**10**	0.05	**10**	0.07	**10**	0.14	**10**	1.03
0.025	51	26	LR	**8**	0.60	9	0.05	**8**	0.06	**8**	0.13	**8**	0.85
0.025	51	26	RC	**9**	0.91	10	0.05	10	0.07	**9**	0.15	**9**	1.00
0.025	51	26	RR	**7**	0.65	**7**	0.04	**7**	0.06	**7**	0.11	**7**	0.84
0.05	51	26	LC	**6**	0.57	7	0.05	**6**	0.05	6.8	0.11	**6**	1.03
0.05	51	26	LR	**4**	0.44	**4**	0.04	5	0.05	4.4	0.07	**4**	0.79
0.05	51	26	RC	**6**	0.58	7	0.06	7	0.05	6.2	0.12	**6**	1.14
0.05	51	26	RR	**5**	0.38	**5**	0.04	**5**	0.05	**5**	0.08	**5**	0.94
0.1	51	26	LC	**4**	0.49	5	0.05	**4**	0.05	**4**	0.09	**4**	1.32
0.1	51	26	LR	**3**	0.32	**3**	0.04	**3**	0.04	**3**	0.06	**3**	1.17
0.1	51	26	RC	**4**	0.42	**4**	0.05	**4**	0.05	**4**	0.07	**4**	1.30
0.1	51	26	RR	**3**	0.31	**3**	0.04	**3**	0.05	**3**	0.06	**3**	1.17
0.01	152	231	LC	60	27.34	63.8	3.48	60.8	2.76	**58**	15.34	59.4	16.77
0.01	152	231	LR	**33**	20.84	33.6	2.10	33.2	1.66	**33**	6.56	**33**	7.85
0.01	152	231	RC	57	27.33	61.2	3.48	58.2	2.66	**55.6**	14.90	56.8	14.16
0.01	152	231	RR	37.2	18.71	38.4	2.32	38	1.83	37.4	8.03	**37**	9.99
0.025	152	231	LC	28.4	23.36	30.2	2.67	28.6	1.55	**28.2**	7.63	**28.2**	12.28
0.025	152	231	LR	**17**	9.76	**17**	1.71	18	1.08	17.4	3.48	17.2	6.57
0.025	152	231	RC	28.4	24.05	29.4	2.74	29	1.57	**27.4**	7.99	27.6	10.31
0.025	152	231	RR	**17.6**	8.25	18	1.87	18	1.08	18	3.71	**17.6**	5.80
0.05	152	231	LC	18.2	12.46	18.4	2.49	**18**	1.16	**18**	5.49	18.2	10.12
0.05	152	231	LR	**11**	5.91	12	1.78	**11**	0.88	**11**	2.61	**11**	5.60
0.05	152	231	RC	17.4	11.59	17.2	2.66	17	1.13	**16.4**	5.12	17.4	11.03
0.05	152	231	RR	10.6	5.90	11	1.73	**10**	0.89	11	2.41	10.4	5.93
0.1	152	231	LC	11	7.48	11	2.38	11	0.92	**10.4**	3.09	10.8	10.37
0.1	152	231	LR	7	3.79	7	1.85	7	0.85	**6.6**	1.81	**6.6**	8.17
0.1	152	231	RC	10.2	6.90	**10**	2.65	10.4	0.96	10.4	3.48	11	8.80
0.1	152	231	RR	**6.8**	4.03	7	1.98	7	0.94	7	1.68	7	6.44
0.01	225	506	LC	80.4	76.31	83.8	14.84	80.6	10.04	**77.4**	46.15	78	45.95
0.01	225	506	LR	43	66.10	43.8	7.81	43.6	5.75	**42.8**	17.80	43	20.22
0.01	225	506	RC	76.6	85.52	81.6	14.93	77.6	9.68	**75.2**	44.06	75.8	36.30
0.01	225	506	RR	41	75.33	42.2	7.70	43.8	5.71	**40.6**	17.16	41.2	19.18
0.025	225	506	LC	39.2	84.69	41	11.60	40.4	5.77	**38.4**	22.44	40	23.32
0.025	225	506	LR	21.6	36.93	21.6	6.28	24	3.56	21.4	9.34	**21.2**	14.93
0.025	225	506	RC	38.6	69.64	40	11.67	39.2	5.69	**37.8**	22.60	38.4	27.07
0.025	225	506	RR	**22**	40.10	22.4	6.64	**22**	3.48	**22**	9.96	22.4	14.51
0.05	225	506	LC	24.8	35.29	24.2	10.56	24	4.08	**23.8**	15.34	24.8	25.49
0.05	225	506	LR	**13.8**	18.42	14	6.40	14	2.67	14	6.91	14.2	13.99
0.05	225	506	RC	23.8	35.06	23.8	11.03	24	4.14	**23.4**	15.23	24.2	23.74
0.05	225	506	RR	**13.6**	20.32	14	6.82	14	2.96	**13.6**	6.57	14	11.53
0.1	225	506	LC	**14.8**	24.09	**14.8**	10.16	15	3.18	**14.8**	9.57	15	23.66
0.1	225	506	LR	9	12.47	9	6.56	10	2.59	**8.8**	4.58	**8.8**	16.61
0.1	225	506	RC	**14.8**	20.02	**14.8**	11.32	15	3.49	15	9.85	15.4	25.19
0.1	225	506	RR	**8.2**	12.39	9	6.94	9	2.88	9	4.45	8.6	15.66
0.005	400	1600	LC	208	850.06	227.4	197.38	215	158.54	**205**	351.47	205.4	173.08
0.005	400	1600	LR	93.2	634.82	97.8	83.38	96	73.69	92.8	133.58	**92.6**	94.12
0.005	400	1600	RC	215.4	911.50	234.8	202.72	218.2	160.72	**214**	382.73	**214**	187.73
0.005	400	1600	RR	**97.2**	584.54	102.8	88.88	101.6	78.11	97.4	137.81	98.6	88.22
0.01	400	1600	LC	136.2	680.22	144.2	164.80	138.2	106.07	**134.2**	256.08	135	175.40
0.01	400	1600	LR	58.4	531.47	59	66.06	61.6	49.67	**57**	77.76	59.4	64.93
0.01	400	1600	RC	135.6	623.13	143.2	165.41	138	106.02	**134.2**	256.83	135.2	136.65
0.01	400	1600	RR	60.8	517.35	62.4	69.92	62.8	50.19	**60**	86.63	60.8	76.98
0.025	400	1600	LC	68.6	396.31	69	124.49	68.6	58.43	**66.2**	125.77	69	111.35
0.025	400	1600	LR	31.2	219.89	31	55.23	31.4	28.53	**30**	46.27	31.4	52.32
0.025	400	1600	RC	67.8	384.34	67.8	124.21	67.6	57.77	**67.4**	128.47	67.6	106.38
0.025	400	1600	RR	**32**	232.73	**32**	57.62	32.6	29.47	**32**	47.94	32.2	52.83
0.05	400	1600	LC	**40.8**	206.09	41	113.74	41	39.38	41.8	86.25	42	92.62
0.05	400	1600	LR	**18**	94.46	**18**	50.57	**18**	19.90	18.8	28.77	19	46.20
0.05	400	1600	RC	40.2	233.07	**40**	115.06	**40**	39.48	41	84.65	41.2	96.07
0.05	400	1600	RR	**19.2**	112.46	20	55.32	20	21.76	20	31.15	20.6	52.82
0.1	400	1600	LC	25	162.27	**24.8**	108.91	25	28.86	25.8	56.68	27.6	79.57
0.1	400	1600	LR	**11**	55.13	**11**	48.59	**11**	16.72	11.8	18.82	11.6	48.34
0.1	400	1600	RC	**24**	179.11	**24**	111.24	24.2	29.53	25.2	54.15	26.6	88.78
0.1	400	1600	RR	**12**	55.07	**12**	57.27	**12**	19.75	12.2	20.04	12.6	56.63
Average runtime				134.29 sec.		35.16 sec.		19.86 sec.		43.26 sec.		37.52 sec.	

Table 9.B.2. Heuristics results on Small-World datasets. n is the number of nodes, m is the number of labels, d is the density, lbl is the average number of labels returned by a heuristic, bst is the best number of labels returned by a heuristic over the 5 modeling runs for each of the 5 instances considered, and sec is the average runtime in seconds of a heuristic.

Datafile				IDP		RMVCA		RRI		MGA		IPC	
d	n	m	type	lbl	sec	lbl	sec	lbl	sec	lbl	sec	lbl	sec
0.04	50	10	SW	**6.4**	0.73	6.8	0.02	**6.4**	0.04	**6.4**	0.08	**6.4**	1.23
0.04	50	55	SW	**18.6**	1.44	18.76	0.13	**18.6**	0.14	18.64	0.27	**18.6**	1.68
0.04	50	100	SW	23.52	1.68	23.6	0.28	23.6	0.23	23.6	0.87	**23.48**	1.93
0.06	50	10	SW	**3.6**	0.44	**3.6**	0.01	**3.6**	0.02	**3.6**	0.05	**3.6**	0.96
0.06	50	55	SW	**10.8**	0.76	11	0.10	11.16	0.10	10.96	0.16	10.88	1.23
0.06	50	100	SW	14.32	0.98	14.52	0.20	14.4	0.16	**14.24**	0.50	**14.24**	1.37
0.08	50	10	SW	**2.6**	0.36	2.8	0.01	**2.6**	0.02	**2.6**	0.04	**2.6**	0.94
0.08	50	55	SW	**7.8**	0.54	**7.8**	0.09	7.92	0.08	**7.8**	0.11	**7.8**	1.02
0.08	50	100	SW	11	0.80	11.4	0.17	11.2	0.14	11.12	0.39	11.08	1.26
0.1	50	10	SW	**2.2**	0.31	2.4	0.02	2.6	0.02	**2.2**	0.04	**2.2**	1.04
0.1	50	55	SW	**6.08**	0.50	6.6	0.08	6.4	0.07	6.16	0.10	**6.08**	0.98
0.1	50	100	SW	**9.4**	0.72	**9.4**	0.16	**9.4**	0.13	**9.4**	0.31	**9.4**	1.15
0.04	100	10	SW	**3**	1.22	**3**	0.05	**3**	0.05	**3**	0.31	**3**	2.08
0.04	100	55	SW	**10**	2.36	10.96	0.23	10.2	0.20	10.2	0.94	10.12	2.64
0.04	100	100	SW	14	3.28	14.88	0.42	14.2	0.34	**14.04**	1.32	14.2	3.19
0.06	100	10	SW	**2.4**	0.96	2.6	0.05	**2.4**	0.05	**2.4**	0.29	**2.4**	2.52
0.06	100	55	SW	**7**	1.66	7.4	0.23	7.8	0.18	7.08	0.72	**7**	2.35
0.06	100	100	SW	**10.08**	2.13	10.4	0.40	10.24	0.28	10.16	1.00	**10.08**	2.67
0.08	100	10	SW	**2**	0.93	**2**	0.05	**2**	0.06	**2**	0.26	**2**	2.92
0.08	100	55	SW	**5.24**	1.45	6	0.23	6	0.17	5.32	0.55	**5.2**	2.37
0.08	100	100	SW	**8**	1.89	8.2	0.40	8.12	0.27	8.04	0.85	**8**	2.63
0.1	100	10	SW	**1.8**	0.70	**1.8**	0.06	**1.8**	0.06	**1.8**	0.26	**1.8**	3.41
0.1	100	55	SW	4.64	1.23	4.8	0.23	4.8	0.17	4.76	0.51	**4.6**	2.54
0.1	100	100	SW	6.68	1.63	7	0.40	7	0.26	6.76	0.73	**6.6**	2.71
0.04	200	10	SW	**2**	3.51	**2**	0.19	**2**	0.16	**2**	0.95	**2**	6.15
0.04	200	55	SW	**6.6**	5.49	7	0.81	6.8	0.43	6.76	2.53	6.68	5.70
0.04	200	100	SW	**10.04**	8.14	10.6	1.39	10.4	0.67	10.2	3.74	10.16	6.45
0.06	200	10	SW	**1.8**	2.36	**1.8**	0.20	**1.8**	0.20	**1.8**	0.92	**1.8**	8.57
0.06	200	55	SW	**5**	4.37	5.2	0.86	**5**	0.46	**5**	1.96	**5**	7.09
0.06	200	100	SW	7.04	6.24	7.4	1.41	7.8	0.67	7.16	2.75	**7**	7.09
0.08	200	10	SW	**1**	0.01	**1**	0.21	**1**	0.20	**1**	0.47	**1**	5.98
0.08	200	55	SW	**4**	3.86	**4**	0.91	**4**	0.55	**4**	1.66	**4**	6.43
0.08	200	100	SW	5.96	4.79	6	1.49	6	0.71	5.96	2.28	**5.92**	6.95
0.1	200	10	SW	**1**	0.01	**1**	0.21	**1**	0.23	**1**	0.48	**1**	7.53
0.1	200	55	SW	**3**	3.42	3.4	0.93	3.6	0.63	3.04	1.39	**3**	7.53
0.1	200	100	SW	**5**	4.42	5.2	1.53	**5**	0.84	**5**	2.04	**5**	7.53
0.04	400	10	SW	**1**	0.04	**1**	0.76	**1**	0.71	**1**	1.75	**1**	13.50
0.04	400	55	SW	4.88	15.37	5	3.55	5	1.74	4.96	7.73	**4.8**	17.73
0.04	400	100	SW	**7**	22.58	**7**	5.95	7.2	2.20	**7**	10.51	7.04	18.62
0.06	400	10	SW	**1**	0.03	**1**	0.80	**1**	0.83	**1**	1.85	**1**	0.05
0.06	400	55	SW	**3.08**	12.71	3.6	3.74	3.4	2.34	3.28	6.02	3.12	23.46
0.06	400	100	SW	**5**	17.13	5.2	6.30	**5**	2.90	**5**	8.09	5.04	22.36
0.08	400	10	SW	**1**	0.03	**1**	0.81	**1**	0.90	**1**	1.84	**1**	0.06
0.08	400	55	SW	**3**	11.48	**3**	3.86	**3**	2.89	**3**	5.46	**3**	27.28
0.08	400	100	SW	**4**	15.49	**4**	6.44	**4**	3.61	**4**	6.88	**4**	27.20
0.1	400	10	SW	**1**	0.04	**1**	0.89	**1**	1.01	**1**	1.98	**1**	0.08
0.1	400	55	SW	**2**	11.25	2.2	4.05	2.2	3.24	**2**	4.08	**2**	31.68
0.1	400	100	SW	**3.48**	14.15	4	6.72	3.6	4.26	3.68	6.84	3.4	35.00
0.04	800	10	SW	**1**	0.13	**1**	3.23	**1**	3.36	**1**	7.21	**1**	0.11
0.04	800	55	SW	**3**	49.93	**3**	15.56	**3**	10.22	**3**	20.93	**3**	58.23
0.04	800	100	SW	**4.72**	65.00	5	26.83	5	13.18	4.84	32.32	4.92	58.23
0.06	800	10	SW	**1**	0.14	**1**	3.60	**1**	3.85	**1**	8.07	**1**	0.16
Average runtime				5.98 seconds		2.06 seconds		1.27 seconds		3.14 seconds		8.89 seconds	

Chapter 10

OPTIMIZING THE NODE DEGREE IN WIRELESS MULTIHOP NETWORKS WITH SINGLE-LOBE BEAMFORMING

Christian Hartmann, Moritz Kiese, and Robert Vilzmann
Institute of Communication Networks, Technische Universität München
{hartmann, moritz.kiese, vilzmann}@tum.de

Abstract   Future wireless networks will be characterized by heterogeneous network architectures, with multihop communication as an important aspect. It is not clear yet how much multihop communication can benefit from the use of beamforming antennas. In this paper, we control the beamforming directions of wireless devices so as to optimize the node degree, i.e., the number of neighbors a wireless device can directly communicate with. The results show the potential of beamforming antennas, and are useful benchmarks for distributed approaches in self-organizing networks.

Keywords: Wireless communication; multihop networks; beamforming; connectivity.

1.   Introduction

Wireless communication networks consist of network infrastructure providing access to a wired backbone, and mobile devices which associate with the infrastructure. This is the case at least with traditional wireless networks: in cellular networks, a network provider covers large areas with wired basestations; in wireless local area networks (WLAN), access points serve as routers and typically provide connection to the Internet.

In contrast to such wireless *singlehop* communication, more than one link between two communicating devices is wireless in *multihop* networks. In the extreme case, mobile devices only communicate by forwarding each others data and no fixed infrastructure is required at all. Such multihop communication is expected to play an important role in future networks for various reasons. Since functions like service discovery and routing then have to be performed completely decentralized and networks can form spontaneously, such networks are often called *ad hoc* networks. If the network comprises many devices (*nodes*) that communicate wirelessly but are immobile and connected to a power line, the term *mesh* network is often used. Today, multihop communication is already of great importance in sensor networks, where small and low-cost sensors interconnect wirelessly, performing all kinds of sensing and monitoring tasks.

The question of *connectivity* is, in singlehop networks, simply a question of coverage: a mobile device can send and receive data as soon as it is in communication range of a basestation or access point. In multihop networks, the probability of connectivity is not simply the fraction of the covered area, but a function of the locations of other nodes. In fact, it turns out that connectivity is one of the most severe limitations of multihop networking. For a given node, it is unclear how many neighbors it can communicate with directly, and whether or not there is a multihop path to a desired communication peer.

There are several different measures available to quantify the connectivity of a network. Most notably the graph theoretical *connectivity*, which defines a network as being connected if and only if there exists a (multihop) path between any node pair in the network. Other measures are the k-*connectivity*, and the *path probability* describing the probability that an arbitrary node pair can establish a (multihop) path between them. In the context of this paper we are interested in the graph theoretical connectivity. There is a close connection between node degree and connectivity, cf. e.g. Penrose, 1997; Penrose, 1999. Penrose was able to show that in geometric graphs with uniformly random node distributions, the network becomes connected with a probability close to one when the range of the nodes becomes just large enough so that there is no *isolated* node left. Similar theorems exist for pure random graphs and for k-connectivity, relating the minimum node degree in the network to the k-connectivity.

In fact, instead of directly tackling the connectivity, which is a specifically difficult task in a self-organizing system such as an ad hoc network, we aim at maximizing the sum of the node degrees in the network.

Existing work shows how the node degree can be controlled by setting the transmission power of the mobile devices (Wattenhofer et al., 2001). The intention of such topology control is to maintain connectivity while minimizing the emitted power. Another way of controlling the topology is to make use of beamforming antennas. Rather than changing the overall emitted power, beamforming antennas change the way of how it is disseminated into space. By increasing the antenna gain towards neighboring nodes, the transmission range can be significantly increased. Beamforming has thus the potential to connect isolated nodes and reduce the number of hops between communicating peers (Vilzmann et al., 2005).

This paper is not concerned with antenna design and signal processing techniques for beamforming. We are rather interested in how a certain antenna characteristic can perform in a multihop scenario.

The use of beamforming antennas can be categorized into two approaches. The first one carries out beamforming on a packet basis. This means that the beamforming may change in the order of milliseconds, since subsequently transmitted or received packets can be destined to or received from different neighbors. According to the second approach, the beamforming pattern of the antenna is maintained on a larger time scale, e.g., for the duration of a complete data flow, a connection between a client and a server, or even for longer time periods. In the following, we will look at the latter, since it can be utilized without changing other network functionalities such as medium access control, and is less complex and energy consuming. It is thus more likely to be adopted.

We assume beamforming approaches that maximize the antenna gain in a desired direction. The antenna pattern, i.e., its radiation characteristic in the far field, is then characterized by an angular direction with high antenna gain, called the *main lobe*. All other directions have a significantly reduced antenna gain. *Single-lobe beamforming* then refers to an antenna which only has one preferred direction for transmission and reception.

The basic question answered in this paper is: In which direction should the mobile devices point their main lobe so as to maximize the sum of the node degrees of all nodes? We formulate this problem as a Mixed Integer Linear Program (MIP) (cf. D. Bertsimas and J. N. Tsitsiklis, 1997; Dantzig, 1963). Even though such a central optimization approach with full system knowledge is not feasible in self-organizing multihop networks, the results obtained through optimization are of great interest: Only by comparison with the global optimum, we are now able to assess the performance of distributed heuristic algorithms, which can be applied to realistic multihop networks. Therefore, this paper is further concerned with a distributed approach for increasing the node degree, and its performance gap to the optimal solution.

Sec. 2 presents the network model of this paper. Sec. 3 formulates the problem of maximizing node degrees as MIP. Sec. 4 discusses a distributed approach for increasing node degrees. Sec. 5 presents optimization results and compares to the performance of the sub-optimal distributed approach. Finally, Sec. 6 provides concluding remarks.

2. Wireless Network Model

We consider a network model that is generic enough to picture a wide range of multihop network scenarios. The most important aspects of the model are summarized in this section.

We also provide an informal introduction to directional antennas, intended for the reader unfamiliar with directional antenna concepts.

2.1   Node Placement

The model for node placement captures essential topological real-world aspects such as the occurrence of node clusters, disconnection and node isolation, but also the occurrence of node disjoint and link disjoint paths. According to the model, n nodes are placed randomly on a two-dimensional system area. The system area has a size of $1000\,\text{m} \times 1000\,\text{m}$. We are particularly interested in clustered scenarios, i.e., inhomogeneous node distributions. To achieve this, five cluster centers are determined in the system area at random following a uniform spatial distribution. Then, the total number of nodes is split evenly among the clusters. For each cluster, the resulting number of nodes is placed around the cluster center according to a two-dimensional Gaussian distribution, centered at the cluster center. The standard deviation of the Gaussian distribution of each cluster is chosen as 10% of the system area width.

2.2   Signal Propagation

Only a fraction of the energy transmitted by a sending node n_1 is captured by a receiver n_2. In free space, the attenuation of the transmitted signal is proportional to the square of the distance (path loss exponent $a = 2$). In order to consider propagation effects of reflection, diffraction and scattering (Rappaport, 2002), the model can be extended to allow for a higher path loss exponent. In the following, we will assume a modified free space path loss model with $a = 3$. Taking into account the signal attenuation over the wireless link l_{n_1,n_2} according to this model, the received power is

$$p_r = p_t \cdot g\left(\gamma_{n_1}\right) \cdot g\left(\gamma_{n_2}\right) \cdot \left(\frac{\lambda}{4\pi \cdot d_{n_1,n_2}}\right)^2 \left(\frac{d_0}{d_{n_1,n_2}}\right)^{a-2}, \qquad (1)$$

where p_t is the transmission power, λ is the carrier wavelength (center frequency of the band used for transmission), d_{n_1,n_2} is the distance between the communicating peers, and d_0 is a reference distance. The factor $g(\gamma_{n_1})$ is the antenna gain of the transmitter n_1 in the direction of the receiver n_2, and $g(\gamma_{n_2})$ is the antenna gain of n_2 in the direction of n_1.

With a reference distance of $d_0 = 1$ m, the received signal power p_r is given as

$$p_r = p_t \cdot g\left(\gamma_{n_1}\right) \cdot g\left(\gamma_{n_2}\right) \cdot \left(\frac{\lambda}{4\pi}\right)^2 \left(\frac{1}{d_{n_1,n_2}}\right)^a. \qquad (2)$$

In logarithmic scale, the received signal power level is

$$P_r = P_t + G\left(\gamma_{n_1}\right) + G\left(\gamma_{n_2}\right) + 10 \cdot \log\left(\frac{\lambda}{4\pi}\right)^2 + 10 \cdot \log\left(d^{-a}\right), \quad (3)$$

with upper-case variables denoting logarithmic scale.

Whether or not a receiver is able to decode a signal is heavily determined by the received signal strength. It can approximately be assumed that a signal can be received if its strength P_r exceeds a receiver-dependent minimum signal power $P_{r,\,min}$. Therefore, two nodes are within communication range if the link budget in equation

$$0 \leq P_{Tx} + G\left(\gamma_{n_1}\right) + G\left(\gamma_{n_2}\right) - P_{L,n_1,n_2} - P_{r,\,min}. \quad (4)$$

is fulfilled. For easier notation in (4) we implicitly defined the logarithmic path loss

$$P_{L,n_1,n_2} = -10 \cdot \log\left(\frac{\lambda}{4\pi}\right)^2 - 10 \cdot \log\left(d^{-a}\right). \quad (5)$$

The maximum transmission range for give angles γ_{n_1}, γ_{n_2} and antenna gains $G\left(\gamma_{n_1}\right)$, $G\left(\gamma_{n_2}\right)$ is then determined from (4) and (5) as

$$d_r = 10^{\frac{1}{10 \cdot a} \cdot \left(-P_{r,\,min} + P_t + G\left(\gamma_{n_1}\right) + G\left(\gamma_{n_2}\right) + 10 \cdot \log\left(\frac{\lambda}{4\pi}\right)^2\right)}. \quad (6)$$

2.3   Antenna

As an important building block of wireless networks, antennas disseminate energy into the propagation medium on transmission, and collect energy on reception. Antenna design allows this coupling with the medium to be direction-dependent. Examples for directional antennas are horn, dish, PCB or Yagi antennas. Even a dipole antenna does not have perfectly omnidirectional, i.e., direction-independent characteristics.

This work is motivated by the use of multi-element antennas. In contrast to the aforementioned antenna types, the directional characteristic of multi-element antennas can be *steered electronically*, as opposed to mechanical steering. This is achieved using a beamforming circuitry, controlling the signals applied to or tapped from the antenna elements. The beamforming circuitry has to be aware of the physical arrangement of the antenna elements. Among the simplest setups is a circular and equidistant arrangement of antenna elements, e.g., simple dipoles, in connection with a phase shift between neighboring elements. By setting the phase shift properly, the transmitted signals of the individual elements will interfere constructively in a desired direction. The very same directional characteristic is achieved on reception by introducing the phase shift between the received signals.

A variety of advanced techniques for beamforming, but also for direction-of-arrival estimation of received signals, have been developed for multi-element antennas. Due to these capabilities, they are often referred to as *smart* antennas.

In antenna theory, the antenna *gain* is a concept to represent the directional characteristic of an antenna. In the above description of the link budget its meaning has already been introduced. Fig. 10.1(a) illustrates the antenna gain of a phased array with a circular arrangement of eight antenna elements, as a function of the angle in a two-dimensional plane. The antenna elements are modeled as ideal isotropic point radiators. As can be seen in the figure, there is an angular direction of high antenna gain, often referred to as *main lobe* or *main beam*. Besides, so-called *side lobes* exist as well. Advanced beamforming techniques can create more than one main lobe and can even allow for quite arbitrary antenna characteristics. It should be noted, however, that the limited number of antenna elements (= degrees of freedom) constrains such antenna response "shaping".

Due to their practical relevance we will only consider directional antennas with one main lobe in this paper. It is our intention to formulate the problem of maximizing node degrees as a Mixed Integer Linear Program (MIP). This is extremely difficult for antenna patterns as in Fig. 10.1(a). To simplify and abstract the antenna model, its characteristic is therefore represented by the *keyhole model*. It has been used repeatedly in the literature (e.g. by Ramanathan, 2001). We assume that the mobile devices are located in a plane, and antennas are perfectly perpendicular to the ground. The keyhole model can thus be limited to two dimensions. It is then characterized by an angular range with high antenna gain G_M (main lobe), and a low antenna gain G_S in the remaining directions (Fig. 10.1(b)). G_S models the side lobes of a realistic antenna. In the following, we assume $G_M = 10 = 10$ dBi within an antenna aperture of $\alpha = 30°$, and $G_S = 0.1 = -10$ dBi outside the aperture.

Although the antenna configuration could be assumed to be different for transmission and reception, we assume that the antenna gain is left unchanged. Then, no asymmetric links occur.

Note that all nodes of the network are assumed to have a directional antenna.

3.   Problem Formulation

For illustrative purposes we will use the scenario depicted in Fig. 10.2. Depending on the direction of the two respective keyholes, the two nodes n_1 and n_2 might be able to build a link over which communication is possible. In the following we will assume n_1 to be the sending and n_2 to be the receiving node.

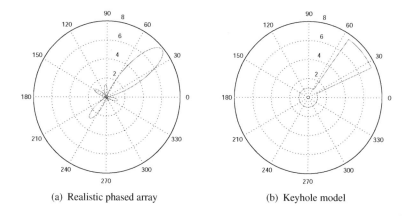

(a) Realistic phased array   (b) Keyhole model

Figure 10.1. Gain patterns

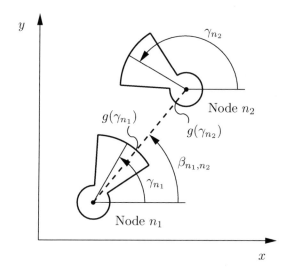

Figure 10.2. Example Scenario

The two nodes $\{n_1, n_2\} \subset \mathcal{N}'$ with respective coordinates (x_{n_1}, y_{n_1}) and (x_{n_2}, y_{n_2}) and Euclidian distance

$$d_{n_1,n_2} = \sqrt{(x_{n_2} - x_{n_1})^2 + (y_{n_2} - y_{n_1})^2} \qquad (7)$$

have individually steerable antennas. The steering direction (center of the main lobe, i.e. the keyhole) is indicated by $\gamma_{n_1}, \gamma_{n_2} \in [0; 2\pi]$, respectively. According to the keyhole model, the antenna gain in decibel is

$$G = \begin{cases} G_\mathrm{M} & \text{within aperture } \alpha. \\ G_\mathrm{S} & \text{else.} \end{cases} \tag{8}$$

The respective antenna gains are effective for reception as well as for transmission, such that links are always bidirectional.

As shown in Section 2, the two nodes n_1 and n_2 will be able to build a connection *iff* the received power P_r is larger than a required minimal reception power $P_{\mathrm{r, min}}$. Closer inspection of (4) suggests three basic cases:

Always out of Range d_{n_1,n_2} is so large that P_r is always smaller than $P_{\mathrm{r, min}}$ independent of the respective γ's. The critical distance is, with (6),

$$d_\mathrm{max} = d_\mathrm{r}\big|_{G(\gamma_{n_1})=G_\mathrm{M},\, G(\gamma_{n_2})=G_\mathrm{M}} . \tag{9}$$

Obviously, node pairs with $d_{n_1,n_2} > d_\mathrm{max}$ are not of interest for the optimization.

Always in Range   In case d_{n_1,n_2} is so small that P_r is sufficient independently of the actual antenna configuration, i.e., smaller than

$$d_\mathrm{min} = d_\mathrm{r}\big|_{G(\gamma_{n_1})=G_\mathrm{S},\, G(\gamma_{n_2})=G_\mathrm{S}} , \tag{10}$$

a link between n_1 and n_2 always exists, and all node pairs falling in this category can be safely ignored by the optimization routine.

In Range in Case of Proper Steering   However, if

$$d_\mathrm{min} \leq d_{n_1,n_2} \leq d_\mathrm{max} , \tag{11}$$

the existence of a link depends on the antenna configuration of n_1 and n_2.

According to Fig. 10.2, we can determine the angle $\beta_{n_1,n_2} \in [0, 2\pi[$ between $\{n_1, n_2\} \subset \mathcal{N}$ via

$$\tan(\beta_{n_1,n_2}) = \frac{y_{n_2} - y_{n_1}}{x_{n_2} - x_{n_1}} . \tag{12}$$

For a given aperture α and an antenna orientation γ_{n_1}, $G(\gamma_{n_1})$ equals G_M (i.e., the signal is amplified by the high antenna gain) *iff*

- for $\frac{\alpha}{2} \leq \gamma_{n_1} \leq 2\pi - \frac{\alpha}{2}$:

$$\beta_{n_1,n_2} \leq \gamma_{n_1} + \frac{\alpha}{2} \quad \wedge \quad \beta_{n_1,n_2} \geq \gamma_{n_1} - \frac{\alpha}{2}, \tag{13a}$$

- for $2\pi - \frac{\alpha}{2} \leq \gamma_{n_1} \leq 2\pi$:

$$\beta_{n_1,n_2} - \frac{\alpha}{2} \leq \gamma_{n_1} \leq 2\pi \quad \vee \quad \beta_{n_1,n_2} \geq \gamma_{n_1} - \frac{\alpha}{2} + 2\pi, \tag{13b}$$

- and for $0 \leq \gamma_{n_1} \leq \frac{\alpha}{2}$:

$$0 \leq \gamma_{n_1} \leq \beta_{n_1,n_2} + \frac{\alpha}{2} \quad \vee \quad \beta_{n_1,n_2} - \frac{\alpha}{2} - 2\pi \leq \gamma_{n_1} \leq 2\pi. \tag{13c}$$

In the following we will use variables with a range of $]-\infty \ldots 1] \subset \mathbb{R}$ repeatedly. In the context of these *indicator variables* a value of 1 will always be used to indicate that a constraint is fulfilled, a link is active, etc. Using an indicator variable $a'_{n_1,n_2} \in]-\infty \ldots 1] \subset \mathbb{R}$ we can reformulate the first inequality of (13a) as

$$a'_{n_1,n_2} \leq \gamma_{n_1} + \frac{\alpha}{2} - \beta_{n_1,n_2} + 1, \tag{14a}$$

where a'_{n_1,n_2} can be 1 *iff* the first part of (13a) is fulfilled. Furthermore, we can put a tighter bound on a'_{n_1,n_2}, because the right-hand side of (14a) can only be as small as $-2\pi + 1 + \frac{\alpha}{2}$ with positive-valued angles. Consequently, a $a'_{n_1,n_2} \in [-2\pi + \frac{\alpha}{2} + 1 \ldots 1]$ will be sufficient to keep (14a) feasible.
In order to be useable in the link-budget later on, we use a'_{n_1,n_2} to set a binary variable b'_{n_1,n_2} to 1 *iff* $a'_{n_1,n_2} \leq 0$ and 0 otherwise, which we achieve with the following constraint[1]:

$$\left(-2\pi + 1 + \frac{\alpha}{2}\right) \cdot b'_{n_1,n_2} - a'_{n_1,n_2} + 1 \leq 0. \tag{14b}$$

The second inequality of (13a) can be formulated in a similar manner using a second indicator variable $a''_{n_1,n_2} \in [-2\pi + \frac{\alpha}{2} + 1 \ldots 1] \subset \mathbb{R}$ and a binary variable b''_{n_1,n_2}:

$$a''_{n_1,n_2} \leq \beta_{n_1,n_2} - \gamma_{n_1} + \frac{\alpha}{2} + 1 \tag{14c}$$

$$\left(-2\pi + \frac{\alpha}{2} + 1\right) \cdot b''_{n_1,n_2} - a''_{n_1,n_2} + 1 \leq 0. \tag{14d}$$

iff both constraints are fulfilled for one node pair n_1, n_2, then b''_{n_1,n_2} and b'_{n_1,n_2} will be able to become 0, allowing $b_{n_1,n_2} \in [0; 1] \subset \mathbb{N}$ to become 1 in the following constraint

$$b_{n_1,n_2} \leq \frac{1}{2} \left(1 - b'_{n_1,n_2}\right) + \frac{1}{2} \left(1 - b''_{n_1,n_2}\right). \tag{15}$$

However, we still need to take care of those cases where β_{n_1,n_2} is in the range of $[2\pi - \frac{\alpha}{2}; 0]$ and $[0; \frac{\alpha}{2}]$, because of the $2\pi \to 0$ overflow as shown in

---

[1] Quite obviously this can all be performed in a single step, however we found this two-step formulation more accessible while not imposing a run-time penalty when solving this MIP with CPLEX

(13b) and (13c). Thus we use the following set of constraints in case $\beta_{n_1,n_2} \geq 2\pi - \frac{\alpha}{2}$ for an indicator variable $c'_{n_1,n_2} \in \left[-\beta_{n_1,n_2} + \frac{\alpha}{2} + 1 \ldots 1\right]$:

$$c'_{n_1,n_2} \leq \gamma_{n_1} - \left(\beta_{n_1,n_2} - \frac{\alpha}{2}\right) + 1 \tag{16a}$$

Again, a binary variable b'_{n_1,n_2} is generated by

$$\left(-\beta_{n_1,n_2} + \frac{\alpha}{2} + 1\right) \cdot b'_{n_1,n_2} - c'_{n_1,n_2} + 1 \leq 0. \tag{16b}$$

While the last constraint detects the obvious case where $\gamma_{n_1} \geq \beta_{n_1,n_2} - \frac{\alpha}{2}$ it is also possible that $\gamma_{n1} \leq \beta_{n_1,n_2} + \frac{\alpha}{2} - 2\pi$ which will be detected via c''_{n_1,n_2}:

$$c''_{n_1,n_2} \leq \left(\beta_{n_1,n_2} + \frac{\alpha}{2} - 2\pi\right) - \gamma_{n_1} + 1, \tag{16c}$$

and a binary variable will be analogously set according to fulfillment of the previous constraints in

$$\left(-4\pi + \beta_{n_1,n_2} + \frac{\alpha}{2}\right) \cdot b''_{n_1,n_2} - c''_{n_1,n_2} + 1 \leq 0. \tag{16d}$$

iff one of the two binary indicator variables $b'_{n_1,n_2}, b''_{n_1,n_2}$ is zero, the opposing node n_2 will be in the keyhole of the antenna, which we again indicate by

$$b_{n_1,n_2} \leq 1 - b'_{n_1,n_2} + 1 - b''_{n_1,n_2}. \tag{17}$$

The case where $\beta_{n_1,n_2} \leq \frac{\alpha}{2}$ (shown in (13c)) is formulated in a similar manner:

$$c'_{n_1,n_2} \leq \beta_{n_1,n_2} + \frac{\alpha}{2} - \gamma_{n_1} + 1 \tag{18a}$$

$$\left(-2\pi + \beta_{n_2}n_2 + \frac{\alpha}{2}\right) \cdot b'_{n_1,n_2} - c''_{n_1,n_2} + 1 \leq 0 \tag{18b}$$

$$c''_{n_1,n_2} \leq \gamma_{n_1} - \left(\beta_{n_1,n_2} - \frac{\alpha}{2} + 2\pi\right) + 1 \tag{18c}$$

$$\left(-\beta_{n_1,n_2} + \frac{\alpha}{2} - 2\pi + 1\right) \cdot b''_{n_1,n_2} - c''_{n_1,n_2} + 1 \leq 0 \tag{18d}$$

$$b_{n_1,n_2} \leq 1 - b'_{n_1,n_2} + 1 - b''_{n_1,n_2}. \tag{19}$$

At this point, we are able to formulate the conditioned link budget according to (4) as a linear constraint

$$\begin{aligned} 0 \leq &P_{\text{Tx}} + (1 - b_{n_1,n_2}) \cdot G_{\text{S}} + b_{n_1,n_2} \cdot G_{\text{M}} + \\ &+ (1 - b_{n_2,n_1}) \cdot G_{\text{S}} + b_{n_2,n_1} \cdot G_{\text{M}} \\ &- l_{n_1,n_2} \cdot P_{L,n_1,n_2} - P_{\text{r, min}} . \end{aligned} \tag{20}$$

All node pairs $\{n_1, n_2\} \subset \mathcal{N}$ can satisfy the above constraint by setting the binary link indicator variable l_{n_1,n_2} to zero. In order for a link to become active (e.g., $l_{n_1,n_2} = 1$) the link budget has to be sufficient. Maximizing the number of active links with

$$\max \sum_{\{n_1;n_2\} \subset \mathcal{N}} l_{n_1,n_2} \tag{21}$$

will now cause the MIP solver to try to set as many l_{n_1,n_2} to 1 as possible. This requires nodes that are not always in range to turn their beamforming direction such that b_{n_1,n_2} can be set to 1 (representing a node in the main lobe), thereby finding a configuration with as many links as theoretically possible.

3.1 Complete Formulation

Consequently for a given link-budget as in (4), a set of nodes $\mathcal{N}$, and corresponding (precomputed) sets of distances $d_{n_1,n_2} \in \mathbb{R}_0^+ \; \forall \{n_1; n_2\} \subset \mathcal{N}'$ and angles between nodes relative to the y-axis $\beta_{n_1,n_2} \in [0\ldots 2\pi] \; \forall \{n_1; n_2\} \subset \mathcal{N}'$ the complete mixed-integer program reads as follows:

$$\max \sum_{\{n_1;n_2\} \subset \mathcal{N}} l_{n_1,n_2} \tag{22}$$

subject to

- $\forall \{n_1; n_2\} \subset \mathcal{N} : \beta_{n_1,n_2} < \frac{\alpha}{2} \wedge d_{\min} < d_{n_1,n_2} \le d_{\max}$

$$c'_{n_1,n_2} \le \beta_{n_1,n_2} + \frac{\alpha}{2} - \gamma_{n_1} + 1 \tag{23a}$$

$$\left(-2\pi + \beta_{n_2 n_2} + \frac{\alpha}{2}\right) \cdot b'_{n_1,n_2} - c''_{n_1,n_2} + 1 \le 0 \tag{23b}$$

$$c''_{n_1,n_2} \le \gamma_{n_1} - \left(\beta_{n_1,n_2} - \frac{\alpha}{2} + 2\pi\right) + 1 \tag{23c}$$

$$\left(-\beta_{n_1,n_2} + \frac{\alpha}{2} - 2\pi + 1\right) \cdot b''_{n_1,n_2} - c''_{n_1,n_2} + 1 \le 0 \tag{23d}$$

$$b_{n_1,n_2} \le 1 - b'_{n_1,n_2} + 1 - b''_{n_1,n_2} \tag{23e}$$

with

$$c'_{n_1,n_2} \in \left[-2\pi + \beta_{n_2 n_2} + \frac{\alpha}{2} \ldots 1\right] \subset \mathbb{R},$$

$$c''_{n_1} n_2 \in \left[-\beta_{n_1,n_2} + \frac{\alpha}{2} - 2\pi + 1 \ldots 1\right],$$

$$b'_{n_1,n_2}, b''_{n_1,n_2}, b_{n_1,n_2} \in [0; 1] \subset \mathbb{N}$$

- $\forall \{n_1; n_2\} \subset \mathcal{N} : \frac{\alpha}{2} \le \beta_{n_1,n_2} \le 2\pi - \frac{\alpha}{2} \wedge d_{\min} < d_{n_1,n_2} \le d_{\max}$

$$a'_{n_1,n_2} \le \gamma_{n_1} + \frac{\alpha}{2} - \beta_{n_1,n_2} + 1 \tag{24a}$$

$$\left(-2\pi + 1 + \frac{\alpha}{2}\right) \cdot b'_{n_1,n_2} - a'_{n_1,n_2} + 1 \le 0 \tag{24b}$$

$$a''_{n_1,n_2} \le \beta_{n_1,n_2} - \gamma_{n_1} + \frac{\alpha}{2} + 1 \tag{24c}$$

$$\left(-2\pi + \frac{\alpha}{2} + 1\right) \cdot b''_{n_1,n_2} - a''_{n_1,n_2} + 1 \le 0 \tag{24d}$$

$$b_{n_1,n_2} \le \frac{1}{2}\left(1 - b'_{n_1,n_2}\right) + \frac{1}{2}\left(1 - b''_{n_1,n_2}\right) \tag{24e}$$

with

$$a'_{n_1,n_2} \in \left[-2\pi + \frac{\alpha}{2} + 1 \dots 1\right] \subset \mathbb{R},$$

$$a''_{n_1,n_2} \in \left[-2\pi + \frac{\alpha}{2} + 1 \dots 1\right] \subset \mathbb{R},$$

$$b'_{n_1,n_2}, b''_{n_1,n_2}, b_{n_1,n_2} \in [0; 1] \subset \mathbb{N}$$

- $\forall \{n_1; n_2\} \subset \mathcal{N} : 2\pi - \frac{\alpha}{2} < \beta_{n_1,n_2} \wedge d_{\min} < d_{n_1,n_2} \le d_{\max}$

$$c'_{n_1,n_2} \le \gamma_{n_1} - \left(\beta_{n_1,n_2} - \frac{\alpha}{2}\right) + 1 \tag{25a}$$

$$\left(-\beta_{n_1,n_2} + \frac{\alpha}{2} + 1\right) \cdot b'_{n_1,n_2} - c'_{n_1,n_2} + 1 \le 0 \tag{25b}$$

$$c''_{n_1,n_2} \le \left(\beta_{n_1,n_2} + \frac{\alpha}{2} - 2\pi\right) - \gamma_{n_1} + 1 \tag{25c}$$

$$\left(-4\pi + \beta_{n_1,n_2} + \frac{\alpha}{2}\right) \cdot b''_{n_1,n_2} - c''_{n_1,n_2} + 1 \le 0 \tag{25d}$$

$$b_{n_1,n_2} \le 1 - b'_{n_1,n_2} + 1 - b''_{n_1,n_2} \tag{25e}$$

with

$$c'_{n_1,n_2} \in \left[-\beta_{n_1,n_2} + \frac{\alpha}{2} + 1 \dots 1\right] \subset \mathbb{R},$$

$$c''_{n_1,n_2} \in \left[-4\pi + \beta_{n_1,n_2} + \frac{\alpha}{2} \dots 1\right] \subset \mathbb{R},$$

$$b'_{n_1,n_2}, b''_{n_1,n_2}, b_{n_1,n_2} \in [0; 1] \subset \mathbb{N}$$

- $\forall \{n_1; n_2\} \subset \mathcal{N} : d_{\min} < d_{n_1,n_2} \le d_{\max}$

$$\begin{aligned} 0 \le & P_{\text{Tx}} + (1 - b_{n_1,n_2}) \cdot G_{\text{S}} + b_{n_1,n_2} \cdot G_{\text{M}} + \\ & + (1 - b_{n_2,n_1}) \cdot G_{\text{S}} + b_{n_2,n_1} \cdot G_{\text{M}} \\ & - l_{n_1,n_2} \cdot P_{L,n_1,n_2} - P_{\text{r, min}} \cdot \end{aligned} \tag{26}$$

with

$$l_{n_1,n_2} [0; 1] \subset \mathbb{N} .$$

4. Distributed Algorithms for Multihop Networks

Optimizing beamforming parameters as described in the previous section is obviously infeasible in ad hoc networks. It would require a central entity with global knowledge about, e.g., the path loss values between all possible node pairs in the network. Furthermore it would require a means for distributing the result of the optimization process to all nodes in the network, such that the nodes can adjust their beam patterns appropriately. In an ad hoc context, we rather rely on distributed algorithms which adjust parameters based on local knowledge. To this end we devise a distributed algorithm named *Maximum Node Degree Beamforming* (MNDB): Each node initially chooses a random direction ϕ_0, uniformly distributed between 0 and 2π. The node now steers its beam, such that the chosen direction coincides with the center of the main lobe. Next, the node checks how many direct neighbors it has, i.e., to how many nodes it can establish a link with the current beam pattern. This is done by overhearing beacons that are periodically transmitted by all nodes in the network: If a node can decode a beacon received from another node, a link to that node can be established. Now the node changes its beam pattern by changing the steering direction from ϕ_0 to $\phi_1 = \phi_0 + \Delta\phi$, and again checks for the number of neighbors. The node repeats this process of changing the steering direction by a margin of $\Delta\phi$ and checking for the number of neighbors until the whole range between ϕ_0 and $\phi_0 + 2\pi$ has been sampled. This angular sampling is called beam sweeping, and $\Delta\phi$ is named the sweeping angle. Finally, the node chooses the steering direction for which the maximum number of neighbors among all sample directions was discovered. If there is a tie between several directions, it is resolved by choosing a random solution among the candidate directions.

This algorithm strives to maximize the node degree locally at each node. Simulative investigations (Vilzmann et al., 2006) could show that the described algorithm is practical for self-organized ad hoc networks, that it is able to improve connectivity in such networks, and that the solution converges after few iterations. Those investigations, however, did not reveal how far the solutions of the distributed algorithm deviate from the global optimum. In providing the required benchmarking results, the merit of the optimization model becomes obvious: It can help answering the question whether improved distributed algorithms are necessary, or whether approaches like MNDB are sufficient.

5.   Results and Discussion

We have investigated three different scenarios with $n \in \{30, 40, 50\}$ nodes randomly placed in the system area as described in Sec. 2. To each scenario we applied the optimization as well as the distributed MNDB algorithm with the beamforming parameters specified in Sec. 2. The sweeping angle for MNDB was chosen as $\Delta\phi = 15°$. The results are graphically represented in Figs. 10.3 to 10.5, where the lines indicate connected nodes. The beam patterns shown in the figures are not linear gains but rather represent the directive range of each node, assuming that the partner node would have an omnidirectional pattern. By this, we try to provide an intuitive illustration as possible, although beam-forming antennas on both communication ends do not allow for the notion of a coverage area.

Comparing the resulting connectivity graphs for optimization and for MNDB we realize that the specific beam directions and connections differ. How-ever, the overall impression of the graphs is similar in the sense that we have connected clusters of similar size in each scenario for optimization as well as for MNDB. Let us take a closer look at the 30 node case (Figs. 10.3(a) and 10.3(b)). We see a similar network partitioning in both cases. However, inspecting for instance the upper left node cluster, it is much better connected with optimal beamforming directions than with MNDB, resulting in higher node degrees. This showcases the limitation of the local and heuristic node de-gree maximization which MNDB performs: the limited information does not allow for the sort of cooperation between neighboring nodes which is neces-sary to establish the maximum number of links possible.

It is worth noting however, that the difference between MNDB and the MIP-based solution relative to the number of links is clearly smaller in the 40 node example (Figs. 10.4(b) and 10.4(a)) — due to the higher node density, the need for cooperation between nodes becomes less important to achieve a high connectivity.

In the 50 node scenario (Figs. 10.5(b) and 10.5(a)) only the MIP-based ap-proach is able to create connections between the two clusters, even though the gap to optimality is still huge.

Table 10.1 compares the sum of the node degrees for each scenario obtained with optimization and MNDB, respectively. In addition, it shows the upper bounds of the sum node degree. The upper bounds represent the residual op-timality gap. Running the optimization to completion would further improve the upper bound and/or the best solution, and it is clear that the optimum will lie in between the values given in Table 10.1 for the upper bound and the best solution, respectively.

The 30 and the 40 node scenario were solved to optimality in less than 2 minutes, the 50 node test sample was interrupted after 12 hours. Similarly to

Table 10.1. Sum of the node degrees for three sample multihop networks

Number of nodes	Optimization		Distributed MNDB
	Upper bound	Best solution	
30	65	65	51
40	113	113	99
50	339	205	178

the 30 node case, the best (known) solution was found relatively early in the optimization, indicating a need for stronger upper bounds which are part of on-going work.

The MIP formulation of Sec. 3 was implemented using CPLEX/Concert 9.0. Simulations were performed on an AMD Opteron 2218 workstation with 6 GByte RAM.

In all three scenarios we obtain better results in terms of the sum node degree in the network when we apply optimization. But most importantly we can state that the results obtained with the practical MNDB approach are relatively close to the optimized results, in particular for higher network sizes. This is despite the fact that MNDB is a fully distributed algorithm which can rely on local information only.

6. Conclusions

In this paper we presented a method to optimize the sum of the node degrees in a wireless multihop network, assuming beamforming antennas with a single-lobe characteristic. We studied three different network scenarios and compared to a distributed, self-organizing approach. The results show that the distributed approach yields node degrees close to the optimal solution when the node density is not too low.

In multihop networks, more important than the node degree, and even more important than connectivity of the entire network, is the probability that a communication path to a desired communication peer exists. Our current and future work therefore considers this problem and tries to optimize path probabilities. This problem is yet more advanced and computationally complex than the one presented in this paper, but can be treated with a similar methodology.

The presented work can also be extended to conclude which antenna characteristic would be particularly useful to increase the node degree and path probability in multihop networks. For instance, a smaller main lobe aperture allows for a higher directive gain, and it is yet unclear which configuration would perform best in a particular scenario.

Although we were able to solve the MIP for up to 40 nodes to optimality, the huge increase in running time when moving to the 50 node test-case (caused by the increase of possible links) has to be addressed by improving the formulation of our optimization problem. Finding suitable cuts causing a notable improvement in the running time however, has proven to be rather difficult and is thus still on-going work. Another approach to reduce the running time would be to start with a reduced number of possible links and iteratively adding improving links in a branch-and-price algorithm, but again, finding a suitable solution-strategy for the appearing pricing problem will be future work.

References

D. Bertsimas and J. N. Tsitsiklis (1997). *Introduction to Linear Optimization*. Athena Scientific Optimization and Computation Series. Athena Scientific, Cambridge, MA, USA, 1st edition.

Dantzig, George Bernard (1963). *Linear Programming and Extensions*. Princeton University Press, Princeton, NJ, USA.

Penrose, M. D. (1997). The longest edge of the random minimal spanning tree. *Annals of Applied Probability*, 15(2):145–164.

Penrose, M. D. (1999). On k-connectivity for a geometric random graph. *Random Structures and Algorithms*, 15(2):145–164.

Ramanathan, R. (2001). On the performance of ad hoc networks with beamforming antennas. In *Proc. ACM MobiHoc*, Long Beach, USA.

Rappaport, T. S. (2002). *Wireless Communications: Principles and Practice, Second Edition*. Prentice-Hall, Inc.

Vilzmann, R., Bettstetter, C., Medina, D., and Hartmann, C. (2005). Hop distances and flooding in wireless multihop networks with randomized beamforming. In *Proc. ACM Intern. Workshop on Modeling, Analysis, and Simulation of Wireless and Mobile Systems (MSWiM)*, Montreal, Canada.

Vilzmann, R., Widmer, J., Aad, I., and Hartmann, C. (2006). Low-complexity beamforming techniques for wireless multihop networks. In *Proc. IEEE Conf. on Sensor, Mesh and Ad Hoc Communications and Networks (SECON)*, Reston, USA.

Wattenhofer, R., Li, L., Bahl, P., and Wang, Y.-M. (2001). Distributed topology control for power efficient operation in multihop wireless ad hoc networks. In *Proc. IEEE Infocom*, volume 3, pages 1388–1397.

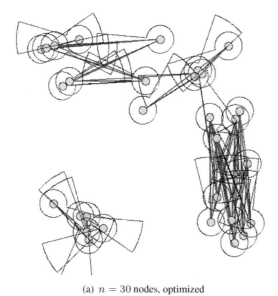

(a) $n = 30$ nodes, optimized

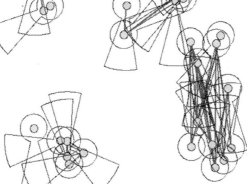

(b) $n = 30$ nodes, MNDB

Figure 10.3. Main lobe directions and resulting links

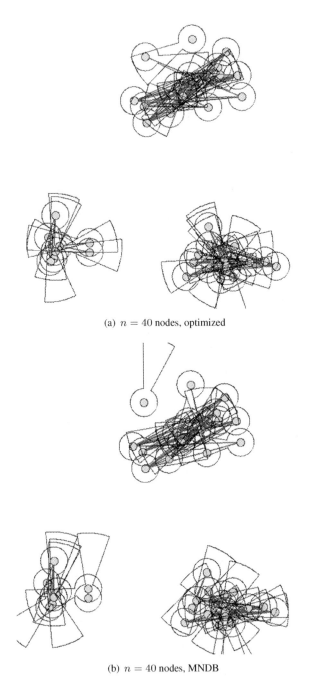

(a) $n = 40$ nodes, optimized

(b) $n = 40$ nodes, MNDB

Figure 10.4.   Main lobe directions and resulting links

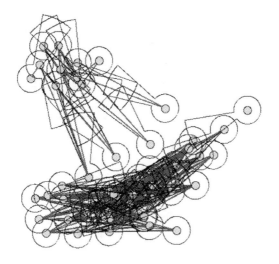

(a) $n = 50$ nodes, optimized

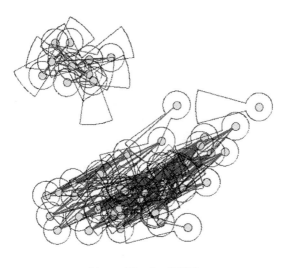

(b) $n = 50$ nodes, MNDB

Figure 10.5.   Main lobe directions and resulting links

Chapter 11

FLUID MODEL OF AN INTERNET ROUTER UNDER THE MIMD CONTROL SCHEME

Urtzi Ayesta
LAAS-CNRS, Toulouse, France
urtzi@laas.fr

Alexei B. Piunovskiy
Department of Mathematical Sciences, University of Liverpool, Liverpool, UK
piunov@liverpool.ac.uk

Y. Zhang
Department of Mathematical Sciences, University of Liverpool, Liverpool, UK
zy1985@liv.ac.uk

Abstract   We study the interaction between an MIMD (Multiplicative Increase Multiplicative Decrease) congestion control algorithm and a Drop Tail buffer. We consider the problem in the framework of deterministic hybrid models. We first show that the hybrid model of the interaction between the MIMD congestion control and bottleneck router always converges to a cyclic behavior that can be of only two different types. Second, we characterize the minimum buffer size required such that the bottleneck link is fully utilized. In particular, our analysis indicates that an MIMD algorithm requires smaller buffer sizes than AIMD in order to fully utilize the link capacity.

Keywords: Internet router; MIMD control; beamforming; fluid model.

1.   Introduction

Most traffic in the Internet is governed by TCP/IP (Transmission Control Protocol and Internet Protocol) [Allman et al 1999; Jacobson 1988]. Data packets of an Internet connection travel from a source node to a destination node via a series of routers. Some routers, particularly edge routers, experience periods of congestion when packets spend a non-negligible time waiting in the router buffers to be transmitted over the next hop. The TCP protocol tries to adjust the sending rate of a source to match the available bandwidth along the path. During the principle Congestion Avoidance phase, standard TCP uses an AIMD (Additive Increase Multiplicative Decrease) binary feedback congestion control scheme. In the absence of congestion signals from the network, TCP increases the congestion window linearly in time, and upon the reception of a congestion signal TCP reduces the congestion window by a multiplicative factor.

It has been shown that the AIMD algorithm underutilizes the resources in High-Speed networks [Floyd 2003]. Thus, in recent years researchers have proposed and studied different versions of congestion control for the Internet such as HS-TCP [Floyd 2003] and Scalable TCP [Kelly 2003]. These algorithms have in common that in the absence of congestion, the sources increase the congestion window in a much more aggressive fashion than does standard TCP. We note that Scalable TCP is a particular instance of an MIMD (Multiplicative Increase Multiplicative Decrease) congestion control algorithm, and thus, in the absence of congestion signals, the algorithm increases the congestion window exponentially.

On the other hand, most of the routers in the Internet are of Drop-Tail type. In basic Drop Tail routers, apart from the router capacity, the buffer size is the only parameter to tune. In fact, the buffer size is one of the few parameters of the TCP/IP network that can be managed by network operators. This makes the choice of the router buffer size a very important problem in the TCP/IP network design. This choice has recently received considerable attention [Appenzeller et al 2004; Avrachenkov et al 2002; Dhamdhere et al 2005; Gorinsky et al 2005; Vu-Brugier et al 2007; Avrachenkov et al 2005; Avrachenkov et al 2007]. All these works assume an AIMD congestion control protocol.

In this paper we study the interaction of MIMD congestion control algorithms with Drop-Tail buffers. We consider the problem in the framework of deterministic hybrid models. Dynamical systems that combine both discrete and continuous behavior are known as Hybrid Systems. Recently, hybrid models have been successfully applied to the modeling of communication networks [Hespanha et al 2001; Bohacek et al 2003]. We show that the hybrid model of the interaction between the MIMD congestion control and bottleneck router always converges to a cyclic behavior that can be of only two different types. Then we characterize the minimum buffer size required such that the bottleneck link is fully utilized. In particular, our analysis indicates that an MIMD algorithm requires smaller buffer sizes than AIMD in order not to waste resources.

The remainder of the paper is organized as follows. In Section 2 we develop the hybrid model. In Section 3 we present the main results. Section 4 contains sketches of the various proofs, and Section 5 contains some numerical experiments.

2.   Mathematical Model

Let n long-lived TCP connections share a bottlenecked Internet router with buffer size B and transmission capacity μ. Denote by $\lambda_i(t)$ the instantaneous sending rate of connection $i = 1, ..., n$ at time $t \in [0, \infty)$. We consider a fluid model. Namely, data is represented by a fluid that flows into the buffer with rate $\lambda(t) = \sum_{i=1}^{n} \lambda_i(t)$, and it leaves the buffer with constant rate μ, if there is a backlog in the buffer. Denote by $x(t)$ the amount of data in the buffer at time $t \in [0, \infty)$. Then, the evolution of x is described by the following differential equation

$$\dot{x}(t) = \begin{cases} \lambda(t) - \mu, & \text{if } x(t) > 0, \text{ or if } x(t) = 0 \text{ and } \lambda(t) > \mu, \\ 0, & \text{if } x(t) = 0 \text{ and } \lambda(t) \leq \mu. \end{cases} \tag{1}$$

If $x(t) < B$, the sending rate of connection i increases exponentially in time with rate r_i. We assume that $r_i \equiv r$. Thus, if $x(t) < B$,

$$\dot{\lambda}(t) = \sum_{i=1}^{n} \dot{\lambda}_i(t) = r\lambda(t). \tag{2}$$

When $x(t)$ reaches B, a congestion signal is sent to one or several TCP connections. Upon the reception of the congestion signal at time t, the TCP connection reduces its sending rate by a multiplicative factor $\beta_0 \in (0, 1)$, that is, $\lambda_i(t + 0) = \beta_0 \lambda_i(t - 0) = \beta_0 \lambda_i(t)$: we assume that all the functions are left-continuous. For example, in Scalable TCP, $r_i = 0.01/\text{'}\mathbf{RTT}\text{'}$ and $\beta_0 = 0.875$ [Kelly 2003], where '$\mathbf{RTT}$' denotes the round-trip-time of the corresponding TCP connection. We assume that the sending rates of connections at the congestion moment are distributed uniformly and that congestion signals are sent to $\{1, ..., \tilde{n}\} \subset \{1, ..., n\}$ connections. Then we have

$$\begin{aligned} \sum_{i=1}^{n} \lambda_i(t + 0) &= \sum_{i=1}^{\tilde{n}} \lambda_i(t + 0) + \sum_{i=\tilde{n}+1}^{n} \lambda_i(t + 0) \\ &= \beta_0 \sum_{i=1}^{\tilde{n}} \lambda_i(t - 0) + \sum_{i=\tilde{n}+1}^{n} \lambda_i(t - 0) \\ &= (\beta_0 - 1) \sum_{i=1}^{\tilde{n}} \lambda_i(t - 0) + \sum_{i=1}^{n} \lambda_i(t - 0) \end{aligned}$$

$$= \sum_{i=1}^{n} \lambda_i(t-0) \left((\beta_0 - 1) \frac{\sum_{i=1}^{\tilde{n}} \lambda_i(t-0)}{\sum_{i=1}^{n} \lambda_i(t-0)} + 1 \right)$$

$$\approx \sum_{i=1}^{n} \lambda_i(t-0) \left((\beta_0 - 1) \frac{\tilde{n}}{n} + 1 \right),$$

and the total sending rate is reduced on average by the factor

$$\beta = 1 - (1 - \beta_0) \frac{\tilde{n}}{n}. \tag{3}$$

Since in the fluid model all variables stand for average values, we can write that $\lambda(t + 0) = \beta\lambda(t - 0)$, where t is a moment of congestion. We call such moments 'jump moments' (of component λ).

Let us now formulate performance criteria. On one hand, we are interested in obtaining as large throughput as possible. That is, we are interested to maximize the average sending rate

$$\bar{\lambda} = \lim_{t\to\infty} \frac{1}{t} \int_0^t \lambda(s)ds.$$

On the other hand, we are interested to make the delay of data in the buffer as small as possible. That is, we are also interested in minimizing the average amount of data in the buffer

$$\bar{x} = \lim_{t\to\infty} \frac{1}{t} \int_0^t x(s)ds.$$

Clearly, these two objectives are contradictory, and the goal of the current research is to construct the Pareto set for this multicriteria problem. We accept that all the parameters of the system are fixed, and only the buffer size B is under control. Clearly, if B is big enough the average sending rate $\bar{\lambda}$ is close to μ, but in this case $\bar{x}$ can become too big. If we reduce the value of B, the average amount of data $\bar{x}$ decreases, but $\bar{\lambda}$ also decreases because the (small) buffer can be empty during long time intervals. Remind that Pareto set is the collection of all non-dominated solutions to a multiple-objective problem. Its graphical representation is known as a trade-off curve on the plane $(\bar{\lambda}, \bar{x})$.

For the sake of simplicity we put $r = 1$, $\mu = 1$. In the general case, one should make change of variables: $\tilde{t} = rt$, $\tilde{x} = (r/\mu)x$, $\tilde{\lambda} = \lambda/\mu$. Clearly, $\bar{\lambda}$ and $\bar{x}$ must be multiplied by μ and by μ/r respectively.

In what follows, we investigate the trajectories of dynamical system (1), (2) which turn to converge to (stable) cycles. Remember that $\lambda(t+0) = \beta\lambda(t-0)$, where t is such that $x(t - 0) = B$, $\lambda(t - 0) > 1$, and in principle there can be several instant jumps meaning that β above should be replaced by β^k.

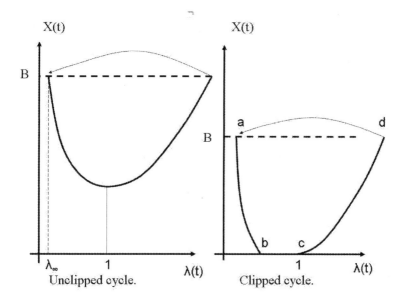

Figure 11.1. Possible cycles.

Definition 1 A trajectory of (1), (2) on a finite interval $t \in [0, T]$ is called a cycle if $x(0) = B$, $\lambda(0) < 1$, $x(T) = B$, $\lambda(T) \geq 1$ and $\lambda(0) = \beta^k \lambda(T)$, where $k \geq 1$ is such that $\beta^{k-1}\lambda(T) > 1$. A cycle is called simple if $k = 1$ and $\forall t \in (0, T)$ $x(t) < B$. (One cannot exclude in advance the situation when a cycle has several different loops resulting from the jumps of λ to several different points.) Cycles with component x being zero during a positive time interval are called clipped (Figure 11.1).

Actually, a cycle is a one period of the vector-valued periodic function $(x(t), \lambda(t))$, but it is better to represent it graphically as a phase portrait: $x(t)$ against $\lambda(t)$. For clipped cycles, $\bar{\lambda}$ and $\bar{x}$ both increase as B increases. The trade-off of $\bar{x}$ versus $\bar{\lambda}$ is described in Theorem 3.

As it will be shown in Theorem 2, only a simple cycle can exist which is clipped/unclipped depending on the values of parameters B and β.

If $x(0) = B$, $\lambda(0) = \lambda_\infty$ is the starting point of a cycle then obviously $x(kT + 0) = B$, $\lambda(kT + 0) = \lambda_\infty$ for all integer $k \geq 0$.

It will be also shown that for fixed values of B and β, only one (simple) cycle exists which is stable in the following sense. Suppose $x(0)$ and $\lambda(0)$ are arbitrary and let λ_i be the value of $\lambda(t)$ immediately after the i-th jump. Then $\lim_{i \to \infty} \lambda_i = \lambda_\infty$. To put it different, any trajectory converges to the cycle which will be sometimes called 'limiting cycle'.

3.   **Main Results**

Theorem 1 Let

$$B_0 \stackrel{\triangle}{=} \ln \frac{\beta - 1}{\beta \ln \beta} - \frac{\beta \ln \beta}{1 - \beta} - 1. \tag{4}$$

Then unclipped (clipped) cycle exists iff $B \geq B_0$ ($B < B_0$). The duration of the cycle equals $T = -\ln \beta$, for all $B \geq 0$.

B_0 denotes the minimal buffer size such that the queue is never empty, see Figure 11.1. Thus it is natural to call B_0 'critical' buffer size. In the desynchronized case, i.e. $\tilde{n} = 1$, from equation (3) we get $\beta = 1 - \frac{0.125}{n}$ for the case of Scalable TCP ($\beta_0 = 0.875$).

Remark 1 If $r \neq 1$, $\mu \neq 1$ then the 'critical' buffer size will become $\tilde{B}_0 = (\mu/r)B_0$.

Lemma 1 In the desynchronized case with $\beta = 1 - \frac{1}{2n}$, $\lim_{n \to \infty} n^2 B_0 = \frac{1}{32}$ meaning that B_0 decreases to zero as $\frac{1}{n^2}$.

Theorem 2 Let λ_k be the value of $\lambda(t)$ immediately after the k-th jump. Then, starting from any initial value λ_0, $\lim_{k \to \infty} \lambda_k = \lambda_\infty$.
    (a) If $B \geq B_0$ then $\lambda_\infty = \frac{-\beta \ln \beta}{1 - \beta}$.
    (b) If $B < B_0$ then $\lambda_\infty = \beta e^\theta$, where θ is the single non-negative solution to $e^\theta - 1 - \theta = B$. In this case $\lambda_2 = \lambda_3 = \ldots = \lambda_\infty$.
    (c) There exist only simple limiting cycles shown in figure 11.1, i.e. instant series of more than one jump are never realized, and all the values of $\lambda(t)$ immediately after a jump coincide with λ_∞ for the trajectory starting from $x_0 = B$, $\lambda_0 = \lambda_\infty$. The limiting cycle is stable.

Remark 2 The meaning of variables can be understood from Fig.11.1: θ is the time interval corresponding to part c-d, δ is the time interval corresponding to the part a-b.

Theorem 3 If $B \geq B_0$ then

$$\bar{\lambda} = 1; \quad \bar{x} = B + \frac{\ln \beta}{2} + \frac{\beta \ln \beta}{1 - \beta} + 1.$$

If $B < B_0$ then

$$\bar{\lambda} = \frac{e^\theta(\beta - 1)}{\ln \beta}; \quad \bar{x} = -\frac{\delta e^\theta(1 - \beta) - \frac{1}{2}(\delta + \theta)^2}{\ln \beta},$$

where θ is defined in Theorem 2 and δ is the minimal positive solution to $\beta e^\theta e^\delta - \beta e^\theta - \delta + B = 0$.

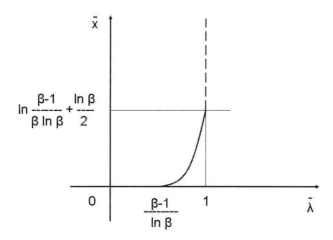

Figure 11.2. Tradeoff curve.

Corollary 1 Let $B < B_0$. Then θ, δ, $\bar\lambda$ and $\bar x$ monotonously increase with B. If B approaches zero then

$$\bar x \to 0; \quad \bar\lambda \to \frac{\beta - 1}{\ln \beta}.$$

If B approaches B_0 then

$$\bar x \to \ln \frac{\beta - 1}{\beta \ln \beta} + \frac{\ln \beta}{2}; \quad \bar\lambda \to 1.$$

Now it is clear that the Pareto set for objectives $(\bar x, \bar\lambda)$ is realized for $0 \leq B \leq B_0$: the minimal value of $\bar x$ equals zero and corresponds to $B = 0$; the maximal value of $\bar\lambda$ equals 1 and corresponds to $B = B_0$. If $B > B_0$ then $\bar x$ increases with B and $\bar\lambda = 1$ remains the same. Thus, solutions on the vertical dashed line (Fig.11.2), when $B > B_0$, are obviously dominated.

3.1 Comments on the Results

As the term "scalable" suggests, the cycle duration T for the MIMD scheme does not depend on the capacity of the link (see Theorem 1). We recall that the cycle duration for the AIMD scheme does depend on the link capacity [Avrachenkov et al 2005].

In the case of a general link capacity $\mu \neq 1$, from equation (4) and Remark 1 we see that the 'critical' buffer size (4) depends linearly on the value of μ. In contrast, the expression for B_0 in the AIMD case has the factor μ^2. This shows that MIMD not only scales well with the capacity of the link but that also requires smaller buffer size in high speed networks. In particular, for the Scalable TCP flavor, when there is only one connection ($n = 1$ $\beta = \beta_0 = 0.875$ and $r = 0.01/'\textbf{RTT}'$), from (4) and Remark 1 we get

$$\tilde{B}_0 = 0.22\mu \cdot '\textbf{RTT}'.$$

The most important rule-of-thumb for dimensioning buffers on the Internet suggests that the size of the queues should be equal to the bandwidth-delay product, that is, $\mu \cdot '\textbf{RTT}'$ [Villamizar and Song 1994]. Thus, the fluid model suggests that a single Scalable TCP connection requires a 78% smaller buffer than what the previous rule-of-thumb indicated. The simulation results of Section 4 suggest that in practice the value of $\tilde{B}_0$ could even be smaller.

The performance of several synchronized MIMD connections with the same '\textbf{RTT}' are equivalent to a single MIMD connection [Altman et al 2005]. If the MIMD connections are not synchronized, from Lemma 1 we know that B_0 decreases to zero as $1/n^2$. As in the AIMD congestion control scheme (see [Avrachenkov et al 2005]), the multiplexing of non-synchronized MIMD connections helps to reduce significantly the minimal required buffer space for the full utilization of the link capacity.

When $B \to 0$, from Corollary 1 we know that $\bar{\lambda} \to \mu(\beta - 1)/\ln(\beta)$. When $n = 1$ $\beta = \beta_0 = 0.875$, and we obtain that $\bar{\lambda} = 0.94\mu$, that is, with Scalable TCP, the minimal guaranteed link utilization will be equal to 94%.

4.   Simulation Results

We perform network simulations with the help of NS-2, the widely used open-source network simulator [Network Simulator]. We consider the following benchmark example of a TCP/IP network with a single bottleneck link. The topology may for instance represent an access network. The capacity of the bottleneck link is denoted by μ and its propagation delay is denoted by d. The capacities of N links leading to the bottleneck link are supposed to be large enough (or the load on each access link is small enough) so that they do not hinder the traffic. Each of these N links has a propagation delay d_i. We assume that in each access link there is one persistent TCP connection.

In the NS simulations we use the following values for the network parameters: bottleneck capacity is $\mu = 100$Mbps, bottleneck link propagation delay $d = 1$ms, the access link capacity and delay are 100Mbps and 1ms, respectively. The packet size is 500bytes. As examples of AIMD and MIMD congestion control schemes, we consider New Reno [Allman et al 1999] and Scalable TCP [Kelly 2003] flavors, respectively. The number of access links is equal to

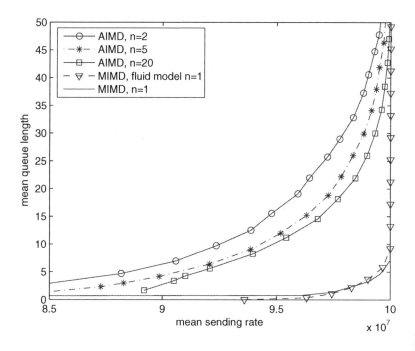

Figure 11.3. The trade-off curves for AIMD ($N = 2$, $N = 5$, $N = 20$) and MIMD $N = 1$.

the number of connections. The fact that the delays in the access links are the same implies that the TCP connections will be synchronized.

In Figure 11.3 we depict the Pareto set for the cases of AIMD with $N = 2$, $N = 5$ and $N = 20$ connections, and MIMD with just one connection. We recall that several symmetric synchronized MIMD connections are equivalent to a single MIMD connection. The qualitative shape of the curves agrees with what our model predicts (Figure 11.2). In particular, MIMD achieves the full link utilization with a much smaller buffer size than in the case of AIMD.

We also display the theoretical trade-off curve for the mathematical model with parameters $\beta = 0.875$, 'RTT'= 4 ms, $r = 0.01/$'RTT'= 2.5 ms^{-1}, $\mu = 10^8$ b/s. It turns to be close to the curve coming from simulations. Anyway, when comparing the results obtained from the analytical model and from simulations we have observed differences. For example, when the buffer size is zero, the simulated average sending rate is smaller than the one obtained with the fluid model. Similarly, in the simulated scenario the minimal buffer size that guarantees full utilization of the link is larger than the one the fluid model predicts. These differences can be explained by the fact that the aggregated traffic in the simulations is not as smooth as the fluid model that we have used.

5.   Conclusions

In this paper we have formulated the problem of choosing the buffer size of routers in the Internet as a multi-criteria optimization problem. A rigorous mathematical analysis of the interaction between the DropTail buffer and an MIMD congestion control algorithms have been provided. In agreement with previous works for AIMD congestion control, our model suggests that as the number of long-lived MIMD connections sharing the common link increases, the minimal buffer size required to achieve full link utilization reduces. Furthermore, our model suggests that MIMD congestion control scheme requires much less buffer space than AIMD. The Pareto set obtained with the help of our model could allow to dimension the IP router buffer size to accommodate real time traffic as well as data traffic.

Appendix: Sketch of the Proofs of the Main Statements

<u>Proof of Theorem 1.</u> Clearly, the first jump (or the first instant series of jumps) of the trajectory starting from $\lambda(0) = \lambda_0$, $x(0) = x_0$ results in the value $\lambda_1 \in [\beta, 1)$. Assuming the trajectory is not clipped and has no jumps on $[0, t]$, equations (1),(2) imply

$$\lambda(t) = \lambda_0 e^t, \quad x(t) = \lambda_0 e^t - t + x_0 - \lambda_0. \quad (11.A.1)$$

Equations $x_0 = x(T) = B$, $\beta\lambda(T) = \lambda_0$ result in formulae

$$T = \ln \frac{1}{\beta} \quad \text{(the duration of the cycle)} \; ; \quad \lambda_0 = \frac{-\beta \ln \beta}{1 - \beta}.$$

The minimal value x_{min} of trajectory (11.A.1) starting from $(\lambda_0 = \frac{-\beta \ln \beta}{1-\beta}, x_0 = B)$ corresponds to $t^* = \ln \frac{1-\beta}{-\beta \ln \beta}$. Therefore an unclipped cycle exists iff

$$x_{min} = x(t^*) = B - B_0 \geq 0.$$

In what follows, we use denotation $\lambda_\infty = \frac{-\beta \ln \beta}{1-\beta}$ since the initial value λ_0 may be arbitrary.

In case $B < B_0$, starting from $(\lambda_0 = 1, x_0 = 0)$, the trajectory reaches level $x(\theta) = B$ at moment θ satisfying equation $e^\theta - 1 - \theta = B$, and initial values $(\lambda_0 = \beta e^\theta, x_0 = B)$ generate the trajectory with $x_{min} < 0$ meaning that we have constructed the clipped cycle. Conversely, if the clipped cycle exists then the above reasoning must lead to $x_{min} < 0$ which is equivalent to $B < B_0$. Note that the duration of the cycle equals $T = -\ln \beta$ for any $B \geq 0$. ∎

<u>Proof of Lemma 1.</u>   Calculations   are   straightforward,   based   on   the L'Hopital's rule. ∎

<u>Proof of Theorem 2.</u> (a) Consider case $B \geq B_0$. For an arbitrary $\lambda_0 \in [\beta, 1)$ we define

$$\varphi(\lambda_0) = \beta\lambda_0 e^{T(\lambda_0)}, \quad (11.A.2)$$

where $T(\lambda_0)$ is the single positive solution to equation

$$F(\lambda_0, T) = \lambda_0 e^T - \lambda_0 - T = 0. \quad (11.A.3)$$

Here $T(\lambda_0)$ is the time interval up to the next jump assuming this part of trajectory is not clipped. This function $T(\lambda_0)$ is decreasing as well as $\varphi(\lambda_0)$. One can show that $T(\beta) <$

$-2 \ln \beta$. Indeed, function $F(\beta, \cdot)$ has a single minimum and the value $F(\beta, -2\ln\beta)$ is already positive. Therefore $\varphi(\beta) = \beta^2 e^{T(\beta)} < 1$ meaning that in fact $\varphi : [\beta, \varphi(\beta)] \to [\beta, \varphi(\beta)]$. Another important consequence: starting from λ_1, instant series of more than one jump are never realized. (See Item (c).)

In case the trajectory is clipped, component $x(t)$ reaches the value of B earlier, the new value $\lambda_2 \le \varphi(\lambda_1)$ and again $\lambda_2 \in [\beta, \varphi(\beta)]$. One can show that the trajectory starting from $(\lambda_2, x_0 = B)$ cannot be clipped.

Since φ is decreasing, the double iteration $\psi(\lambda_0) \overset{\triangle}{=} \varphi(\varphi(\lambda_0))$ is an increasing function meaning that the sequence $\lambda_2, \lambda_4, \lambda_6, \ldots$ is monotonous and hence converges to λ_∞ such that $\psi(\lambda_\infty) = \lambda_\infty$. We intend to prove that $\varphi(\lambda_\infty) = \lambda_\infty$. Suppose $\varphi(\lambda_\infty) = \lambda'_\infty \ne \lambda_\infty$ and let T_1 and T_2 be non-negative solutions to equations

$$\lambda_\infty e^{T_1} - \lambda_\infty - T_1 = 0, \quad \lambda'_\infty e^{T_2} - \lambda'_\infty - T_2 = 0. \tag{11.A.4}$$

We know that $\beta^2 \lambda_\infty e^{T_1+T_2} = \lambda_\infty$, hence $\beta = e^{-(T_1+T_2)/2}$. Since

$$\lambda'_\infty = \varphi(\lambda_\infty) = \beta \lambda_\infty e^{T_1} = \beta e^{T_1} \frac{T_1}{e^{T_1} - 1},$$

we have from (11.A.4): $\lambda'_\infty = \frac{T_2}{e^{T_2}-1} = \frac{\beta T_1 e^{T_1}}{e^{T_1}-1}$. Finally, using the formula for β we conclude that

$$\frac{T_1 e^{T_1/2}}{e^{T_1}-1} = \frac{T_2 e^{T_2/2}}{e^{T_2}-1}.$$

But function $g(\tau) = \frac{\tau e^{\tau/2}}{e^\tau - 1}$ is monotonous, hence $T_1 = T_2$ and $\lambda_\infty = \lambda'_\infty$.

Equation $\varphi(\lambda_\infty) = \lambda_\infty$ results in formulae

$$T = \ln\frac{1}{\beta} \quad \text{(the duration of the cycle)} ; \quad \lambda_\infty = \frac{-\beta \ln\beta}{1-\beta},$$

and no other unclipped cycle exists. Since

$$\frac{d\varphi}{d\lambda_0} = \frac{\beta e^T (T - e^T + 1)}{T e^T - e^T + 1},$$

where T is given by (11.A.3), we conclude that at the stable point

$$\left. \frac{d\varphi}{d\lambda_0} \right|_{\lambda_\infty} = \frac{\beta - 1 - \beta \ln\beta}{\beta - 1 - \ln\beta} > -1$$

meaning that $\left| \frac{d\varphi}{d\lambda_0} \right| < 1$ in the neighborhood of λ_∞, so that the limiting cycle is stable.

(b) If $B < B_0$ then, maximum after one jump (starting from λ_1), the trajectory is clipped, because otherwise we would have faced a sequence $\lambda_1, \lambda_2, \ldots$ resulting in unclipped trajectories and, according to (a), there would have existed an unclipped limiting cycle. Therefore, $\lambda_2 = \lambda_3 = \ldots = \lambda_\infty$, and the value $\lambda_\infty = \beta e^\theta$ follows from equation $x(\theta) = e^\theta - 1 - \theta = B$ describing the trajectory starting from $(\lambda_0 = 1, x_0 = 0)$.

(c) The last statement follows from the previous reasoning. ∎

<u>Proof of Theorem 3.</u> According to Theorems 1,2, the trajectories converge to a single cycle with initial values $(\lambda_0 = \lambda_\infty, x_0 = B)$. Hence

$$\bar{\lambda} = \frac{1}{T} \int_0^T \lambda(t)dt, \quad \bar{x} = \frac{1}{T} \int_0^T x(t)dt.$$

In case $B \ge B_0$, the further calculations are straightforward having in mind formulae (11.A.1) and $T = -\ln\beta$.

Case $B < B_0$. Here one has to calculate the integrals along branches a-b, b-c and c-d (Fig.11.1). Equation for δ comes from condition $x(\delta) = 0$ for trajectory starting from ($\lambda_0 = \lambda_\infty = \beta e^\theta$, $x_0 = B$). One can show that it has exactly two positive solutions. The further calculations are routine. ■

Proof of Corollary 1. The monotonicity of θ follows directly from its equation. δ is the first moment when coordinate $x(t)$ becomes zero. As B and $\lambda_\infty = \beta e^\theta$ increase, the value $x(t)$ at an arbitrary t corresponding to the part a-b (Fig.11.1) increases with B meaning that δ increases. The reasoning presented implies that the value of the integral $\int_0^T x(t)dt$ increases, and hence $\bar{x}$ increases. (Remember $T = -\ln\beta$ is constant.) The value of $\bar{\lambda}$ increases because θ increases. If $B \to 0$ then $\theta \to 0$ and $\delta \to 0$. If $B \to B_0$ then

$$\theta \to \ln\left(\frac{-\ln\beta}{1-\beta}\right); \quad \delta \to T - \theta = -\ln\beta - \ln\left(\frac{-\ln\beta}{1-\beta}\right) = -\ln\left(\frac{-\beta\ln\beta}{1-\beta}\right).$$

Calculations of the limits are straightforward. ■

References

M. Allman, V. Paxson and W. Stevens, TCP congestion control, *RFC 2581*, April 1999, available at http://www.ietf.org/rfc/[Allman et al 1999].txt.

E. Altman, K. Avrachenkov, and B. Prabhu, "Fairness in MIMD Congestion Control Algorithms", in Proceedings of IEEE Infocom, March, 2005.

G. Appenzeller, I. Keslassy and N. McKeown, "Sizing Router Buffers", ACM SIGCOMM '04, Portland, Oregon, September 2004. Also in Computer Communication Review, Vol. 34, No. 4, pp. 281-292, October 2004.

K. Avrachenkov, U. Ayesta, E. Altman, P. Nain, and C. Barakat, "The effect of router buffer size on the TCP performance", in the Proceedings of LONIIS workshop, St. Petersburg, Jan. 29 - Feb. 1, 2002.

K. Avrachenkov, U. Ayesta, A. Piunovskiy, "Optimal choice of the buffer size in the Internet Routers", in Proceedings of IEEE CDC-ECC 2005.

K. Avrachenkov, U. Ayesta and A. Piunovskiy, "Convergence and Optimal Buffer Sizing for Window Based AIMD Congestion Control", INRIA Research Report RR-6142, Available at: http://hal.inria.fr/inria-00136205.

S. Bohacek, J.P. Hespanha, J. Lee, and K. Obraczka, "A hybrid systems modeling framework for fast and accurate simulation of data communication networks", in Proceedings of ACM SIGMETRICS 2003, pp.58-69.

A. Dhamdhere, H. Jiang, and C. Dovrolis, "Buffer Sizing for Congested Internet Links", in the Proceedings of IEEE Infocom, Miami FL, March 2005.

S. Floyd, "HighSpeed TCP for Large Congestion Windows", *RFC 3649*, December 2003, available at http://www.ietf.org/rfc/rfc3649.txt.

S. Gorinsky, A. Kantawala, and J. Turner, "Link buffer sizing: a new look at the old problem", in Proceedings of IEEE Symposium on Computers and Communications (ISCC 2005), June 2005.

J.P. Hespanha, S. Bohacek, K. Obraczka, and J. Lee, "Hybrid modeling of TCP congestion control", In *Hybrid Systems: Computation and Control*, LNCS v.2034, pp.291-304, 2001.

V. Jacobson, Congestion avoidance and control, *ACM SIGCOMM'88*, August 1988.

T. Kelly, "Scalable TCP: Improving performance in highspeed wide area networks", *Computer Comm. Review*, v.33, no.2, pp.83-91, 2003.

"Network Simulator, Ver.2, (NS-2) Release 2.18a", Available at: http://www.isi.edu/nsnam/ns/index.html.

C. Villamizar and C. Song, "High Performance TCP in the ANSNET", *ACM SIGCOMM Computer Communication Review*, v.24, no.5, pp.45–60, November 1994.

G. Vu-Brugier, R.S. Stanojevic, J. Leith, and R.N. Shorten, "A critique of recently proposed buffer-sizing strategies", *ACM SIGCOMM Computer Communication Review*, v.37(1), pp.43-48, 2007.

Chapter 12

OPTIMAL SURVIVABLE ROUTING WITH A SMALL NUMBER OF HOPS

Luís Gouveia

CIO and Departamento de Estatística e Investigação Operacional
Faculdade de Ciências da Universidade de Lisboa
legouveia@fc.ul.pt

Pedro Patrício

CIO and Departamento de Matemática
da Universidade da Beira Interior
pedrofp@mat.ubi.pt

Amaro de Sousa

Instituto de Telecomunicações
Universidade de Aveiro
asou@av.it.pt

Abstract   Consider a given network defined by an undirected graph with a capacity value associated with each edge and a set of traffic commodities that must be routed through the network. Assume that the network contains at least D hop-constrained node disjoint routing paths between the origin and the destination nodes of each commodity. This paper addresses the minimum hop survivability routing problem, *i.e.*, the determination of the routing paths optimizing hop related objective functions applied to the Δ minimum hop routing paths of each commodity, where $1 \leq \Delta \leq D$. We propose ILP formulations addressing two objective functions: the minimization of the average number of hops and the minimization of the maximum number of hops. In both cases, the proposed models let us address two common survivability mechanisms: the case with $\Delta = D$ corresponds to the Path Diversity mechanism and the case with $\Delta = D - 1$ corresponds to the Path Protection mechanism. We present computational results using pre-dimensioned networks based on the NSF network for given estimated commodity demands. We study two traffic engineering issues: i) the relationship between the total commodity demand and the optimal values of the objective functions and ii) the impact of demand estimation errors on the feasibility of pre-dimensioned network design solutions. Concerning the efficiency of the proposed formulations, the results show that when $\Delta = D$ the proposed models are very efficient in all cases; the results also show that when $\Delta = D - 1$ the proposed models are efficient when the total commodity demand is as much as 97.5% of the network capacity and become harder to solve when total demand reaches the limit of the network capacity.

Keywords: Routing optimization; hop constraints; survivability.

1.   Introduction

The evolution of telecommunication services is introducing new requirements on the networks that must be efficiently dealt with by network operators. In this work, we consider two of these requirements. Let us consider a telecommunication network composed by a set of nodes and a set of point-to-point links connecting all nodes.

Concerning the first requirement, the network must efficiently support delay sensitive services like voice or video. A data packet traveling through a set of links from its origin to its destination suffers a total delay given by multiple factors: queuing and transmission on the interfaces and propagation on the links. Besides total delay, jitter (a measure of the delay variation) is also an important factor and the impact of queuing is usually dominant over transmission and propagation concerning both total delay and jitter (for example, propagation has no impact on jitter since each link introduces a constant delay on each packet). Therefore, it is desirable to route demand commodities on the smallest possible number of traversed links, which is equivalent to minimizing the number of hops of each routing path. We consider two optimization objectives: in the first case, the operator aims to minimize the average number of hops among all routing paths achieving the best global quality of service and, in the second case, the operator aims to minimize the maximum number of hops among all routing paths in order to guarantee the best quality of service for the worst case commodity.

Concerning the second requirement, the network must provide reliable services, *i.e.*, the network must provide multiple routing paths and include a survivability mechanism to deal efficiently with failure scenarios. In this work, we assume single node failures, *i.e.*, routing must consider the survivability when a single network node fails. We present Integer Linear Programming (ILP) formulations that let us address two common survivability mechanisms – Path Diversity and Path Protection – which differ in the way the operator wishes to protect total demand. Path Diversity is suitable to enhance demand protection but total protection is not required while Path Protection is preferred when protection of all demand is required.

In this paper, we consider a given network defined by an undirected graph $N = (X, U)$ with a capacity value b_e associated with each edge $e \in U$, a given set of commodities with origin/destination nodes $p, q \in S \subset X$ and a demand matrix $R = [r_{pq}]$ $(p, q \in S)$. We assume that N contains at least D hop-constrained node disjoint paths (more precisely, each path has H hops at most) for every commodity. The aim is to route all demands r_{pq} over the network N, under the survivability mechanism one wishes to consider, through D hop-constrained node disjoint paths for every commodity and complying with the installed capacity on each edge. An optimal routing is the one that minimizes either the average or the maximum number of hops of the Δ $(1 \leq \Delta \leq D)$ minimum hop routing paths between any pair of nodes $p, q \in S$ (as will be seen later, the $\Delta = D$ case corresponds to the Path Diversity mechanism and the $\Delta = D - 1$ case corresponds to the Path Protection mechanism).

We present ILP formulations based on a hop-indexed formulation that was previously explored in the context of network design problems with hop constraints and survivability requirements [1, 2]. As noted then, this formulation is suitable to model problems with hop constraints. Here, we further explore the hop-indexed formulation to derive appropriate ILP formulations to optimize the routing paths on a given network. The hop-indexed formulation uses loop variables associated with the destination node of each commodity that have relevant information for defining the objective functions that are addressed in this work.

The routing optimization of a given demand matrix on a given telecommunications network has been generically designated as traffic engineering. The proposed ILP formulations are used in pre-dimensioned MPLS networks computed in our previous work [1] and based on the NSF network for given estimated commodity demands. On that work, we have assumed that the MPLS links are implemented over an optical WDM network and this optical layer is responsible for link survivability. Therefore, for each MPLS commodity, the D paths can share common links when they do not contain intermediate nodes (more precisely, when the path connecting node pairs corresponds to a single link). We study two traffic engineering issues: i) the relationship between the total traffic demand and the optimal values of the objective functions and ii) the impact of traffic estimation errors on the feasibility of pre-dimensioned network design solutions. The computational results let us also study the efficiency of the proposed formulations.

There are very few references dealing with delay optimization and the reader is referred to [3, 6, 7, 9] for heuristic techniques dealing with delay related traffic engineering methods. Many other works deal mainly with optimization criteria related to the minimization of network link loads as a means to improve the capacity of the network to recover from failures. In our work, the survivability requirements are guaranteed by the solution and optimizing the routing hops becomes a more important objective. Survivability mechanisms were first proposed to optical networks. Besides the traditional $1 + 1$ dedicated protection or the $1 : n$ shared protection (one backup lightpath to protect n working lightpaths with the same end nodes), the recent Demand-wise Shared Protection mechanism [4] is an example of a more efficient mechanism that considers routing the lightpaths between the same end nodes through multiple paths, while guaranteeing that if a single path fails, there is a required percentage of lightpaths that do not fail. More recently, protection mechanisms have been proposed for modern packet switched networks [5, 8] which are straightforward adaptations of the optical $1 + 1$ dedicated and $1 : n$ shared mechanisms.

This paper is organized as follows. Section 2 describes the Path Diversity and Path Protection survivability mechanisms. Section 3 presents the hop-indexed formulation that models the constraints of our problem. In Section 4, we model the two addressed optimization criteria, accordingly, completing the description of the suitable formulations. Section 5 presents the computational results obtained with different testing instances based on the NSFNet network and, finally, some conclusions are drawn in Section 6.

2.   Survivability Mechanisms

In this work, we consider two types of survivability mechanisms – Path Diversity and Path Protection – both requiring the existence of D node disjoint paths between p and q, for all $p, q \in S$.

The Path Diversity mechanism is appropriate when total protection is not a requirement. The demand r_{pq} of each commodity is equally split by the D node disjoint paths, which ensures that $(D - 1)/D \times 100\%$ of the total demand is guaranteed if a single network element fails. When $D = 2$, each of both paths between p and q support half of the traffic r_{pq} and, thus, 50% of the total demand is protected. When $D = 3$, each path supports one third of r_{pq} and, so, 66% of the total demand is protected.

Path Protection is the preferred mechanism when total demand protection is needed, since it ensures that the D node disjoint paths between any pair of nodes $p, q \in S$ support a capacity such that if one path fails, the remaining ones accommodate the total demand. When $D = 2$, each path is able to support the total demand (this is equivalent to the traditional $1 + 1$ or $1 : 1$ protection). In this case, the best path (the one with fewer hops) is used as the service path and the other path is used as a protection (backup) path (it is used whenever the service path fails). When $D = 3$, each path is able to support half the demand. In this case, the two best paths (the ones with fewer hops) are used as service paths (the total demand is equally split by the two service paths) and the other path is used as a protection (backup) path. Path Protection can be seen as a particular case of the more general Demand-wise Shared Protection mechanism [4] applied to node-disjoint paths.

In both mechanisms, we assume that the demand r_{pq} of each commodity is equally split between different paths. This equally split rule can be assumed without any lack of generalization in modern packet switched networks since a commodity demand is, in practice, given by the aggregate of a large number of individual packet flows between customers connected to the origin node and costumers connected to the destination node. If reception of data packets out of order is not a problem, then, the demand packets can be routed through the different paths with a simple round-robin algorithm. If packets of each individual flow are required to be routed on a single path, due to the fine granularity of individual flows with respect to the total commodity demand, we can assume that the individual flows can be assigned on the capacity reserved for each path with a round-robin rule.

Note that the survivability mechanisms define the Δ minimum hop routing paths, among the D paths between p and q ($p, q \in S$), that will be subject to the optimization criteria considered in this paper. Under the Path Diversity mechanism, all D node disjoint paths support traffic between any pair of nodes $p, q \in S$, which implies that all paths are relevant with respect to the two optimization criteria. Therefore, in the Path Diversity case, we consider $\Delta = D$. Under the Path Protection mechanism, the backup paths support traffic only when a failure occurs and during the period until the failure is fixed. For this reason, we consider that the service paths are the ones relevant with respect to the two optimization criteria (note that a minimum quality of service is guaranteed by the model for the protection path since it ensures that all routing paths, the protection path included, have H hops at most). Thus, in the Path Protection case, we consider $\Delta = D - 1$.

3. Modeling the Constraints

In this section, we present a set of linear inequalities that model the constraints of our problem, that is, i) a traffic demand matrix R must be routed through D hop-constrained node disjoint paths, under either the Path Diversity or the Path Protection mechanism, ii) this routing must not exceed link capacities and iii) each path of each commodity must not exceed a maximum allowable number of hops, denoted by H.

In the following, we define a (p, q)-H-path as a path with at most H arcs (hops) and we define a path as a sequence $\{(i_1, j_1), ..., (i_k, j_k)\}$ of arcs such that $i_1 = p$, $j_k = q$ and $j_s = i_{s+1}$ for $s = 1, ..., k - 1$. Following [2], consider a single set of integer hop-indexed variables, w_{ij}^{hpq} ($e = \{i, j\} \in U; h =$

$1, ..., H; p, q \in S$), that represent the number of (p, q)-H-paths traversing edge $\{i, j\}$ in the direction from i to j, in the hth position. Note that some of the D (p, q)-H-paths may contain fewer than H arcs (that is, $w_{jq}^{hpq} \geq 1$ for some $j \in X \setminus \{q\}$ and $1 \leq h \leq H - 1$), hence, we also consider the so-called "loop" flow variables w_{qq}^{hpq} ($h = 2, ..., H$) to represent such situations. We may then model the constraints of our problem, as follows:

$$\sum_{j:\{p,j\}\in U} w_{pj}^{1pq} = D, \ p, q \in S \tag{1a}$$

$$w_{qq}^{2pq} - w_{pq}^{1pq} = 0, \ p, q \in S \tag{1b}$$

$$\sum_{j:\{i,j\}\in U} w_{ij}^{h+1,pq} - \sum_{j:\{i,j\}\in U} w_{ji}^{hpq} = 0,$$
$$i \neq p, q; h = 1, ..., H - 1; p, q \in S \tag{1c}$$

$$w_{qq}^{h+1,pq} - \sum_{j:\{j,q\}\in U} w_{jq}^{hpq} - w_{qq}^{hpq} = 0, \ h = 2, ..., H - 1; p, q \in S \tag{1d}$$

$$\sum_{j:\{j,q\}\in U} w_{jq}^{Hpq} = D, \ p, q \in S \tag{1e}$$

$$\sum_{i:\{i,j\}\in U} \sum_{h=1,...,H} w_{ij}^{hpq} \leq 1, \ j \in X \setminus \{p, q\}; p, q \in S \tag{2}$$

$$\sum_{p,q\in S} \beta r_{pq} \left(\sum_{h=1,...,H} w_{ij}^{hpq} + \sum_{h=1,...,H} w_{ji}^{hpq} \right) \leq b_e, \ e = \{i, j\} \in U \tag{3}$$

$$w_{ij}^{hpq}, w_{ji}^{hpq} \in \{0, 1, ..., D\}, \ e = \{i, j\} \in U; h = 1, ..., H; p, q \in S \tag{4a}$$

$$w_{qq}^{hpq} \in \{0, 1, ..., D\}, \ h = 2, ..., H; p, q \in S \tag{4b}$$

Constraints **(1a)**-**(1e)** (see [2]) are the typical constraints of a hop-indexed model. They guarantee that each commodity is supported by D paths, each of which with at most H hops. For all $p, q \in S$ the constraints guarantee that i) D units of flow emanate from node p in position 1; ii) if any node $i \neq p, q$ is reached through an edge traversed in position h, then an edge must be traversed from i in position $h + 1$, with $h = 1, ..., H - 1$; and iii) D units of flow reach node q, at most, in position H. As noted in [2], for all $p, q \in S$, each set of constraints **(1a)**-**(1e)** corresponds to a network flow model in an expanded layered graph. Thus, for each commodity, the extreme points of the feasible solution set of the linear relaxation of constraints **(1a)**-**(1e)** are integer valued.

Constraints **(2)** guarantee that the D paths supporting each commodity are node disjoint, since any node j (other than p or q) is visited by at most one of the D paths between p and q. Notice that in the presence of constraints **(2)** we could think of restricting the w_{ij}^{hpq} ($\{i,j\} \in U \setminus \{p,q\}$; $h = 1, ..., H$; $p, q \in S$) variables to binary values. However, since there may exist a direct link between p and q, we remark that the w_{pq}^{1pq} ($p, q \in S$) variables may assume integer values in $\{0, 1, ..., D\}$. Additionally, notice that the so-called "loop" flow variables may also assume integer values in $\{0, 1, ..., D\}$ since there may be up to D paths reaching node q with fewer than H hops. These loop variables will play a crucial role in defining the objective functions for the traffic engineering models discussed in Section 4 since they contain relevant information on the length of each path supporting each commodity.

To comply with the installed capacity (b_e) on each edge $e \in U$, we must consider constraints (**3**). They state that the total amount of traffic demand flowing through each edge is properly accommodated. These constraints, together with (**2**), account for the degree of survivability that one wishes to guarantee since the β coefficient is used to model the two survivability mechanisms. Recall that under Path Diversity each demand is equally split by D paths, and under Path Protection if a path fails then the remaining $D - 1$ paths must accommodate total demand. Thus, for $D = 2$ we must consider $\beta = 1/2$ for Path Diversity and $\beta = 1$ for Path Protection. For $D = 3$, we must consider $\beta = 1/3$ for Path Diversity and $\beta = 1/2$ for Path Protection. Finally, constraints (**4a**) and (**4b**) are domain constraints.

4. Modeling the Objective Functions

For each commodity, we assume (as previously mentioned) that there are D node disjoint routing paths connecting p and q. Among these D paths we want to optimize a hop related criterion regarding the Δ minimum hop routing paths, $1 \leq \Delta \leq D$, that is, the Δ paths with least number of hops. Consider, then, the following two different objective functions: i) Minimize the average number of hops of the Δ minimum hop routing paths for all $p, q \in S$; ii) Minimize the maximum number of hops of the Δ minimum hop routing paths for all $p, q \in S$.

As mentioned before, the loop variables used in the hop-indexed model provide information on the length of the D paths associated with each commodity. In fact, each loop variable w_{qq}^{hpq} represents the number of paths (starting in p and ending in q) that have less than h hops. We will use these variables to derive appropriate objective functions and inequalities to add to (**1a**)-(**4b**) in order to obtain valid models for the two previously mentioned hop related minimization problems. In the following, we address separately the two different objective functions.

4.1   Minimization of the Average Number of Hops

We start by pointing out that minimizing the average number of hops of all the Δ minimum hop routing paths of every commodity is equivalent to minimizing the sum of the number of hops. Note that for each commodity, the condition $w_{qq}^{hpq} > \Delta$ implies that all the Δ minimum hop routing paths reach the destination q with less than h hops. On the contrary, the condition $w_{qq}^{hpq} \leq \Delta$ means that only the w_{qq}^{hpq} minimum hop routing paths reach the destination q with less than h hops. Let us consider the variables V^{hpq} defined as follows:

$$V^{hpq} = \begin{cases} 1, & \text{if } w_{qq}^{hpq} > \Delta \\ 0, & \text{if } w_{qq}^{hpq} \leq \Delta \end{cases}, \quad h = 2, ..., H; p, q \in S \quad \textbf{(A)}$$

We, first, note that by including the linking inequalities $V^{hpq} \leq w_{qq}^{hpq}$ $(p, q \in S; h = 2, ..., H)$ condition **(A)** is enforced and the new variables V^{hpq} have the required meaning. Then, for each commodity, the sum of the V^{hpq} variables for all possible h is inversely proportional to the sum of the number of hops of the Δ best paths among all D paths. Notice that according to **(A)** the value $\sum_{h=2,...,H} V^{hpq}$ increases if for some h the value w_{qq}^{hpq} also increases, which, in turn (by constraints **(1a)-(1e)**), means that one of the Δ best paths reaches node q with less than h hops. Therefore, an appropriate objective function for the average minimization criterion is given by the sum of V^{hpq} for all values of h and for all $p, q \in S$. These observations prove the validity of the Average Number of Hops Minimization (ANHM) model:

$$Max \sum_{p,q \in S} \sum_{h=2,...,H} V^{hpq}$$

subject to:

$$V^{hpq} \leq w_{qq}^{hpq}, \ p, q \in S; h = 2, ..., H$$

(1a)-(4b)

$$V^{hpq} \in \{0, 1, ..., \Delta\}, \ p, q \in S; h = 2, ..., H$$

Given an optimal solution of ANHM with an optimal value represented by $v(ANHM)$, its average number of hops can, then, be computed as follows. If we denote by n the total number of paths subject to the average number of hops minimization criterion, we have $n = m \times \Delta$, where $m = |S| \times (|S| - 1)/2$ is the total number of commodities. So, we determine the average number of hops (which is the real optimal value) by computing $[nH - v(ANHM)]/n$.

To illustrate the meaning of the new variables, Figure 12.1 depicts an exam-

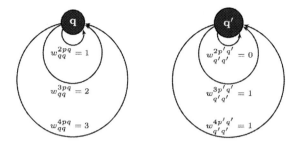

Figure 12.1. Example of two commodities, with destination nodes q and q', where the values of the loop flow variables are presented next to each arc

ple considering two commodities with destination nodes q and q', $H = 4$ and $D = 3$. The values of the loop flow variables are presented next to each arc.

Now, consider $\Delta = 2$. In this case, we want to minimize the average number of hops of the two minimum hop routing paths among the $D = 3$ paths of every commodity. According to **(A)**, we have for the first commodity: i) $V^{2pq} = w_{qq}^{2pq} = 1$, as only the best path reaches q with less than two hops; ii) $V^{3pq} = w_{qq}^{3pq} = 2$, since "only" the two minimum hop routing paths reach q with less than three hops; and iii) $V^{4pq} = \Delta = 2$, as all the two minimum hop routing paths reach q with less than four hops. Similarly, for the second commodity, we have $V^{2p'q'} = 0$, $V^{3p'q'} = 1$ and $V^{4p'q'} = 1$. Notice that these values for the V^{hpq} and $V^{hp'q'}$ variables are obtained considering the formulation presented above. Additionally, notice that $\sum_{h=2,3,4} V^{hpq} = 5$ and $\sum_{h=2,3,4} V^{hp'q'} = 2$ represent the number of loops performed by the two (Δ) minimum hop routing paths of each commodity at the respective destination nodes q and q'. If this is the optimal solution, then, the optimal value of the ANHM model is 7. In this case, $m = 2$, $\Delta = 2$, $H = 4$, and, therefore, $n = 4$. Computing $(4 \times 4 - 7)/4$, we may state that the average number of hops is 2.25.

We also remark that in the particular case of $\Delta = D$, the inequality $w_{qq}^{hpq} \leq \Delta$ is always true and then condition **(A)** is reduced to $V^{hpq} = w_{qq}^{hpq}$. Therefore, in this particular case, we can use this equality to eliminate the variables V^{hpq} of the ANHM model obtaining the intuitive objective function given by $Max \sum_{p,q \in S} \sum_{h=2,\dots,H} w_{qq}^{hpq}$.

4.2 Minimization of the Maximum Number of Hops

When considering the maximum number of hops minimization criterion, we are interested in optimizing only the worst path (that is, the path with most hops) among the Δ minimum hop routing paths of each commodity. For each commodity $p, q \in S$ the condition $w_{qq}^{hpq} \geq \Delta$ implies that all the Δ minimum hop routing paths reach the destination q with less than h hops – notice that the worst path among the Δ minimum hop routing paths is obviously included. In contrast, the condition $w_{qq}^{hpq} < \Delta$ means that only the w_{qq}^{hpq} minimum hop routing paths reach the destination q with less than h hops, which in turn means that the worst path of the Δ best paths reaches node q with h or more hops. Thus, let us consider the binary variables Y^{hpq} defined as follows:

$$Y^{hpq} = \begin{cases} 1, & \text{if } w_{qq}^{hpq} \geq \Delta \\ 0, & \text{if } w_{qq}^{hpq} < \Delta \end{cases}, \ h = 2, ..., H; p, q \in S \qquad \textbf{(B)}$$

The linking constraints $\Delta Y^{hpq} \leq w_{qq}^{hpq}$, $p, q \in S; h = 2, ..., H$, guarantee the condition stated in **(B)**. Observe that, for each commodity $p, q \in S$, the summation $\sum_{h=2,...,H} Y^{hpq}$ represents the number of loops at node q of the worst path. If our aim is to minimize the maximum number of hops of the Δ best paths for all $p, q \in S$, then an appropriate objective function is given by $Max \, Y$, where Y cannot be greater than each value $\sum_{h=2,...,H} Y^{hpq}$, for all $p, q \in S$. These observations prove the validity of the Maximum Number of Hops Minimization (MNHM) model:

$$Max \, Y$$

subject to:

$$\Delta Y^{hpq} \leq w_{qq}^{hpq}, \ p, q \in S; h = 2, ..., H$$

$$\sum_{h=2,...,H} Y^{hpq} \geq Y, \ p, q \in S$$

(1a)-(4b)

$$Y^{hpq} \in \{0, 1\}, \ p, q \in S; h = 2, ..., H$$

$$Y \geq 0 \text{ and integer}$$

Given an optimal solution of MNHM with an optimal value given by Y, its maximum number of hops (which is its real optimal value) is given by $H - Y$.

Again, for illustration purposes, consider the example pictured in Figure 12.1 and let $\Delta = 2$. In this case, we want to minimize the number of hops of the worst path among the two minimum hop routing paths of every commodity. According to **(B)**, we have for the first commodity: i) $Y^{2pq} = 0$, as $w_{qq}^{2pq} = 1 < \Delta$, that is, the worst path among the two minimum hop routing paths reaches q with two or more hops; ii) $Y^{3pq} = 1$, since $w_{qq}^{3pq} = 2 \geq \Delta$, which means that the worst path among the two minimum hop routing paths reaches q with less than three hops (precisely with two, taking into account i)); and iii), similarly to ii), $Y^{4pq} = 1$, since $w_{qq}^{4pq} = 2 \geq \Delta$. Analogously, for the second commodity, we have $Y^{2p'q'} = Y^{3p'q'} = Y^{4p'q'} = 0$. We remark that these values for the Y^{hpq} and $Y^{hp'q'}$ variables are obtained considering the MNHM model. Notice that $Y = 0$ since $\sum_{h=2,3,4} Y^{hpq} = 2$ and $\sum_{h=2,3,4} Y^{hp'q'} = 0$ (that is, the worst of the two (Δ) minimum hop routing paths of each commodity perform two and zero loops at q and q', respectively). If this is the optimal solution and since $H = 4$, then, the maximum number of hops is $H - Y = 4 - 0 = 4$.

5.   Computational Results

For our computational experiments, we assume that the graph representing the network contains at least D hop-constrained node disjoint routing paths between the end nodes of each commodity. In order to obtain valid testing instances, we have used the network design solutions determined in our previous work [1] obtained using the NSFNet network. In that work, we have determined a minimum cost MPLS over WDM network solution that guarantees D hop-constrained node disjoint routing paths with a maximum number of H hops for every routing path and enough installed capacity on every link to guarantee survivability through one of the survivability mechanism considered here. The input to that problem is a graph $G = (V, E)$ representing the WDM network, a set of MPLS edge nodes $S \subset V$ (the set $V \setminus S$ represents the set of candidate locations for additional MPLS nodes) and a given set of commodities with origin/destination nodes $p, q \in S$ with an associated demand matrix $T = [t_{pq}]$ ($p, q \in S$). The output is a set of MPLS nodes and the connections between them (routed through the underlying WDM network) with a capacity value given by the number of WDM lightpaths multiplied by the capacity of each lightpath. In this paper, this solution defines the graph $N = (X, U)$ and the capacity value b_e associated with each edge $e \in U$ of each testing instance.

In [1], we have also considered two main scenarios in the computational tests for the NSFNet network: $|S| = 6$ and $|S| = 8$. In all scenarios, we have considered a maximum number of hops $H = 4$ for both survivability mechanisms (Path Diversity and Path Protection). Within each main scenario and for all $p, q \in S$, four different demand matrices were generated with different average demands. The t_{pq} values of the demand matrices were randomly generated with uniform distributions in the intervals: $[0, 0.4]$, $[0, 0.6]$, $[0, 0.8]$ and $[0, 1.0]$ where the upper limit is normalized with respect to the capacity of a lightpath. In [1], we have shown that the case with $D > 3$ produces more expensive solutions for both Path Diversity and Path Protection survivable mechanisms.

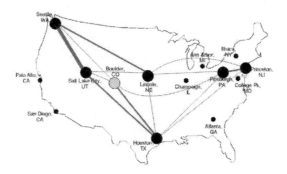

Figure 12.2. Example of a $N = (X, U)$ network. One of the NSFNet networks obtained in [1] with $|S| = 6$, $H = 4$ and $D = 3$. Black nodes represent traffic demand end nodes (that is, nodes in S) and the grey node is a node in $X \backslash S$. Edges in bold have a greater installed capacity

Therefore, in the computational results reported here, we have used the network design solutions obtained for $D = 2$ and $D = 3$. Figure 12.2 depicts one such solution, where $|S| = 6$ and $D = 3$.

Note that we can obtain a lower bound on the value of each objective function by ignoring the capacity constraints (3) on the corresponding models. This lower bound is only imposed by the topology of the network $N = (X, U)$ (therefore, we name it the "topological" lower bound) and gives the optimal solution value when the traffic demands are well below the ones for which the network was optimally designed.

We have conducted two sets of computational results. In the first set, we have considered that each new demand r_{pq} $(p, q \in S)$ ranges from 90 to 97.5% of the original demands in 2.5% steps. That is, $r_{pq} = (1-\delta)t_{pq}$ $(p, q \in S)$, with $\delta = 0.025, 0.05, 0.075$ and 0.1. The comparison of these optimal values with the corresponding topological lower bounds enables us to study the relationship between the total traffic demand and the optimal values of the objective functions. Moreover, we aim also to study the efficiency of the proposed models when the traffic demands are below the demands for which the network was dimensioned.

In the second set, we have generated each new demand r_{pq} $(p, q \in S)$ with a uniform distribution between $(1 - \epsilon)t_{pq}$ and $(1 + \epsilon)t_{pq}$, with $\epsilon = 0, 0.05, 0.1, 0.15$ and 0.2 (parameter ϵ represents the maximum relative error of the initial estimated demands t_{pq}). With these results we aim to study the impact of traffic estimation errors on the feasibility of pre-dimensioned network design solutions as well as the efficiency of the proposed models when the traffic demands are close to the limit of the network capacity. In the following subsections, we present separately each set of computational results.

All computational results were obtained using CPLEX 10.2 software-package with a maximum computational time set to two days. The results were obtained on an Intel Core 2 Duo at 2.0GHz with 512Mb of RAM. We remark that when constraints (3) are ignored, the resulting models were solved in all cases with a computational time under a second of CPU time and their optimal values are the topological lower bounds previously defined.

5.1 First Set of Computational Results

Tables 12.1 and 12.2 present the computational results of the testing instances with $|S| = 6$ under the Path Diversity and Path Protection mechanisms respectively, and, similarly, tables 12.3 and 12.4 contain the computational results obtained with $|S| = 8$. All tables contain two columns for each optimization model, either the ANHM or the MNHM model, one for $D = 2$ and another for $D = 3$. For each tested instance, all tables contain the values of the linear programming relaxation gap in percentage ("gap" value), the optimal solution CPU time in seconds ("CPU" value) and the associated penalty in percentage ("pen" value). The penalty is given by the difference between the optimal solution value of the instance and its topological lower bound divided by the topological lower bound. Both "gap" and "pen" values are based on the real values of the solutions (previously explained on Section 4).

Concerning the relationship between the total commodity demand and the optimal values of the objective functions, let us consider the penalty results. For the case where minimizing the maximum number of hops is the objective, the results exhibit a 0% penalty in almost all instances (there is only one case in table 12.3, corresponding to instances with traffic matrices higher than 92.5% where the topological lower bound is equal to 3 and the best maximum number of hops is equal to 4). These results show that the best maximum number of hops is almost always optimal and independent of the demand values. For the case where minimizing the average number of hops is the objective, the results show that as δ decreases (that is, when the traffic matrix R is closer to the original traffic matrix T), the penalty associated with each instance increases (*i.e.*, we have to route more commodities over longer paths to comply with the fixed capacities of each edge). However, the results show that the increase is 13.2% at most on all tested instances. The average penalty among all cases for $\delta = 0.1$ is 1.21% (independently of the survivability mechanism and the value D), which is still a rather small value. This indicates that routing up to 90% of the demand matrices T does not penalize significantly the optimal average number of hops given by the topological lower bound. Moreover, the average penalties for $\delta = 0.025$ (the matrices closer to the original traffic matrices T) are 3.60% for Path Diversity and $D = 2$, 4.90% for Path Diversity and $D = 3$, 0.93% for Path Protection and $D = 2$ and 1.89% for Path Protection

Table 12.1.   Results of tested instances with $|S| = 6$ under Path Diversity

demands	δ		Min Average		Min Maximum	
			$D = 2$	$D = 3$	$D = 2$	$D = 3$
$[0, 0.4]$	0.1	gap (CPU)	0.0% (< 1)	0.0% (< 1)	25.0% (< 1)	33.3% (< 1)
		pen	0.0%	0.0%	0.0%	0.0%
	0.075	gap (CPU)	0.0% (< 1)	0.0% (< 1)	25.0% (< 1)	33.3% (< 1)
		pen	0.0%	0.0%	0.0%	0.0%
	0.05	gap (CPU)	0.0% (< 1)	0.0% (< 1)	25.0% (< 1)	33.3% (< 1)
		pen	0.0%	0.0%	0.0%	0.0%
	0.025	gap (CPU)	0.0% (< 1)	0.0% (< 1)	25.0% (< 1)	33.3% (< 1)
		pen	0.0%	0.0%	0.0%	0.0%
$[0, 0.6]$	0.1	gap (CPU)	0.0% (< 1)	0.0% (< 1)	16.7% (< 1)	33.3% (< 1)
		pen	0.0%	0.0%	0.0%	0.0%
	0.075	gap (CPU)	0.0% (< 1)	1.2% (< 1)	16.7% (< 1)	33.3% (< 1)
		pen	0.0%	1.4%	0.0%	0.0%
	0.05	gap (CPU)	6.1% (< 1)	1.0% (< 1)	16.7% (< 1)	33.3% (< 1)
		pen	6.7%	1.4%	0.0%	0.0%
	0.025	gap (CPU)	7.0% (< 1)	0.8% (< 1)	16.7% (< 1)	33.3% (< 1)
		pen	8.9%	1.4%	0.0%	0.0%
$[0, 0.8]$	0.1	gap (CPU)	4.8% (< 1)	0.3% (< 1)	25.0% (< 1)	33.3% (< 1)
		pen	6.5%	1.4%	0.0%	0.0%
	0.075	gap (CPU)	4.1% (< 1)	2.7% (< 1)	25.0% (< 1)	33.3% (< 1)
		pen	6.5%	4.2%	0.0%	0.0%
	0.05	gap (CPU)	3.3% (< 1)	3.3% (< 1)	25.0% (< 1)	33.3% (< 1)
		pen	6.5%	5.6%	0.0%	0.0%
	0.025	gap (CPU)	4.5% (< 1)	6.4% (< 1)	25.0% (< 1)	33.3% (< 1)
		pen	8.7%	9.9%	0.0%	0.0%
$[0, 1.0]$	0.1	gap (CPU)	0.0% (< 1)	4.8% (< 1)	0.0% (< 1)	11.0% (< 1)
		pen	0.0%	11.8%	0.0%	0.0%
	0.075	gap (CPU)	0.0% (< 1)	5.2% (< 1)	0.0% (< 1)	11.0% (< 1)
		pen	0.0%	13.2%	0.0%	0.0%
	0.05	gap (CPU)	0.0% (< 1)	4.5% (< 1)	0.0% (< 1)	11.0% (< 1)
		pen	0.0%	13.2%	0.0%	0.0%
	0.025	gap (CPU)	0.0% (< 1)	3.7% (< 1)	0.0% (< 1)	11.0% (< 1)
		pen	0.0%	13.2%	0.0%	0.0%

and $D = 3$. These results show that: i) Path Protection is less penalized with growing demand values than Path Diversity is (due to the fact that the protection paths of the Path Protection mechanism do not influence the objective function) and ii) a survivability mechanism based on more D disjoint paths is also less penalized.

Table 12.2. Results of tested instances with $|S| = 6$ under Path Protection

demands	δ		Min Average $D = 2$	$D = 3$	Min Maximum $D = 2$	$D = 3$
[0, 0.4]	0.1	gap (CPU)	0.0% (< 1)	0.0% (< 1)	0.0% (< 1)	16.7% (< 1)
		pen	0.0%	0.0%	0.0%	0.0%
	0.075	gap (CPU)	0.0% (< 1)	3.6% (< 1)	0.0% (< 1)	16.7% (< 1)
		pen	0.0%	4.4%	0.0%	0.0%
	0.05	gap (CPU)	0.0% (< 1)	2.9% (< 1)	0.0% (< 1)	16.7% (< 1)
		pen	0.0%	4.4%	0.0%	0.0%
	0.025	gap (CPU)	0.0% (< 1)	4.2% (< 1)	0.0% (< 1)	16.7% (< 1)
		pen	0.0%	6.7%	0.0%	0.0%
[0, 0.6]	0.1	gap (CPU)	0.0% (< 1)	0.0% (< 1)	0.0% (< 1)	16.7% (< 1)
		pen	0.0%	0.0%	0.0%	0.0%
	0.075	gap (CPU)	0.0% (< 1)	0.0% (< 1)	0.0% (< 1)	16.7% (< 1)
		pen	0.0%	0.0%	0.0%	0.0%
	0.05	gap (CPU)	0.0% (< 1)	0.0% (< 1)	0.0% (< 1)	16.7% (< 1)
		pen	0.0%	0.0%	0.0%	0.0%
	0.025	gap (CPU)	0.0% (< 1)	2.4% (< 1)	0.0% (< 1)	16.7% (< 1)
		pen	0.0%	2.4%	0.0%	0.0%
[0, 0.8]	0.1	gap (CPU)	0.0% (< 1)	0.0% (< 1)	0.0% (< 1)	16.7% (< 1)
		pen	0.0%	0.0%	0.0%	0.0%
	0.075	gap (CPU)	0.0% (< 1)	0.0% (< 1)	0.0% (< 1)	16.7% (< 1)
		pen	0.0%	0.0%	0.0%	0.0%
	0.05	gap (CPU)	0.0% (< 1)	0.0% (< 1)	0.0% (< 1)	16.7% (< 1)
		pen	0.0%	0.0%	0.0%	0.0%
	0.1	gap (CPU)	4.8% (< 1)	0.0% (< 1)	0.0% (< 1)	16.7% (< 1)
		pen	5.0%	0.0%	0.0%	0.0%
[0, 1.0]	0.1	gap (CPU)	0.0% (< 1)	2.0% (< 1)	0.0% (< 1)	16.7% (< 1)
		pen	0.0%	2.4%	0.0%	0.0%
	0.075	gap (CPU)	0.0% (< 1)	1.8% (< 1)	0.0% (< 1)	16.7% (< 1)
		pen	0.0%	2.4%	0.0%	0.0%
	0.05	gap (CPU)	0.0% (< 1)	1.7% (< 1)	0.0% (< 1)	16.7% (< 1)
		pen	0.0%	2.4%	0.0%	0.0%
	0.025	gap (CPU)	0.0% (< 1)	3.8% (< 1)	0.0% (< 1)	16.7% (< 1)
		pen	0.0%	4.9%	0.0%	0.0%

Concerning the efficiency of the proposed ANHM and MNHM models, we start by observing that the optimal solution CPU times are quite small for most of the cases. Note, however, that the CPU times of some of the bigger instances (with $|S| = 8$) and with Path Protection were up to a few hundreds of seconds. Under the Path Diversity survivability mechanism, the average

Table 12.3.   Results of tested instances with $|S| = 8$ under Path Diversity

demands	δ		Min Average		Min Maximum	
			$D = 2$	$D = 3$	$D = 2$	$D = 3$
[0, 0.4]	0.1	gap (CPU)	0.0% (< 1)	0.5% (< 1)	0.0% (< 1)	16.7% (< 1)
		pen	0.0%	0.6%	0.0%	0.0%
	0.075	gap (CPU)	0.0% (< 1)	0.3% (< 1)	0.0% (< 1)	16.7% (< 1)
		pen	0.0%	0.6%	0.0%	0.0%
	0.05	gap (CPU)	0.0% (< 1)	0.2% (< 1)	0.0% (< 1)	16.7% (< 1)
		pen	0.0%	0.6%	0.0%	0.0%
	0.025	gap (CPU)	0.0% (< 1)	0.0% (< 1)	0.0% (< 1)	16.7% (< 1)
		pen	0.0%	0.6%	0.0%	0.0%
[0, 0.6]	0.1	gap (CPU)	0.4% (< 1)	0.1% (< 1)	0.0% (< 1)	25.0% (< 1)
		pen	1.0%	0.6%	0.0%	0.0%
	0.075	gap (CPU)	0.3% (< 1)	0.6% (< 1)	25.0% (< 1)	25.0% (< 1)
		pen	1.0%	1.3%	33.3%	0.0%
	0.05	gap (CPU)	1.2% (< 1)	1.1% (< 1)	25.0% (< 1)	25.0% (< 1)
		pen	2.1%	1.9%	33.3%	0.0%
	0.025	gap (CPU)	2.0% (< 1)	2.7% (< 1)	25.0% (< 1)	25.0% (< 1)
		pen	3.1%	3.8%	33.3%	0.0%
[0, 0.8]	0.1	gap (CPU)	1.6% (< 1)	3.9% (< 1)	0.0% (< 1)	16.7% (< 1)
		pen	3.1%	4.7%	0.0%	0.0%
	0.075	gap (CPU)	1.3% (< 1)	3.7% (< 1)	0.0% (< 1)	16.7% (< 1)
		pen	3.1%	5.4%	0.0%	0.0%
	0.05	gap (CPU)	2.0% (< 1)	2.8% (< 1)	25.0% (21)	16.7% (< 1)
		pen	4.1%	6.0%	33.3%	0.0%
	0.025	gap (CPU)	3.4% (2)	1.9% (< 1)	25.0% (3)	16.7% (< 1)
		pen	6.1%	6.7%	33.3%	0.0%
[0, 1.0]	0.1	gap (CPU)	0.7% (< 1)	1.6% (< 1)	25.0% (< 1)	25.0% (< 1)
		pen	1.0%	2.1%	0.0%	0.0%
	0.075	gap (CPU)	1.6% (< 1)	1.9% (< 1)	25.0% (< 1)	25.0% (< 1)
		pen	2.0%	2.9%	0.0%	0.0%
	0.05	gap (CPU)	1.3% (< 1)	2.1% (< 1)	25.0% (< 1)	25.0% (< 1)
		pen	2.0%	3.6%	0.0%	0.0%
	0.025	gap (CPU)	1.0% (< 1)	1.7% (< 1)	25.0% (2)	25.0% (< 1)
		pen	2.0%	3.6%	0.0%	0.0%

linear programming gap of the average number of hops minimization case is 1.7%, and that of the maximum number of hops minimization case is 19.9%. Under the Path Protection mechanism, the average gaps are tighter (0.6% and 5.2%, respectively for the average and maximum number of hops minimization cases). Although ANHM has much smaller gaps than MNHM, the CPU

Table 12.4. Results of tested instances with $|S| = 8$ under Path Protection

demands	δ		Min Average		Min Maximum	
			$D = 2$	$D = 3$	$D = 2$	$D = 3$
$[0, 0.4]$	0.1	gap (CPU)	0.0% (< 1)	0.0% (< 1)	0.0% (< 1)	0.0% (< 1)
		pen	0.0%	0.0%	0.0%	0.0%
	0.075	gap (CPU)	0.0% (< 1)	0.0% (< 1)	0.0% (156)	0.0% (< 1)
		pen	0.0%	0.0%	0.0%	0.0%
	0.05	gap (CPU)	0.0% (< 1)	0.0% (3)	0.0% (400)	0.0% (< 1)
		pen	0.0%	0.0%	0.0%	0.0%
	0.025	gap (CPU)	0.0% (14)	0.0% (< 1)	0.0% (9)	0.0% (2)
		pen	0.0%	0.0%	0.0%	0.0%
$[0, 0.6]$	0.1	gap (CPU)	0.0% (< 1)	0.7% (< 1)	0.0% (< 1)	0.0% (< 1)
		pen	0.0%	1.1%	0.0%	0.0%
	0.075	gap (CPU)	0.0% (< 1)	0.6% (< 1)	0.0% (97)	0.0% (< 1)
		pen	0.0%	1.1%	0.0%	0.0%
	0.05	gap (CPU)	0.0% (< 1)	0.5% (< 1)	0.0% (66)	0.0% (4)
		pen	0.0%	1.1%	0.0%	0.0%
	0.025	gap (CPU)	0.0% (28)	0.4% (1)	0.0% (59)	0.0% (175)
		pen	0.0%	1.1%	0.0%	0.0%
$[0, 0.8]$	0.1	gap (CPU)	0.0% (< 1)	0.0% (< 1)	0.0% (< 1)	0.0% (11)
		pen	0.0%	0.0%	0.0%	0.0%
	0.075	gap (CPU)	0.0% (< 1)	0.0% (68)	0.0% (5)	0.0% (246)
		pen	0.0%	0.0%	0.0%	0.0%
	0.05	gap (CPU)	0.0% (91)	0.0% (3)	0.0% (6)	0.0% (1)
		pen	0.0%	0.0%	0.0%	0.0%
	0.025	gap (CPU)	0.0% (3)	0.0% (8)	0.0% (< 1)	0.0% (2414)
		pen	0.0%	0.0%	0.0%	0.0%
$[0, 1.0]$	0.1	gap (CPU)	1.6% (< 1)	0.0% (< 1)	0.0% (< 1)	16.7% (< 1)
		pen	2.4%	0.0%	0.0%	0.0%
	0.075	gap (CPU)	1.5% (2)	0.0% (< 1)	0.0% (< 1)	16.7% (< 1)
		pen	2.4%	0.0%	0.0%	0.0%
	0.05	gap (CPU)	1.4% (< 1)	0.0% (2)	0.0% (< 1)	16.7% (3)
		pen	2.4%	0.0%	0.0%	0.0%
	0.025	gap (CPU)	1.3% (38)	0.0% (39)	0.0% (4)	16.7% (55)
		pen	2.4%	0.0%	0.0%	0.0%

times are similar, which means that they exhibit similar efficiency. It is interesting to point out that although the linear programming gaps are smaller for the Path Protection instances, these are more difficult to solve (that is, the CPU times to solve the integer model are bigger). One possible explanation for this is that under the Path Diversity mechanism ($\Delta = D$) all paths are relevant with respect to the optimization criteria while under the Path Protection mechanism ($\Delta = D-1$) only the service paths are relevant with respect to the optimization criteria and in the proposed models for Path Protection, the w_{ij}^{hpq} path variables do not make any distinction between service and protection paths.

5.2   Second Set of Computational Results

Tables 12.5 and 12.6 present the computational results of the testing instances with $|S| = 6$ and $|S| = 8$, respectively, under the Path Diversity and Path Protection mechanisms. In both tables the meaning of each line is similar to the previous tables: each column contains the linear programming relaxation gap value (in percentage) and, between parentheses, the CPU time (in seconds). In table 12.6, some of the gap values are indicated with a "*" for those instances where CPLEX was not able to provide an upper bound on their optimal value within two days of CPU time.

Concerning the impact of traffic estimation errors on the feasibility of predimensioned network design solutions, the results show diverse results. There are cases when the network design solutions become infeasible for a maximum error of 5% ($\epsilon = 0.05$) but there are also a few cases that are still feasible with maximum errors of 20% ($\epsilon = 0.2$). In table 12.7, we present the number of feasible instances for each survivability mechanism and each value of ϵ and D (for $\epsilon = 0$, all cases are feasible since they correspond to the original traffic matrices for which the networks were designed). From this table, it is possible to see that for small values of ϵ there are much more feasible solutions when the Path Diversity mechanism is considered (irrespective to the number D of paths) and when $D = 3$ paths are considered (irrespective to the survivability mechanism). Therefore, we can conclude that these cases are less sensitive to estimation errors. For larger values of ϵ the number of feasible instances is very small and this does not allow us to make any relevant conclusion.

Concerning the efficiency of the ANHM and MNHM models, the results are similar to the ones reported for the first set of results: i) similar efficiency between them, ii) both models are efficient in solving all Path Diversity tested instances and iii) bigger instances (with $|S| = 8$) with Path Protection are, in general, hard to solve by both models. In these cases, though, the difficult cases have rather huge CPU times and some could not be solved within two days. Concerning the Path Diversity mechanism, the results show that we have obtained average linear programming gaps of 3.4% and 21.1%, respectively for the average and the maximum number of hops minimization cases. Under the Path Protection mechanism, the average gaps are tighter (1.8% and 7.0%, respectively for the average and maximum number of hops minimization cases) but, as in the results of the previous section, these are the most difficult cases. Note that these average gaps are higher than the ones of the first set of results,

Table 12.5. Results for $|S| = 6$ under Path Diversity (PD) and Path Protection (PP)

demands	ϵ		Min Average		Min Maximum	
			$D = 2$	$D = 3$	$D = 2$	$D = 3$
	0.00		0.0% (< 1)	0.0% (< 1)	25.0% (< 1)	33.3% (< 1)
	0.05		0.0% (< 1)	0.0% (< 1)	25.0% (< 1)	33.3% (< 1)
[0, 0.4]	0.10	PD	0.0% (< 1)	0.0% (< 1)	25.0% (< 1)	33.3% (< 1)
	0.15		infeasible	0.0% (< 1)	infeasible	33.3% (< 1)
	0.20		infeasible	0.0% (< 1)	infeasible	33.3% (< 1)
	0.00		7.6% (< 1)	0.6% (< 1)	16.7% (< 1)	33.3% (< 1)
	0.05		infeasible	0.7% (< 1)	infeasible	33.3% (< 1)
[0, 0.6]	0.10	PD	11.3% (< 1)	0.2% (< 1)	16.7% (< 1)	33.3% (< 1)
	0.15		6.4% (< 1)	0.8% (< 1)	16.7% (< 1)	33.3% (< 1)
	0.20		infeasible	0.5% (< 1)	infeasible	33.3% (< 1)
	0.00		3.8% (< 1)	12.4% (< 1)	25.0% (< 1)	33.3% (< 1)
	0.05		infeasible	11.8% (< 1)	infeasible	33.3% (< 1)
[0, 0.8]	0.10	PD	infeasible	infeasible	infeasible	infeasible
	0.15		infeasible	infeasible	infeasible	infeasible
	0.20		infeasible	infeasible	infeasible	infeasible
	0.00		0.0% (< 1)	3.9% (< 1)	0.0% (< 1)	11.0% (< 1)
	0.05		0.0% (< 1)	3.3% (< 1)	0.0% (< 1)	11.0% (< 1)
[0, 1.0]	0.10	PD	0.0% (< 1)	infeasible	0.0% (< 1)	infeasible
	0.15		1.7% (< 1)	infeasible	0.0% (< 1)	infeasible
	0.20		9.7% (< 1)	infeasible	0.0% (< 1)	infeasible
	0.00		0.0% (< 1)	3.6% (< 1)	0.0% (< 1)	16.7% (< 1)
	0.05		infeasible	3.7% (< 1)	infeasible	16.7% (< 1)
[0, 0.4]	0.10	PP	infeasible	3.6% (< 1)	infeasible	16.7% (< 1)
	0.15		infeasible	infeasible	infeasible	infeasible
	0.20		infeasible	infeasible	infeasible	infeasible
	0.00		0.0% (< 1)	2.4% (< 1)	0.0% (< 1)	16.7% (< 1)
	0.05		0.0% (< 1)	2.4% (< 1)	0.0% (< 1)	16.7% (< 1)
[0, 0.6]	0.10	PP	0.0% (< 1)	infeasible	0.0% (< 1)	infeasible
	0.15		0.0% (< 1)	2.4% (< 1)	0.0% (< 1)	16.7% (< 1)
	0.20		infeasible	infeasible	infeasible	infeasible
	0.00		4.8% (< 1)	0.0% (< 1)	0.0% (< 1)	16.7% (< 1)
	0.05		infeasible	infeasible	infeasible	infeasible
[0, 0.8]	0.10	PP	infeasible	infeasible	infeasible	infeasible
	0.15		infeasible	infeasible	infeasible	infeasible
	0.20		infeasible	infeasible	infeasible	infeasible
	0.00		0.0% (< 1)	8.0% (< 1)	0.0% (< 1)	16.7% (< 1)
	0.05		infeasible	infeasible	infeasible	infeasible
[0, 1.0]	0.10	PP	infeasible	infeasible	infeasible	infeasible
	0.15		infeasible	infeasible	infeasible	infeasible
	0.20		infeasible	infeasible	infeasible	infeasible

Table 12.6.   Results for $|S| = 8$ under Path Diversity (PD) and Path Protection (PP)

demands	ϵ	Surv.	Min Average $D = 2$	$D = 3$	Min Maximum $D = 2$	$D = 3$
	0.00		0.0% (< 1)	2.7% (< 1)	0.0% (< 1)	16.7% (< 1)
	0.05		infeasible	2.7% (< 1)	infeasible	16.7% (< 1)
[0, 0.4]	0.10	PD	infeasible	infeasible	infeasible	infeasible
	0.15		infeasible	3.3% (< 1)	infeasible	16.7% (< 1)
	0.20		infeasible	infeasible	infeasible	infeasible
	0.00		5.6% (< 1)	4.4% (< 1)	25.0% (< 1)	25.0% (< 1)
	0.05		infeasible	infeasible	infeasible	infeasible
[0, 0.6]	0.10	PD	infeasible	infeasible	infeasible	infeasible
	0.15		infeasible	infeasible	infeasible	infeasible
	0.20		infeasible	infeasible	infeasible	infeasible
	0.00		5.5% (4)	2.9% (2)	25.0% (2)	16.7% (3)
	0.05		7.1% (5)	infeasible	25% (3)	infeasible
[0, 0.8]	0.10	PD	infeasible	infeasible	infeasible	infeasible
	0.15		infeasible	infeasible	infeasible	infeasible
	0.20		infeasible	infeasible	infeasible	infeasible
	0.00		4.1% (< 1)	3.8% (2)	25.0% (2)	25.0% (< 1)
	0.05		infeasible	4.8% (2)	infeasible	25.0% (< 1)
[0, 1.0]	0.10	PD	infeasible	infeasible	infeasible	infeasible
	0.15		infeasible	infeasible	infeasible	infeasible
	0.20		infeasible	infeasible	infeasible	infeasible
	0.00		4.4% (1258)	0.0% (5)	0.0% (38)	0.0% (3)
	0.05		infeasible	infeasible	infeasible	infeasible
[0, 0.4]	0.10	PP	infeasible	infeasible	infeasible	infeasible
	0.15		infeasible	infeasible	infeasible	infeasible
	0.20		infeasible	infeasible	infeasible	infeasible
	0.00		2.4% (6017)	0.3% (28)	33.3% (64363)	0.0% (50)
	0.05		infeasible	1.3% (2714)	infeasible	0.0% (22331)
[0, 0.6]	0.10	PP	infeasible	infeasible	infeasible	infeasible
	0.15		infeasible	infeasible	infeasible	infeasible
	0.20		infeasible	infeasible	infeasible	infeasible
	0.00		2.3% (77)	0.0% (15583)	0.0% (8)	0.0% (284)
	0.05		infeasible	0.0% (1587)	infeasible	0.0% (16487)
[0, 0.8]	0.10	PP	infeasible	0.0% (1373)	infeasible	* (2 days)
	0.15		infeasible	infeasible	infeasible	infeasible
	0.20		infeasible	infeasible	infeasible	infeasible
	0.00		3.5% (30)	1.1% (766)	0.0% (13)	16.7% (1487)
	0.05		infeasible	* (2 days)	infeasible	* (2 days)
[0, 1.0]	0.10	PP	infeasible	infeasible	infeasible	infeasible
	0.15		infeasible	infeasible	infeasible	infeasible
	0.20		infeasible	infeasible	infeasible	infeasible

Table 12.7. Number of feasible instances for each mechanism and each value of ϵ and D

ϵ	Min Average		Min Maximum	
	$D = 2$	$D = 3$	$D = 2$	$D = 3$
		Path Diversity		
0.05	3	5	3	5
0.10	3	2	3	2
0.15	2	2	2	2
0.20	1	1	1	1
		Path Protection		
0.05	1	4	1	4
0.10	1	2	1	1
0.15	1	1	1	1
0.20	0	0	0	0

which is the reason why CPU times are also higher.

As a concluding remark for both sets of results, first and second, we note that: i) when $\Delta = D$ (the Path Diversity case) the proposed models are very efficient in solving all the tested cases and ii) when $\Delta = D - 1$ (the Path Protection case) the proposed models are efficient when the total commodity demand is as much as 97.5% of the network capacity and become harder to solve when total demand reaches the limit of the network capacity.

6. Conclusions

In this paper, we have addressed the minimum hop survivability routing problem, *i.e.*, the problem of minimizing the (average or maximum) number of hops of the Δ minimum hop routing paths, among the D hop-constrained node disjoint paths supporting each commodity of a set of commodities (with $1 \leq \Delta \leq D$). For each optimization criterion, we propose a different Integer Linear Programming formulation that is able to address two common survivability mechanisms – Path Diversity and Path Protection. The models described in this paper – the ANHM and MNHM models – contain loop flow hop-indexed variables, which contain crucial information allowing us to model the problems addressed in this work. In our computational experience, we have considered different problem instances that are pre-dimensioned networks based on the NSFNet network, enabling us to characterize the efficiency of the proposed models. Future work includes trying to close the obtained gaps, especially those of the maximum number of hops minimization problems. The computational results show that under the Path Protection survivability mechanism the problems that minimize either the average or maximum number of hops are more difficult to solve. As future work, we will address this issue.

As a final remark, we have addressed network survivability for single network node failures since it is by far the most likely failure case. In this case, the Path Protection mechanism relies on a single backup path to protect demand when one of the service paths fails and this case is correctly modeled using $\Delta = D - 1$. If the operator requires demand protection for multiple failures, the Path Protection mechanism must rely on more than one backup path and this requirement can be easily accommodated in the proposed models using $\Delta < D - 1$ and with the appropriate values of β in constraints (**3**).

Acknowledgment.   The authors thank the referees for useful comments which have improved the paper.

References

[1] Gouveia, L. E.; Patrício, P.F.; de Sousa, A.F., *Hop-Constrained Node Survivable Network Design: an Application to MPLS over WDM*, to appear in NETS special issue on telecommunications, related to the INFORMS 2006 Telecom conference.

[2] Gouveia, L., Patrício, P.F., Sousa, A.F., *Compact models for hop-constrained node survivable network design* In Telecommunications Network Planning: Innovations in Pricing, Network Design and Management, ed. S. Raghavan and G. Anandaligam, Springer, 2006.

[3] Juttner, A., Szviatovski, B., Mecs, I., Rajko, Z., *Lagrange relaxation based method for the QoS routing problem*, Proceedings of INFOCOM 2001, Vol. 2, pp. 859-868, 2001.

[4] Koster, A., Zymolka A, Jager, M., and Hulsermann, R., *Demand-wise shared protection for meshed optical networks*, Journal of Network and Systems Management, Vol. 13, No. 1, pp. 35-55, 2005.

[5] Mannie, E., *Generalized Multi-Protocol Label Switching (GMPLS) Architecture*, RFC 3945, Internet Engineering Task Force, October 2004.

[6] Orda, A., *Routing with end to end QoS guarantees in broadband networks*, IEEE/ACM Transactions on Networking, Vol. 7, No. 3, pp. 365-374, 1999.

[7] Ramakrishnan, K. G., Rodrigues, M. A., *Optimal routing in shortest-path data networks*, Bell Labs Technical Journal, Vol. 6, No. 1, pp. 117-138, 2001.

[8] Sharma, V., Hellstrand, F., *Framework for Multi-Protocol Label Switching (MPLS) – based Recovery*, RFC 3469, Internet Engineering Task Force, February 2003.

[9] Yuan, X., *Heuristic Algorithms for multiconstrained quality-of-service routing*, IEEE/ACM Transactions on Networking, Vol. 10, No. 2, pp. 244-256, 2002.

Chapter 13

COMMUNICATION CONSTRAINTS AND AD HOC SCHEDULING

Steven Weber*

Dept. of ECE, Drexel University, Philadelphia PA 19104

sweber@ece.drexel.edu

Abstract   Communication constraints, in the context of scheduling in a wireless ad hoc (multi-hop) network, are a set of rules defining permissible concurrent transmissions. These rules may be imposed either by technological limitations of the transceiver, or by the operational mode of the network. This paper considers 24 distinct communication constraint sets (CCS) by comparing the average cardinality of a maximal schedule under each CCS using a greedy edge selection heuristic. The average cardinality as a function of the network size is studied via Monte Carlo simulation. The simulation results are useful for network and transceiver designers by identifying the sensitivity of scheduling performance to the CCS. In particular, the results illuminate that the performance gain obtainable by removing each constraint is highly dependent upon the overall CCS.

Keywords: Ad hoc networks; scheduling; communication constraints; combinatorial optimization.

1.   Introduction

Communication constraints, in the context of scheduling in a wireless ad hoc (multi-hop) network, are a set of rules defining permissible concurrent transmissions. These rules may be imposed either by technological limitations of the transceiver, or by the operational mode of the network. Several of these constraints are listed in Table 13.1. As shown there, none of the constraints is by nature fundamental. Although technologies exist to circumvent

*This work is supported under NSF grant #0635003 and by the DARPA IT-MANET program, grant W911NF-07-1-0028.

each of these constraints, they are overcome at a cost, possibly measured in terms of additional hardware requirements (and the associated higher monetary cost), processing time (*e.g.*, of complex algorithms), or performance (*e.g.*, reduced transmission rate). In practical network deployments these costs may be prohibitive, and the designers may elect to deploy networks that must operate subject to some of these constraints. Given the breadth of possible ad hoc network designs, it is not surprising that researchers have employed a wide variety of communication constraint sets (CCSs) in their mathematical models. A thorough review of the scheduling literature confirms that there has been no *systematic* study of the algorithmic and performance impacts of these models. The *algorithmic* impact of a CCS relates to the computational complexity of scheduling under that CCS, and the viability of distributed polynomial time approximation algorithms (for NP problems). The *performance* impact of a CCS relates to bounds on, say, the cardinality of an optimal schedule achievable under the CCS, and the performance improvement obtained by each constraint's removal. A systematic constraint impact study is a vital next step for next generation ad hoc transceiver and protocol design: it will illuminate fundamental design limitations and suggest areas for design improvement.

This paper is a first step towards a systematic study of the various CCSs. We restrict our attention to unidirectional point to point communication, leaving bidirectional and broadcast communication for future work. The ideal performance metric for this study is the Monte Carlo average cardinality of a *maximum* schedule under each CCS; unfortunately finding the maximum schedule is NP-Complete for many CCSs, and thus computationally infeasible for even small to moderate sized networks. Instead, our performance metric is the Monte Carlo average cardinality of a maximal[1] schedule under each CCS, using a greedy heuristic edge selection rule. In particular, the edges in the communication graph (indicating *potential* communication) are sorted from strongest to weakest (*i.e.*, shortest to longest), and an edge is added if the resulting schedule satisfies each constraint in the CCS. This heuristic is somewhat arbitrary (other greedy approaches may work as well or better), but is certainly a reasonable low complexity approximation of the maximum schedule. A further justification of the greedy heuristic is that practical low-complexity schedules in real networks are likely to employ greedy (distributed) heuristics to find (locally) maximal schedules, rather than seek optimal schedules.

The average cardinality of a maximal schedule is studied as a function of the network size. The simulation results identify the sensitivity of the schedule

---

[1] A schedule is maximum if its cardinality is at least as large as that of all other feasible schedules. A schedule is maximal if adding any additional transmissions will violate one or more of the constraints. Finding maximum schedules often requires searching over the entire space of possible schedules, while maximal schedules are easily found by greedy algorithms (like the sorting heuristic employed here).

Table 13.1. Description of, reasons for, and means to circumvent communication constraints.

Constraint	Description
Half-duplex	A node can not concurrently transmit and receive.
Single reception	A node can not concurrently receive from multiple transmitters.
Unicast	A node can not concurrently transmit distinct information to multiple receivers.
Exclusive node	A node can not concurrently communicate (tx or rx) with more than one node.
Interference	(Physical): A node can not receive if its SINR is below a specified threshold.
Interference	(Protocol): A node can not receive if there is any interfering transmission in its vicinity.

Constraint	Reason for constraint	To circumvent constraint
Half-duplex	Transceiver design	Full-duplex transceiver, multiple channels
Single reception	Receiver design	Multi-user detection
Unicast	Source/channel code design	Broadcast channel codes
Interference	Receiver design, lack of CSI, channel conditions	Interference cancelation, error correction, reduced data rates, spread spectrum

cardinality to each constraint by quantifying the performance improvement obtainable through each constraint's removal. This sensitivity analysis is of value to network protocol and transceiver designers who may accept the cost of removing a constraint if the performance sensitivity of a particular constraint in a CCS is high. Similarly, designers may elect to accept a particular constraint if the benefit of its removal is seen to be small.

The rest of this paper is structured as follows. Sec. 2 defines the three primary and two secondary constraints giving rise to the 24 CCSs. Sec. 3 presents the simulation results on the average schedule cardinality versus the network size. Sec. 4 discusses a portion of the large body of related work, and Sec. 5 offers a brief conclusion with an outline for future work.

2. Communication Constraints and Combinatorial Optimization

In this section we formally define the combinatorial optimization problems corresponding to each communication constraint set (CCS). Consider a wireless ad hoc network of N nodes located in an arena $\mathcal{A}$. The *scheduling problem* is to identify a compatible set of concurrent transmissions at each instant in time so as to optimize some performance objective. There are several reasonable choices for the performance objective, *e.g.*, maximize the number of concurrent transmissions at each time, minimize the time to empty the network, maximize the stability region, maximize the capacity region. Wireless networks significantly benefit from cross-layer design, and so scheduling is often jointly optimized along with the congestion control, power control, and routing algorithms. Moreover, there is a wide range of possible assumptions regarding the available network state information, *e.g.*, global (centralized) vs. local (decentralized), or fluid rates (static) vs. queue lengths (dynamic). Variations in the performance objectives, cross-layer designs, and available network state information notwithstanding, the common underlying problem is to maximize the number of concurrent transmissions subject to the governing CCS. The following discussion presents constraints for unidirectional point to point, bidirectional point to point, and broadcast communication, although our simulations are restricted to unidirectional point to point communication.

Communication graph. Assume for simplicity that each node employs unit transmission power. For *unidirectional* transmissions, the *communication graph* $G_c = (V_c, E_c)$ (with $|V_c| = N$) is directed (in general), and an edge from s to t indicates that s is capable of successfully transmitting to t *in the absence of interference*. For *bidirectional* transmissions the graph is undirected, and an edge between s and t indicates that s and t are capable of (alternately) transmitting to each other, again in the absence of interference. More specifically, define the noise power N-vector $\boldsymbol{\eta} = (\eta_t, t \in V)$, where $\eta_t \in \mathbb{R}^+$ is the noise power at vertex t, and define the $N \times N$ channel matrix $\mathbf{H}$ with entries $H_{st} \in \mathbb{R}^+$ giving the power attenuation factor of the channel from s to t at a particular instant in time. For a specified SNR constraint of β_c, a directed edge (s, t) is added if the SNR from s to t is acceptably high, $H_{st}/\eta_t > \beta_c$. An undirected edge requires in addition that $H_{ts}/\eta_s > \beta_c$. If channel attenuation is due strictly to pathloss, then all directed edges come in pairs, and the communication graph simply adds an edge between each pair of nodes separated by a distance less than some threshold.

Transmission vector. In the case of *point to point* transmissions, the scheduling problem requires identification of an optimal subset of *edges* from the communication graph, $E_S^* \subseteq E_c$ (S for schedule). The feasible set is in general exponentially large in N, *i.e.*, $E_S^* \in \mathcal{P}(E_c)$, the power set of E_c, where $|\mathcal{P}(E_c)| = 2^M$, for $M = |E_c| = O(N^2)$ the size of G_c. In the case of *broadcast* transmissions, the scheduling problem requires identification of an optimal subset of *nodes* from the communication graph, $V_S^* \subseteq V$, where $V_S^* \in \mathcal{P}(V)$ and $|\mathcal{P}(V)| = 2^{|N|}$ is also exponentially large in N. The *transmission vector* for a particular point to point schedule, say E_S, is a $\{0, 1\}$-valued M-vector, $\mathbf{x} = (x_1, \ldots, x_M)$, with elements $x_e = 1$ if edge $e \in E_S$. The transmission vector for a particular broadcast schedule, say V_S, is a $\{0, 1\}$-

valued N-vector, $\mathbf{y} = (y_1, \ldots, y_N)$ with elements $y_v = 1$ if vertex $v \in V_S$. The transmission vector is the *decision variable* of the scheduling combinatorial optimization problem.

Performance objective. As mentioned above, multiple performance objectives are possible; for simplicity we restrict our attention to the simple but natural linear weight objective. For *point to point* transmissions, the weight vector $\mathbf{a} = (a_1, \ldots, a_M)$ has elements $a_m \in \mathbb{R}^+$ denoting the relative value of activating each edge, and the scheduling objective is to maximize $\mathbf{a}^\mathsf{T}\mathbf{x}$. It is a significant assumption to assume, as we do here, that the a_e are independent of $\mathbf{x}$. This assumption holds if, say, $a_{(s,t)}$ is the SNR at t from s, but fails if, say, $a_{(s,t)}$ is the SINR at t from s, which depends upon $\mathbf{x}$. The maximum cardinality objective corresponds to $\mathbf{a} = \mathbf{1}$. For *broadcast* transmissions, the weight vector $\mathbf{b} = (b_1, \ldots, b_N)$ has elements $b_v \in \mathbb{R}^+$ denoting the relative value of activating each vertex, and the objective is to maximize $\mathbf{b}^\mathsf{T}\mathbf{y}$.

2.1 Communication Constraints

Each of the communication constraints is defined below; see Fig. 13.1. The constraints are presented in quadratic form ($\mathbf{x}^\mathsf{T}\mathbf{A}\mathbf{x} = 0$ for point to point communication, $\mathbf{y}^\mathsf{T}\mathbf{B}\mathbf{y} = 0$ for broadcast communication), but may be equivalently represented in linear form (say, $\tilde{\mathbf{A}}\mathbf{x} \leq 1, \tilde{\mathbf{B}}\mathbf{y} \leq 1$), often at the expense of larger matrices. All matrices below are $\{0, 1\}$-valued, granting the equivalence:

$$\mathbf{x}^\mathsf{T}\mathbf{A}\mathbf{x} = 0 \quad \Leftrightarrow \quad x_e A_{ef} x_f = 0, \ \forall\, e, f \in E_c^2,$$
$$\mathbf{y}^\mathsf{T}\mathbf{B}\mathbf{y} = 0 \quad \Leftrightarrow \quad y_u B_{uv} y_v = 0, \ \forall\, u, v \in V^2. \tag{1}$$

That is, the entries of $\mathbf{A}$ ($\mathbf{B}$) indicate incompatible pairs of edges (nodes), *i.e.*, $A_{ef} = 1$ ($B_{uv} = 1$) means edges e and f (nodes u and v) cannot be simultaneously active as they together violate one or more of the governing constraints. The mathematical formulation of the communication constraints allow us to express the point to point scheduling problem as a family of combinatorial optimization problems, shown below. The objective is to maximize $\mathbf{a}^\mathsf{T}\mathbf{x}$ over all possible transmission vectors $\mathbf{x} \in \{0, 1\}^M$, subject to any of the eight combinations of primary constraints, and possibly subject to either the physical or protocol interference constraint. There is an analogous family of optimization problems for broadcast communications.

maximize	$\mathbf{a}^\mathsf{T}\mathbf{x}$
over	$\mathbf{x} \in \{0,1\}^M$
subject to	
any subset of	$\mathbf{x}^\mathsf{T}\mathbf{A}^{\mathrm{HD}}\mathbf{x} \;=\; 0$
(primary constraints)	$\mathbf{x}^\mathsf{T}\mathbf{A}^{\mathrm{SR}}\mathbf{x} \;=\; 0$
	$\mathbf{x}^\mathsf{T}\mathbf{A}^{\mathrm{UC}}\mathbf{x} \;=\; 0$
and none or one of	$\mathbf{A}^{\mathrm{Iph}}\mathbf{x} \;\leq\; \mathbf{c}$
(secondary constraints)	$\mathbf{x}^\mathsf{T}\mathbf{A}^{\mathrm{Ipr}}\mathbf{x} \;=\; 0$

$$(2)$$

Primary communication constraints. There are three possible primary communication constraints.

Half-duplex: a node can not concurrently transmit and receive. Define the $M \times M$ symmetric matrix $\mathbf{A}^{\mathrm{HD}}$ with entries $A^{\mathrm{HD}}_{ef} = 1$ if $e = (u, v), f = (v, w)$ or $f = (u, v), e = (v, w)$, *i.e.*, e, f are head to tail. The constraint is $\mathbf{x}^\mathsf{T}\mathbf{A}^{\mathrm{HD}}\mathbf{x} = 0$.

Single reception: a node can not concurrently receive from multiple transmitters. Define the $M \times M$ symmetric matrix $\mathbf{A}^{\mathrm{SR}}$ with entries $A^{\mathrm{SR}}_{ef} = 1$ if $e = (u, v), f = (w, v)$, *i.e.*, e, f have a common head. The constraint is $\mathbf{x}^\mathsf{T}\mathbf{A}^{\mathrm{SR}}\mathbf{x} = 0$.

Unicast: a node can not concurrently transmit distinct information to multiple receivers. Define the $M \times M$ symmetric matrix $\mathbf{A}^{\mathrm{UC}}$ with $A^{\mathrm{UC}}_{ef} = 1$ if $e = (v, u), f = (v, w)$, *i.e.*, e, f have a common tail. The constraint is $\mathbf{x}^\mathsf{T}\mathbf{A}^{\mathrm{UC}}\mathbf{x} = 0$.

The following exclusive node model is equivalent to communication subject to all three of the above primary constraints.

Exclusive node: a node can not concurrently communicate (tx or rx) with more than one node. Although unidirectional point to point communication in general requires directed graphs (as for the three constraints above), the exclusive node constraint is modeled on an undirected graph (because "communicates with" is a symmetric relation). Define the $M \times M$ symmetric matrix $\mathbf{A}^{\mathrm{EN}}$ with entries $A^{\mathrm{EN}}_{ef} = 1$ if e, f are adjacent edges. The constraint is $\mathbf{x}^\mathsf{T}\mathbf{A}^{\mathrm{EN}}\mathbf{x} = 0$. Moreover, $\mathbf{A}^{\mathrm{EN}} = \mathbf{A}^{\mathrm{HD}} + \mathbf{A}^{\mathrm{SR}} + \mathbf{A}^{\mathrm{UC}}$; the EN constraint is equivalent to the above three constraints.

Secondary (interference) communication constraints. There are two possible secondary communication constraints. Whereas primary constraints have to do with "logical" requirements on concurrent transmissions, secondary constraints have to do with capturing the negative effect of interference on communication. In contrast with the primary constraints, at most one secondary constraint can hold. The selection of which secondary constraint (if any) is often decided based on the tractability of the corresponding mathematical model.

Interference (physical): a node can not receive if its signal to interference plus noise ratio (SINR) is below a specified threshold. A transmission set, modeled as a corresponding transmission vector $\mathbf{x}$, is *incompatible* with the interference constraint if the SINR at one or more receivers active under $\mathbf{x}$ is below β_c. That is, $\mathbf{x}$ is incompatible if and only if

$$\exists\, s, t : x_{(s,t)} = 1 \text{ and } \text{SINR}_t = \frac{H_{st}}{\sum_{u \neq s} \delta_u(\mathbf{x}) H_{ut} + \eta_t} < \beta_c, \qquad (3)$$

where $\delta_u(\mathbf{x}) = 1$ if u is a transmitter (to one or more receivers) under $\mathbf{x}$. A *minimally incompatible* transmission set (MITS) is such that no subset of the transmission set is incompatible, *i.e.*, removing any active edge makes the transmission set compatible. Let $\mathcal{I} = (I_1, \ldots, I_K)$ be the system of MITSs, where each $I_k \subseteq E_c$. Define the $K \times M$ matrix $\mathbf{A}^{\text{Iph}}$ with entries $A_{ke}^{\text{Iph}} = 1$ if $e \in I_k$. The physical interference constraint is $\mathbf{A}^{\text{Iph}}\mathbf{x} \leq \mathbf{c}$, where $\mathbf{c} = (c_1, \ldots, c_K)$ has entries $c_k = |I_k|$. In words, no MITS is fully activated under $\mathbf{x}$. The physical interference constraint may be generalized beyond the SINR requirement used here; a system of MITSs may be constructed under a different definition of compatibility. This is the only constraint not in quadratic form. All the other constraints identify *pairs* of incompatible nodes or edges, while the physical interference constraint identifies incompatible *sets*.

Interference (protocol): a node can not receive if there is any interfering transmission in its "vicinity", where an interfering transmitter for a receiver t is any node s whose interference to noise ratio (INR) at t is above a specified threshold β_i. Formally, define the *node-interference graph* $G_i = (V_i, E_i)$ with $|V_i| = N$ and edge set $E_i = \{(s, t) : H_{st}/\eta_t \geq \beta_i\}$. Define the symmetric $M \times M$ matrix $\mathbf{A}^{\text{Ipr}}$ with entries $A_{ef}^{\text{Ipr}} = 1$ if $e = (s, t) \in E_c, f = (u, v) \in E_c$, and either $g = (u, t)$ or $g = (s, v)$ is in E_i. That is, e, f interfere if the INR at either receiver from the interfering transmitter exceeds β_i. The constraint is $\mathbf{x}^\mathsf{T}\mathbf{A}^{\text{Ipr}}\mathbf{x} = 0$.

2.2 Combinatorial Optimization

Several of the optimization problems in (2) are classical problems in graph theory.

Maximum weighted matching (MWM). A matching is a set of edges not sharing a common vertex. Optimization for bidirectional point to point communication subject to the primary (exclusive node) constraint corresponds to the MWM problem. Adding the secondary protocol interference constraint yields the distance-2 MWM problem: no two active edges may be within distance 2 of each other. The distance-1 MWM problem may be solved in polynomial time.

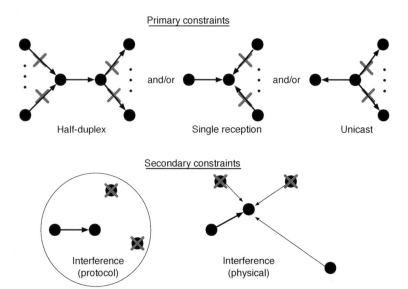

Figure 13.1. Pictorial representation of the communication constraints. **Top:** *the primary constraints are the half-duplex (HD), single reception (SR), and unicast (UC) constraints. In each case the* ✕ *identifies those edges that are incompatible with the edge shown.* **Bottom:** *the secondary constraints are the physical interference and protocol interference constraints. The protocol interference constraint requires no interferers within a certain area of an active receiver; the* ✕ *through the nodes indicates all edges emanating from those nodes are forbidden. The physical interference constraint requires the SINR computed at each active receiver exceed a specified threshold. The* ✕ *through the two transmitters means indicates all edges emanating from that node are forbidden. It is important to understand that the two nodes with the* ✕ *may be individually acceptable, but jointly unacceptable. This is captured through the use of the corresponding minimally incompatible transmission set (MITS).*

Degree constrained subgraph problem (DCSP). The DCSP is to find an optimal subgraph subject to constraints on the degree of each node in the subgraph. Optimization subject to either the single reception (in-degree at most one) or the unicast (out-degree at most one) constraint is a DCSP problem. DCSPs are solvable as MWMs.

Maximum weighted independent set (MWIS). An independent set is a set of vertices not sharing a common edge. Optimization for bidirectional broadcast subject to the primary constraint corresponds to the MWIS problem. Adding the protocol interference constraint yields the distance-2 MWIS problem: no two active nodes may be within distance 2 of each other. Maximization subject to the interference graph constraint corresponds to the MWIS problem on the edge-interference graph. Distance 1 and distance 2 MWIS problems are NP-Complete.

3.   Average Schedule Cardinality vs. Network Size

This section presents Monte Carlo[2] averages of the maximal schedule cardinality under the greedy edge selection heuristic as a function of the network size, N. Each of the 24 CCSs for unidirectional point to point communication is considered. There are 8 distinct combinations of the three primary constraints (HD, SR, UC), and for each combination there are 3 possibilities for the secondary constraint: none, physical, and protocol. Fig. 13.2 shows a sample realization for the 8 primary CCSs under the physical secondary constraint with $\beta_c = 0.2$ and $N = 50$. A close examination of the figures reveals the individual impact of each constraint on the schedule. For example, all head-to-tail arrow pairs in the Iph CCS (top left) are forbidden under the Iph+HD CCSS (top right).

All simulation results employ a square arena $\mathcal{A}$ of 100×100 square meters. A variable number N of nodes are placed uniformly at random in the arena. The communication graph $G_c = (V_c, E_c)$ is created using an SNR requirement of $\beta_c = 0.2$ for Fig. 13.2, and $\beta_c = 2$ for Figs. 13.3 and 13.4. The smaller $\beta_c = 0.2$ in Fig. 13.2 is to encourage more edges which more dramatically illustrates the impact of the various primary constraints, while the larger $\beta_c = 2$ is more realistic for narrowband communication. The noise power is a common constant $\eta_t = \eta = 8 \times 10^{-6}$ Watts. All channels are pure pathloss with an attenuation constant of $\alpha = 4$ and a distance decay of $H_{st}(d_{st}) = 1/(1 + d_{st}^\alpha)$; the more common $H_{st} = d_{st}^{-\alpha}$ has the drawback of a singularity at $d_{st} = 0$ meters. All simulation points are averages over 100 independent realizations of the network. The running time to compute the maximal schedule for a given topology on a desktop computer grows with N, but is at most a few seconds, even for $N = 100$.

Fig. 13.3 shows the growth in the average maximal schedule size versus the network size, N, for the three possible secondary constraints, where $\beta_c = 2$. The two bottom plots show results for the protocol interference constraint with $\beta_i = 4$ on the left and $\beta_i = 16$ on the right. The top left (no interference constraint) plot shows that the average maximal schedule cardinality is convex in N under either no constraints or under the HD constraint (at least for $N \le 100$). In contrast, the scaling is more or less linear in N under the other six primary CCSs. All eight primary CCSs show linear growth under the physical interference constraint (top right), and concave growth under the protocol interference constraint. The anomalous convex growth for the two cases under no interference constraint is because the number of edges in the communication graph $G_c = (V_c, E_c)$ satisfies $|E_c| = O(N^2)$ in this special case. A

---

[2] A Monte Carlo average is obtained by taking a performance average over a large number of independent realizations of the network.

secondary interference constraint, either physical or protocol, precludes "long" edges across the network. Similarly, in the no interference constraint case, the SR and UC constraints respectively limit the incoming and outgoing degree of any node to at most one.

Consider the two bottom protocol interference constraint plots in Fig. 13.3. First note that increasing β_i yields higher cardinality schedules. This is explained by recalling that under the protocol interference model an edge may be added provided there is no active transmission causing an INR above β_i at the proposed receiver. More interesting is to note that for both plots the differentiating factor is the presence or absence of the HD constraint. In particular, the top four curves are those where the HD constraint is binding, and the bottom four curves are those where the HD constraint is absent. Note that for large N the lower curve is almost exactly at half the height of the upper curve. This result is natural when one considers that the protocol constraint effectively enforces both a SR and UC constraint by excluding nearby interferers. As such the presence or absence of those constraints has little impact on performance. The takeaway for the network designer is that effort spent on removing primary constraints from transceivers is better spent on removing the HD constraint than on the SR, UC constraints.

Fig. 13.4 shows the same growth in N but with a distinct plot for each primary CCS, where the three curves correspond to the three possible secondary constraints, where $\beta_i = 16$. Fig. 13.4 illustrates that the performance under the physical and protocol constraints are roughly equivalent for $\beta_i = 16$ and $\beta_c = 2$, with the notable exception for the HD and (HD,SR) cases. In these two cases the growth is more or less linear under the physical constraint and concave under the protocol constraint. The figure also illustrates distinct performance gains are obtainable through relaxation of the secondary constraints depending upon the primary CCS. The top right HD plot shows that relaxation of a secondary constraint promises extensive performance improvement, whereas the bottom right (HD,SR,UC) plot shows that minimal performance improvement is obtainable by relaxation of the secondary constraint.

4.   Related Work

Scheduling in ad hoc networks has received extensive attention since the early 1980s. This section attempts to characterize the wide variety of models, algorithms, and results that have been obtained. Space limitations permit only the crudest summary. An extensive review of the scheduling literature confirms that there has been no *systematic* study of the impact of the CCS on the corresponding schedule cardinality.

A scheduling rate vector, $\mathbf{r}$, has elements indicating the average arrival rate of messages on each edge in the communication graph. The *capacity region*,

$C \subset \mathbb{R}_+^M$ is the set of achievable arrival rates, *i.e.*, $\mathbf{r} \in C$ means there exists a scheduling policy that stabilizes all queues for arrival rates $\mathbf{r}$, while $\mathbf{r} \notin C$ means no such policy exists. The seminal paper by Arikan [1] (1984) showed finding C is NPC under the interference graph model. The optimal schedule under the interference graph model requires solving a MWIS problem, which is NPC.

Several different interference constraint models are found in the literature. Grönkvist [2] (2001) show scheduling under the interference graph model may lead to links that are incompatible under the (more realistic) physical interference model. Behzad [3] (2003) demonstrate that finding a maximum matching (under the protocol interference model) does not necessarily correspond to maximization of the actual throughput (under the physical interference model). Negi [4] (2003) study the impact of the communication and interference radii in the interference graph, G_i, subject to pure pathloss attenuation. Jain [5] (2005) presents the *conflict graph*, a generalization of the interference graph to include sets of incompatible edges.

Although many scheduling problems are NPC in general, some problems become tractable when restricted to the geometric communication graphs induced by connecting points on the plane. Ramanathan [6] (1993) develop efficient distributed algorithms exploiting the fact that network topologies are in practice *nearly planar*. Their earlier work [7] (1992) establishes a P-time approximation algorithm for distance 2 coloring of planar graphs. Tassiulas [8] (1997) considers constantly changing topologies. The interesting problem of distributed scheduling brings its own challenges; see the book by Peleg [9].

5. Conclusions

This paper has studied the impact of 24 distinct CCSs on unidirectional point to point ad hoc scheduling. These results are a first step towards a systematic performance study of how CCSs affect scheduling in ad hoc networks. A systematic performance study is of use to network designers by identifying where their efforts on improving transceiver design are likely to be profitable, at least measured in terms of scheduling.

There are many directions for future work. A natural question is to seek to compare the maximum schedule sizes instead of comparing maximal sizes. In many cases this is infeasible since the corresponding combinatorial optimization problem is NP-Complete, and in some cases inapproximable. Nonetheless, the literature has piecemeal addressed these problems, and a systematic characterization is needed to shed light on the overall picture. Such a study naturally leads to joint comparison of both the performance impact (the schedule cardinality) as well as the algorithmic impact (the computational complexity) of each CCS. Finally, these algorithms need to be distributed for practical deployment, and the literature contains extensive work on distributed scheduling. Again, however, there is no systematic study of the performance and complexity of distributed algorithms under a consistent set of assumptions.

References

[1] E. Arikan, "Some complexity results about packet radio networks," *IEEE Transactions on Information Theory*, vol. IT-30, no. 4, pp. 681–685, July 1984.

[2] J. Grönkvist and A. Hannson, "Comparison between graph-based and interference-based STDMA scheduling," in *Proceedings of ACMMobiHoc*, Long Beach, CA, October 2001, pp. 255–258.

[3] A. Behzad and I. Rubin, "On the performance of graph-based scheduling algorithms for packet radio networks," in *Proceedings of IEEE GlobeCom*, vol. 6, San Francisco, CA, December 2003, pp. 3432–3436.

[4] R. Negi and A. Rajeswaran, "Physical layer effect on MAC performance in ad-hoc wireless networks," in *Proceedings of CIIT*, Scottsdale, AZ, November 2003, pp. 1–6.

[5] K. Jain, J. Padhye, V. Padmanabhan, and L. Qiu, "Impact of interference on multi-hop wireless network performance," *Wireless Networks*, vol. 11, no. 4, pp. 471–487, 2005.

[6] S. Ramanathan and E. Lloyd, "Scheduling algorithms for multihop radio networks," *IEEE/ACM Transactions on Networking*, vol. 1, no. 2, pp. 166–177, April 1993.

[7] E. Lloyd and S. Ramanathan, "On the complexity of distance-2 coloring," in *Proceedings of IEEE ICC*, Chicago, IL, May 1992, pp. 71–74.

[8] L. Tassiulas, "Scheduling and performance limits of networks with constantly changing topology," *IEEE Transactions on Information Theory*, vol. 43, no. 3, pp. 1067–1073, May 1997.

[9] D. Peleg, *Distributed computing: a locality–sensitive approach*. Philadelphia, PA: Society for Industrial and Applied Mathematics, 2000.

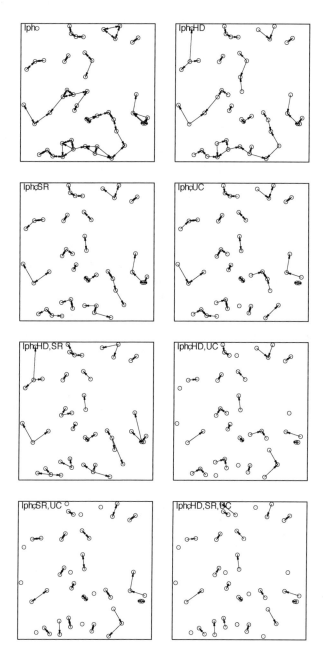

Figure 13.2. Sample realization of maximal schedules under eight distinct CCSs for $N = 50$. The eight boxes show the eight possible combinations of primary constraints (HD, SR, UC) combined with the physical SINR constraint with $\beta_c = 0.2$. A close examination of the figures reveals the individual impacts of each constraint on the schedule.

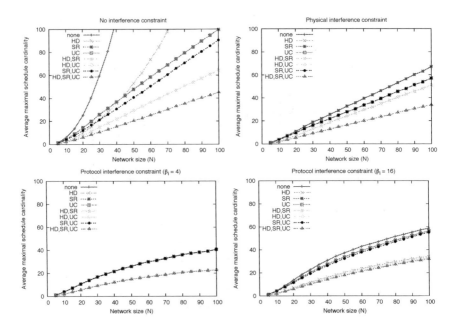

Figure 13.3. Average cardinality of a maximal schedule using the greedy heuristic for the eight possible combinations of primary constraints (HD, SR, UC). The top left shows results for no interference constraint, the top right for a physical interference constraint with $\beta_c = 2$, the bottom shows results under the protocol interference constraint ($\beta_i = 4$ on the left and $\beta_i = 16$ on the right).

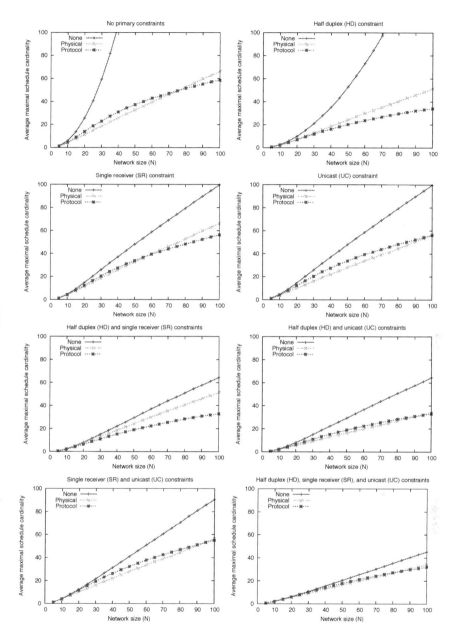

Figure 13.4. Average cardinality of a maximal schedule using the greedy heuristic for the eight possible combinations of primary constraints (HD, SR, UC). Each of the eight plots shows a combination of primary constraints, the three curves on each plot represent three possible secondary constraints (none, physical (with $\beta_c = 2$), and protocol (with $\beta_i = 16$)).

Chapter 14

TOPOLOGY CONTROL IN A FREE SPACE OPTICAL NETWORK

Yohan Shim*, Steven Gabriel*, Stuart Milner*, Christopher Davis**
*Department of Civil and Environmental Engineering, University of Maryland, College Park, MD 20742
**Department of Electrical and Computer Engineering, University of Maryland, College Park, MD 20742

Abstract: We describe a pointing, acquisition, and tracking (PAT) technique and efficient heuristic algorithms for autonomous physical and logical reconfiguration (Topology Control) in a free space optical communication network. First, we show a GPS-based pointing technique to steer the local directional laser beam of an optical transceiver to a target optical transceiver at a remote node, where the pointing accuracy is in the milliradian range. Second, we present fast heuristics for the congestion minimization problem and a multiobjective optimization problem (jointly minimizing the two objectives of physical network cost and congestion) for a bi-connected ring network topology. Finally, we present a GPS-based autonomous reconfiguration scenario for mobile nodes, which combines the PAT technique and heuristic algorithms.

Keywords: Topology control; dynamic reconfiguration; ring topologies.

1.   INTRODUCTION

Free Space Optical communication has been recognized as a high-speed bridging technology to current fiber optics network (Davis et al., 2003), and a valuable technology in commercial and military backbone networks (Milner et al., 2003). FSO communication systems involve direct line-of-sight and point-to-point links with optical transceivers (e.g., Canobeam DT-130-LX 1.25 Gbps) through the atmosphere. Their high-speed wireless properties are an attractive solution to the first or last mile problem in current fiber optics network (Davis et al., 2003). However its bright prospects depend on the performance of pointing, acquisition, and tracking (PAT) technology, and autonomous reconfiguration algorithms dealing with the effects of node mobility and atmospheric obscuration. In this paper we present a GPS-based precise pointing technique and fast heuristic methods for the autonomous reconfiguration algorithms.

1.1   The Main Challenge in FSO Network

An FSO network is characterized by frequent changes in its link states due to the dynamic performance of optical wireless links, which depend on the effect of node mobility and atmospheric obscuration (e.g., dense fog, dust, or snow) and sudden changes in traffic demands. Thus, it must be capable of autonomous physical and logical reconfiguration responding to degradation in one or more links; this is called *Topology Control* (Davis et al., 2003). This reconfiguration occurs both physically, by means of pointing, acquisition and tracking (PAT), and logically, by using autonomous reconfiguration algorithms. For example, Figure 1 presents how topology control works against a degradation problem. Because of a sudden change in link or traffic states, physical reconfiguration is necessary. Then, the reconfiguration algorithms yield an optimal topology which minimizes cost or congestion on the network. Subsequently, the PAT technique creates a new topology in accordance with the solution.

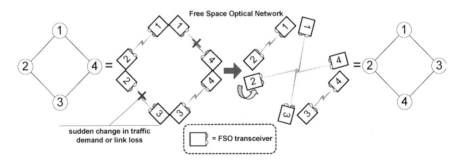

Figure 1. Degradation scenario and respective action taken by topology control (Example of bi-connected ring network topology with directional optical link)

1.2 Physical Reconfiguration: Pointing, Acquisition, and Tracking

FSO communication networks include a link using narrow, directional laser beams. It is essential to steer FSO transceivers (i.e., laser beams) precisely between two nodes, as shown in Figure 2. This process is referred as "pointing." If the link is available, "acquisition" is complete. If either node is mobile, then the node is tracked by the other node to maintain the established link - "tracking." The tracking is achieved by estimating (predicting) the future position and velocity of the mobile node.

Figure 2. Pointing between FSO transceivers in nodes A and B

The pointing requires microradian (i.e., 0.000057°) to milliradian (i.e., 0.057°) accuracy, which is a challenging problem unless both nodes are close to each other. For example, 1 milliradian accuracy corresponds to an error circle of 1 meter radius (r) with d =1000 meters in Figure 2. In this case manual alignment is straightforward and can be guided by the use of optical beacons or image based pointing. However, if the link distance is more than a few kilometers, then these techniques become increasingly difficult to implement. Hence, it is essential to have complete information as to where nodes are (position coordinates) as well as where they are heading (pointing vectors) as shown in Figure 3. The use of various kinds of position and angular sensor devices is therefore natural in pointing techniques (Epple, 2006; Ho et al., 2006; Wilkerson et al., 2006; Yee et al. 1998). A GPS (Global Positioning System) might be the alternative for providing such complete information for all weathers and global regions. Centimeter level positioning accuracy can be provided by real-time kinematics (RTK) GPS, which has been used in applications requiring precise location, navigation, and tracking (Buick, 2006; Cohen et al., 2993; Lachapelle et al., 1996; Park et al. 1998).

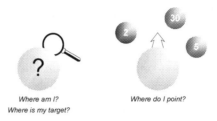

Where am I?
Where is my target?

Where do I point?

Figure 3. Questions in pointing

We have been developing a precise pointing method applicable to mobile and static nodes using RTK GPS and local angular sensors (e.g., tilt sensors or INS). With a medium range (264 m) pointing experiment between two buildings (roof-to-roof) on the University of Maryland campus at College Park, "dead-reckoning" pointing accuracy in the milliradian range (i.e., the pointing error is within 0.264 m) was obtained (et al., 2007b). We conduct a reliability test with an automatic pointing system equipped with a two-axis gimbal (step size per axis: 0.0072°). The test tells us how quickly (in seconds) and successfully (percentage success) the pointing method can obtain such milliradian accuracy. The RTK GPS provides centimeter level positioning accuracy on-the-fly; its high accuracy will improve the performance of position and velocity estimation of a mobile node for tracking. GPS and INS are conventional air navigation sensors. The precise heading information from RTK GPS can be combined with the roll and pitch outputs from INS mounted on an aircraft (Lee et al., 1998; 2001); thus enabling us to use the pointing technique in a dynamic environment.

1.3   Logical Reconfiguration: Topology Optimization

In logical reconfiguration, an optimal topology in an FSO network is determined by a graphical mapping of the configuration of its network elements (nodes and links). Given the cost matrix for each possible link (Figure 4 (b)) and the traffic matrix for all origin-destination nodes pair in the network (Figure 4 (c)), the mapping of the network elements is related to an optimization problem whose objective is finding an optimal topology minimizing overall cost (e.g., transmission power) or congestion. Since existence or utilization of a link (i, j) between two nodes i and j is represented by binary variables, the optimization problem is a mixed-integer linear program (MILP) which may have many feasible solutions, subsequently requiring a large amount of computer time to find global optimum such as the Network Layer Topology Control Problem (Shim et al., 2007a). This is not attractive in topology control demanding near-real time solutions; thus, a fast heuristic approach providing a near-optimal solution would be preferable in this case.

With a precise pointing technique for physical reconfiguration, we consider a logical reconfiguration algorithm with the aim of *i)* minimizing congestion due to varying traffic demands (called the *Network Layer Topology Control Problem*) and *ii)* simultaneously optimizing the two objectives of the physical network cost (due to node mobility and atmospheric obscuration) and congestion (called the *Multiobjective Optimization Problem*). The Network Layer Topology Control Problem (NLTCP) is defined as the congestion minimization problem at the network layer (Shim et al., 2007a). Its solution is the best ring topology with an optimal routing strategy responding to a given traffic demands between origin (source) and destination node pairs in a ring network. The traffic demand in the network is given in the form of a traffic matrix (e.g., Figure 4 (c)). The Multiobjective Optimization Problem (MOP) is defined by selecting the best ring topology that minimizes both physical layer cost and network layer congestion with uncertain traffic demands (Gabriel et al., 2007). The cost matrix (e.g., Figure 4 (b)) is generated by obscuration scenarios considering link distance and a cloud model (Gabriel et al., 2007). The uncertainty in the traffic patterns is represented by a set of probabilities (i.e., $\{p_1, ..., p_K\}$) assigned to K traffic matrices (stochastic load).

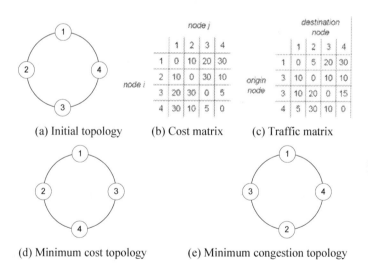

(a) Initial topology   (b) Cost matrix   (c) Traffic matrix

(d) Minimum cost topology   (e) Minimum congestion topology

Figure 4. Example of logical reconfiguration

The assumption in the logical reconfiguration algorithm is that *(i)* all possible links are feasible, *(ii)* the capacity on all possible links is not limited; thus the NLTCP and MOP are a uncapacitated network design problems, *(iii)* the shortest hop route is chosen when a longer path exists between origin and destination nodes, and *(iv)* the number of nodes and the cost and traffic matrices are known (or continuously updated). To justify assumption (ii), a central node can measure maximum load in a link given traffic demands in a centralized network in which it decides a best ring topology and routing scheme based on cost and traffic information collected from network nodes (see Section 3 more details). If the maximum load in a link (i.e., the sum of all traffic demands passing through the link) is above an available capacity for the link, then the central node may reduce the size of the traffic demands passing through the link into the smaller ones whose sum does not exceed the available link capacity. The shortest hop route in the assumption (iii) is unidirectional and considers a multi-hop path by which to send data from origin-node to destination-node through two or more links.

2.   TOPOLOGY OPTIMIZATION

A Free-Space Optical (FSO) network must be capable of autonomous physical and logical reconfiguration responding to changes in its link or traffic states due to node mobility and atmospheric obscuration (e.g., dense fog, dust, or snow). The purpose of this section is as follows: First, we review the relevant literature to the topology optimization under consideration; second, we will provide logical reconfiguration algorithms with the aim of minimizing congestion due to varying traffic demands to solve the NLTCP; third, similar algorithms will be applied to simultaneously optimize the two objectives of physical network cost (due to node mobility and atmospheric obscuration) and congestion, i.e., solving the MOP.

2.1   Literature Review

2.1.1   Synchronous Optical Network

A Synchronous Optical NETwork (SONET) is equipped with a high-speed add-drop multiplexing capability up to 9.953 Gbps (Optical Carrier-192). Its Self-Healing Ring architecture (SHR) provides a self-healing capability, which automatically restores disrupted services caused by damage to an optical fiber link. The self-healing capability is provided by a second protection ring parallel to the working ring as 1:1 Unidirectional SHR (Figure 5 (a)), or by a single ring where its half capacity is reserved for protection as in Bidirectional SHR /2 (BSHR/2) (Figure 5 (b)).

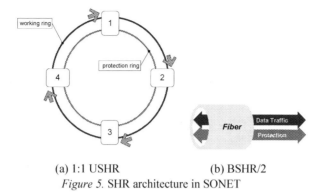

(a) 1:1 USHR   (b) BSHR/2
Figure 5. SHR architecture in SONET

In BSHR/2, SONET consists of a single fiber ring; working traffic utilizes half of the capacity and the rest is reserved for protection. Hence load balancing is required so that any traffic on the fiber should not exceed half the capacity of the ring. An associated optimization problem is called the Ring Loading Problem (RLP).

RLP is defined on an undirected ring network $R = (N, A)$ with a node set $N = \{1, 2, ..., n\}$ and an arc set A. The goal of RLP is to minimize the maximum traffic load on a link by considering how to route the traffic demand between origin-destination pairs. This is accomplished by routing in *i)* either of two directions (clockwise or counter-clockwise), or *ii)* routing a fraction (a, where $0 < a < 1$) of the traffic demand in clockwise and the rest fraction $(1-a)$ of traffic demand in counter-clockwise (Goldschmidt et al., 2003; van Hoesel, 2005; Karunanithi et al., 1994; Lee et al., 1997; Myung et al., 1997; Schrijver et al., 1998; Myung et al., 2004; Wang, 2005). The problem in which each demand is entirely routed in the clockwise or counter-clockwise is called the RLPWO problem and has been shown to be NP-complete (Cosares et al., 1992). RLP is a routing problem that finds optimal routing for a fixed physical topology.

2.1.2   Wavelength Division Multiplexed Network

A Wavelength Division Multiplexed (WDM) network provides multi-channel capacity using multiple wavelengths on a single optical fiber to utilize the high capacity of optical fiber. Given that the physical topology of WDM is fixed, each wavelength is assigned between two nodes to make a lightpath. For instance, a wavelength λ_2 is assigned between node-i and node-k as shown in Figure 6 (b); it forms a lightpath consisting of physical links (i, j) and (j, k) and a wavelength λ_2 assigned on the two links. There are two constraints to form a lightpath:

- A lightpath is spanned by the same wavelength;
- Lightpaths passing the same physical link must have different wavelengths to avoid conflict (interference).

Figure 6 (c) shows an example of wavelength assignment with those two constraints and its corresponding logical topology consisting of four wavelengths and seven lightpaths. Any origin-destination (or source-destination) node pairs in traffic demand that are not directly connected by a lightpath routes its data packets through two or more lightpaths (multi-hopping). For instance, traffic demand between origin node 4 and destination node 5 can be routed through multiple lightpaths: (4,2) →(2,1) →(1,5), (4,3) →(3,1) →(1,5) or (4,2) →(2,6) →(6,5). New logical topology is obtained by rearranging the lightpaths (i.e., using different wavelength assignments) as shown in Figure 6 (d).

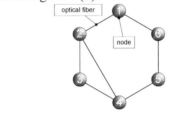

(a) Physical Topology

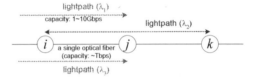

(b) Multiple-channel transmission on physical links (optical fibers)

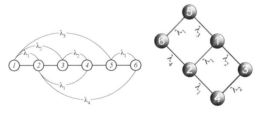

(c) Wavelength assignment and its corresponding logical topology

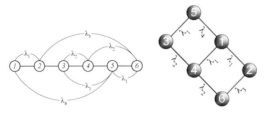

(d) New topology creation by rearranging the lightpaths

Figure 6. WDM network

In a WDM network, the logical topology is dynamically reconfigured corresponding to traffic pattern changes, network element failures and network element additions. The logical topology reconfiguration is carried out to minimize the network congestion (Ramaswami et al., 1996), or minimize the average packet delay due to queuing delays at the intermediate nodes with link propagation delays (Mukherjee et al., 1996). An associated mixed-integer linear optimization problem can be solved that consists of two subproblems: a logical topology design problem and a routing problem, but as shown previously it is NP-complete (Banerjee et al., 2004; Chlamtac et al., 1993; Narula-Tam et al., 2000). Because it is impractical to determine the optimal topology with optimal routing by solving a mixed-integer linear program, heuristic approaches have been introduced: a local search by applying 2-branch exchange or 3-branch exchange (Labourdette et al., 1991; Narula-Tam et al., 2000) or a combination of simulated annealing and flow deviation (Mukherjee et al., 1996). Narula-Tam et al. (2000), Mukherjee et al. (1996), Ramaswami et al. (1996), and Zhang et al. (1995) used shortest hop routing in their heuristic algorithms to simplify the routing subproblem.

2.2 Free-Space Optical Network: Dynamic Reconfiguration of Ring Network Topologies

RLP in SONET BSHR/2 is a routing problem in which the physical topology is fixed. In a WDM network, the physical topology is also fixed, however, the logical topology is reconfigured to minimize the network congestion or the average packet delay between any origin-destination node pairs in traffic demand.

In an FSO network, the physical topology is not fixed because it involves mobile nodes. Due to the node mobility, the physical distance between nodes and the atmospheric conditions surrounding each node vary. If the physical distance is large or the atmospheric obscuration (e.g., dense fog, dust, or snow) is so high that directional links experience excessive optical signal attenuation, then this causes link failure or requires a large increase in transmission power to compensate for attenuation. The physical distance and atmospheric obscuration can be construed as network costs (Llorca et al., 2004a). With such an approach an optimization problem can be solved that seeks the minimum cost topology, given the network cost of all possible physical links in the network. Such a problem is called the *Physical Layer Topology Control Problem* (PLTCP) (Llorca et al., 2004b). In contrast, logical topology is reconfigured responding to changes in traffic pattern. The reconfiguration is carried out to minimize the network congestion defined as the sum of loads on all active links in the network. An associated optimization problem to solve is called the *Network Layer Topology Control Problem* (Shim et al., 2007a). In a bi-connected FSO network (a ring network), the Network Layer Topology Control Problem (NLTCP) finds a best ring network topology (i.e., physical links between nodes) whose congestion is minimal by assuming that all possible optical links between any two nodes in the network are feasible (no optical signal attenuation). The PLTCP and NLTCP are described more in detail at the following:

Physical Layer Topology Control Problem

At the physical layer, performance is measured in terms of bit-error-rate (BER), which is a function of the received power at the FSO transceiver. As an example, an FSO link is considered to be feasible if its BER is less than 10^{-9}. Link distance and obscuration are the main factors that cause attenuation of the optical signal, which results in increased (i.e., worse) BER. The higher the link attenuation, the more power needs to be transmitted in order to maintain a given BER. Thus the objective at the physical layer is to compute a topology with minimum overall cost (e.g., transmission power). In a bi-connected FSO network, the PLTCP is reduced to finding an optimal ring network topology with minimum cost and is known to be NP complete (Llorca et al. 2004a)

Network Layer Topology Control Problem

In contrast, logical topology is reconfigured responding to changes in traffic patterns. The reconfiguration is carried out to minimize the network congestion, defined as either the sum of loads on all active links in the network or the maximum load on an active link in the network. In a bi-connected FSO network (a ring network), the NLTCP finds a best ring network topology (i.e., physical links between nodes) whose congestion is minimal, by assuming that all possible optical links between any two nodes in the network are feasible (no optical signal attenuation). See Shim et al. (2007a) for details of the description and formulation of NLTCP. In this paper, the authors mentioned that NLTCP is a computationally hard problem as the number of nodes n increases. Because it is a binary linear program, we applied branch-and-bound technique to solve the problem with a commercial solver (e.g., XPRESS-MP). Two new approaches were used: *Shortest Path Constraints* and *Partition Constraints,* to solve the problem efficiently. The Shortest Path Constraints and Partition Constraints increase the lower bound of the LP relaxation, thereby reducing the number of branches in the branch-and-bound tree in the MIP search. They showed that the two constraints speed up the solution time in the solver for networks with $n \leq 10$ nodes.

Multiobjective Optimization Problem

For the dynamic reconfiguration of an FSO network, a multiobjective optimization approach is necessary to find a best topology whose network cost and congestion is as low as possible. The MOP deals with both PLTCP and NLTCP at the same time. However, as shown in Figures 4 (d) and (e), the minimum cost topology for PLTCP and the minimum congestion topology for NLTCP may be different. The objective of MOP is to balance these two competing objectives. For this purpose, Gabriel et al. (2007) generated a Pareto optimal (Cohon, 1978) set of ring topologies in which the cost objective must come at the expense of the congestion objective; the notion of Pareto optimality is described in the paper. They considered uncertain traffic demands for the congestion minimization subproblem. The uncertainty in the traffic demand was represented by a set of K scenarios $\{1,...,K\}$ with a traffic matrix R^k for scenario k; the traffic matrix consisted of a random load between origin-destination nodes (OD) pair (the number of OD pairs are $n(n-1)$ for a ring network with n nodes). The objective function of MOP was:

$$w \times \cos t + (1-w) \times \left(\sum_{k=1}^{K} p^k \times congestion^k \right),$$

where p^k is the probability of scenario k and $\sum_{k=1}^{K} p^k = 1$.

The weighting method (Cohen, 1978) is applied to combine both cost objective and congestion objective for k-th scenario using a positive weight w. In the objective function, the weight w is fixed at a real value between 0<w<1. The weight w represents relative importance (or preference) of cost or congestion objective. Since the best weight sets $(w, 1-w)$ which provide the entire Pareto optimal set are unknown, it would be useful to proceed by first with large step sizes (Δw) for the weights to find a rough approximation of the Pareto-optimal solutions. Then, the process should repeat with a smaller step size for a range of weight sets of particular interest (Cohon, 2003). The MOP Heuristic expedites that process to provide near-Pareto optimal solutions.

2.3   Heuristic Algorithms for Dynamic Reconfiguration of Ring Network Topologies

The logical topology reconfiguration problem of a WDM network for a ring network topology (Narula-Tam et al., 2000), discussed in *Section A,* is similar to NLTCP in that it also requires an exhaustive search of all possible ring network topologies to find a best ring network topology with optimal routing scheme.   However, sometimes it is not possible to ever compute optimal solutions as was the case in Narula-Tam et al. (2000), where only a 16-node ring networks was tried, or in the case of Labourdette et al. (1991), Mukherjee et al. (1996), Ramaswami et al. (1996), and Zhang et al. (1995). Shim et al. (2007a) also discussed the lack of a performance measure for optimal solutions in the Uncapacitated Network Design Problem (UNDP), such as the optimization problem in WDM network. Since NLTCP does not impose any capacity constraint in a link to limit the sum of traffic flows through it, NLTCP is an UNDP.   In this section, we present heuristic methods for the logical reconfiguration of ring network topologies in FSO networks and their performance accuracy (i.e., optimality gaps), which considerably contributes to the solutions of UNDP.

2.3.1   Heuristics for NLTCP

The heuristic algorithm for NLTCP is based on a two-node swapping method and an iterative improvement to find a better solution. As long as an improved solution exists, it is adopted and the iterative procedure is repeated from the new solution.   The overall procedure is as follows:

1. Generate a random feasible solution (a ring network topology) and compute its corresponding objective function value. Step 1 in Figure 7 shows this procedure.   A feasible topology is randomly chosen and its initial objective function value ($TTC_{init} = 834$) is restored.

2. Then swap two nodes from this random solution. Compute and record the improvement in the objective function value (TTC) for the topology with the swapped nodes (i.e., the objective function value is improved when $TTC_{diff} = TTC - TTC_{init} \leq 0$).   Do this for every two node swapping possibility. The number of two node swapping applied in this step is $(n-1)(n-2)$. Step 2 in Figure 7 displays this procedure.

3. Order, in a list, the improvements in the objective function based on this swapping method from largest (the most improved) to smallest (the least improved). If the length of the list is greater than or equal to four, then the top two and bottom two topologies can be always selected from the

list. Thus, picking out the top two and bottom two topologies from the list can be more practical than selecting the topologies that show improvement in the objective function in a regular manner (i.e., selecting the *i*-th, *j*-th, *k*-th, and *l*-th topology from the list), although this is somewhat arbitrary. These four ring network topologies that have been selected become new feasible solutions. Step 3 in Figure 7 shows the list of topologies whose objective function value is improved by at least zero. The top two topologies (*1-2-5-4-3* and *1-2-4-3-5*) and bottom two topologies (*1-4-3-2-5* and *1-3-2-4-5*) are selected as new feasible solutions.

4. Apply the same procedure from 2 and 3, to each new feasible solution in parallel, except choosing the most improved topology and considering it as a new solution. This continues until a best topology is found. Step 4 in Figure 7 illustrates this procedure. For the rightmost feasible topology, 2 and 3 are repeated until there is no improvement in the objective function value.

The core of the NLTCP Heuristic is step 3, in which the search direction for a local or global minimum is diversified as the number of the feasible topologies picked out from the list. Each feasible topology provides a different search direction, and this is called *RULE*. The search direction is more diversified by increasing the number of RULEs to more than four or by replacing $TTC_{diff} \leq 0$ with $TTC_{diff} \leq \alpha$ (where $\alpha > 0$) in the step 2.

A more formal version of the procedure stated above is presented at Shim et al. (2007a), in which the performance of the NLTCP Heuristic was tested for networks of size 8 to 15 nodes. For each node, ten $n \times n$ traffic matrices were randomly generated and best solutions from the heuristic code implemented by MATLAB were compared with the optimal solutions from XPRESS-MP or with an enumeration code in MATLAB. 56 cases out of a total of 60 trials showed an optimality gap within 1.5 % and 58 cases out of the 60 trials were within a 2.0 % optimality gap, while the optimality gaps of the whole 60 cases were within 2.5% (Table 1). In addition, most of the search times to find the best integer solution were less than 60 seconds, with the exception for two cases for the 15 ring network topology, where the search times were more than 60 seconds (the most was 73 seconds). See Shim et al. (2007a) for more details.

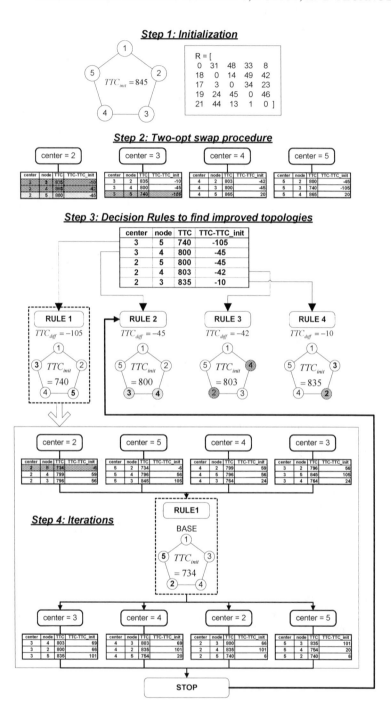

Figure 7. Example of NLTCP Heuristic procedure

2.3.2 Heuristics for MOP

The heuristic algorithm for MOP is almost same as the NLTCP Heuristic. The difference between the two heuristic algorithms is the input and objective function formats. Inputs to the heuristic algorithm are both a cost matrix and the expected traffic demand; the traffic demand is expressed by $p^k R^k$, where a traffic matrix R^k is multiplied by the probability p^k for the k-th scenario. Gabriel et al. (2007) showed that the heuristic procedure achieved near-Pareto optimality with a reduction in time complexity for a wide range of traffic patterns and obscuration scenarios: in 55% of test cases, they achieved an optimality gap less than 0.1%, and 100% of the cases are within 1.2% optimality gap (Table 1). See Gabriel et al. (2007a) for more details.

Table 1. Performance accuracy of heuristic methods

	Network Size (number of nodes)	# of Test Problems	Optimality Gap	Solution Time (n=number of nodes)
NLTCP Heuristic (MATLAB version 7.0)	8,9,10,12,14,15	60	≤ 2.5%	6 sec (n=8) ~ 60 sec (n=15)
MOP Heuristic (MATLAB version 7.0)	8,10	162	≤ 1.2%	6 sec (n=8) ~ 12 sec(n=10)

3. GPS-BASED AUTONOMOUS RECONFIGURATION SCENARIO

This section presents an example of autonomous reconfiguration with the physical reconfiguration (by the precise pointing technique with GPS and local angular sensors) and the logical reconfiguration (by the NLTCP Heuristic and MOP Heuristic) at the phase of initial link establishment. Assume that there exist six nodes in a coverage area in which they can continuously track at least five common GPS satellites, and a central node can move around the coverage area to collect all information necessary for initial link establishment. This is shown in Figure 8.

The autonomous reconfiguration may work in the following scenario:
1. Each node broadcasts its packet data (Figure 8) to neighbor nodes.
2. A central node collects all information (costs and traffic demands) from the nodes that participate in the network (Figure 9). The information is displayed on the screen of an automatic vehicle location system (AVLS).

For a bi-connected ring network with n nodes, there exist $(n-1)!/2$ ring topologies. The heuristic algorithms for NLTCP and MOP yield a near-optimal topology and the associated routing table based on the input cost and traffic matrices (Figure 9). The heuristics are based on the shortest path (hop) routing scheme. For example, Figure 10 shows a ring network topology solution and its routing table from the heuristic for NLTCP or MOP. The routing table is made up of the sequence of links from origin-node to destination-node on the ring network, and it contains the shortest hop routing direction for each traffic demand of origin-destination pairs.

3. The central node broadcasts an initial link establishment command with an RF data transmitter or relays the command with an FSO transceiver. For example, the link command would be *1-3-4-5-6-2-1* (Figure 11). According to the command, each node establishes its directional link with the pointing technique described by Shim et al. (2007b).

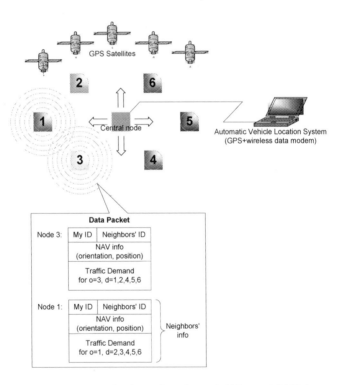

Figure 8. Centralized Topology Control (Shim et al. 2007c)

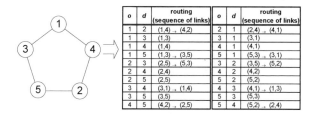

Node	Neighbors
1	2, 3, 4, 5, 6
2	1, 3, 4, 5, 6
3	1, 2, 4, 5, 6
4	1, 2, 3, 5, 6
5	1, 2, 3, 4, 6
6	1, 2, 3, 4, 5

(a) Possible links   (b) Cost matrix   (c) Traffic matrix

Figure 9. Node information and input matrices (Shim et al. 2007c)

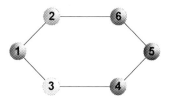

o	d	routing (sequence of links)	o	d	routing (sequence of links)
1	2	(1,4) → (4,2)	2	1	(2,4) → (4,1)
1	3	(1,3)	3	1	(3,1)
1	4	(1,4)	4	1	(4,1)
1	5	(1,3) → (3,5)	5	1	(5,3) → (3,1)
2	3	(2,5) → (5,3)	3	2	(3,5) → (5,2)
2	4	(2,4)	4	2	(4,2)
2	5	(2,5)	5	2	(5,2)
3	4	(3,1) → (1,4)	4	3	(4,1) → (1,3)
3	5	(3,5)	5	3	(5,3)
4	5	(4,2) → (2,5)	5	4	(5,2) → (2,4)

Figure 10. The shortest hop routing for a ring network topology with $n = 5$ (Shim et al. 2007c)

Figure 11. Link command (Shim et al. 2007c)

4. SUMMARY

In this paper we have presented a PAT technique and efficient heuristic algorithms for the autonomous physical and logical reconfiguration (Topology Control) in a free space optical communication network.

A GPS-based precise pointing technique has obtained a "dead-reckoning" pointing accuracy in the milliradian range (i.e., the pointing error is within 0.264 m) in a medium range (264 m) experiment. The pointing technique utilizes GPS and local angular sensors (tilt sensors, INS or inertial measurement units); thus the technique can be used in a dynamic environment with mobile nodes such as terrestrial and aeronautical vehicles.

We will conduct a reliability test with an automatic pointing system equipped with a two-axis gimbal. The test will tell us how quickly (in seconds) and successfully (percentage success) the pointing method can obtain such milliradian accuracy.

With a precise pointing technique for physical reconfiguration, we have introduced efficient heuristic algorithms for dynamic reconfiguration of ring network topologies in FSO networks, which are NLTCP Heuristic and MOP Heuristic. Shim et al. (2007a) showed that the NLTCP Heuristic achieved a 0.5% optimality gap in 50% of the test problems and less than 2.5% in 100% of the test problems. The MOP Heuristic provided near-Pareto optimal solutions for the multiobjective optimization problem with various types of network cost and stochastic traffic load. The numerical results in Gabriel et al. (2007) showed that 100% of the test problems were within a 1.2% optimality gap. The heuristic improvement algorithm for NLTCP Heuristic and MOP Heuristic improved the optimality gaps even more.

There has been no known result in the literature to our knowledge that compares solutions obtained by heuristic procedures of UNDP against the true optimal solutions of that problem. Finding a heuristic and presenting performance accuracy of the heuristic was one of the objectives of this paper, which makes a significant contribution to the solutions of UNDP.

Lastly, we have presented a GPS-based autonomous reconfiguration scenario for mobile nodes. A central node equipped with an automatic vehicle location system (AVLS) using GPS and wireless data modem collects all information (orientation, position, costs and traffic demands of each node participating in the network) necessary for the initial link establishment. The NLTCP Heuristic or MOP Heuristic yields near-optimal topology and its associated routing table according to the input costs and traffic demands. The precise pointing technique is used to establish the wireless optical link.

REFERENCES

Banerjee N, Mehta V and Pandey S (2004). A Genetic Algorithm Approach for Solving the Routing and Wavelength Assignment Problem in WDM Networks. In 3rd IEEE/IEE International Conference on Networking, ICN 2004, Paris, Feb-March, pp 70-78.

Chlamtac I, Ganz A and Karmi G (1993). Lightnets: Topologies for High-Speed Optical Networks. Journal of Lightwave Technology 11(5/6): 951-961.

Buick R (2006). White Paper: RTK base station networks driving adoption of GPS +1/-1 inch automated steering among crop growers. Trimble Navigation Limited.

Cohen C, McNally BD and Parkinson BW (1993). Flight Tests of Attitude Determination using GPS compared against an Inertial Navigation Unit. Presented at the ION National Technical Meeting, San Francisco, California.

Cohon JL (1978). Multiobjective Programming and Planning, Dover Publications, Inc., Mineola, NY (reprinted 2003).

Cosares S and Saniee I (1992). An optimization problem related to balancing loads on SONET rings. Technical Memorandum. Bellcore, Morristown, NJ 07962.

Davis CC, Smolyaninov II and Milner SD (2003). Flexible optical high data rate wireless links and networks, IEEE Communications Magazine, March.

Epple B (2006). Using a GPS-aided Inertial System for Coarse-Pointing of Free-Space Optical Communication Terminals. Proceedings of SPIE 2006, San Diego

Gabriel S, Shim Y, Llorca J and Milner S (2007). A Multiobjective Optimization Model for Dynamic Reconfiguration of Ring Topologies with Stochastic Load. Networks and Spatial Economics. Accepted for publication.

Goldschmidt O, Laugier A and Olinick EV (2003). SONET/SDH ring assignment with capacity constraints, Discrete Applied Mathematics 129 99 – 128.

Ho TH and Davis C (2006). Three-dimensional Optical Pointing System Encoded by Radial Trifocal Tensor. Proceedings of SPIE 2006, San Diego.

Karunanithi N, Carpenter T (1994). A ring loading application of genetic algorithms. Proceedings of the 1994 ACM symposium on applied computing 227-231.

Labourdette JP and Acampora AS (1991). Logically Rearrangeable Multihop Lightwave Networks. IEEE Transactions on Communications 39(8): 1223-1230.

Lachapelle G, Cannon ME, Lu G and Loncarevic B (1996). Shipborne GPS Attitude Determination During MMST-93. IEEE Journal of Oceanic Engineering 21(1).

Lee CY and Chang SG (1997). Balancing loads on SONET rings with integer demand splitting. Computers and Operations Research 24(3) 221-229.

Lee S, Yoo C, Shim Y and Kim J (2001). Performance Testing of Integrated Strapdown INS and GPS. KSAS International Journal 2(1).

Lee S, Shim Y, Kim D, Kang C, Yoo C, Tunik AA and Kim J (1998). RDGPS-based Automatic Landing System for Light and Commuter Aircraft. The 14th IFAC Symposium on Automatic Control in Aerospace.

Llorca J, Desai A, Baskara E, Milner S and Davis C (2005). Optimizing Performance of Hybrid FSO/RF Networks in Realistic Dynamic Scenarios. Free-Space Laser Communications V. Proceedings of the SPIE, 5892, 52-60.

Llorca J, Desai A, Vishkin U, Davis CC, Milner SD (2004a). Reconfigurable optical wireless sensor networks, Optics in Atmospheric Propagation and Adaptive Systems VI, J.D. Gonglewski and K. Stein, eds., Proceedings of SPIE 5237, 136-146.

Llorca J, Desai A, Milner S (2004b). Obscuration Minimization In Dynamic Free Space Optical Networks Through Topology Control. Proc. IEEE MILCOM.

Mukherjee B, Banerjee D, Ramamurthy S and Mukherjee A (1996). Some Principles for Designing a Wide-Area WDM Optical Network. IEEE/ACM Transactions on Networking 4(5): 684-696

Myung YS and Kim HG (2004). On the ring loading problem with demand splitting. Operations Research Letters 32 167-173.

Myung YS, Kim HG and Tcha DW (1997). Optimal load balancing on SONET bidirectional rings. Operations Research 45(1) 148-152.

Narula-Tam A and Modiano E (2000). Dynamic Load Balancing in WDM Packet Networks With and Without Wavelength Constraints. IEEE Journal on Selected Areas in Communications 18(10): 1972-1979.

Milner SD, Thakkar S, Chandrashekar K and Chen W (2003). Performance and Scalability of Wireless Base-Station-Oriented Networks. Invited paper, Mobile Computing and Communications Review.

Park C and Kim I (1998). Integer ambiguity resolution for GPS based attitude determination system. SICE '98. Proceedings of the 37th SICE Annual Conference. International Session Papers: 1115-1120.

Ramaswamy R and Sivarajan K (1996). Design of logical topologies for wavelength routed optical networks, IEEE Journal on Selected Areas in Communications, 14 (5), 840-851.

Schrijver A, Seymour P and Winkler P (1998). The ring loading problem. SIAM Journal on Discrete Mathematics 11(1) 1-14.

Shim Y, Gabriel SA, Desai A, Sahakij P and Milner S (2007a). A Fast Heuristic Method for Minimizing Traffic Congestion on Reconfigurable Ring Topologies. Journal of the Operational Research Society (JORS) advance online publication 7 February 2007; doi: 10.1057/palgrave.jors.2602360

Shim Y, Milner SD and Davis CC (2007b). A Precise Pointing Technique For Free Space Optical Networking. MILCOM. In review.

Shim Y, Milner SD and Davis CC (2007c). A Precise Pointing Technique for FSO Links and Networks using Kinematic GPS and Local Sensors. The Free-Space Laser Communications VII conference. Proceedings of the SPIE. San Diego. CA. in review.

van Hoesel SPM (2005). Optimization in telecommunication networks, The Statistica Neerlandica 59(2) 180-205.

Wang B-F (2005). Linear time algorithms for the ring loading problem with demand splitting. Journal of Algorithms 54 45-57.

Wilkerson BL, Giggenbach D and Epple B (2006). Concepts for Fast Acquisition in Optical Communications Systems. Proceedings of SPIE 2006, San Diego

Yee R and Robbins F (1998). Inertial Pointing and Positioning System. US Patent 5809457.

Zhang Z and Acampora AS (1995). A Heuristic Wavelength Assignment Algorithm for Multihop WDM Networks with Wavelength Routing and Wavelength Re-Use. IEEE/ACM Transactions on Networking 3(3): 281-288.

Chapter 15

A LOCAL SEARCH HYBRID GENETIC ALGORITHM APPROACH TO THE NETWORK DESIGN PROBLEM WITH RELAY STATIONS

Sadan Kulturel-Konak, Abdullah Konak
Penn State Berks, Tulpehocken Road, P.O. Box 7009, Reading, PA 19610, US

Abstract: The network design problem with relay stations arises in telecommunication and logistic systems. The design problem involves selecting network links and determining the location of the relay stations to minimize the design cost. A constraint is imposed on the distance that a signal can travel without being regenerated by a relay station. An efficient hybrid meta-heuristic approach is presented to solve large sized problems.

Keywords: Network design; telecommunications; genetic algorithms; meta-heuristics.

1.   INTRODUCTION

The network design problem with relay stations (NDPRS) is briefly defined as follows. A undirected network $G=(V, E)$ with node set $V=\{1, 2, ..., n\}$ and edge set $E=\{(i, j): i, j \in V, i<j\}$ is given. Each edge (i, j) has an installation cost of $c_{i,j}$ and a length of $d_{i,j}$. K commodities, representing point-to-point traffics, are simultaneously routed on the network; each commodity k has a single source node $s(k)$ and a single destination node $t(k)$. All traffic from node $s(k)$ to node $t(k)$ is routed through a single path. Being different from a regular network design problem, some nodes of the network have to be dedicated as relay stations in which the communication signal is regenerated. An upper bound λ is imposed on the distance that a commodity k can travel without visiting a relay station on a path from node $s(k)$ to node $t(k)$. A fixed cost f_i is occurred when a relay station is located at node i. The objective function of the NDPRS is to minimize the network design cost while making sure that each traffic commodity k is routed from node $s(k)$ to node $t(k)$ through a path on which the distances between node $s(k)$ and the

first relay station, between any two consecutive relay stations, and between node $t(k)$ and the last relay station are less than the upper bound λ. A network flow based formulation of the NDPRS on a directed network $G=(V,E)$ where edge set E includes both edges (i, j) and (j, i) is given as follows:

Decision Variables:

$x_{i,j}$ binary edge decision variable such that $x_{i,j}=1$ if edge (i, j) is selected in the solution, 0 otherwise.

y_i binary relay station variable such that $y_i=1$ if a relay station is located at node i, 0 otherwise.

$\overline{x}_{i,j}^k$ binary flow decision variable such that $\overline{x}_{i,j}^k =1$ if edge (i, j) is used by commodity k, 0 otherwise.

$u_{k,i}$ total distance traveled by commodity k to node i without visiting a relay station.

$u_{k,i}'$ total distance traveled by commodity k after node i without visiting a relay station.

Problem NDPRS:

$$\text{Min } z = \sum_{i\in V} f_i y_i + \sum_{(i,j)\in E, i<j} c_{i,j} x_{i,j} \tag{1}$$

$$\sum_{(i,j)\in E} \overline{x}_{i,j}^k - \sum_{(j,i)\in E} \overline{x}_{j,i}^k = \begin{cases} 1 & i = s(k) \\ -1 & i = t(k) \\ 0 & otherwise \end{cases} \qquad k \in K, i \in V \tag{2}$$

$$u_{k,i} \ge u_{k,j}' + d_{j,i} - (1-\overline{x}_{j,i}^k)M \qquad k \in K, i \in V, (j,i) \in E \tag{3}$$

$$u_{k,i} \le \lambda \qquad k \in K, i \in V \tag{4}$$

$$u_{k,i}' \ge u_{k,i} - My_i \qquad k \in K, i \in V \tag{5}$$

$$\sum_{k\in K}(\overline{x}_{i,j}^k + \overline{x}_{j,i}^k) \le Mx_{i,j} \qquad (i,j) \in E, i < j \tag{6}$$

$$y_i, x_{i,j}, \overline{x}_{i,j}^k \in \{0,1\}$$

$$u_{k,i}, u_{k,i}' \ge 0$$

In the formulation above, constraint set (2) is the node flow balance constraints to make sure that one unit flow is sent from node $s(k)$ to node $t(k)$. Constraint (3) is used to calculate the total distance traveled by each commodity without visiting a relay station. Constraints (4) is the relay station constraint that makes sure that the total distance traveled by any commodity without visiting a relay station is less than λ at each node.

Constraint (5) resets the total distance traveled by commodity k until node i to zero if node i is a relay station. Constraint (6) makes sure that edge (i, j) cannot be used by any commodity if it is not included in the solution.

The NDPRS is first introduced by Cabral *et al.* [1] in the context of a real life telecommunication network design problem. Cabral *et al.* [1] formulate a path based integer programming model of the problem and propose a column generation approach. Unfortunately, the column generation approach cannot be practically used to find the optimal solution in the case of large problem instances since all feasible paths and relay station locations combinations have to be generated as a priori. Therefore, Cabral *et al.* [1] recommend using a subset of all feasible paths and relay station combinations. Although this approach does not guarantee optimality, superior solutions can be found in reasonable CPU times. In addition, they proposed four different construction heuristics in which a solution is constructed by taking into consideration one commodity at a time.

Although the NDPRS was studied first time by Cabral *et al.* [1], it is closely related to well-known network design problems such as the Steiner tree problem, the hop-constrained network design problem, the constrained shortest path problem, and the facility location problem. In the hop constrained network design problem, hop constraints impose an upper bound on the number of edges between source and destination node pairs due to reliability [2] or performance concerns [3]. Several papers [4-6] address optical network design problem considering restricted transmission range due to optical impairments, which is one of the main motivations in the NDPRS as well.

Similar to the Steiner tree problem, all nodes are not required to be connected in the NDPRS. Voss [7] considers hop-constrained Steiner tree problem and proposes a solution approach based on tabu search and mathematical programming. Gouveia and Magnanti [8] consider the diameter-constrained minimum spanning and Steiner tree problems where an upper-bound is imposed on the number of edges between any node pairs. Gouveia [9] provides two different mathematical models for the hop-constrained minimum spanning tree problem; and, in addition, he proposes Lagrangean relaxation and heuristic approaches to solve the problem. Later, Gouveia and Requejo [10] develop an improved Lagrangean relaxation approach to the problem. In a sense, the NDPRS is a generalization of the hop-constrained network design problem where $d_{i,j}=1$ for each edge and λ is an integer. In addition, due to relay station decision variables, the NDPRS is closely related to the facility location problem [11].

The objective of this paper is to develop a meta-heuristic approach for the NDPRS to solve large problem instances effectively and efficiently. After experimenting with a few different meta-heuristics approaches such as

Genetic Algorithms (GA), Simulated Annealing, and Ant Colony Approach, the best results were found by a local search hybrid genetic algorithm. It should be noted that no meta-heuristic approach has been previously applied to this problem. We report the results found by a local search hybrid genetic algorithm.

2.   A HYBRID GENETIC ALGORITHM APPROACH FOR THE NETWORK DESIGN WITH RELAY STATIONS

In this section, we describe a hybrid genetic algorithm to find good solutions to the NDPRS. The algorithm is called local search hybrid genetic algorithm (LSHGA) since a local search is used to explore new solutions in addition to the traditional GA operators, crossover and mutation. The parameters and notation used in the LSHGA are given as follows:

z	a solution
$z.x_{i,j}$	edge decision variable of solution z such that $z.x_{i,j}=1$ if edge (i,j) is selected in solution z, 0 otherwise.
$z.y_i$	relay decision variable of solution z such that $z.y_i=1$ if a relay station is located at node i, 0 otherwise.
$E(z)$	edge set of solution z, $E(z){\subset}E$
$V(z)$	node set of solution z, $V(z){\subset}V$
μ	population size
$tc_{i,j}$	temporary cost of edge (i,j)
t_{max}	maximum number of generations (stopping criteria)
P	population
OP	offspring population
$P[i]$	the ith solution in the population
U	uniform random number between 0 and 1
N	number of nodes, $|V|$
M	number of edges, $|E|$

2.1   Encoding, Fitness, and Solution Evaluation

A binary encoding based on the edge and relay decision variables of the NDPRS is used to represent a solution z as described above. By definition, a feasible solution to the NDPRS does not have to be a connected network. A solution is feasible if at least one path exists between the source and destination nodes of each commodity and the commodities are routed no longer than λ distance without visiting a relay station. The crossover/mutation operators and local search procedures of the LSHGA ensure that the source and destination nodes of each commodity are always connected. However, the feasibility of solutions with respect to the relay station distance constraint is not guaranteed. Therefore, the feasibility of solutions is checked using a depth-first search. The number of commodities that violate the relay station distance constraint of the problem NDPRS is used as a measure of infeasibility. Infeasible solutions are not discarded from the population, but penalized using a ranking schema as follows: (*i*) between two feasible solutions, the one with the lower cost is superior; (*ii*) between an infeasible and a feasible solution, the feasible solution is superior; (*iii*) between two infeasible solutions, the one with a smaller constraint violation is superior. Instead of assigning a fitness value, the population is ranked according to these three rules. This ranking procedure is simple and does not require any parameters unlike penalty function approaches.

2.2   Crossover and Mutation

In GA, the function of crossover is to create new solutions by recombining the characteristics of existing solutions. In our initial experiments with GA, traditional GA crossover operators such as single-point or uniform crossover did not provide promising results since they generated highly disconnected and infeasible solutions. Therefore, a specialized crossover based on random shortest paths between source and destination nodes was developed. An offspring solution z is constructed from two parent solutions $P[p_1]$ and $P[p_2]$ by considering one commodity at a time in a random order of commodities. After randomly selecting indexes p_1 and p_2 for parent solutions, temporary cost $tc_{i,j}$ is assigned to each edge as follows: for each edge $(i, j) \in E$, if $P[p_1].x_{i,j}=1$ or $P[p_2].x_{i,j}=1$, then set $tc_{i,j}:=U \times (c_{i,j}+f_i+f_j)$; else, set $tc_{i,j}:=\infty$. Then, the shortest path $p(k)$ from node $s(k)$ to node $t(k)$ with respect to temporary costs is found for each commodity k in a random order of commodities. After finding the shortest path $p(k)$, each edge $(i, j) \in p(k)$ is added to the offspring while setting its temporary cost $tc_{i,j}$ to zero in order to encourage unassigned commodities to use the edges already included in the offspring. This process is repeated until all commodities are routed. Finally, the locations of the relay stations on path $p(k)$ are determined based on the relay stations of parents $P[p_1]$ and $P[p_2]$. To do so, starting from node $s(k)$, each edge $(i, j) \in p(k)$ is sequentially examined whether a relay station should be located at node i or not. After examining edge (i, j), a relay station is located at node i if and only if the total distance from the previous relay station on path $p(k)$ to node j is more than λ and either of the parents has a relay station located at node i.

The LSHGA has also a specialized mutation operator. The function of mutation in GA is to avoid local minima by preventing solutions to become too similar to each other. The mutation operator of the LSHGA randomly modifies a solution while making sure that a path exists between the source and destination nodes of commodities. To achieve this, mutation is applied within the crossover operator. First, an edge (i, j) such that $(i, j) \notin E(P[p_1])$, $(i, j) \notin E(P[p_2])$, $i \in \{V(P[p_1]) \cup V(P[p_2])\}$, and $j \in \{V(P[p_1]) \cup V(P[p_2])\}$ is randomly selected, and then its temporary cost $tc_{i,j}$ is set to zero before applying the crossover. By randomly selecting an edge that does not exist in either of the parents and setting its cost to zero, it is expected that the offspring will include a different edge than its parents. Mutation is applied to ρ percent of the population. The procedure of the crossover/mutation operator is given as follows:

Procedure Crossover_Mutation()

Randomly select two solutions $P[p_1]$ and $P[p_2]$ from P.
for each edge $(i, j) \in E$ **do** {
    if $P[p_1].x_{i,j} = 1$ or $P[p_2].x_{i,j} = 1$ **then** $tc_{i,j} := U \times (c_{i,j} + f_i + f_j)$ **else** $tc_{i,j} := \infty$
    }
if $(\rho < U)$ **then** {
    randomly select an edge (i, j) such that $(i, j) \notin E(P[p_1])$,
    $(i, j) \notin E(P[p_2])$, $i \in \{V(P[p_1]) \cup V(P[p_2])\}$, & $j \in \{V(P[p_1]) \cup V(P[p_2])\}$.
    set $tc_{i,j} := 0$
    }
for each commodity k in a random sequence of commodities **do** {
    find the shortest path $p(k)$ from node $s(k)$ to node $t(k)$ using
    temporary costs $tc_{i,j}$.
    set $Q := 0$
    for each edge $(i, j) \in p(k)$ **do** {
        set $z.x_{i,j} := 1$
        $Q := Q + d_{i,j}$
        if $Q > \lambda$ and $(P[p_1].y_i = 1$ or $P[p_2].y_i = 1)$ **then** {set $z.y_i := 1$ and
                                      $Q := d_{i,j}$}
        set $tc_{i,j} := 0$
        }
    }

2.3   Local Search

As mentioned earlier, the LSHGA also uses local search to investigate new solutions in addition to crossover and mutation. In the local search, a set of neighborhood solutions of each solution in the population is searched by applying a graph perturbation operator, and the best solution in the neighborhood, which is determined by the population ranking rules given in Section 2.1, is selected as the offspring. It should be noted that the best solution in a neighborhood might be worse than the original solution. Therefore, the local search also prevents getting mired at local optima. We considered several local search operators and after initial experiments four different types were selected to be used in the LSHGA. These four different local search procedures are described as follows:

Node Swap Local Search: This local search is based on a node swap operator which replaces a node that is in the solution with another node that is not. For a solution z, swapping nodes i and j is said to be admissible if $i \in V(z)$, $j \notin V(z)$, and edge $(j, k) \in E$ for each edge $(i, k) \in E(z)$. The node swap operator for an admissible node pair i and j is given as follows:

node_swap(i, j)
for each edge $(i, k) \in E(z)$ **do** {
    set $z.x_{j,k} := 1$ and $z.x_{i,k} := 0$
    }
set $z.y_j := z.y_i$

For a solution z, all admissible node_swap(i, j)s are performed, and the best solution is added to the offspring population.

Relay Station Local Search: In this local search, the values of the relay station decision variables are flipped (i.e., $z.y_i = 1 - z.y_i$) one node at a time for each node $i \in V(z)$. As a result, the best solution is returned.

Edge Swap/Node Add Local Search: In this local search, a solution z is modified by removing an edge $(i, j) \in E(z)$ and adding two new edges (i, k) and (j, k). Node k is included in the solution if it does not exist in the solution. This perturbation is permissible only if $(i, k) \in E$ and $(j, k) \in E$. As a result of this perturbation, nodes i and j are connected through node k instead of being directly connected; therefore, the connectivity of solution z is not disturbed. Similarly, after performing all permissible perturbations, the best solution is added to the offspring population.

Edge Swap/Node Delete Local Search: This local search is the opposite of the edge swap/node add local search. Basically, two edges $(i, j) \in E(z)$ and $(j, k) \in E(z)$ are removed from a solution z, and new edge $(i, k) \notin E(z)$ is added (i.e, set $z.x_{i,j} := 0$, $z.x_{i,k} := 0$, and $z.x_{i,j} := 1$). Deletion of edges (i, j) and (j, k) is permissible if

- $(i, k) \in E$ and $(i, k) \notin E(z)$, and
- node j has a node degree of two, and
- node j is neither a source node nor a destination node.

The local search is applied to all permissible node triples i, j, and k, and the best solution is added to the offspring population.

2.4   Overall Algorithm

The important features of the LSHGA are given as follows:
- Initial solutions are randomly generated in a similar fashion to the crossover operator on the complete edge and node sets. A uniform random number is assigned to each edge ($tc_{i,j}:=U$ for each $(i, j) \in E$), and the shortest path from node $s(k)$ and node $t(k)$ is found for each commodity k in a random order of commodities. After finding the shortest path from node $s(k)$ to node $t(k)$, the nodes on the shortest path is sequentially analyzed starting from node $s(k)$ in order to determine the location of relay stations on the shortest path. The edges on the shortest path and relay nodes are added to the solution, and $tc_{i,j}:=0$ for each edge included in the solution.
- The LSHGA is a generational GA where the entire parent population is replaced by offspring generated by either the crossover/mutation or the local search. In initial experiments, significantly better solutions were obtained with a generational GA than with a steady-state GA where the population retains the best solutions of earlier generations. The LSHGA retains only the best feasible solution found so far in the population between iterations. All other solutions in the next generation are newly generated.
- Duplicate solutions are discouraged in the population. If a solution happens to have multiple copies in the offspring population, only one of them is considered while ranking offspring solutions, and the others are automatically assigned a low rank (i.e., they are pushed back in the offspring population). Thereby, the population is discouraged from converging to a single solution, which is usually the case in GA. In our initial experiments, however, we found better results by avoiding identical solutions in the population.
- In the local search, one of the four local search procedures given in Section 2.3 is randomly and uniformly selected.
- In the selection procedure, the offspring population is sorted according to the solution ranking rules given in Section 2.1. The best μ-1 offspring are selected for the next generation.

The pseudo code of the LSHGA is given as follows:

Procedure LSHGA

Randomly generate μ solutions
for $t:=1..t_{max}$ **do** {
  //Crossover
  $i:=0$
  do {
    Randomly select two distinct integers p_1 and p_2 in $[1, \mu]$
    $OP[i]:=$Crossover_Mutation($P[p_1]$, $P[p_2]$)
    Evaluate $OP[i]$
    $i:=i+1$
  } **while** ($i < \mu$)
  // Local Search
  for $j:=1..\mu$ **do** {
    Randomly and uniformly select a local search procedure
    Apply local search, set $OP[i]:=$Local_Search($P[j]$)
    $i:=i+1$
    }
  Rank and sort OP according to the ranking rules (consider a single copy of identical solutions while ranking OP and assign a low ranking to the others)
  for $j:=1..\mu$ **do** set $P[j]:=OP[j]$
}

3. EXPERIMENTAL RESULTS

In the experimental study, 20 problem instances of five groups of different number of nodes, the smallest with 40 nodes and 198 edges and the largest with 160 nodes and 3624 edges, are used. For each problem group, the x and y coordinates and relay station cost f_i of each node i are randomly generated from integer numbers between 0 and 100. Cost $c_{i,j}$ and distance $d_{i,j}$ of edge (i, j) are defined as the Euclidian distance between nodes i and j. Two different values of λ and K are used. The source and the destination nodes of each commodity for each problem group are randomly selected while making sure that the problems are not trivial (source and destinations nodes are selected apart from each other). The settings for the problems are given in Table 1. In this section, we refer to individual problems using problem parameters N-K-λ. For example, $160N$-$10K$-35λ refers to the problem with 160 nodes, 10 commodities, and $\lambda=35$.

We compared the performance of the LSHGA with the Construction Heuristic 1 (CH1) and Construction Heuristic 2 (CH2) developed by Cabral et al. [1]. In the CH1, a solution is constructed by considering one commodity at the time in a random order of commodities. Cabral *et al.* [1] used a path based integer programming formulation to solve the NDPRS with a single commodity. The NDPRS with a single commodity is called the subproblem of in the CH1. This formulation approach requires that all feasible path and relay station location combinations between a source node and a destination node are generated a priori and input to the model. Unfortunately, generating all feasible path and relay station location combinations is computationally infeasible for the size of problems studied in this paper. In such cases, Cabral *et al.* [1] recommend using a subset of all feasible path and relay station location combinations to find good solutions to the subproblems without guaranteeing optimality. Fortunately, we were able to optimally solve the problem NDPRS with a single commodity for all problem instances using CPLEX 9.0. It should be noted that since the subproblems of the CH1 are solved to the optimality in this paper, the CH1 run longer than the CPU times reported in [1].

The CH2 provides the best results among the four construction heuristics given in [1]. The CH2 uses the CH1 as a subroutine and analyzes each edge and node one at the time to test whether an edge or node should be included in the final solutions or not. Therefore, the CH2 is a computationally very expensive heuristic. In order to solve problem $160N\text{-}10K\text{-}35\lambda$, for example, the CH2 requires minimum of $10 \times (160+3624)$ calls to the CH1 (at least 10 calls for each node and edge). Cabral *et al.* [1] recommend using the CH1 if the CPU time is premium. Due to the time constraints, we were able to implement CH2 for all instances of the 40, 50, 60-node problems and only one instance of the 80-node problem, but not for 160-node problems.

The total costs for the best solutions found by the LSHGA, CH1, and CH2 are given in Table 1. The parameters of the LSHGA were $\mu=50$, $\rho=0.50$, and $t_{max}=100$ in all runs. For each problem setting, 10 random replications were performed. The average cost of 10 random replications for each problem is also given in the table. To be consistent, the CH1 was run for 10 random replications and the best solution found in 10 replications is reported in Table 1. As seen in the table, the best solutions found by the LSHGA are superior to those found by the CH1 and CH2, excluding problem $80N\text{-}5K\text{-}30\lambda$. For this problem, the CH2 found a better solution. In some cases, even the average costs of 10 random replications are better than the best objective function values found by the CH1 and CH2. In every problem, the average cost of 10 random replications is very close to the best objective function value found. This shows the robustness of the LSHGA over random replications.

In Table 1, the CPU times given for the LSHGA are averaged over 10 replications. The CPU time results show that the LSHGA is highly scaleable. The CPU time requirement was only doubled from the smallest (with 198 edges) to the largest problem (with 3624 edges) while the problem size increased in 18-fold. The CPU time requirement for the CH2 was in the range of several hours since subproblems were solved to optimality using the problem NDPRS.

Table 1. Results of the test problems

				LSHGA (10 Replications)			CH1	CH2
						Average		
				Best	Average	CPU	Best	Best
N	K	λ	M	Cost	Cost	Seconds*.	Cost	Cost
40	5	30	198	473.80	475.57	391	486.55	486.55
40	5	35	272	354.57	356.56	457	361.49	381.27
40	10	30	198	518.98	519.16	443	567.76	547.20
40	10	35	272	399.76	409.16	491	446.45	434.56
50	5	30	279	283.78	283.78	392	341.34	320.31
50	5	35	372	260.23	260.23	383	260.23	267.31
50	10	30	279	540.39	550.03	581	592.71	594.29
50	10	35	372	407.49	418.72	688	467.50	481.46
60	5	30	305	509.90	524.02	433	525.41	538.38
60	5	35	412	377.02	377.14	481	404.51	397.44
60	10	30	305	694.89	732.11	642	714.65	731.41
60	10	35	412	499.64	512.88	645	595.86	596.16
80	5	30	641	356.65	360.70	412	372.29	341.72
80	5	35	853	328.80	332.18	455	347.05	
80	10	30	641	464.99	482.81	514	501.45	
80	10	35	853	436.75	459.84	539	516.90	
160	5	30	2773	287.84	292.27	538	297.25	
160	5	35	3624	270.22	274.27	569	314.51	
160	10	30	2773	408.10	431.60	643	458.37	
160	10	35	3624	409.93	433.29	775	479.87	

*The computational experiments were performed in the Lion-XM system of the High Performance Computing Group at the Pennsylvania State University (http://gears.aset.psu.edu/hpc/systems/lionxm/). The implementation code was not paralyzed over multiple processors. Therefore, the CPU times are comparable with a single 3.2 GHz Intel Xeon Processor with 4GB memory.

Figures 1 and 2 illustrate the best solutions found for problems $80N$-$10K$-30λ and $80N$-$10K$-35λ by the LSHGA, respectively. On both figures, the source and destination nodes are also identified. In both cases, the best solutions are spanning trees.

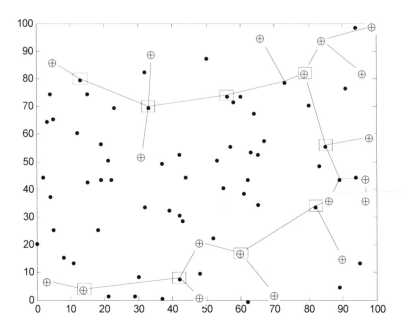

Figure 1. The best solution found for problem 80*N*-10*K*-30λ (●: location of nodes, □: relay station node, and ⊕: source or destination node)

4.   CONCLUSIONS AND FUTURE RESEARCH

In this paper, to our best knowledge, a meta-heuristic based approach was applied to the network design problem with relay stations for the first time.   Our initial experiments with traditional GA and local search approaches did not provide promising results. Therefore, a hybrid approach was developed.   The proposed hybrid GA approach has specialized crossover and mutation operators, and four different local search procedures are used. The experimental results showed that the proposed hybrid GA with the local search heuristics was effective to find good solutions in reasonable CPU times. Compared to the CH1 and CH2 [1], the proposed approach was superior.

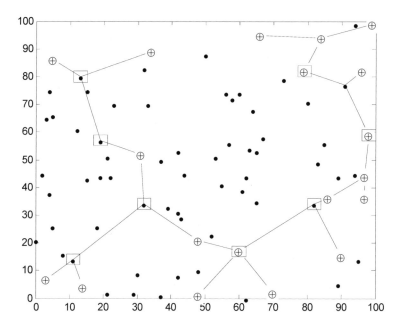

Figure 2. The best solution found for problem 80*N*-10*K*-35λ (●: location of nodes, ☐: relay station node, and ⊕: source or destination node)

References:

1. E. A. Cabral, E. Erkut, G. Laporte, and R. A. Patterson, The network design problem with relays. *European Journal of Operational Research* 180(2), 834-844, (2007).
2. L. LeBlanc and R. Reddoch, Reliable link topology/capacity design and routing in backbone telecommunication networks. *First ORSA Telecommunications SIG Conference*, (1990).
3. A. Balakrishnan and K. Altinkemer, Using a hop-constrained model to generate alternative communication network design. *ORSA Journal on Computing* 4(2), 192-205, (1992).
4. S. Choplin, Virtual path layout in ATM path with given hop count. *Proceedings of the First International Conference on Networking-Part 2*, Colmar, France, 527-537, (2001).
5. L. Kwangil and M. A. Shayman, Optical network design with optical constraints in IP/WDM networks. *IEICE Transactions on Communications* E88-B(5), 1898-905, (2005).
6. M. Randall, G. McMahon, and S. Sugden, A simulated annealing approach to communication network design. *Journal of Combinatorial Optimization* 6(1), 55-65, (2002).
7. S. Voss, The Steiner tree problem with hop constraints. *Annals of Operations Research* 86(0), 321-345, (1999).
8. L. Gouveia and T. L. Magnanti, Network flow models for designing diameter-constrained minimum spanning and Steiner trees. *Networks* 41(3), 159-73, (2003).

9. L. Gouveia, Multicommodity flow models for spanning trees with hop constraints. *European Journal of Operational Research* 95(1), 178-90, (1996).

10. L. Gouveia and C. Requejo, A new Lagrangean relaxation approach for the hop-constrained minimum spanning tree problem. *European Journal of Operational Research* 132(3), 539-52, (2001).

11. S. L. Hakimi, Optimum locations of switching centers and absolute centers and medians of graph. *Operations Research* 12(3), 450-459, (1964).

Chapter 16

DYNAMIC BANDWIDTH RESERVATION IN A VIRTUAL PRIVATE NETWORK UNDER UNCERTAIN TRAFFIC

Hélène Le Cadre and Mustapha Bouhtou

Orange Labs
$38 - 40$, *rue du Général Leclerc*
92794 *Issy-les-Moulineaux Cedex* 9
FRANCE
helene.lecadre@orange-ftgroup.com, mustapha.bouhtou@orange-ftgroup.com

Abstract   A Virtual Private Network (VPN) is a telecommunication network, built by an operator, between distant sites of a customer's firm. The aim of the operator is to manage optimally his network. The originality of the article lies in the representation of the problem as an iterative two side game. Indeed, the network operator wants to provide dynamically the best Quality of Service to his customers, while saving his resources. Consequently, he must be able to forecast the worst traffic evolution, so as to optimize dynamically bandwidth allocation. We use Markov Decision Processes to model the traffic uncertainty and Bellman optimality equation to determine optimal policies. Finally, to manage the curse of dimensionality due to the state space growth, we introduce techniques of simulation based on optimization over the policy space.

Keywords: Hose model; Markov decision process; Bellman optimality principle; stochastic games; linear programming.

1.   Introduction

The starting point of the idea to model the traffic evolution as a stochastic game, comes from the original article [9]. Nilim and El Ghaoui studied extensively the problem of managing airplane traffic flows between two airports, under constraints. More precisely, the airport operator should be able to define *optimal* trajectories for each airplane, so as to minimize the expected delay of the overall system. Indeed, there are two major constraints: at first, the airport operator should prevent the airplanes from collision risks into another one, by associating fixed capacities to each sector between the two airports. Secondly, the operator should also be able to cope with a storm, occurring at two different places. The originality of the article lies in the idea to model the storm as a Markov chain, whose transition probabilities are updated, using weather forecasting information. Actually, the storm zones are not seen anymore as mere obstacles, but the operator might choose to drive his airplane through the storm, provided its intensity is not too strong.

Judging from the surrounding literature, we can note that there are three major ways to treat the problem of the dynamic evolution of a Virtual Private Network. The first traditional approach (see [16]), is to use traffic matrices to realize link reservations, so as to make capacity-savings. During the last decades, many methods have been developed to tackle the rather hard problem of traffic matrix estimation (see [18], [19], [21] and [20] for a presentation of the subject). The study of this rich field is out of the scope of this article. Briefly, traffic matrices are not known by the network manager, and should be estimated on-line using various statistical techniques. This approach relies strongly on the link traffic data available to the operator. Besides, it doesn't take into account the uncertainty with which such measures are known.

A second interesting approach has been introduced, through the articles [1], [2], and [7]. Indeed, the authors supposed that the traffic is uncertain, and consequently, the traffic matrix belongs to a polytope of uncertainty. For example, the hose model enables the network operator to define an uncertainty polytope. Then, the operator determines an optimal routing, using operations research techniques, so as to minimize a global cost, on the overall network. The main drawback of this method, lies in the fact that at first glance, we don't know how the uncertainty polytope will evolve in the future. Consequently, it seems difficult to develop stochastic approaches in such a context.

Finally, there is a third elegant point of view (see [6], [8], and [22]), which considers the whole telecommunication network, under a system oriented point of view. More precisely, the idea is not anymore to study the data resulting from the system, but to model the system as a set of actors, interacting with one another. The aim of this model is of course, to define the best strategies to follow for each player, so as to drive the whole system in a global equilibrium. The spirit of this approach relies deeply in the world of game theory.

Practically, [16] determines the relative importance of mechanisms (i.e. admission control, signalling, traffic matrix estimation) that positively affect the operational efficiency of the VPN provisioning, while [1] and [2] define the hose model as a performance and flexible model to manage resources. [3] introduces a tree structure to optimize the total bandwidth reserved on edges of the VPN tree, dramatically reducing bandwidth requirements in many instances.

Virtual Private Networks (VPNs) are networks built between geographically distant Internet Protocol (IP)-sites of a firm. With the help of this technology, distant sites of the same firm are able to communicate via secured tunnels. Indeed, the data should be transmitted via the Internet, which is a public infrastructure shared by many operators. In order to guarantee the security of his client, the data will be encrypted and sent along virtual tunnels using Multi-Protocol Label Switching (MPLS) technology. Besides, a *Service Level Agreement* (SLA) should be defined between the network provider and his client. The aim of this contract is to specify bounds on admissible levels of QoS. To perform such a task, the operator should have some precise knowledge about the spatial and temporal traffic distributions to drive his system into states satisfying the QoS constraints. Unfortunately, the traffic matrix accuracy relies mainly on the quality of the estimate itself and of the data, which can be quite hazardous. Then, the solution we have chosen to get a rough characterization of the traffic, is to use the hose model, introduced for the first time in [1].

The client is asked to merely specify:
- the amount of traffic going out each of his web sites,
- the relationships between all his web points (source → destination).

We can check that, although the hose model is quite simple to specify from the client point of view, it is full of uncertainty for the manager. Indeed, for each source node, for example, the operator ignores how the traffic is shared between the different destination nodes, which constitutes in itself a spatial uncertainty. Furthermore, due to the roughness of this approach, he does not know how the traffic should evolve under this assumption. Consequently, we have chosen to model the dynamic evolution of the traffic as a Markov decision process (MDP), which enables us to introduce uncertainty, in our model.

The article is organized as follows: in section 1, we explain how to represent traffic as a Markov Decision Process, which enables us to introduce, later, the iterative game between bandwidth reservation and traffic allocation. In a second section, we apply our theoretical results to the management of a 3 site VPN, and prove the existence of stationary strategies. Furthermore, numerical results of simulations are presented. Finally, to prevent us from the curse of dimensionality, resulting from the use of dynamic programming, we have introduced parameterized strategies, whose parameters should be optimized over the policy space, in section 3.

2.   A Model to Cope with Uncertain Traffic Evolution

2.1   The Representation of Traffic as an MDP

Let $\{X^{(t)}\}_{t\in\mathbb{N}}$, be the discrete time, discrete state space, stochastic process, representing the traffic in the network. The VPN network will be represented by an oriented graph: $G = (\mathcal{N}, \mathcal{L})$, where $\mathcal{N}$ is the set of the nodes modeling the sites of the network, and $\mathcal{L}$, is the directed link set of the VPN.

Let $X_{ij}^{(t)}$ denotes the traffic going from the node i, to the node j, at the instant t.

At time period t, the whole traffic is represented by a vector $X^{(t)}$, i.e.:[1]

$$X^{(t)} = \left(\begin{array}{ccccccc} X_{12}^{(t)} & X_{13}^{(t)} & \cdots & X_{|\mathcal{N}|\,1}^{(t)} & \cdots & X_{|\mathcal{N}|(|\mathcal{N}|-2)}^{(t)} & X_{|\mathcal{N}|(|\mathcal{N}|-1)}^{(t)} \end{array} \right)^T . \tag{1}$$

The traffic on the links is obtained via the matrix equation:

$$\left(\begin{array}{cccc} L_1^{(t)} & L_2^{(t)} & \cdots & L_{|\mathcal{L}|}^{(t)} \end{array} \right)^T = R(t) \left(\begin{array}{cccc} X_{12}^{(t)} & X_{13}^{(t)} & \cdots & X_{|\mathcal{N}|\,(|\mathcal{N}|-1)}^{(t)} \end{array} \right)^T , \tag{2}$$

where, $R(t)$, models the routing matrix, which can remain constant or change with the time. The rather intuitive notation $L_l^{(t)} = \left(R(t)\, X^{(t)} \right)_l$, $l \in \mathcal{L}$, represents the traffic flowing through the link l.

The state space is defined using a simplified version of the hose model. Indeed, the client gives a rather tight upper bound on the traffic going out of each node. As we are supposed to be in the worst case, we should assume that this bound is reached. As an example, in the three-node case, we get a system of relationships:

$$\begin{cases} X_{12}^{(t)} + X_{13}^{(t)} = t_1^{\text{out}} \\ X_{21}^{(t)} + X_{23}^{(t)} = t_2^{\text{out}} \\ X_{31}^{(t)} + X_{32}^{(t)} = t_3^{\text{out}} \\ X_{ij}^{(t)} \geq 0, \ \forall i, j \in \{1, 2, 3\}, \ i \neq j , \end{cases} \tag{3}$$

where, the constant t_i^{out}, $i = 1, 2, 3$, represents the volume of traffic leaving the site i of the VPN. We just need to deal with the 3 components $X_{12}^{(t)}$, $X_{21}^{(t)}$ and $X_{31}^{(t)}$, since the others are deduced from the first. The state space is represented geometrically as the union of the three independent segments defined by the system (3). Consequently, we will note the continuous state space under the form:

$$\left(\mathbf{S^X} \right)^{\text{continuous}} = \left(\mathbf{S_1^X} \right)^{\text{continuous}} \times \left(\mathbf{S_2^X} \right)^{\text{continuous}} \times \left(\mathbf{S_3^X} \right)^{\text{continuous}} .$$

Every element of $\left(\mathbf{S^X} \right)^{\text{continuous}}$ could be represented under a 3-dimensional vector form: $s = (s_1, s_2, s_3)$, where, s_i takes its values in the state space $\left(\mathbf{S_i^X} \right)^{\text{continuous}}$, $i = 1, 2, 3$.

---

[1] A^T is the transpose of the matrix, A.

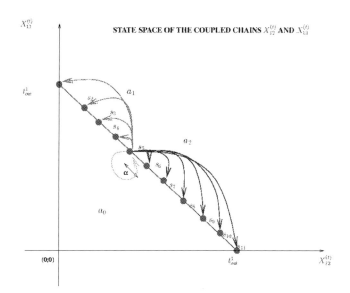

Figure 16.1. Discrete state space S_1^X, and action space.

To be more explicit, $\left(\mathbf{S_1^X}\right)^{\text{continuous}} = \left\{(X_{12}^{(t)}, X_{13}^{(t)}) | X_{12}^{(t)} + X_{13}^{(t)} = t_1^{\text{out}}\right\}$, represents the continuous state space associated with the stochastic process $\{X_{12}^{(t)}\}_t$, while $\left(\mathbf{S_2^X}\right)^{\text{continuous}}$ and $\left(\mathbf{S_3^X}\right)^{\text{continuous}}$ define the continuous state spaces associated with the processes $\{X_{21}^{(t)}\}_t$ and $\{X_{31}^{(t)}\}_t$, respectively. In order to get a discrete state space, the operator should fix *a fiability parameter* $\alpha > 0$, which would characterize the accuracy with which he desires to know the traffic flowing through its links. Then, each of the 3 segments is discretized using the parameter α. The discrete state space resulting, will be logically noted: $\mathbf{S^X} = \mathbf{S_1^X} \times \mathbf{S_2^X} \times \mathbf{S_3^X}$. The discrete state space associated with the stochastic process $X_{12}^{(t)}$, has been represented on Figure 16.1. In the following sections, $|S_i^X|$ will denote the number of elements in the ith state space.

For ease of notation, we will represent the traffic leaving the site i of the VPN, as a stochastic process:

$$X_i^{(t)} = \left(X_{ij}^{(t)}, X_{ik}^{(t)}\right), \ i \neq j, i \neq k, j \neq k \ , \ i = 1, 2, 3 \ .$$

The action space associated with the stochastic process $\left\{X_i^{(t)}\right\}_t$, is reduced to 3 distinct motions, that will be denoted: $\mathbf{A} = \{a_0; a_1; a_2\}$. Let us describe the nature of these actions.

- If we choose $a_0 = (0; 0)$, the process stays in the same state.
- But, if we choose $a_1 = (a_1(1), a_1(2))$, the traffic decreases in the first component, with an uncertainty on the state transition.

Indeed, we suppose that if the process is in the state $s_i \in \mathbf{S_i^X}$, $i = 1, 2, 3$ at time t, then it will jump up on one of the adjacent states: s_{i-k}, $1 \le k \le (i - 1)$, $i \ge 2$, according to an exponential distribution, decreasing with the distance between these two states[2]. Using the numerotation given on Figure 16.1, we draw a normalized ordered sample of the transition probabilities: $(p(s_{i-1}|s_i, a_1), p(s_{i-2}|s_i, a_1), ..., p(s_1|s_i, a_1))$. More explicitly:

$$\begin{cases} p(s_{i-k}|s_i, a_1) \sim \mathcal{E}(\lambda_1), \ \lambda_1 \in \mathbb{R}^+, \ k \in \{1, 2, ..., (i-1)\} \ , \ i \ge 2 \ , \\ p(s_{i-1}|s_i, a_1) \ge p(s_{i-2}|s_i, a_1) \ge ... \ge p(s_1|s_i, a_1) \ , \end{cases}$$

under the normalizing constraint: $\displaystyle\sum_{k=1}^{(i-1)} p(s_{i-k}|s_i, a_1) = 1$.

Recall that $\mathcal{E}(\lambda_1)$ symbolizes the exponential distribution of parameter $\lambda_1 \in \mathbb{R}^+$:

$$X \sim \mathcal{E}(\lambda_1) \ \Leftrightarrow \ f(x; \lambda_1) = \lambda_1 \exp(-\lambda_1 \ x) \ \mathbf{1}_{\mathbb{R}^+}(x) \ .$$

- Finally, if we choose $a_2 = (a_2(1), a_2(2))$, the traffic increases in its first component. Formally, we set:

$$\begin{cases} p(s_{i+k}|s_i, a_2) \sim \mathcal{E}(\lambda_2), \lambda_2 \in \mathbb{R}^+, k \in \{1, 2, ..., (|S_i^X| - i)\}, \\ p(s_{i+1}|s_i, a_2) \ge p(s_{i+2}|s_i, a_2) \ge ... \ge p\left(s_{|S_i^X|}|s_i, a_2\right), i \le (|S_i^X| - 1), \end{cases}$$

we still have a normalizing constraint of the form:

$$\sum_{k=1}^{(|S_i^X|-i)} p(s_{i+k}|s_i, a_2) = 1 \ .$$

$\mathcal{E}(\lambda_2)$ symbolizes the exponential distribution of parameter $\lambda_2 \in \mathbb{R}^+$:

$$X \sim \mathcal{E}(\lambda_2) \ \Leftrightarrow \ f(x; \lambda_2) = \lambda_2 \exp(-\lambda_2 \ x) \ \mathbf{1}_{\mathbb{R}^+}(x) \ .$$

2.2   Iterative Game Between Bandwidth Reservation and Traffic Allocation

We remind the reader that a strategy specifies for each state $s \in \mathbf{S_i^X}$ and each time instant t, the probability to choose one of the three actions. Under

---

[2]The transition probabilities can also be restricted to a maximum number of states, for example, at most three.

the vector form, we obtain:

$$\forall t \in \mathbb{N}, \ \forall s \in \mathbf{S_i^X}, \ F_t^{X_i}(s) = \left(f_t^{X_i}(s, a_0) \ f_t^{X_i}(s, a_1) \ f_t^{X_i}(s, a_2) \right)^T$$

$$i = 1, 2, 3 \ .$$

However, this probability vector is stochastic, and consequently, must satisfy the following constraints of normalization, and non negativity:

$$\begin{cases} \sum_{a \in \mathbf{A}} f_t^{X_i}(s, a) = 1, \ \forall t \in \mathbb{N}, \ \forall s \in \mathbf{S_i^X}, \\ f_t^{X_i}(s, a) \geq 0, \forall t \in \mathbb{N}, \ \forall s \in \mathbf{S_i^X}, \ \forall a \in \mathbf{A} \ . \end{cases}$$

For each time period t, the strategy is represented by an associated matrix $F_t^{X_i}$:

$$\begin{aligned} F_t^{X_i} &= \left(F_t^{X_i}(1) \ F_t^{X_i}(2) \ ... \ F_t^{X_i}(|S_i^X|) \right) \\ &= \begin{pmatrix} f_t^{X_i}(1, a_0) & f_t^{X_i}(2, a_0) & \cdots & f_t^{X_i}(|S_i^X|, a_0) \\ f_t^{X_i}(1, a_1) & f_t^{X_i}(2, a_1) & \cdots & f_t^{X_i}(|S_i^X|, a_1) \\ f_t^{X_i}(1, a_2) & f_t^{X_i}(2, a_2) & \cdots & f_t^{X_i}(|S_i^X|, a_2) \end{pmatrix} \ . \end{aligned}$$

We begin to recall basic definitions, which may be very useful for a proper understanding of the rest of the article.

Definition 16.1. *A strategy is stationary, if it is time invariant, i.e.:*

$$\forall t \in \mathbb{N}, \forall s \in \mathbf{S_i^X}, \ f_t^{X_i}(s, a) = f^{X_i}(s, a) \ , \ \forall a \in \mathbf{A} \ , \ i = 1, 2, 3 \ ,$$

*and **deterministic** or **pure**, if there exists a unique optimal action for each state, at each time instant t. Which means that:*

$$\forall s \in \mathbf{S_i^X}, \ f_t^{X_i}(s, a) \in \{0; 1\}, \ a \in \mathbf{A} \ , \ i = 1, 2, 3 \ .$$

Hypothesis. At first, we deal with deterministic strategies only. Furthermore, we suppose that the horizon is finite.

We note: $\pi^{X_i} = (F_0^{X_i}, F_1^{X_i}, ..., F_T^{X_i})$, the sequence of stationary strategies associated with the stochastic process $\left\{ X_i^{(t)} \right\}_t$, $i = 1, 2, 3$, defined on $[0; T]$.

To begin with, we consider a simple model of a 3 site network (see Figure 16.2). The sites will be numbered

$$\mathcal{N} = \{1, 2, 3\} \ ,$$

and are associated with nodes. The IP site of Rennes will be defined as being the site 1 of the VPN, while the nodes of Toulouse and Nice will keep the numbers 2 and 3 respectively. The directed links are stored in the set:

$$\mathcal{L} = \{(1, 2); (1, 3); (2, 1); (2, 3); (3, 1); (3, 2)\} \ .$$

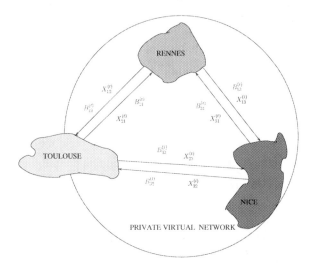

Figure 16.2.   A simple model of a 3 site VPN.

Furthermore, we suppose that the routing is time invariant, and that between each couple of nodes, the only possible path is the directed link joining these two nodes. We will see in section 3, how this assumption could be overcome.

We have chosen to cope with an objective function modeling the delay on the whole network, which is one fundamental parameter in the QoS requirements. In fact, due to the simple structure of the example (see Figure 16.2), each link is associated with a $M/M/1$ queue, and consequently the global delay on the whole Virtual Private Network, takes the form:

$$C_t^X \left(X^{(t)} \right) = \sum_{\{i,j \in \mathcal{N}, \, i \neq j\}} \left[\frac{X_{ij}^{(t)}}{\left(B_{ij}^X \right)^{(t)} - X_{ij}^{(t)}} \right. $$
$$\left. + p_{ij}^X \left((B_{ij}^X)^{(t)} - (B_{ij}^X)^{(t-1)} \right) \right] , \quad (4)$$

with,

$$C_t^{X_i} \left(X_i^{(t)} \right) = \left[\frac{X_{ij}^{(t)}}{\left(B_{ij}^X \right)^{(t)} - X_{ij}^{(t)}} + p_{ij}^X \left((B_{ij}^X)^{(t)} - (B_{ij}^X)^{(t-1)} \right) \right]$$
$$+ \left[\frac{X_{ik}^{(t)}}{\left(B_{ik}^X \right)^{(t)} - X_{ik}^{(t)}} + p_{ik}^X \left((B_{ik}^X)^{(t)} - (B_{ik}^X)^{(t-1)} \right) \right] ,$$
$$i \neq j, \, i \neq k, \, k \neq j, \, i,j,k = 1,2,3 .$$

$(B_{ij}^X)^{(t)}$ is the reserved bandwidth on the directed link (i,j), at the time instant t, by the network manager[3]. The second part of the global cost equation (4) stands for a penalty criteria. Indeed, the traffic values being fixed, in order to minimize the first part of the equation, the operator should choose to increase infinitely far the reserved amount of bandwidth, which seems not realistic, economically speaking. Fortunately, the second part, introduces a fixed price $p_{ij}^X > 0$, linked with the variations of the reserved bandwidth. Under this assumption, the manager's interest should be not to increase too fast the amounts of reserved bandwidths[4]. The second equation represents the cost associated with the traffic flow leaving the site i, of the VPN. We can note that the global cost, i.e. the first equation, is the sum of all the costs associated with the traffic flows leaving the sites 1, 2, and 3 respectively, of the VPN.

Since, the global equation in (4) can be cut into 3 independent parts (one for each amount of traffic, issued of each of the 3 sites), our problem takes the formal form:

$$
\left(\pi^{X_i}\right)^\star = \arg \min_{B_{X_i} \geq X_i} \arg \max_{\pi^{X_i}} \mathbf{E}_{\pi^{X_i}} \left[\sum_{t=0}^{T} \beta^t\, C_t^{X_i}(X_i^{(t)}, F_t^{X_i}) | X_i^{(0)} = s \right],
$$

$$
\text{with, } B_{X_i} = (B_{X_i}^{(0)}, B_{X_i}^{(1)}, ..., B_{X_i}^{(T)}) \text{ and } \pi^{X_i} = (F_0^{X_i}, F_1^{X_i}, ..., F_T^{X_i}). \qquad (5)
$$

$s \in \mathbf{S_i^X}$, $B_{X_i}^{(t)} = \left((B_{ij}^X)^{(t)}, (B_{ik}^X)^{(t)} \right)$, contains the reserved amounts of bandwidth on the directed links (i,j) and (i,k), of the VPN.
$X_i = \left(X_i^{(0)}, X_i^{(1)}, ..., X_i^{(T)} \right)$, and $\forall t \geq 0$, $X_i^{(t)} = (X_{ij}^{(t)}, X_{ik}^{(t)})$. Naturally, the reserved amounts of bandwidth must be superior to the traffic flowing through the link.

Remark. Since the strategies are deterministic, at each time instant t, there is a unique optimal action, associated with each state. This is the reason why we would rather use the notation: $F_t^{X_i}(s) = a_s$, to denote the optimal action

---

[3]However, it is possible to choose another QoS measure such as loss or jitter. Moreover, the only required assumption on the cost function, is that it is differentiable and admits a unique minimum in $\left(B_{ij}^X\right)^{(t)}$, with $\left(B_{ij}^X\right)^{(t)} \geq X_{ij}^{(t)}$.

[4]The problem is envisaged as a stochastic game, since reserved bandwidth being fixed, the traffic evolves following the *worst* behavior, and then, the operator minimizes the resulting delay. The economic coefficient p_{ij}^X is tuned by operational considerations. The optimization of this parameter deals with pricing and power relations between sites, which is beyond the scope of this article. Hence, it will be supposed fixed. Moreover, the penalty can be either positive if the bandwidth has to be increased on some links, either negative, since the release of bandwidth on some links is seen as profitable, for example, to route other lucrative applications.

in the state s, at the time instant t, for the MDP $\left\{ X_i^{(t)} \right\}_t$.

Besides, note that each element of $\mathbf{S}_i^{\mathbf{X}}$, $i = 1, 2, 3$, is represented as a 2-dimensional vector: $s = (s_{ij}, s_{ik})$. However, s_{ik} is easily deduced from s_{ij}, and from the fact that $s_{ij} + s_{ik} = t_i^{\text{out}}$, (see the system (3)). Consequently, we would rather represent the elements of the state space $\mathbf{S}_i^{\mathbf{X}}$, by their first component values. If we incorporate in the cost function, the actions to be taken on each traffic flow $\left\{ X_i^{(t)} \right\}_t$, $i = 1, 2, 3$, we get the following expression:

$$
\mathcal{C}_t^{X_i}\left(X_i^{(t)}, F_t^{X_i} \right) = \left[\frac{X_{ij}^{(t)} + F_t^{X_i}(X_{ij}^{(t)})}{\Phi\left(X_{ij}^{(t)} + F_t^{X_i}(X_{ij}^{(t)}) \right) - X_{ij}^{(t)}} \right.
$$
$$
\left. + p_{ij}^X \left(\Phi\left(X_{ij}^{(t)} + F_t^{X_i}(X_{ij}^{(t)}) \right) - \Phi\left(X_{ij}^{(t)} \right) \right) \right]
$$
$$
+ \left[\frac{X_{ik}^{(t)} + F_t^{X_i}(X_{ik}^{(t)})}{\Phi\left(X_{ik}^{(t)} + F_t^{X_i}(X_{ik}^{(t)}) \right) - X_{ik}^{(t)}} + p_{ik}^X \left(\Phi\left(X_{ik}^{(t)} + F_t^{X_i}(X_{ik}^{(t)}) \right) - \Phi\left(X_{ik}^{(t)} \right) \right) \right],
$$

$i \neq j, i \neq k, k \neq j, i, j, k = 1, 2, 3$, where:

$$
\left(B_{ij}^X \right)^{(t+1)} = \Phi\left(X_{ij}^{(t)} + F_t^{X_i}(X_{ij}^{(t)}) \right),
$$

and

$$
\left(B_{ik}^X \right)^{(t+1)} = \Phi\left(X_{ik}^{(t)} + F_t^{X_i}(X_{ik}^{(t)}) \right),
$$

are in fact, the results of the optimization problem (5), traffic values being fixed. The parameter $\beta \in [0; 1[$, often called *discount factor*, captures the natural notion that a reward of 1 unit at a time of $(t + 1)$, is worth only β of what it was worth at time t.

In order to simplify the expression (5), a quite natural idea might be to isolate the sum into two parts. Hence, following our intuition, we write:

$$
\left(\pi^{X_i} \right)^* = \arg\min_{B_{X_i} \geq X_i} \arg\max_{\pi^{X_i}} \left\{ \mathbf{E}_{\pi^{X_i}} \left[\mathcal{C}_0^{X_i}(X_i^{(0)}, F_0^{X_i}) | X_i^{(0)} = s \right] \right.
$$
$$
\left. + \mathbf{E}_{\pi^{X_i}} \left[\sum_{t=1}^{T} \beta^t \, \mathcal{C}_t^{X_i}(X_i^{(t)}, F_t^{X_i}) | X_i^{(0)} = s \right] \right\}.
$$

$$(6)$$

Then, it comes easily that:

$$\left(\pi^{X_i}\right)^\star = \arg\min_{B_{X_i} \geq X_i} \left\{\arg\max_{F_0^{X_i}} \left[\mathcal{C}_0^{X_i}(s, F_0^{X_i})\right]\right.$$

$$+ \arg\max_{F_1^{X_i}, F_2^{X_i}, \dots, F_T^{X_i}} \left(\mathbf{E}_{\pi^{X_i}}\left[\sum_{t=1}^{T} \beta^t \, \mathcal{C}_t^{X_i}(X_i^{(t)}, F_t^{X_i}) | X_i^{(0)} = s\right]\right)\right\}.$$

If we repeat once more the same decomposition, we get the expression:

$$\left(\pi^{X_i}\right)^\star = \arg\min_{B_{X_i} \geq X_i} \left\{\arg\max_{F_0^{X_i}} \left[\mathcal{C}_0^{X_i}(s, F_0^{X_i})\right] + \arg\max_{F_1^{X_i}} \sum_{s' \in S_i^X} [\beta \, \mathcal{C}_1^{X_i}(s', F_1^{X_i})\right.$$

$$\left. p(s'|s, F_1^{X_i})] + \arg\max_{F_2^{X_i}, F_3^{X_i}, \dots, F_T^{X_i}} \mathbf{E}_{\pi^{X_i}}\left[\sum_{t=2}^{T} \beta^t \, \mathcal{C}_t^{X_i}(X_i^{(t)}, F_t^{X_i}) | X_i^{(0)} = s\right]\right\}. \quad (7)$$

The equation (7) captures the essence of the principle of optimality, which is based on the recursive nature of the equation, and the introduction of the value function $V_t^i(s)$, $s \in \mathbf{S}_i^X$. In fact, solving (5) is equivalent to computing a solution to Bellman optimality equation, which takes the following special setting:

$$V_t^i(s) = \min_{B_{X_i}^{(t)} \geq X_i^{(t)}} \max_{a \in A} \left\{\mathcal{C}_{T-t}^{X_i}(s, a) + \beta \sum_{s'=1}^{|S_i^X|} p(s'|s, a) \, V_{t-1}^i(s')\right\}, \; \forall s \in \mathbf{S}_i^X,$$

$$\forall t \in \{0, 1, 2, \dots, T\}. \quad (8)$$

To solve the recursive equation (8), we proceed by backward induction.
• To begin with, we suppose that at $t = T$, the reserved bandwidth is fixed. Then **in each state s**, we have to find the set of actions on each link, which maximizes the equation:

$$a_s^{T-1} = \arg\max_{a \in A} \left\{\left[\frac{s_{ij} + a(1)}{(B_{ij}^X)^{(T)} - (s_{ij} + a(1))} + p_{ij}^X \left((B_{ij}^X)^{(T)} - (B_{ij}^X)^{(T-1)}\right)\right]\right.$$

$$\left. + \left[\frac{s_{ik} + a(2)}{(B_{ik}^X)^{(T)} - (s_{ik} + a(2))} + p_{ik}^X \left((B_{ik}^X)^{(T)} - (B_{ik}^X)^{(T-1)}\right)\right]\right\}. \quad (9)$$

The traffic being fixed to its new value: $X_i^{(T)} := X_i^{(T-1)} + a^{(T-1)}$ (i.e. optimal actions have been chosen on each VPN link), we would like to find the minimal amount of bandwidth to be reserved on each link[5]. Consequently, we

---

[5]The equation modeling the traffic evolution is purely formal. In reality, on each link (i, j), we have:
$$X_{ij}^{(T)} = \sum_{s' \in S_i^X} p(s'|X_{ij}^{(T-1)}, a^{(T-1)}(1)) \, s' \; .$$ Practically, to simulate the traffic evolution, we stock
by increasing order the conditional transition probabilities: $p(s'|X_{ij}^{(T-1)}, a_j^{(T-1)})$, $s' \in S_i^X$, draw a random uniform variable, $U \sim \mathcal{U}[0; 1]$, and let: $u = s' \Leftrightarrow u \in [p(s'|X_{ij}^{(T-1)}, a^{(T-1)}(1)); p(s' + \alpha|X_{ij}^{(T-1)}, a^{(T-1)}(1))[$.

must solve the optimization problem[6]:

$$
B_{X_i}^{(T)} = \arg\min_{B \geq X^{(T)}} \left\{ \left[\frac{X_{ij}^{(T)}}{B_{ij} - X_{ij}^{(T)}} + p_{ij}^X \left(B_{ij} - B_{ij}^{(T-1)} \right) \right] \right.
$$
$$
\left. + \left[\frac{X_{ik}^{(T)}}{B_{ik} - X_{ik}^{(T)}} + p_{ik}^X (B_{ik} - B_{ik}^{(T-1)}) \right] \right\}. \tag{10}
$$

The solution of this continuous optimization problem can be obtained analytically. This is the reason why we express it as a function of the worst traffic allocation, at time T:

$$
B_{X_i}^{(T)} = \Phi \left(X_i^{(T)} \right). \tag{11}
$$

Finally, substituting (11) in the equation (9), we get the simpler expression:

$$
F_{T-1}^{X_i} \left(x_i^{(T-1)} \right) = \arg\max_{a \in \mathbf{A}} \left\{ \left[\frac{x_{ij}^{(T-1)} + a(1)}{\Phi(x_{ij}^{(T-1)} + a(1)) - (x_{ij}^{(T-1)} + a(1))} \right. \right.
$$
$$
\left. + p_{ij}^X \left(\Phi(x_{ij}^{(T)}) - \Phi(x_{ij}^{(T-1)}) \right) \right]
$$
$$
\left. + \left[\frac{x_{ik}^{(T-1)} + a(2)}{\Phi(x_{ik}^{(T-1)} + a(2)) - (x_{ik}^{(T-1)} + a(2))} + p_{ik}^X \left(\Phi(x_{ik}^{(T)}) - \Phi(x_{ik}^{(T-1)}) \right) \right] \right\}, \tag{12}
$$

where, $x_i^{(T-1)}$ is a realization of the traffic process $X_i^{(T-1)}$ in the state space $\mathbf{S}_i^X$.

Now, the value can be easily computed, and we set:

$$
V_1^i(s) = C_{T-1}^{X_i}(s, a_s^{T-1}), \ \forall s \in \mathbf{S}_i^X, \ i = 1, 2, 3.
$$

• Then, at the iteration $(T - t)$, $t > 1$, we proceed exactly the same way. An optimal action, and the associated optimal rewards are known, for the last $(t - 1)$ stages. Then, with t stages to go, the only thing we need to do, is to maximize the immediate expected reward and the maximal expected payoff for the remainder of the process with $(t - 1)$ stages to go. As a result, we obtain the expression:

$$
a_{x_i^{(T-t)}}^{T-t} = \arg\max_{a \in \mathbf{A}} \left\{ \left[\frac{x_{ij}^{(T-t)} + a(1)}{\Phi(x_{ij}^{(T-t)} + a(1)) - (x_{ij}^{(T-t)} + a(1))} \right. \right.
$$
$$
\left. + p_{ij}^X \left(\Phi(x_{ij}^{(T-(t-1))}) - \Phi(x_{ij}^{(T-t)}) \right) \right]
$$
$$
+ \left[\frac{x_{ik}^{(T-t)} + a(2)}{\Phi(x_{ik}^{(T-t)} + a(2)) - (x_{ik}^{(T-t)} + a(2))} + p_{ik}^X \left(\Phi(x_{ik}^{(T-(t-1))}) - \Phi(x_{ik}^{(T-t)}) \right) \right]
$$
$$
\left. + \beta \sum_{s'=1}^{|\mathbf{S}_i^X|} p(s'|x_i^{(T-t)}, a) V_{(t-1)}(s') \right\} \tag{13}
$$

---

[6]We use the convention: $B \geq X \Leftrightarrow B_{ij} \geq X_{ij}, \ \forall i, j$.

And, for $x_i^{(T-t)} = s \in S_i^X$, the value takes the form:

$$
V_t^i(s) = \left\{ \left[\frac{x_{ij}^{(T-t)} + a_{x_i^{(T-t)}}^{(T-t)}(1)}{\Phi(x_{ij}^{(T-t)} + a_{x_i^{(T-t)}}^{(T-t)}(1)) - (x_{ij}^{(T-t)} + a_{x_i^{(T-t)}}^{(T-t)}(1))} \right. \right.
$$
$$
\left. + p_{ij}^X \left(\Phi(x_{ij}^{(T-(t-1))}) - \Phi(x_{ij}^{(T-t)}) \right) \right]
$$
$$
+ \left[\frac{x_{ik}^{(T-t)} + a_{x_i^{(T-t)}}^{(T-t)}(2)}{\Phi(x_{ik}^{(T-t)} + a_{x_i^{(T-t)}}^{(T-t)}(2)) - (x_{ik}^{(T-t)} + a_{x_i^{(T-t)}}^{(T-t)}(2))} \right.
$$
$$
\left. \left. + p_{ik}^X \left(\Phi(x_{ik}^{(T-(t-1))}) - \Phi(x_{ik}^{(T-t)}) \right) \right] + \beta \sum_{s'=1}^{|S_i^X|} p(s'|x_i^{(T-t)}, a_{x_i^{(T-t)}}^{(T-t)}) V_{(t-1)}(s') \right\}.
$$

We go back with the same idea, until $t = T$. Finally, we have proved the following useful proposition:

Proposition 1. *Solving the optimization problem* (5),

$$
\left(\pi^{X_i} \right)^\star = \arg \min_{B_{X_i} \geq X_i} \arg \max_{\pi^{X_i}} \left\{ \mathbf{E}_{\pi^{X_i}} \left[\sum_{t=0}^{T} \beta^t \, C_t^{X_i}(X_i^{(t)}, F_t^{X_i}) | X_i^{(0)} = s \right] \right\},
$$

$s \in S_i^X$, *is equivalent to computing a solution to Bellman optimality principle* (8):

$$
V_t^i(s) = \min_{B_{X_i}^{(t)} \geq X_i^{(t)}} \max_{a \in A} \left\{ C_{T-t}^{X_i}(s, a) + \beta \sum_{s'=1}^{|S_i^X|} p(s'|s, a) V_{t-1}^i(s') \right\}, \quad \forall s \in S_i^X,
$$
$$
\forall i \in \{1, 2, 3\}, \forall t \in \{0, 1, 2, ..., T\}. \tag{14}
$$

3. Application to the Management of a 3 Site VPN

3.1 Stable and Mono-path Routing

To model this simple system, we introduce 3 MDPs, called respectively $X_1^{(t)} = (X_{12}^{(t)}, X_{13}^{(t)})$, $X_2^{(t)} = (X_{21}^{(t)}, X_{23}^{(t)})$ and, $X_3^{(t)} = (X_{31}^{(t)}, X_{32}^{(t)})$. In fact, these MDPs are not really bi-dimensional, since we only need to take into account the first components. Indeed, the second ones are deduced from the first ones, using the set of equalities (3). Since the routing is supposed to be constant, we note that these three MDPs are completely independent of one another. Consequently, our initial problem can be separated into three disjoint sub-problems:

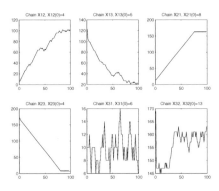

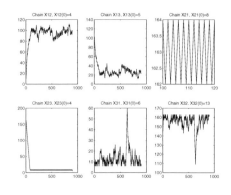

Figure 16.3. Dynamic evolution of the traffic on the six links for $t \leq 100$, $\beta = 0.9$.

Figure 16.4. A few iterations later ($t \leq 900$, $\beta = 0.9$), a stationary behavior appears.

$$
(\pi^{X_i})^\star = \arg \min_{\left(B_{ij}^X, B_{ik}^X\right)} \arg \max_{\pi^{X_i}} \left\{ \mathbf{E}_{\pi^{X_i}} \left[\sum_{t=0}^{T} C_t^{X_i}(X_i^{(t)}, F_t^{X_i}) | X_i^{(0)} = s \right] \mid s \in \mathbf{S_i^X} \right\},
$$

$$
i, j, k \in \{1, 2, 3\}, \ i \neq j, \ i \neq k, \ j \neq k. \quad (15)
$$

To solve these equations, we apply Bellman optimality equation, and backward induction. On Figure 16.5, we have drawn a numerical example, for the first VPN site. Starting at the time instant $(T - 1) = 7$, we determine the optimal actions in each state a_s^{T-1}, and infer the values of the Value function: $V_1^1(s)$, $s \in S_1^X$. Then, going backward, at each time instant $(T - t) \geq 1$, using the values of the Value function at the instant $(t - 1)$, we compute the optimal actions for each states a_s^{T-t}, and the associated values of the Value function: $V_t^1(s)$, $s \in S_1^X$. We go back until $t = 1$. Finally, knowing the initial state of the traffic process, the worst traffic evolution is simulated, by generating the new state in each time $t \geq 1$, using the optimal computed action: $x_1^{(t)} := x_1^{(t-1)} + a_{x_1^{(t-1)}}^{(t-1)}$, $t \geq 2$.

We have represented on Figure 16.3, the dynamic evolution of the stochastic processes $X_{12}^{(t)}$, $X_{21}^{(t)}$ and $X_{31}^{(t)}$, during the first 100 iterations, having previously fixed initial states $X_{12}^{(0)}$, $X_{21}^{(0)}$ and $X_{31}^{(0)}$. The state spaces S_1^X, S_2^X and S_3^X, are of cardinality 60, 100 and 100, respectively. If we increase the number of iterations, we see on Figure 16.4, that stationary behaviors appear, which means that whenever we enter the same state, the optimal action is the same.

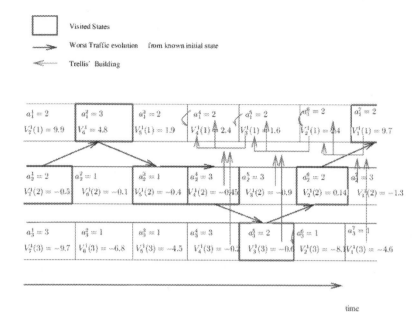

Figure 16.5. Prediction of the worst dynamic traffic evolution.

3.2 Existence of Stationary Strategies

The notion of stability is fundamental in the theory of dynamical systems. The usual idea is to prove the convergence of the system towards an equilibrium point. Transposed to the theory of Markov chains, equilibrium points are associated with invariant measures. Finally, in the theory of MDPs, these invariant measures become stationary strategies.

We will start by computing the stationary strategies using the elegant approach developed in more details in [5].

Theorem 16.2. *For every state* $s \in \mathbf{S}_i^{\mathbf{X}}$*, we determine the optimal stationary strategy, by solving the linear program:*

$$
(\mathcal{D}_\beta) := \begin{cases}
\max \sum_{s=1}^{|\mathbf{S}_i^{\mathbf{X}}|} \sum_{a \in \mathbf{A}} \mathcal{C}^{X_i}(s,a)\, x_{sa} \\
\sum_{s=1}^{|\mathbf{S}_i^{\mathbf{X}}|} \sum_{a \in \mathbf{A}} [\delta(s,s') - \beta p(s'|s,a)] x_{sa} = \gamma(s),\ s' \in \mathbf{S}_i^{\mathbf{X}} \\
x_{sa} \geq 0,\ a \in \mathbf{A},\ s \in \mathbf{S}_i^{\mathbf{X}}.
\end{cases}
\tag{16}
$$

Then, for each state $s \in \mathbf{S}_i^X$, the strategy obtained from computing: $f^{X_i}(s,a)$
$= \dfrac{x_{sa}}{\displaystyle\sum_{a \in \mathbf{A}} x_{sa}}$, $a \in \mathbf{A}$, *is a stationary strategy associated with the recursive equation* (8).

Furthermore, if the solution of the above linear program is obtained via the simplex algorithm, then the resulting strategy is deterministic.

Proof. Let V^i be an arbitrary vector taking values in the state space $\mathbf{S}_i^X$. Using the definition of the optimality equation, we know that in each state $s \in \mathbf{S}_i^X$, the value function should satisfy the inequality:

$$V^i(s) \geq C^{X_i}(s,a) + \beta \sum_{s'=1}^{|\mathbf{S}_i^X|} p(s'|s,a)V^i(s'), \ \forall a \in \mathbf{A}, \ \forall s \in \mathbf{S}_i^X . \quad (17)$$

Remark. The function C^{X_i} is actually independent of the time, since the strategy should be stationary.

If we multiply the above inequalities by $f^{X_i}(s,a)$, and sum over all the $a \in \mathbf{A}$, we get:

$$V^i(s) \geq C^{X_i}(s, F^{X_i}) + \beta \sum_{s'=1}^{|\mathbf{S}_i^X|} p(s'|s, F^{X_i})V^i(s'), \ \forall s \in \mathbf{S}_i^X ,$$

with, $C^{X_i}(s, F^{X_i}) = \displaystyle\sum_{a \in \mathbf{A}} C^{X_i}(s,a)f^{X_i}(s,a)$, and $p(s'|s, F^{X_i}) = \displaystyle\sum_{a \in \mathbf{A}} p(s'|s,a)f^{X_i}(s,a)$.

In matrix form, the set of inequalities becomes:

$$V^i \geq C^{X_i}(F^{X_i}) + \beta \, P(F^{X_i})V^i ,$$

where, the reward function under the strategy F^{X_i}, can be written under the vector form:

$$C^{X_i}(F^{X_i}) = \begin{pmatrix} C^{X_i}(1, F^{X_i}) \\ C^{X_i}(2, F^{X_i}) \\ \vdots \\ C^{X_i}(|\mathbf{S}_i^X|, F^{X_i}) \end{pmatrix},$$

and the probability transition matrix becomes,

$$P(F^{X_i}) = \begin{pmatrix} p(1|1, F^{X_i}) & p(2|1, F^{X_i}) & \cdots & p(|\mathbf{S}_i^X||1, F^{X_i}) \\ p(1|2, F^{X_i}) & p(2|2, F^{X_i}) & \cdots & p(|\mathbf{S}_i^X||2, F^{X_i}) \\ \vdots & \vdots & \vdots & \vdots \\ p(1||\mathbf{S}_i^X|, F^{X_i}) & p(2||\mathbf{S}_i^X|, F^{X_i}) & \cdots & p(|\mathbf{S}_i^X|||\mathbf{S}_i^X|, F^{X_i}) \end{pmatrix}.$$

Upon substituting the above inequality into itself k times, and taking the limit as $k \rightarrow \infty$, we obtain:

$$V^i \geq [I - \beta \, P(F^{X_i})]^{-1} C^{X_i}(F^{X_i}) \, .$$

But,

$$\sum_{t=0}^{\infty} \beta^t \mathbf{E}_{F^{X_i}}[C^{X_i}(X_i^{(t)}, F^{X_i})|X_i^{(0)} = s] =$$

$$\sum_{t=0}^{\infty} \beta^t \, p_t(s'|s, F^{X_i}) C^{X_i}(s', F^{X_i}) = \sum_{t=0}^{\infty} \beta^t [P^t(F^{X_i}) C^{X_i}(F^{X_i})|X_i^{(0)} = s],$$

since the transition probabilities are time homogeneous. Going back to our matrix formulation, we get:

$$\begin{pmatrix} \sum_{t=0}^{\infty} \beta^t \mathbf{E}_{F^{X_i}}[C^{X_i}(X_i^{(t)}, F^{X_i})|X_i^{(0)} = 1] \\ \sum_{t=0}^{\infty} \beta^t \mathbf{E}_{F^{X_i}}[C^{X_i}(X_i^{(t)}, F^{X_i})|X_i^{(0)} = 2] \\ \vdots \\ \sum_{t=0}^{\infty} \beta^t \mathbf{E}_{F^{X_i}}[C^{X_i}(X_i^{(t)}, F^{X_i})|X_i^{(0)} = |\mathbf{S}_i^{\mathbf{X}}|] \end{pmatrix}$$

$$= [I - \beta \, P(F^{X_i})]^{-1} C^{X_i}(F^{X_i}) \, .$$

We see that an arbitrary vector V^i satisfying (17), is an upper bound on the discounted value vector due to any stationary strategy F^{X_i}. Consequently, we naturally think that the discounted value vector might be the optimal solution of the primal linear program:

$$(\mathcal{P}_\beta) := \begin{cases} \min \sum_{s=1}^{|\mathbf{S}_i^{\mathbf{X}}|} \gamma(s) V^i(s) \\ V^i(s) \geq C^{X_i}(s, a) + \beta \sum_{s'=1}^{|\mathbf{S}_i^{\mathbf{X}}|} p(s'|s, a) V^i(s'), \ a \in \mathbf{A}, \ s \in \mathbf{S}_i^{\mathbf{X}} \end{cases}$$

with $\gamma(s)$ $\left(\gamma(s) > 0 \text{ and } \sum_{s \in \mathbf{S}_i^{\mathbf{X}}} \gamma(s) = 1 \right)$, being the probability that the process begins in state $s \in \mathbf{S}_i^{\mathbf{X}}$. By duality, we get:

$$(\mathcal{D}_\beta) := \begin{cases} \max \sum_{s=1}^{|\mathbf{S}_\mathbf{i}^\mathbf{X}|} \sum_{a \in \mathbf{A}} c^{X_i}(s, a) \, x_{sa} \\ \sum_{s=1}^{|\mathbf{S}_\mathbf{i}^\mathbf{X}|} \sum_{a \in \mathbf{A}} [\delta(s, s') - \beta p(s'|s, a)] x_{sa} = \gamma(s), \ s' \in \mathbf{S}_\mathbf{i}^\mathbf{X} \\ x_{sa} \geq 0, \ a \in \mathbf{A}, \ s \in \mathbf{S}_\mathbf{i}^\mathbf{X} \, . \end{cases} \tag{18}$$

x_{sa}, $s \in \mathbf{S}_\mathbf{i}^\mathbf{X}$, $a \in \mathbf{A}$, which is the dual variable, can be heuristically interpreted as the long-run fraction of decision epochs at which the system is in the state s, and action a is made.

Remark. It can be shown (see [5]), that if the variables x_{sa} are obtained using the simplex algorithm, as the solution of the above linear program, then the associated stationary strategy is indeed a *deterministic stationary* strategy. We note, $x_s = \sum_{a \in \mathbf{A}} x_{sa}$, for each $s \in \mathbf{S}_\mathbf{i}^\mathbf{X}$. In our context, we get the following system of equalities:

$$\begin{cases} x_{1a_0} + x_{1a_1} + x_{1a_2} = x_1 \\ x_{2a_0} + x_{2a_1} + x_{2a_2} = x_2 \\ \vdots \\ x_{|\mathbf{S}_\mathbf{i}^\mathbf{X}|a_0} + x_{|\mathbf{S}_\mathbf{i}^\mathbf{X}|a_1} + x_{|\mathbf{S}_\mathbf{i}^\mathbf{X}|a_2} = x_{|\mathbf{S}_\mathbf{i}^\mathbf{X}|} \\ x_{sa} \geq 0, \ \forall s \in \mathbf{S}_\mathbf{i}^\mathbf{X}, \ \forall a \in \mathbf{A} \, . \end{cases} \tag{19}$$

However, as $x^0 = \left(x^0_{1a_0} x^0_{1a_1} x^0_{1a_2} \mid x^0_{2a_0} x^0_{2a_1} x^0_{2a_2} \mid \cdots \mid x^0_{|\mathbf{S}_\mathbf{i}^\mathbf{X}|a_0} x^0_{|\mathbf{S}_\mathbf{i}^\mathbf{X}|a_1} x^0_{|\mathbf{S}_\mathbf{i}^\mathbf{X}|a_2} \right)$, is an optimal basic feasible solution for the simplex algorithm, it is necessarily an extreme point of the space defined by the system (19). Using the definition of an extreme point, for all $s \in \mathbf{S}_\mathbf{i}^\mathbf{X}$, there exists a unique $i \in \{0; 1; 2\}$ such that $x^0_{sa_i} = x^0_s$, and $x^0_{sa_j} = 0$, for $j \in \{0; 1; 2\}, j \neq i$. Consequently, the stationary control $F_0^{X_i}$ constructed from x^0, by setting

$$f_0^{X_i}(s, a) = \frac{x^0_{sa}}{\sum_{a \in \mathbf{A}} x^0_{sa}} , \ \forall a \in \mathbf{A}, \ \forall s \in \mathbf{S}_\mathbf{i}^\mathbf{X},$$

is deterministic.

□

We have proved the existence of a stationary strategy for our problem. But, are we sure that the set of feasible strategies determined on $[0; T]$ with the help of Bellman optimality equation converges asymptotically to these values? Basically, *a system is said to be ergodic*, if all the specific realizations of the dynamic evolution of the system are asymptotically and statistically the same. In fact, ergodicity is synonymous with equality between spatial and temporal means. Transposed to the MDP context, the property of ergodicity is defined conditionally to the choice of an action. The theoretic definition below introduces the notion of ergodicity from a measure theoretic point of view (see [17]).

Definition 16.3. *Conditionally to the choice of an action* $a \in \mathbf{A}$, *the Markov chain* $(\mathbf{S_i^X}, \{p(s'|s, a)\}_{s,s' \in \mathbf{S_i^X}})$ *is ergodic if:*

$$|p[X_i^{(t+1)} \in \mathbf{B}|X_i^{(0)} = s] - \mu^\star(\mathbf{B})| \to 0, \forall s \in \mathbf{S_i^X}, \forall \mathbf{B} \in \mathcal{B}(\mathbf{S_i^X}), i = 1, 2, 3,$$
(20)

where, $\mu^\star(\mathbf{B}) = \int \mu(dx) \mathbf{P}[X_i^{(t+1)} \in \mathbf{B} \mid X_i^{(0)} = x] . \mathcal{B}(\mathbf{S_i^X})$, *is a countably generated σ-field on* $\mathbf{S_i^X}$, *while μ is a given probability measure on* $\mathcal{B}(\mathbf{S_i^X})$.

Besides, a well known result states that in the case of an ergodic MDP, the set of strategies $\{f_t^{X_i}(s, a)|s \in \mathbf{S_i^X}, a \in \mathbf{A}\}_t$, converges to a set of stationary strategies $\{f^{X_i}(s, a)|s \in \mathbf{S_i^X}, a \in \mathbf{A}\}$, i.e. strategies which are time invariant. Now, we will introduce the important theorem, which states that the strategies obtained through the resolution of the dual linear program $(\mathcal{D}_\beta)$ (see (18)), are the same as those obtained for a large number of iterations in Bellman optimality equation.

Theorem 16.4. *Conditionally to the choice of an action* $a \in \mathbf{A}$, *the Markov chains* $\left(\mathbf{S_1^X}, \{p(s'|s, a)\}_{s,s' \in \mathbf{S_1^X}}\right)$, $\left(\mathbf{S_2^X}, \{p(s'|s, a)\}_{s,s' \in \mathbf{S_2^X}}\right)$, $\left(\mathbf{S_3^X}, \{p(s'|s, a)\}_{s,s' \in \mathbf{S_3^X}}\right)$ *are ergodic. Consequently, under such hypotheses, the set of strategies converges to a set of stationary strategies:*

$$\begin{cases} f_t^{X_1}(s, a) \to f^{X_1}(s, a) , \forall s \in \mathbf{S_1^X} , \\ f_t^{X_2}(s, a) \to f^{X_2}(s, a) , \forall s \in \mathbf{S_2^X} , \\ f_t^{X_3}(s, a) \to f^{X_3}(s, a) \forall s \in \mathbf{S_3^X} . \end{cases}$$

Besides, we show that these stationary strategies coincide with the ones obtained, for T large enough, in Bellman optimality equation (8).

Proof. In practice, we would rather use the fundamental result evoked before, which states that to prove the ergodicity of a Markov chain, it suffices to establish the equality between temporal and spatial order means. Since conditionally to the choice of an action $(\mathbf{S_i^X}, \{p(s'|s, a)\}_{s,s' \in \mathbf{S_i^X}})$ is a Markov chain, we are able to transpose this result to the theory of MDP. Then, for every $a \in \mathbf{A}$, we have to check that:

$$\forall k \in \mathbb{N}, \lim_{t \to \infty} \sum_{s \in \mathbf{S}_i^X} s^k f_t^{X_i}(s, a) = \lim_{T \to \infty} \sum_{s \in \mathbf{S}_i^X} s^k \frac{\hat{x}_{sa}^i}{T}, \text{ almost everywhere },$$

(21)

$i = 1, 2, 3$. The second part of the equality is obtained by drawing all the possible traffic trajectories for T large enough. Indeed, using Bellman optimality principle, and for T large, we are given a set of optimal deterministic strategies on $[0; T]$: $\pi^{X_i} = \left(F_0^{X_i}, F_1^{X_i}, ..., F_T^{X_i} \right)$. Using these optimal strategies (cf the trellis in Figure 16.5), we infer the worst possible traffic evolutions, issued from every initial state. Then, we just have to choose a distribution on the initial states, and compute the number of times that the traffic is in state s, and evolve according to the action a, i.e. $\hat{x}_{sa}^i$. The results of the simulation, drawn on Figure 16.6, show that the second order means of the MDPs $\{X_1^{(t)}\}_t$, $\{X_2^{(t)}\}_t$, $\{X_3^{(t)}\}_t$, conditionally to the choices of actions a_1, a_2, and a_0 respectively, converge towards a limit. To compute the first part of the equation, since the first term is positive, we can interchange the sum and the limit. And, to determine $f^{X_i}(s, a)$, we use linear programming. Indeed, the linear program (18), introduced previously, gives us the values of the optimal parameters $\{x_{sa}^i \mid s \in \mathbf{S}_i^X, a \in \mathbf{A}\}$, via the simplex algorithm. The strategies obtained using the normalizing ratio:

$$f^{X_i}(s, a) = \frac{x_{sa}^i}{\sum_{a \in \mathbf{A}} x_{sa}^i}, \quad \forall s \in \mathbf{S}_i^X, \forall a \in \mathbf{A},$$

are stationary and deterministic. Since the empirical and the statistical means coincide asymptotically, we deduce that the sequence of optimal strategies determined by dynamic programming, converges to the stationary strategy obtained using linear programming.

□

Remark. How does this model look like, if we suppose that the routing is multi-path and changing? We notice that the three MDPs are not independent anymore. Consequently, the equation (4) can't be separated into 3 different parts anymore. Besides, the state space and the action space are made of all the combinations of 3 elements taken from the state space $\mathbf{S}^X = \mathbf{S}_1^X \times \mathbf{S}_2^X \times \mathbf{S}_3^X$, and the initial action space $\mathbf{A}$, respectively. Let $\mathcal{L}$, be the set of links of the network, and $R(t)$, the routing matrix at time instant t. The optimality equation remains unchanged on the form, but the cost function is more complicated.

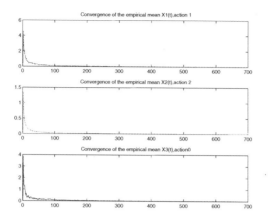

Figure 16.6. Convergence of the empirical means of the MDPs conditionally to the choice of actions, $t \leq 300$, $k = 2$.

Indeed, the value function takes the form:

$$V_t(s) = \min_{B_X^{(t)} = \left(B_{X_1}^{(t)}, B_{X_2}^{(t)}, B_{X_3}^{(t)} \right) \geq X^{(t)}} \max_{a \in \mathbf{A}^3} \left\{ \mathcal{C}_{T-t}^X(s, a) + \sum_{s'=1}^{|\mathbf{S}^X|} p(s'|s, a) \, V_{t+1}(s') \right\},$$

$$\forall s \in \mathbf{S}^X, \forall t \in \{0, 1, 2, ..., T\}, \tag{22}$$

where,

$$C_t^X(X^{(t)}) = \sum_{l=1}^{|\mathcal{L}|} \left[\frac{(R(t) \, X^{(t)})_l}{(B_l^L)^{(t)} - (R(t) \, X^{(t)})_l} + p_l \left((R(t) \, X^{(t)})_l - (R(t-1) \, X^{(t-1)})_l \right) \right],$$

$p_l > 0$, is the price associated with the link l.

Besides, conditionally to the choice of a 3-dimensional action, we make the assumption that the transition probabilities are independent of one another, i.e.:

$$p\left((s_1', s_2', s_3') \mid (s_1, s_2, s_3), (a_1, a_2, a_3) \right) = \prod_{i=1}^{3} p\left(s_i' \mid (s_i, a_i) \right),$$

$\forall (s_1, s_2, s_3), (s_1', s_2', s_3') \in \mathbf{S}^X$. We have represented the dynamic evolution of the traffic issued from the 3 sites, given initial states. Furthermore, we have supposed that the instants of changing routing were pre-defined, periodically distributed, and that the routing weights composing the routing matrix were distributed according to an exponential law (see Figure 16.7), or a normal distribution (see Figure 16.8). We can see that the changes of routing prevents the system from adopting a stationary behavior. But, it depends of course, of how often the routing is updated.

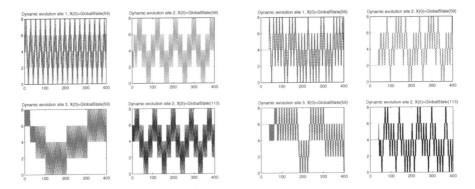

Figure 16.7. Dynamic evolution of the traffic on the VPN for a changing routing, with exponentially distributed weights.

Figure 16.8. Dynamic evolution of the traffic on the VPN for a changing routing, with normally distributed weights.

4.   The Curse of Dimensionality and Optimization in Policy Space

The use of Markov decision processes and the associated dynamic programming methodology become rapidly limited, due to the high cardinality of the state space. A solution to such a problem, lies in the introduction of parametric representations. There are three main methods to tackle the problem of dimensionality. The first well-known method called neuro-dynamic programming, or reinforcement learning, requires the introduction of weights in the value function. In each state $s \in \mathbf{S}$, the value function takes the form: $V(s, r), \ r \geq 0$. The idea is to tune the weights, so as to obtain a good approximation of the value function, and to infer a policy as close as possible to the optimal one. The second method, essentially developed in [14], considers a class of policies described by a parameter vector $\theta \in \mathbb{R}^K$. The policy is improved by updating θ in a gradient direction, via simulation. The third and last one, called actor-critic, combines the principles of both approaches.

In this article, we concentrate our study on the improvement of the parameterized policy through the policy space. We extend the framework of section 2, to the case of more than 3 nodes. Our performance metric will be the average reward function, which is slightly different from the objective function previously considered. The main reason to use such an expression, is that the methodology developed in [14] requires it, in order to introduce the steady state probabilities in the performance function and later, to derive a proper estimate for the gradient function. The long term average reward is commonly denoted:

$$\lambda^i(\theta) = \lim_{T\to\infty} \frac{1}{T}\mathbf{E}\left[\sum_{t=0}^{T} \mathcal{C}_t^{X_i}(X_i^{(t)}, \theta)|X_i^{(0)} = s\right], \ i \in \mathcal{N} \qquad (23)$$

where, we still have:

$$\mathcal{C}_t^{X_i}(X_i^{(t)}) = \sum_{\{j\in\mathcal{N},\, i\to j\}} \frac{X_{ij}^{(t)}}{\Phi(X_{ij}^{(t)}) - X_{ij}^{(t)}} + p_{ij}^{X} \left(\Phi(X_{ij}^{(t)}) - \Phi(X_{ij}^{(t-1)})\right), i \in \mathcal{N}. \tag{24}$$

At the instant t, we define a parametric matrix of strategies $F_t^{X_i}(\theta)$. Let $\theta := \theta^{\text{site } i} = \left(\theta_1^{\text{site } i}, ..., \theta_{|A|}^{\text{site } i}\right) \in \mathbf{R}^{|A|}$, be a parameter vector of size $|A|$. Each parameter $\theta_k^{\text{site } i}$, $k \in A$, is associated with the choice of the action k in the state i. We define $f_t^{X_i}(s, a, \theta)$, as the probability to be in the state $s \in \mathbf{S_i^X}$, while we choose the action $a \in A$, at the decision epoch t. The parameterized transition probabilities and reward function, take the form:

$$\begin{cases} p_\theta^{X_i}(s, s') = \sum_{a\in\mathbf{A}} f_t^{X_i}(s, a, \theta)\, p(s'|s, a)\,, \ \forall s, s' \in \mathbf{S_i^X}\,, \\ \mathcal{C}_t^{X_i}(s, \theta) = \sum_{a\in\mathbf{A}} f_t^{X_i}(s, a, \theta)\, \mathcal{C}_t^{X_i}(s, a)\,, \ \forall s \in \mathbf{S_i^X}\,. \end{cases} \tag{25}$$

We denote, $\mathcal{P}_i = \left\{P^{X_i}(\theta) = (p_\theta^{X_i}(s, s'))_{s,s'\in\mathbf{S_i^X}}, \ \theta \in \mathbf{R}^{|A|}\right\}$, the set of transition probabilities, and $\bar{\mathcal{P}}_i$, its closure which is also composed of stochastic matrices. Furthermore, we make the following assumption, required to prove the convergence of the associated algorithm:

Hypothesis. The Markov chain corresponding to every $P^{X_i} \in \bar{\mathcal{P}}_i$, is aperiodic, which means that the GCD of the length of all its cycles is one. Besides, there exists a state $s^\star \in \mathbf{S_i^X}$, which is recurrent for every such Markov chain.

Our purpose is presently, to maximize the average reward:

$$\theta^\star = \arg\max_\theta \left\{\lambda^i(\theta)\right\}$$

$$= \arg\max_\theta \left\{\lim_{T\to\infty} \frac{1}{T}\mathbf{E}\left[\sum_{t=0}^{T} \mathcal{C}_t^{X_i}(x_i^{(t)}, \theta)|x_i^{(0)} = s\right]\right\}, \tag{26}$$

where $x_i^{(t)}$, represents a realization of the stochastic process $\{X_i^{(t)}\}_t$, at the instant t. The expectation is computed relatively to the randomized strategy $F_t^X(\theta)$. The first idea is to introduce the well-known gradient algorithm, to get an estimate of the parameter.

$$\theta(t+1) \;=\; \theta(t) \;+\; \gamma_t \, \nabla_\theta \, \lambda^i \left(\theta(t)\right), \; \gamma_t \;=\; \frac{1}{t}, \; t \in \mathbb{N} \,.$$

Unfortunately, we can't compute analytically the gradient of the performance function, and must resort to simulation. The algorithm developed in [14], updates at every time step the value of the parameter, and uses a biased estimate (whose bias asymptotically vanishes) of the gradient of the performance metric.

$$\begin{cases} \theta(t+1) = \theta(t) + \gamma_t \left[\nabla_\theta C_t^{X_i}(x_i^{(t)}, \theta(t)) + \left(C_t^{X_i}(x_i^{(t)}, \theta(t)) - \tilde{\lambda}_t^i \right) z_t \right], \\ \tilde{\lambda}_{t+1}^i = \tilde{\lambda}_t^i + \eta\gamma_t \left[C_t^{X_i}(x_i^{(t)}, \theta(t)) - \tilde{\lambda}_t^i \right]. \end{cases}$$

$$(27)$$

$\eta > 0$, is a parameter which enables us to scale the stepsize of our algorithm for updating $\tilde{\lambda}_t^i$ by a positive constant. Then, we simulate a transition to the next state $x_i^{(t+1)}$ following the transition probabilities $\left\{ p_{\theta(t+1)}^{X_i}(x_i^{(t)}, s), \; s \in \mathbf{S_i^X} \right\}$.

At the same time, z is updated according to the following rules:

$$z_{t+1} \;=\; \begin{cases} 0, \; \text{if } x_i^{(t+1)} = s_i^\star, \\ z_t + L_{\theta(t)}\left(x_i^{(t)}, x_i^{(t+1)} \right), \; \text{otherwise}, \end{cases} \qquad (28)$$

where $L_{\theta(t)}(x_i^{(t)}, x_i^{(t+1)}) \;=\; \dfrac{\nabla_\theta p_{\theta(t)}^{X_i}(x_i^{(t)}, x_i^{(t+1)})}{p_{\theta(t)}^{X_i}(x_i^{(t)}, x_i^{(t+1)})}, \; \text{if } p_{\theta(t)}^{X_i}(x_i^{(t)}, x_i^{(t+1)}) > 0, \; 0$

otherwise. This term can be interpreted as a Likelihood-ratio derivative term.

In the case of a multi-site VPN, we choose simple parametric strategies. For the site $i \in \mathcal{N}$, we set:

$$\begin{cases} (f_t^a)^{\text{site } i} \;=\; f_t^{\text{site } i}(X_i^{(t)}, a, \theta) \;=\; \dfrac{1}{1+\exp\left[\left(\sum_{\{j \in \mathcal{N} | i \to j\}} \Phi(X_{ij}^{(t)})\right) - \theta_a^{\text{site } i}\right]}, \\ \text{the probability to choose the action } a \in A \text{ for the chain } \{X_i^{(t)}\}_t \,. \end{cases}$$

$$(29)$$

It can be observed on Figure 16.9 that:

$$(f_t^a)^{\text{site } i} \geq 0.5 \;\Leftrightarrow\; \left(\sum_{\{j \in \mathcal{N} | i \to j\}} \Phi(X_{ij}^{(t)}) \right) \leq \theta_a^{\text{site } i}, \; a \in A \,. \qquad (30)$$

As a result, the parameters $\theta_a^{\text{site } i}, \; a \in A$ can be interpreted as fuzzy bounds for the system, since they determine the probability to choose the action a.

We remind the reader that the analytical expression of $C_t^{X_i}(X_i^{(t)}, \theta(t))$ is inferred from (25) and (24). In Figure 16.10, we have applied our method

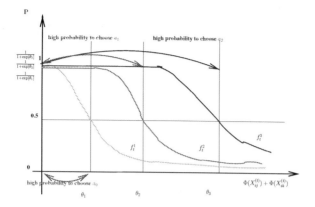

Figure 16.9. Belief functions, or parameterized strategies in the case of 3 actions, the communication scheme being of the form: $i \to j$ and $i \to k$.

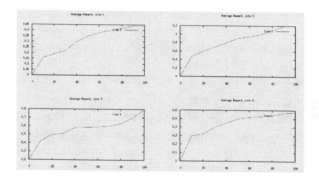

Figure 16.10. Convergence of the average rewards for each site.

to the case of a 4 node VPN, the communication scheme being of the form: $1 \to \{2,3,4\}$, $2 \to \{1,3\}$, $3 \to \{2,1,4\}$, $4 \to \{3,1\}$. We check that the average rewards converge towards finite values.

5. Conclusions

We have developed an original approach to provide decision aid, under uncertainty. The choice of optimizing a QoS criterion such as delay is rather arbitrary, and could be extended to various objective functions. This article gives us rules to control optimally a VPN so as to minimize the delay under the assumption that the traffic follows the worst possible evolution. We first determine a solution on a finite horizon $[0; T]$, using extensively Bellman principle. But, asymptotically, we would rather apply linear programming, since under such an assumption the strategies can be assumed stationary.

A curious point which could be evoked, is that the system evolved without any observation, since all the possible behaviors should be predicted and kept in memory before the system enters its initial state. In fact, the system evolution is blind. An interesting idea should be to introduce observations, so as to adapt the evolution of the system. The introduction of Partially Observed Markov Decision Processes (see [10], [11], [12], [13]) might also be quite promising, but rather hard to put in application due to the large cardinality of our state spaces.

Indeed, the curse of dimensionality appears as soon as we have to manage a complex network of numerous sites or VPNs. The state space rapidly becomes huge, and Bellman principle gets quite difficult to put in application. Fortunately, techniques of simulation based on optimization over the policy space ([14]) introduced briefly in the last section, represent an alternative approach that we have tested successfully. The idea is to introduce parameterized strategies, that depend on a set of unknown parameters. In a practical point of view, the use of this approach is all the more interesting, since to our knowledge, it has been tested only on few concrete case studies.

Finally, on the overall network, each VPN evolves independently and selfishly (cf [22] for an analogy with selfish routing). Consequently, some links might be shared between the traffics issued from various VPNs. Bandwidth might be reserved locally on each VPN link, by the VPN provider, or by a central unit also called regulator, whose aim should be to make reservations on the links. The conflict then, results from the management of the distinct QoS satisfaction levels defined by the clients, while minimizing the global amount of reserved bandwidth on the whole network. In such problems, hierarchical MDPs, or control switching game approaches might be envisaged.

References

[1] Duffield, Goyal, Greenberg. (1999). *A Flexible model for Resource Management in Virtual Private Networks.* ACM SIGCOMM.

[2] Naldi (2005). *Risk Reduction in the Hose Model for VPN Design.* EURONGI Workshop on QoS and Traffic Control.

[3] Kumar, Rastogi et al. (2002). *Algorithms for provisioning Virtual Private Networks in the Hose Model.* IEEE Transactions on Networking.

[4] Hiriart-Urruty (1996). *L'Optimisation.* Presses Universitaires de France.

[5] Filar, Vrieze (1996). *Competitive Markov Decision Processes.* Springer.

[6] Zhang, Liu, Gong, Towsley (2005). *On the Interaction Between Overlay Routing and Traffic Engineering (MPLS), Conflicts in Routing Games.* INFOCOMM.

[7] Ben-Ameur, Kerivin (2005). *Routing of Uncertain Traffic Demands.* Springer Science & Business Media, Optimization and Engineering.

[8] Korilis, Lazar, Orda (1997). *Achieving Network Optima Using Stackelberg Routing Strategies.* IEEE/ACM Transactions on Networking. Vol.5.

[9] Nilim, El Ghaoui (2004). *Algorithms for Air Traffic Flow Management under Stochastic Environments*. Proceedings of American Control Conference.

[10] Smallwood, Sondik (1973). *The Optimal Control of Partially Observable Markov Processes over a Finite Horizon*. Operational Research. vol 21. pp.1071-1088.

[11] Monahan (1982). *A Survey of POMDPs: Theory, Models, and Algorithms*. Management Science, Vol.28.

[12] Lovejoy (2005). *A survey of Algorithmic Methods for POMDPs*. Annals of Operations Research. Springer Netherlands.

[13] Pineau, Gordon, Thrun (2003). *Point-based value iteration: An anytime algorithm for POMDPs*. UAI.

[14] Marbach, Tsitsiklis (2001). *Simulation-Based Optimization of Markov Reward Processes*. IEEE Transactions on Automatic Control. Vol.46.

[15] Marbach, Tsitsiklis (2003). *Approximate Gradient Methods in Policy-Space Optimization of Markov Reward Process*. Journal of Discrete Event Dynamical Systems. Vol.13.

[16] Raghunath, Ramakrishnan et al. (2005). *Trade-offs in Resource Management for Virtual Private Network*. IEEE INFOCOMM.

[17] Melo, Ribeiro (2006). *Convergence of Classical Reinforcement learning Algorithms and Partial Observability*. Technical Report.

[18] Gunnar, Johansson, Telkamp (2004). *Traffic Matrix Estimation on large IP Backbone- A comparison on Real Data*. IMC'04.

[19] Medinan, Salamatian, Battacharyya, Diot (2002). *Traffic Matrix Estimation: Existing techniques and New Directions*. SIGCOMM'02.

[20] Vaton, Bedo, Gravey (2005). *Advanced Methods for the Estimation of the Origin-Destination Traffic matrix, Performance evaluation and Planning Methods for the Next Generation Internet*. Book of the 25th GIRARD's birthday.

[21] Zhang, Roughan, Donoho (2003). *An Information-Theoretic Approach to Traffic Matrix Estimation*. in Proceedings ACM SIGCOMM.

[22] Roughgarden, Tardos (2000). *How Bad is Selfish Routing?*. IEEE Symposium on Foundations of Computer Science.

Chapter 17

EVALUATION AND DESIGN OF BUSINESS MODELS FOR COLLABORATIVE PROVISION OF ADVANCED MOBILE DATA SERVICES: A PORTFOLIO THEORY APPROACH

Alexei A. Gaivoronski

Norwegian University of Science and Technology, Trondheim, Norway

Alexei.Gaivoronski@iot.ntnu.no

Josip Zoric

Telenor R&D, Trondheim, Norway

Josip.Zoric@telenor.com

Abstract   Design of platforms for provision of advanced mobile data services is at the center of current industrial and academic research in mobile telecommunications. Provision of such services requires combination of different types of expertise and capabilities and for this reason needs a concerted effort of different industrial actors. While the main research focus has been on the engineering of services and technological design, much less is done for understanding of business and economic issues which such collaboration between different actors with different interests entails.

   In this paper we develop quantitative tools for evaluation and design of business models for collaborative service provision. These methods are based on the notions of modern investment theory and risk management and use advances in decision support under uncertainty, in particular stochastic optimization. While stochastic optimization component is relatively simple in the present paper, it sets the stage for further developments in this direction.

Keywords: Business models; mobile data: portfolio theory; stochastic optimization.

1.   Introduction

Design of advanced mobile data services to be carried on 3G networks and the networks of further generations is the hot topic in telecommunication industry and academy. This is because the business success of provision of such services will define the business success of the mobile operators and other relevant industrial actors in the near to medium future. In this respect considerable attention is given to design and development of service provision platforms which support a set of tools and basic services that facilitate development, deployment and customization of specialized services by service providers and even nonprofessional end users.

Deployment and operation of service provision platforms and provision of individual services requires collaboration of different industrial actors who contribute to the common goal with their individual capabilities and expertise. One can think about fixed network operators, mobile operators, providers of different information content, internet providers, software developers and other actors who will join forces to provide a successful service. Provision of a service involves assuming different roles and industrial actors can combine such roles. All this gives a rich picture of service provision environment where a multitude of actors cooperate and compete in order to deliver to customers a wide range of services in a profitable manner.

Understandably, the main research and development effort so far has been concentrated on technological and engineering aspects which enable the provisioning of advanced mobile data services. The history of information technology testifies, however, that the possession of the best technological solution is not necessarily enough to assure the business success of an enterprize. Very important and sometimes neglected aspect is design and evaluation of appropriate business model which would support the service provision. Business models for provision of a service requiring a single actor are pretty well understood, both organizationally and economically. This is the case, for example, of provisioning of the traditional voice service over fixed network. When an actor evaluates the economic feasibility of entering the provision of such service, he can employ quantitative tools developed by investment science, like estimation of the Net Present Value of such project [11]. Usually an actor should choose between several service provisioning projects, each providing return on investment and generating the risky cash flows. Then the portfolio theory [12] suggests the way to balance between return and risk and select the best portfolio of projects taking into account the actor's risk attitudes. The adequate risk management is especially important in a highly volatile telecommunication environment and the industrial standards in this respect are starting to emerge, originating from the financial industry [1]. Industrial projects in hightech industries are often characterized by considerable uncertainty and at the same time carry different flexibilities. The real options approach [17] allows to take these flexibilities into account while making evaluation of the profitability of the project. Stochastic programming [3], [8], [10] provide the optimization models for adequate treatment of uncertainty in the planning of service provision.

Business models for cooperative service provision involving different constellations of actors are studied to much lesser extent. The understanding of their importance has lead to some qualitative analysis in [6], [9], but the quantitative analysis similar to what exists for the single actor case remains a challenge. The methods mentioned above are all developed to be used by a single actor engaged in the selection and risk management of his portfolio of industrial projects. The influence of other actors is present only implicitly on the stage of estimation of the future cash flows. This is not enough for adequate analysis of collaborative service provision. Suppose, for example, that a service provider delivers a service to a population of users and receives a revenue for this delivery. If a service is composed from modules and enablers provided by different actors then this service provider has to decide about the revenue division between the actors which will make it attractive to them to participate in the service provision. This revenue sharing decision together with a concept of what is attractive to other actors he should explicitly incorporate in the evaluation of profitability of this project.

The aim of this paper is to contribute to the adaptation and further development of the methods of evaluation and risk management of business models and industrial projects for the case of the collaborative service provision. We look at the actors engaging in a service provision as making a decision about the composition of their portfolio of services to which they are going to contribute. They do this independently following the risk management framework of portfolio theory. The pricing and revenue sharing schemes induce the actors to contribute the right amount of provision capacity to participation in the service provision. We develop a two tier modeling framework which results in selection of pricing and revenue sharing in the optimal way. This is done by utilizing the approach of stochastic optimization with bilevel structure [2], combining it with portfolio theory. In this paper we lay the foundation for this integrated approach and for the purposes of clarity we have limited ourselves to the cases where the stochastic optimization component is relatively simple and can be described by expected values. More detailed consideration of stochastic optimization issues is relegated to the subsequent paper.

The rest of the paper is organized as follows. Section 2 describes different aspects of mobile data services and service platforms providing the background for the quantitative discussion of the latter sections. The introductory model with simplified cost structure and exogenous service pricing is presented in sections 3 and 4. Section 3 provides the basic modeling framework and the discussion of the application of portfolio theory for selection of service portfolios. The modeling issues related to selection of the revenue sharing scheme are considered in the section 4. More detailed service provision model with fixed and variable costs and pricing decision is developed in the section 5. The section 6 contains discussion of the properties of the models, brief information about decision support system which implements our approach and the results of the case study performed with Edition 1 of this system. The paper concludes with the summary and acknowledgement.

2.   Cooperative Provision of Advanced Mobile Data Services

Service platform for provision of Information technology (IT)and communication services is one of the central elements of the modern telecommunications environment. The service platform (SP) hosts services and enabling services (enablers) and provides them to users. The SP has several dimensions: it can be a firm, a technical system, user can see it as a portfolio of services supporting user's activities, service providers can see it as a set of enablers they use to provide end-user service etc. For the purposes of this paper the service platform can be described as follows.

- Service platform hosts and provides services to end-users.

- Services are heterogeneous, distributed and organized as service portfolios.

- Service platform also provides services and enabling services to 3rd party service providers, who combine them with their own enabling services and provide them as their own services to end-users.

- Service is composed of a set of enabling services or *enablers*.

The general service composition model is presented in Figure 17.1. It is based on [18],[19]. It is modeled in unified modeling language (UML), and Figure 17.1 presents the main service platform activities with the outline of the information flows exchanged between the activities in the service delivery process. It can be described in the following way: service discovery provides a list of enablers, based on the service context and other service related information, service brokering assists in choosing the appropriate enablers, mediation prepares them and service composition composes them for the end-user service delivery. Once delivered to the end-user, the service life-cycle mechanisms follow their performance and quality of service, by QoS and A4C management processes, until the service is complete. More on this can be found in [18] and [19].

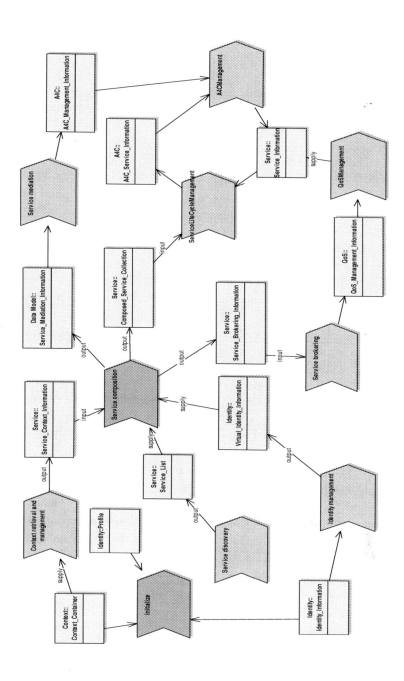

Figure 17.1.   The General Service Composition Model

EXAMPLE 17.1 *Mobile guide service is composed of several enablers: network, service context, multimedia content, messaging enabler and presence enabler.*

Enablers here denote distinctive and composable functionalities that service platform mechanisms discover, broker, mediate and compose to construct end-user services. Enablers can also be a subtype of services. Enablers are described by:

(i) Technical functionality and related technical parameters.

(ii) Quality of Service (QoS) and Quality of Information (QoI) they provide.

(iii) Business and economical parameters (e.g. various costs, income, pricing).

(iv) Enablers have related architecture entities that host and provide them, and for that consume/produce resources (services).

Figure 17.1 shows the general service composition model. The purpose of this model is to approximate the service platform architectures and functionality by the simplified model, which is convenient for the mathematical modeling and simulation. Modern service architectures are very complex, multilayered, distributed and heterogeneous. Their evolution in directions of pervasiveness (ubiquity) and ambience introduce also the aspects of service dynamics. Direct analysis of such complex systems is not plausible. They have to be simplified and prepared for the business modeling and analysis. Such analysis should give a possibility to: (1) analyze particular service platform solutions and (2) compare various service platforms and their service portfolios. For this reason the service composition model is more convenient than the direct work on the service platforms. We shall address these issues in more detail in our next paper.

Services and enablers are provided by several business and system actors. They are network provider (NP), service context provider (CtxtP), content provider (ConP), service provider (SP), Identity management provider (IdP), 3rd party service provider (3PSP) and others. One business and system actor can provide several enablers (and play several roles), e.g. network and service provider at the same time. This is the case of majority of telecom operators today. Usually these actors are independent business entities and they should be economically interested in contributing to service provision if the service is to take off.

User's consumption of IT and communication services is often described through various types of *scenarios* obtained through expert-driven interviews, market and user analysis. Usually several user groups are identified with one or more scenarios per user type. Very often scenarios are organized as sub-scenario sets, sometimes called *scenes*. Scenarios can be modeled in various ways. Usually the initial description is provided as template-based scenario stories with the attributed scenario context, and after that the description is made more formal through usage of message sequence charts and sequence diagrams written in UML 2.0.

3. Simplified Model of Selection of the Service Portfolio

In this section we are going to develop a quantitative description of the service provisioning model involving several actors having as the background the environment presented in the previous section.

3.1 Description of Services

As one can see from Figure 17.1, the composition of a service can be quite complex, especially if we take into account that various components of that picture can be services themselves and subject to further disaggregation. For the purposes of clarity we are going to start from a simpler description which still possess the main features of the provision environment important for business modeling. Namely, two levels of the service composition will be considered here as shown in example on Figure 17.2.

In this case the service environment is composed from two types of services. The first type is comprised from services with structure and provision we are interested in and which we are going to consider in some detail. They can be provided in the context of a service platform and therefore they will be referred to as *platform* services. There will be also *3rd party* services whose structure is of no concern to our modeling purposes. They are present in the model for the purposes of the adequate modeling of the environment in which the provisioning of the platform services happens. Let us now consider the model of provisioning of platform services.

The main building blocks of the platform services are service *enablers* indexed by $i = 1 : N$ and *services* indexed by $j = 1 : M$. Enablers are measured in units relevant for their description, like bandwidth, content volume, etc. The relation between enablers and services is described by coefficients λ_{ij} which measure the amount of enabler i necessary for provision of the unit amount of service j. Thus, a service j can be described by vector

$$\lambda_j = (\lambda_{1j}, .., \lambda_{Nj}) \tag{1}$$

This description is obtained from analysis of the usage scenarios described in Section 2. A service j generates a revenue v_j per unit of service. This quantity depends on the service pricing which in its turn depends on the user behavior and market structure. For the moment let us assume that v_j is the random variable with known distribution, later in section 5 we shall describe this revenue in more detail. This distribution can be recovered from the expert estimates and from simulation models which would explore the structure of user prefer-

Service platform

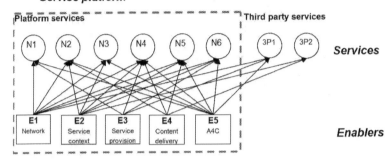

Figure 17.2.　　Service provision for business person on the move.

ences and market features. The random variables v_j can be correlated due to the service substitution, macroeconomic phenomena and other causes.

Services can be provided by different constellations of actors. In this paper we consider one such constellation where the actors are the enterprizes which have the capability to provide service enablers assuming different *roles*, they are indexed by $k = 1 : K$. Actors may choose to join forces to provide a service. Contribution of a given actor consists of taking responsibility for provision of one or more enablers of the service. Sometimes these actors will be referred to as *enabler providers*. There will be an actor who provides the service aggregation functionality and organizes the overall service delivery to the end users, this actor will be referred to as a *service provider*. This actor can provide the whole bundle of platform services and he will decide which services to include in this bundle. Often he will collect the revenue from the end users and distribute it among the enabler providers.

EXAMPLE 17.2 *Service provision for business person on the move. (see Figure 17.2).*

This is a simplified yet realistic example of service provision which was developed on the basis of the project results of the EU project SPICE and NFR project ISIS. The addressed terminal here is a smart mobile phone used by a business person on the move.

We consider here the services which run on the service platform and third party services which partially compete with them, being accessible from the same terminal. We have simplified this example to just total of six native services, two third party services and five enablers (from hundreds of services and dozens of enablers, distributed in several service platforms) available in this service platform. However, services in this platform correspond well to the business offer of a typical service provider. Service bundles have been defined in accordance to the market segments, corresponding customer classes, user behavior, requirements and various subscription schemes. More specifically, we consider the following services.

Native services of the platform:

N1 - Messaging; N2 - Audio conferencing; N3 - Video conferencing; N4 - Location based services; N5 - News; N6 - Point of Interest service.

Third party services.

3P1 - Third party Information service; 3P2 - Third party News service.

The following business actors collaborate in providing the mobile service bundle to the users

1. E1 - *Network provider* – providing the network access.
2. E2 - *Context provider* – service context retrieval and management.
3. E3 - *Service provider* – responsible for service provision.
4. E4 - *Content provider* – content retrieval and management.
5. E5 - *Provider of A4C* (authentication, authorization, auditing, accounting and charging) enabler. This actor will often coincide with the service provider, but one can envisage also the cases when it will be a distinct actor.

Besides, there are one or more providers of the third party services which are in partial competition with the platform services. This example will be treated in some detail in Section 6.

The objective of an enabler provider is to select a portfolio of services to which this actor will make a contribution. This decision is made on the grounds of balance between projected profit from enabler provision balanced against the risk of variations in demand and service acceptance among the prospective users of services. In order to quantify this decision process it is necessary to use a simplified profit model for an actor.

It is assumed that the revenue v_j generated by a unit of service j is distributed among the actors who participate in the creation of service. There can be different schemes for such subdivision. It is assumed here that this distribution is performed using a vector of revenue shares

$$\gamma_j = (\gamma_{1j}, .., \gamma_{Nj}), \gamma = (\gamma_{11}, .., \gamma_{N1}, ..., \gamma_{1M}, .., \gamma_{NM})$$

such that an actor which contributes with the enabler i receives the revenue $\gamma_{ij}v_j$. Determination of these revenue sharing coefficients is one of the objectives of the design of the business model for service provision.

Besides platform services the actors can supply enablers also to the 3rd party services. The structure of these services is not specified and it is assumed that they are fully described by the revenue v_{ij} generated by provision of the unit of enabler i to 3rd party service j, $j = M + 1, ..., \bar{M}$.

3.2   Profit Model of an Actor

Let us consider the situation when all the actors have already developed the capacities for provision of enablers. Thus, for the time being the investment process necessary for creation and expansion of these capacities is not the part of our model, however, it will be considered at the later stages. For this reason at this stage it is enough to consider only variable costs due to the operation of capacities and provision of enablers. Alternatively, one can assume that the cost structure includes both the operational and discounted portion of the investment costs for enabler development, recalculated down to the enabler and the service instances.

For further formulation of the actor's profit model we introduce the following notation.

c_{ik} - unit provision costs for enabler i by actor k;

W_{ik} - provision capability of enabler i of actor k;

x_{ijk} - the portion of provision capability for enabler i of actor k dedicated to participation in provision of service j.

Now the revenue of actor k obtained from contribution to provision of the platform service j can be expressed as follows. The quantity $x_{ijk}W_{ik}$ will be the volume of provision of enabler i dedicated by actor k to service j. Assuming that the required quantity of other enablers is available, this will result in the volume of service j in which the actor k participates to be $x_{ijk}W_{ik}/\lambda_{ij}$. The total revenue from this service will be $v_j x_{ijk}W_{ki}/\lambda_{ij}$ and the part of the revenue which goes to actor k will be $v_j x_{ijk}W_{ik}\gamma_{ij}/\lambda_{ij}$.

For the 3rd party service the revenue will be $v_{ij}x_{ijk}W_{ik}$, and the total costs incurred by actor k for the provision of enabler i to service j will be $x_{ijk}c_{ik}W_{ik}$.

In order to simplify the following discussion let us assume now that the actor k participates in the provision of service j by contributing only one enabler $i = i(k,j)$ or assuming only one role. Taking the profit π_k to be the difference between the revenue and costs, the profit of the actor k can be expressed as follows:

$$\pi_k = \sum_{j=1}^{M} x_{ijk}W_{ik}c_{ik}\left(\frac{v_j\gamma_{ij}}{c_{ik}\lambda_{ij}} - 1\right) + \sum_{j=M+1}^{\bar{M}} x_{ijk}W_{ik}c_{ik}\left(\frac{v_{ij}}{c_{ik}} - 1\right)$$

In the expression above index i depends on the values of indices j and k. Now let us assume that the actor k assumes only one role which consists in the provision of enabler i to different services which require this enabler. Thus, we consider a generic actor whose role is to provide enabler i to different services. Then we can simplify notations by taking $x_{ijk} = x_{ij}$, $W_{ik} = W_i$, $c_{ik} = c_i$,

$\pi_k = \pi_i$. In this case the profit will be

$$\pi_i = W_i c_i \left(\sum_{j=1}^{M} x_{ij} \left(\frac{v_j \gamma_{ij}}{c_i \lambda_{ij}} - 1 \right) + \sum_{j=M+1}^{\bar{M}} x_{ij} \left(\frac{v_{ij}}{c_i} - 1 \right) \right)$$

Dividing the profit by the total costs $W_i c_i$ we obtain the return r_i on investment by a generic actor which assumes the role of provision of enabler i to services which require this enabler.

$$r_i = \sum_{j=1}^{M} x_{ij} \left(\frac{v_j \gamma_{ij}}{c_i \lambda_{ij}} - 1 \right) + \sum_{j=M+1}^{\bar{M}} x_{ij} \left(\frac{v_{ij}}{c_i} - 1 \right) \qquad (2)$$

3.3 Service Portfolio: Financial Perspective

The profit representation (2) allows us to look at the enabler provision from the point of view of financial portfolio theory [12]. The actor with the role to provide the enabler i has to choose the set of services to which provide this enabler from all the possible available services requiring this enabler. In other words, he has to select his service portfolio. This portfolio is defined by shares x_{ij} of his provision capability,

$$x_i = (x_{i1}, ..., x_{i\bar{M}})$$

Return coefficients associated with his participation in each platform service are expressed as

$$r_{ij} = \frac{v_j \gamma_{ij}}{c_i \lambda_{ij}} - 1, \ j = 1 : M \qquad (3)$$

and for the 3rd party services these coefficients are

$$r_{ij} = \frac{v_{ij}}{c_i} - 1, \ j = M + 1 : \bar{M}. \qquad (4)$$

These coefficients depend on the random variables which are mostly the revenue per unit of service v_j and the revenue per component provision v_{ij}. Randomness here is due to the uncertainty in demand and the user acceptance of service. However, both enabler provision costs c_i and even enabler shares λ_{ij} also will be random variables due to uncertainty inherent in the service usage patterns and the evolution of costs. Besides, the costs c_i often will be the estimates of the provision costs of enabler provider i made by some other actor. Such estimates are inherently imprecise and are better described by random variables similarly to how it was done in [2]. The expected return coefficients are

$$\mu_{ij} = \gamma_{ij} \mathbf{E} \frac{v_j}{c_i \lambda_{ij}} - 1, \ j = 1 : M, \ \mu_{ij} = \mathbf{E} \frac{v_{ij}}{c_i} - 1, \ j = M + 1 : \bar{M} \qquad (5)$$

and expected return $\bar{r}_i(x_i)$ of service portfolio is

$$\bar{r}_i(x_i) = \sum_{j=1}^{\bar{M}} \mu_{ij} x_{ij} = \sum_{j=1}^{M} x_{ij} \left(\gamma_{ij} \mathbf{E} \frac{v_j}{c_i \lambda_{ij}} - 1 \right) + \sum_{j=M+1}^{\bar{M}} x_{ij} \left(\mathbf{E} \frac{v_{ij}}{c_i} - 1 \right).$$

(6)

However, the realized return can differ substantially from the expected return due to uncertainty discussed above. This introduces the risk $R(x_i)$ for an actor which assumes the enabler provision role. Financial theory traditionally measures this risk as the variance of portfolio return [12]. Recently several different risk measures were introduced and, in particular Value at Risk (VaR) and its many modifications. The VaR has attained the level of industrial standard in the financial risk management [1]. In this section the variance and the standard deviation of the return will be used as the risk measure because the correct selection of the risk measure in the context of collaborative service provision is outside the scope of this paper and it will be addressed by us in the subsequent papers. What is important here is that the consideration of the risk measures allow an actor to estimate the probability and size of his future losses. Thus, we take

$$R(x_i) = \text{StDev}(r_i(x_i)) = \text{StDev} \left(\sum_{j=1}^{\bar{M}} r_{ij} x_{ij} \right)$$

(7)

where return coefficients r_{ij} are taken from (3),(4).

Portfolio theory looks at the portfolio selection as the trade-off between risk and return. Its application to our problem of service portfolio consists of the following steps.

1. *Construction of efficient frontier.* Some average return target η is fixed. The risk of service portfolio is minimized with constraint on this return target. The risk minimization problem looks as follows.

$$\min_x \text{StDev}^2 \left(\sum_{j=1}^{\bar{M}} r_{ij} x_{ij} \right)$$

(8)

$$\sum_{j=1}^{\bar{M}} \mu_{ij} x_{ij} = \eta$$

(9)

$$\sum_{j=1}^{\bar{M}} x_{ij} = 1, \ x_{ij} \geq 0$$

(10)

Solution of this problem for all admissible values of target return η will provide the set of service portfolios which are the reasonable candidates for selection by actor who provides the enabler j. They constitute the *efficient frontier* of the set of all possible service portfolios. This concept is illustrated on Figure 17.3.

Each service portfolio x can be characterized by pair (risk,return) defined by (7) and (6) respectively. Therefore it can be represented as a point in the risk-return space depicted on Figure 17.3. The set of such points for all possible portfolios describes all existing relations between risk and return and is called *the feasible set*. Which of possible service portfolios an actor should choose? It depends on the objectives which an actor pursues. Here we assume that an actor's decision depends on return and risk only. Namely, an actor will seek the highest possible return among equally risky alternatives and he will seek the lowest possible risk among equally profitable alternatives. This is a simplification because in reality the actors can be driven by other considerations, like increase of market share, revenue, regulatory constraints, etc. However, the consideration of only risk and return provides with the reasonable starting point for analysis of business models. More complex cases can be taken into account in a similar manner by introducing additional constraints on the feasible set or by modifying the concept of performance. For example, suppose that an actor has three objectives: return and market share to maximize and the risk to minimize. Then the market share and the return can be integrated in one performance measure by assigning weights to these objectives. The weights will measure the relative importance of return and market share to the actor. The composite performance measure is obtained by computing the weighted sum of the original objectives. The risk is defined as the variation of this composite measure. This composite performance measure is used in Figure 17.3 instead of return.

Considering Figure 17.3 it becomes clear that some of the service portfolios should be preferred to others. For example, let us consider portfolio x_0 to which corresponds the point in risk-return space inside the feasible set, as in Figure 17.2. It is clear that portfolio x_2 should be preferred to x_0 by an agent who makes his decision on the basis of return and risk. This is because portfolio x_2 has the same risk as portfolio x_0 and larger return. Similarly, portfolio x_1 also should be preferred to x_0 because it provides the same return with the smaller risk. Thus, portfolio x_0 is dominated by both portfolios x_1 and x_2 and should not be taken in consideration. The actor whose decisions are guided by risk and return should consider only nondominated portfolios which constitute *efficient frontier*, depicted by dotted curve on Figure 17.3. This efficient frontier can be computed by solving the problem (8)-(10) for different values of η. This efficient frontier can be viewed also as the solution of the two objective optimization problem of minimizing risk and maximizing return under the constraints (10).

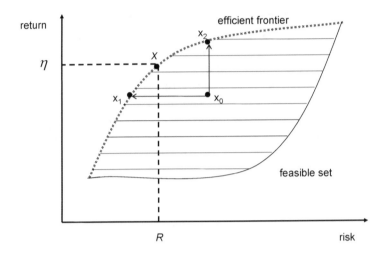

Figure 17.3.   Selection of service portfolio

2. *Selection of the target service portfolio.* The previous step resulted in the selection of much smaller set of efficient service portfolios from the set of all possible service portfolios. These portfolios form the efficient frontier in the risk-return space. An actor selects his target service portfolio from this efficient set by choosing the trade-off between risk and return. One way to achieve this trade-off is to consider the largest risk an actor is willing to take. Suppose that the value of such risk is R (see Figure 17.3). Then the actor should choose the portfolio x on efficient frontier with this value of risk. Suppose that this service portfolio yields return η. No other portfolio yields better return without increasing the risk. If an actor is not satisfied with return η this means that he should increase his risk tolerance or look for opportunities to participate in the service provision not yet described in this model. Or, such actor should seek more advantageous revenue sharing scheme.

From these considerations it is clear that all important opportunities of participation in service provision should be included in this model. For example, suppose that an actor assumes the role of content provision and can contribute his content to advanced mobile data service and at the same time this content can be contributed to, say, traditional newspaper. Both opportunities should be included in the model with the traditional service being modeled as a 3rd party service.

4.   Modeling of Collaborative Service Provision

In the previous section we highlighted the importance of having the adequate forecasts of the cash flows generated by services in order to quantitatively evaluate the economic future of the service and business models which support the service provision. Due to uncertainty inherent in the user response and technological development any such forecast should be given in terms of random variables which assign probabilities to different scenarios of user response and possible evolution of other uncertain parameters. The forecasts should take into account the mutual influence of services which result in correlation between cash flows generated by different services.

Such description allows to look at the providers of different service enablers as actors which independently select the service portfolios having their targets described in terms of return on investment and risk tolerance. However, a service can become a reality only if the participation in its provision will be consistent with these individual targets. This means that all actors which cover the roles indispensable for provision of a particular service should have this service in their efficient service portfolio. In other words, the service portfolios of the relevant actors should be *compatible*. There are several items which affect the risk/return characteristics of a service portfolio and decide whether a particular service will be present in it. One is the cash flow generated by a service j, another is the revenue sharing scheme γ_j. Besides, the enabler provision capacities, industrial risk/return standards, market prices, all play a role in making service portfolios compatible. In this section we are going to characterize the properties which facilitate the service portfolio compatibility and develop a model for selection of the revenue sharing scheme.

4.1   Service Provision Capacities

According to (1) a platform service j is described by vector λ_j of the service enablers. Let us denote by I_j the set of enablers which are present in the service description in nonzero quantities:

$$I_j = \{i : \lambda_{ij} > 0\}$$

For each enabler $i \in I_j$ an actor should be found who is willing to take a role of provision of this enabler. This means that the position j in service portfolio of generic actor who provides enabler $i \in I_j$ should be nonnegative: $x_{ij} > 0$. The value of this position allows to estimate the enabler provision capacity which an actor should possess. Indeed, x_{ij} is a fraction of provision capacity which an actor is going to dedicate to provision of enabler i to service j. Therefore λ_{ij}/x_{ij} is the capacity necessary to provide a unit of service j. Suppose that $B_j^{\min}$ is the minimal volume of provision of service j which makes such provision viable, and B_j is the target volume of service provision for a generic constellation of actors which is going to provide this service. Then we have the following constraints on the service provision capacities of actors:

$$W_i x_{ij} \geq \lambda_{ij} B_j^{\min}, \ i \in I_j \tag{11}$$

if the provision of service j will be viable at all and

$$W_i x_{ij} \geq \lambda_{ij} B_j, \ i \in I_j \tag{12}$$

if only one actor with provision capability of enabler i is desirable in the constellation which provides service j. These constraints can help to make decisions about the nature of the actors which should be encouraged to participate in the provision of different services. For example, some enablers of some services will be provided by established actors with large provision capacity. In such cases the share x_{ij} of capacity dedicated to service j can be small. In other cases the service enablers will be provided by startups with relatively small capacity. In such cases the share x_{ij} should be large or even equal to 1. These shares implicitly depend on the revenue sharing scheme γ_j through the solution of problem (8)-(10) and in the latter case it may be beneficial on the initial stages of service penetration to encourage startups by appropriate adjustment of the revenue sharing scheme.

The constraints (11)-(12) can be also looked at as the constraints on the composition of service portfolio. Suppose that $W_i^{\max}$ is the maximal desirable component provision capacity which an actor providing enabler i should possess. Then the smallest share x_{ij} dedicated to service j should be

$$x_{ij} \geq \lambda_{ij} \frac{B_j^{\min}}{W_i^{\max}}, \ i \in I_j \tag{13}$$

4.2   Risk/Return Industrial Expectations

Provision of advanced mobile data services will involve different actors coming from different backgrounds and industries. There will be many startups, but there will be also established actors from other industrial branches. One example is the content provision where the same content can be provided to newspapers, internet and mobile terminals. Such actors will have the attitudes towards admissible and/or desirable returns on investment and rewards which taking risk should bring. Often such attitudes will be influenced by industrial standards and expectations inherited from their previous activity. One way to express these expectations is to include all generic projects, in which an actor can be involved in his traditional business, as services in the set of all considered 3rd party services in this model. This is especially useful approach if the revenues from the traditional activities will influence and will be influenced by the revenues from the mobile services under consideration. Another possibility is to account for these expectations explicitly. This can be done by introducing the connection between the expected return $\bar{r}_i(x_i)$ and risk $R(x_i)$ from (6) and (7) as follows:

$$\bar{r}_i(x_i) \geq a_i + b_i R(x_i) \tag{14}$$

where a_i will be the return on investment associated with traditional activity while $b_i R(x_i)$ will be the risk premium associated with the participation in provision of advanced mobile data services. The coefficients a_i and b_i will depend also on individual characteristics of an actor like size, market position.

Beside this an actor will have the risk tolerance expressed in terms of the upper bound on risk which he is willing to take irrespective of return:

$$R(x_i) \leq \bar{R} \tag{15}$$

The upper bound on admissible risk $\bar{R}$ will again depend on the characteristics of a particular actor. To put it simply, this is the maximal loss an actor can afford during the time period under consideration.

4.3 Pricing

The revenue per unit of service v_j together with the service composition λ_j and the revenue sharing scheme γ_j defines the unit price p_i of enabler i :

$$p_i = \frac{v_j \gamma_{ij}}{\lambda_{ij}}$$

This is a random variable since the revenue is also random. Therefore the expected price $\bar{p}_i = \mathbf{E} p_i$ will be

$$\bar{p}_i = \frac{\gamma_{ij}}{\lambda_{ij}} \mathbf{E} v_j$$

An actor providing the enabler i may have the target p_i^* for the price of his product and the tolerances Δ^+ and Δ^- within which he is willing to accept a different price. These targets can result from the market prices in established industries, internal market studies, internal cost estimates. This will lead to the following constraints

$$p_i^* - \Delta^- \leq \frac{\gamma_{ij}}{\lambda_{ij}} \mathbf{E} v_j \leq p_i^* + \Delta^+ \tag{16}$$

This constraint should be taken into account while considering the revenue sharing schemes.

4.4   Revenue Sharing Schemes

Now let us look at the problem of selecting the revenue sharing coefficients γ_j which would be compatible with the concerted provision of a platform service. Summarizing the discussion present in the sections 3, 4.1, 4.2 we obtain that the actor which supplies enabler i will select portfolio of services $x_i = (x_{i1}, ..., x_{iM})$ by solving the following problem

$$\max_{x_i} \bar{r}_i(x_i, \gamma_j) \tag{17}$$

subject to constraints

$$\sum_{j=1}^{\bar{M}} x_{ij} = 1, \ x_{ij} \geq 0 \tag{18}$$

$$\bar{r}_i(x_i, \gamma_j) \geq a_i + b_i R(x_i, \gamma_j) \tag{19}$$

$$R(x_i, \gamma_j) \leq \bar{R} \tag{20}$$

where $\bar{r}_i(x_i, \gamma_j)$ is the expected return of the actor on his expenditure and $R(x_i, \gamma_j)$ is the risk defined in (6) and (7) respectively. We emphasize here the dependence of risk and return on the revenue sharing scheme γ_j. Solution of this problem will give service portfolios $x_i(\gamma_j)$ for all generic actors providing enabler i for the platform services $j = 1 : M$. These service portfolios will depend on the revenue sharing schemes γ_j. Let us now concentrate on a particular service with index j. In order that a provision of this service becomes possible it is necessary that all actors which provide the necessary enablers to this service will include it in their service portfolios in desirable proportions. This means that

$$x_i(\gamma_j) \in X_j, \ \forall i \in I_j \tag{21}$$

where the set X_j can be defined, for example, by constraints (13). Constraints (21) define the feasible set of the revenue sharing coefficients and if these constraints are not satisfied then the service will not come into being.

Suppose now that the enabler number 1 of service j is a service aggregation enabler which is provided by an actor which bears overall responsibility for the functioning of service and receives the revenue stream from the end users. His responsibility includes also the division of the revenue stream between the participating actors and the selection for this purpose of the revenue sharing coefficients γ_j. He should select these coefficients in such a way that the constraints (21) are satisfied. Between all such revenue sharing coefficients he would select ones which would maximize his return. This can be formulated as the following optimization problem.

$$\max_{\gamma_j} \bar{r}_1(x_1(\gamma_j), \gamma_j) \tag{22}$$

subject to constraints

$$x_i(\gamma_j) \in X_j, \ \forall i \in I_j \tag{23}$$

$$\gamma_j \in \Gamma_j \tag{24}$$

where the set Γ_j can be defined, for example, by constraints (16). Even simpler, this actor may wish to maximize his revenue share

$$\max_{\gamma_j} \gamma_{1j} \tag{25}$$

under constraints (23)-(24). Observe that the feasible set of this optimization problem depends on the solution of the other actor's optimization problems (17)-(20) similar to how it depends in optimization problems with bilevel structure.

5. Deciding on Price of a Service

So far we have assumed that the revenue stream v_j generated by service j is a fixed random variable with the distribution obtained from the expert estimates and the market research. For this reason the main business decision which the service providing agent makes after establishing of a service is how to divide the revenue stream between the component providers in such a way as all of them are interested in participation. Let us introduce now in our model another important consideration which is the price of a service. Since this model has a strategic application field, various specific pricing schemes and price differentiation are not considered here yet. Instead under the price p_j it will be understood an average price for the unit of service which an average customer pays to the service provider. This will be another decision to take for a service provider of service j. We assume here that the service has some kind of unique features which allows a service provider to change its price as opposed to taking just the market price for a well established service. Usually, this is the case for mobile data services. Besides, for the 3rd party services there will be considered the price p_{ij} which will be the average price which enabler provider gets for delivering the unit of enabler to service j, $j = M+1 : \bar{M}$.

Let us now observe how the explicit introduction of the price will affect different elements of the quantitative business model considered so far. There are two such elements: revenue per unit of service or enabler and demand which in its turn will affect the capacity for delivery of enablers.

Revenue. The actual revenue which a service provider gets for the unit of service delivery is described by a random variable with average p_j. This is because we are looking at generic business model for the provision of future services and p_j is just the average price, while the actual price will differ due to customer heterogeneity and specific pricing schemes. Similar considerations are also valid for the unit enabler price p_{ij}. Thus,

$$\mathbf{E}v_j = p_j, \quad \mathbf{E}v_{ij} = p_{ij} \tag{26}$$

The vector of prices of all platform services is denoted by $P = (p_1, ..., p_M)$.
Demand. Let us denote by d_j the demand for the platform service j and by
d_{ij} the demand for provision of component i to the 3rd party service j. In economic literature one can find different ways to describe how demand depends
on price. One possibility is to follow [8] and look at relatively small price
variations around some reference (market) price p_{0j} to which corresponds a
reference demand d_{0j}. In this case the dependence of demand on price is approximated by a linear dependence as follows:

$$d_j = d_{0j} - w_j(p_j - p_{0j})$$

where w_j is some coefficient to be estimated together with the reference point
(p_{0j}, d_{0j}). These coefficients should be modeled by random variables due to
uncertainties in their determination.

For larger price variations one should follow the traditional microeconomic
approach and consider demand elasticity. In particular, demand for telecommunication services can be reasonably described by constant elasticity ϵ, see
[13]:

$$d_j = \frac{a_j}{p_j^\epsilon}$$

where both a_j and ϵ are uncertain and should be estimated. In any case it will
be assumed that demand is a decreasing function of price

$$d_j = d_j(p_j), \quad d_{ij} = d_{ij}(p_{ij}) \tag{27}$$

which usually will depend on uncertain parameters described by random variables.
Service substitution. Often telecom and information services are catering to the
same or similar needs of consumers. For this reason the demand for a service
may depend not only on its price but also on prices of the services which can
fully or partially substitute it. That is

$$d_j = d_j(p_1, ..., p_M)$$

This function can be quite complicated and dependent on uncertain parameters.
Another way to describe the service substitution is to consider the upper bound
D^{max} on the total aggregated demand and consider only such demand bundles
that do not exceed this bound:

$$\sum_{j=1}^{M} p_j d_j(p_j) \leq D^{\mathrm{max}}$$

where ρ_j are aggregation coefficients which reflect partial substitutability of services. Instead of such bound on aggregated total demand one can consider also bounds on aggregated demand for subsets of mutually substitutable services.

5.1 Risk-performance Trade-off for Enabler Provider

Let us look now into different components of the business model for enabler provider.

Provision costs. In this section we are going to look in more detail on the structure of provision costs for enablers. Namely, we are taking account for economies of scale and the costs of enabler customization for usage in different services. One way to do this is to consider the costs to be dependent on the service and introduce fixed and variable components to the costs. Let us denote
X_{ij} - volume of provision of enabler i to service j;
Y_{ij} - binary variable which equals 1 if nonzero volume of enabler i is contributed to service j, and it equals zero otherwise.

$$X_i = (X_{i1}, ..., X_{i\bar{M}}), \ Y_i = (Y_{i1}, ..., Y_{i\bar{M}})$$

Thus, the total costs $C_{ij}(X_{ij})$ for provision of volume X_{ij} of enabler i to service j will be

$$C_{ij}(X_{ij}) = Y_{ij}c_{0ij} + c_{1ij}X_{ij}$$

where c_{0ij} are fixed costs and c_{0ij} are variable costs per unit of provision. The total cost which bears the provider of enabler i is

$$C_i(X_i) = \sum_{j=1}^{\bar{M}} (Y_{ij}c_{0ij} + c_{1ij}X_{ij})$$

These costs are also uncertain and should be described by random variables, because they are the provision costs for the new data services in rapidly evolving industry. Denoting $\bar{c}_{0ij} = \mathbf{E}c_{0ij}$, $\bar{c}_{1ij} = \mathbf{E}c_{1ij}$ we obtain the *expected provision costs*. These can be the estimates of the internal provision costs made by the actors themselves. Or, in the case when the model is used by the actor responsible for the overall service provision, this can be the best estimate of provision costs of the other participants to the collaborative service provision which this actor can get hold of.

$$\bar{C}_i(X_i) = \sum_{j=1}^{\bar{M}} (Y_{ij}\bar{c}_{0ij} + \bar{c}_{1ij}X_{ij})$$

Measures $F(X_i, Y_i)$ of business performance. This is the important choice for quantitative evaluation of the business models. In the section 3.2 with relatively simple decision and cost structure we took the return on costs as the main performance measure. In the current more advanced model we shall consider revenue and profit as two performance measures while the return preferences will be described in the form of constraint. Revenue will be very reasonable performance measure when the cost structure is well defined, while the profit will be more appropriate in the situation when the costs are uncertain.

Revenue for provision of enabler i to platform and 3rd party services:

$$F_i(X_i, Y_i) = \sum_{j=1}^{M} v_j \frac{\gamma_{ij}}{\lambda_{ij}} X_{ij} + \sum_{j=M+1}^{\bar{M}} v_{ij} X_{ij}$$

Expected revenue taking into account (26) and assuming that the service composition λ_j is deterministic:

$$\bar{F}_i(X_i, Y_i) = \sum_{j=1}^{M} \frac{\gamma_{ij}}{\lambda_{ij}} p_j X_{ij} + \sum_{j=M+1}^{\bar{M}} p_{ij} X_{ij}$$

Profit of provider of enabler i:

$$F_i(X_i, Y_i) = \sum_{j=1}^{M} \left(v_j \frac{\gamma_{ij}}{\lambda_{ij}} - c_{1ij} \right) X_{ij} + \sum_{j=M+1}^{\bar{M}} (v_{ij} - c_{1ij}) X_{ij} - \sum_{j=1}^{\bar{M}} Y_{ij} c_{0ij}$$

Expected profit of provider of enabler i:

$$\bar{F}_i(X_i, Y_i) = \sum_{j=1}^{M} \left(\frac{\gamma_{ij}}{\lambda_{ij}} p_j - \bar{c}_{1ij} \right) X_{ij} + \sum_{j=M+1}^{\bar{M}} (p_{ij} - \bar{c}_{1ij}) X_{ij} - \sum_{j=1}^{\bar{M}} Y_{ij} \bar{c}_{0ij}$$

Risk $R(X_i, Y_i)$ in this setting manifests itself in the deviation of the actual business performance from its expected performance and it translates in the possibility of losses of specific frequency and magnitude. Following the classical approach in finance, this deviation will be measured here in the terms of variance and standard deviation.[12]. Let us define

$$b^i = \left(v_1 \frac{\gamma_{i1}}{\lambda_{i1}}, ..., v_M \frac{\gamma_{iM}}{\lambda_{iM}}, v_{iM+1}, ..., v_{i\bar{M}} \right)$$

for the case when the performance is measured by the revenue and

$$b^i = \left(v_1 \frac{\gamma_{i1}}{\lambda_{i1}} - c_{1i1}, ..., v_M \frac{\gamma_{iM}}{\lambda_{iM}} - c_{1iM}, v_{iM+1} - c_{1iM+1}, ..., \right.$$
$$\left. v_{i\bar{M}} - c_{1i\bar{M}}, -c_{0i1}, ..., -c_{0i\bar{M}} \right)$$

for the case when the performance is measured by the profit. Then the matrix

$$Q^i = \mathbf{E} \left(b^i - \mathbf{E}b^i \right) \left(b^i - \mathbf{E}b^i \right)^T$$

will be the covariance matrix of the respective measures of business performance. Denoting

$$\bar{X}_i = (X_{i1}, ..., X_{i\bar{M}}, Y_{i1}, ..., Y_{i\bar{M}})$$

it is possible to express the risk measured by variance as

$$R_i(X_i, Y_i) = X_i Q^i X_i$$

in the case of the revenue and

$$R_i(X_i, Y_i) = \bar{X}_i Q^i \bar{X}_i$$

in the case of the profit.

Now all elements are in place in order to adapt to this setting the risk/performance decision paradigm developed in finance. The enabler provider will consider the following problem in order to select the composition of his service portfolio:

$$\min_{X_i, Y_i} R_i(X_i, Y_i) \tag{28}$$

$$\bar{F}_i(X_i, Y_i) \geq \eta \tag{29}$$

$$X_{ij} \leq \lambda_{ij} d_j(p_j), \ j = 1 : M \tag{30}$$

$$X_{ij} \leq d_{ij}(p_{ij}), \ j = M + 1 : \bar{M} \tag{31}$$

$$X_{ij} \leq D_i Y_{ij} \tag{32}$$

$$X_{ij} \geq 0, \ Y_{ij} \in \{0, 1\} \tag{33}$$

This problem has the same origins as the problem (8)-(10) from Section 3.3. It minimizes the risk (28) under the constraint on the target performance (29). Constraints (30)-(31) limit the enabler provision to the existing demand for the platform and external services. It fulfills the same role as the constraint (10) from (8)-(10). Constraint (32) connects two groups of decision variables present in the problem. It essentially tells that if decision is taken not to participate in the provision of service j, i.e. $Y_{ij} = 0$, then the volume of provision X_{ij} should be zero. Here D_i is a large number exceeding possible demand on component i.

By solving the problem (28)-(33) for different values of the performance target η one obtains the efficient frontier in the risk-performance space similar to one depicted on Figure 17.3. After that the enabler provider may choose his service portfolio among efficient portfolios from this frontier, taking into account his risk preferences and other considerations.

From the computational point of view the problem (28)-(33) is quite complicated due to the presence of binary variables in the nonlinear objective. These variables disappear if only the variable costs are considered. However, the solution of the full version with the binary variables is facilitated by relatively small dimension of the problem.

5.2   Collaborative Service Provision

Now let us look at the business model of the whole service provisioning, similarly to how this was done in section 4.4. We continue to operate in the setting of Figure 17.2 where the enabler providers select their service portfolios and deliver service enablers to the service providers which provide services to customers, decide about prices, collect the revenue and distribute it among enabler providers. For the sake of simplicity let us assume that a single service provider is responsible for provision of all platform services. Thus, decisions are taken on two levels: the enabler provider level and the service provider level.

1. *Enabler provider level. Service portfolios.*

The basic logic behind decisions about service portfolios taken by enabler providers is contained in the problem (28)-(33) and the efficient frontier approach from Figure 17.2. Here some additional considerations are added. One such consideration is the return which was absent from (28)-(33) due to more complicated structure of the problem. The way to introduce return here is to fix the return target χ and introduce constraint that will force the expected revenue to exceed the expected costs by appropriate multiplier:

$$\sum_{j=1}^{M} \frac{\gamma_{ij}}{\lambda_{ij}} p_j X_{ij} + \sum_{j=M+1}^{\bar{M}} p_{ij} X_{ij} \geq (1+\chi) \sum_{j=1}^{\bar{M}} (\bar{c}_{0ij} Y_{ij} + \bar{c}_{1ij} X_{ij})$$

Summarizing the discussion about considerations that will affect the decisions of the enabler providers we obtain the following problem for definition of the service portfolio by a enabler provider i.

$$\max_{X_i, Y_i} \bar{F}_i(X_i, Y_i, P, \gamma) \qquad (34)$$

subject to constraints

$$R(X_i, Y_i, P, \gamma) \leq \bar{R} \qquad (35)$$

$$\sum_{j=1}^{M} \frac{\gamma_{ij}}{\lambda_{ij}} p_j X_{ij} + \sum_{j=M+1}^{\bar{M}} p_{ij} X_{ij} \geq (1+\chi) \sum_{j=1}^{\bar{M}} (\bar{c}_{0ij} Y_{ij} + \bar{c}_{1ij} X_{ij}) \qquad (36)$$

$$X_{ij} \leq \lambda_{ij} d_j(p_j), \ j = 1 : M \tag{37}$$

$$X_{ij} \leq d_{ij}(p_{ij}), \ j = M + 1 : \bar{M} \tag{38}$$

$$X_{ij} \leq D_i Y_{ij} \tag{39}$$

$$X_{ij} \geq 0, \ Y_{ij} \in \{0, 1\} \tag{40}$$

Here we have emphasized deliberately the dependence of the performance and risk measures on the prices of platform services P and the revenue sharing scheme γ. This problem is solved by all enabler providers which result in the determination of the service portfolio $X_i(P, \gamma)$ for each of them.

2. *Service provider level. Service prices and revenue sharing.*

Let us consider the situation when all the platform services are provided by the same service provider who also provides the service aggregation enabler for each service with index 1. He chooses prices and the revenue sharing schemes guided by two considerations.

(i) Maximization of his business performance measure like revenue, profit or return.

(ii) Balancing of the offer from enabler providers.

The problem is that independent solution of the problem (34)-(40) for arbitrary fixed P and γ will result in imbalance in enabler provision. Namely, a enabler provider i will provide amount $X_{ij}(P, \gamma)$ of this enabler to service j. This will be enough for the total volume X_{ij}/λ_{ij} of provision of service j. Therefore the maximal possible provision volume of service j will be

$$V_i = \min_{i:\lambda_{ij} > 0} \frac{X_{ij}(P, \gamma)}{\lambda_{ij}} \tag{41}$$

If no special effort is made to select appropriate P and γ then the volume V_i from (41) will not satisfy demand $d_j(p_j)$ i.e. there will be $V_i < d_j(p_j)$ and, besides, any enabler provider i which will have $X_{ij}(P, \gamma)/\lambda_{ij} > V_i$ will deliver unnecessary quantity $X_{ij}(P, \gamma) - \lambda_{ij} V_i$ of enabler i to service j. If we assume that all demand should be satisfied then the solution of the following problem will provide the prices and revenue sharing schemes that will satisfy both above requirements.

$$\max_{P, \gamma} \bar{F}_1(X_1(P, \gamma), Y_1(P, \gamma), P, \gamma) \tag{42}$$

$$X_{ij}(P, \gamma) \geq \lambda_{ij} d_j(p_j), \ j = 1 : M, \ i = 1 : N \tag{43}$$

$$\sum_{j=1}^{M} \rho_j d_j(p_j) \leq D^{\max} \tag{44}$$

where the constraint of type (16) can be included.

Let us consider several possibilities how this two tier structure can be actually implemented and used in the collaborative service provision environment and what information flows it implies. We consider two possibilities here among many.

1. *Feasibility study of the service provision by prospective service provider.* Such actor on the stage of feasibility study would like to know what kind of enabler providers he can get interested in the collaborative service provision, what size, cost structures, risk attitudes, profit demands to expect, what room for maneuver he can have with respect to pricing of services and pricing offers to enabler providers, where are his bottlenecks with respect to his knowledge of the environment.

In this case the service provider would need to develop the risk/performance models of the prospective partners, make the plausible estimates of their expectations and costs, develop the provisions for the user acceptance of his service offer. Usually, this will be done by considering several scenarios of the service development. After that he can use the models described above to obtain the answers for what-if questions, explore the impact of different assumptions about prices, partner and user behavior and characteristics. This will be an iterative process resulting in the broad guidelines for the ensuing search for partners and negotiation process.

2. *Operative management of dynamic service provision environment.* Suppose that the collaborating team is already assembled around a service platform and provides a bundle of platform services to user population in competition with 3rd party services. We consider the case when demand for the platform services varies considerably and quickly over time which necessitates dynamic price corrections both for the bundle offered to the end users and the price adjustments between the partners. In this case the models of enabler provider level would reside on the premises of individual partners who would supply them with their proprietary information which will remain unknown to other partners. Enabler providers will run them for different values of the prices for their product and obtain the optimal service portfolios which will be translated in the amounts of respective enablers which they will be willing to supply to the platform for a given price. They will communicate this information to the platform operator whose responsibility will be to choose the prices to end users and to enabler providers which will clear the market and maximize his performance. He will do this by solving the problem (42)-(44) of service provider level which does not require any knowledge of the proprietary information of the enabler providers, only their table of enabler offers.

This process is very similar to one which takes place on the daily basis for more than ten years in the Nordic power industry between electricity producers and Nordic power exchange for the purpose of provision of electricity delivery service to electric power consumers. Now this process is being extended to the rest of Europe and it is already in place in different other countries.

Detailed discussion of these and other modes for the usage of proposed modeling system is beyond the scope of this paper. Another opportunities include support of regulator's decisions who may want to decide on the bounds of pricing for services and enablers in order to encourage/discourage certain patterns of the service offer and usage for the public good.

This is the end of the modeling part of this paper and one final comment is due about the relation between our approach and other modeling approaches relevant in the multiactor environment. One such approach is provided by the game theory which is the natural and traditional choice for study of competing and collaborating multiactor environment, see [16] and further references there for examples of the use of this approach for modeling of different problems in telecommunications and other network industries. In fact, substantial similarity can be noted between our approach and the game theory. For example, the two tier modeling structure just described can be easily identified with the leader-follower games of Stackelberg type. However, we differ substantially from the game theory because we do not employ equilibrium concepts which are in the center of the game theoretical analysis. This is because the equilibrium of any kind is yet to be observed in the highly dynamic and substantially transient world of data service provision. For this reason we have chosen to concentrate on the analysis of the initial stages of the transient behavior instead.

6.   Model Properties, Implementation and Case Study

The models of the previous sections can be looked at as a special type of stochastic optimization problems with bilevel structure [2], where the lower level is composed from the problems of individual component providers (17)-(20) or (34)-(40) while the upper level contains the problem of service provider (22)-(24) or (42)-(44). Stochasticity comes from uncertainty inherent in the information about the characteristics of advanced data services and the user response to them. So far we have adopted a relatively simple treatment of uncertainty substituting the random variables by their expected values in some cases, while in the other cases the special structure of the problem allowed to limit the modeling to the expected values and covariance matrix. This can be viewed as a special type of the deterministic equivalent of stochastic programming problems, a technique widely used in stochastic programming (see [3] for more discussion on different types of deterministic equivalents). More detailed description of this uncertainty can be introduced in these models similar to how it was done in [2]. Different bilevel optimization problems have drawn considerable attention recently, see [4], [5], [14], [15].

The decision support system based on these models is under implementation. It is composed of four components: data and user interface implemented in Excel, a set of service models, a set of mathematical models implemented in Matlab and a library of optimization solvers including some specialized solvers for stochastic programming problems like SQG [7].

The Edition 1 of this system is already functional. This edition includes the models described in Sections 3,4. It was used for analysis of the case study described below.

This case study deals with the analysis of the service provider centric business model for provision of the platform bundle of services to a business person on the move who uses his smart mobile phone to access this service offer. The setting of this case study is described in Example 17.2 introduced in Section 3. The Edition 1 of the prototype of the decision support system implementing models from this paper was used for the analysis of this case study.

Considerable data preparation effort was made for this case study. First of all, we have developed the service composition matrix, showing which enabler participates in which services. This relation between different enablers and services is shown on Figure 17.2. We have obtained also an average estimate of the service usage (in service instances) in a period of interest, and prices per service instance. These data we have estimated by averaging various service composition and business scenarios. On the basis of technical and economic analysis we have obtained the cost estimates and the correlation matrix showing the correlation between the usage of services and the variance of service usage. Details of this analysis will be given in another paper by the authors.

Suppose that the service provider is using our DSS for performing the feasibility study for provision of this bundle of business services similarly to the discussion at the end of Section 5.2. There are many different what-if questions of interest to the prospective service provider to which this DSS can provide the answers. Let us provide a couple of examples of this analysis. Suppose that the service provider feels that the success of the whole enterprize depends critically on the quality and offer of specialized content which can be obtained for his services by engaging prospective content providers (enabler E4 from Figure 17.2). He wants to get insight into the properties of the content providers which may be interested in collaboration with him and in the chances that his service offer in this respect will stand against the competition of the 3rd party services. One way to do this is to look how the service portfolios and risk/profit preferences of prospective partners will depend on correlation and relative pricing of his offer against the offer of competition. Figures 17.4-17.8 provide examples of answers which our modeling system can deliver.

Figures 17.4 and 17.5 show how the characteristics and attitudes of the content providers towards the service platform depend on the alternatives which the competition can offer to them. Figure 17.4 shows risk/profit efficient fron-

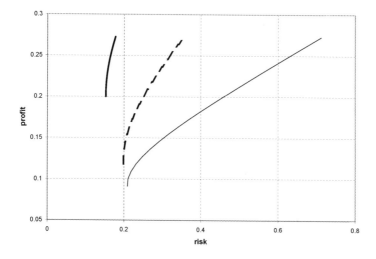

Figure 17.4. Dependence of risk/return preferences of content providers on the strength of competition

tiers similar to frontier presented on Figure 17.3 while Figure 17.5 depicts the percentage share of the content provision capability of the content providers dedicated to the service platform. In other words, the Figure 17.5 shows the market share of the service platform in the market for this specific type of content provision dependent on the risk tolerance of the content providers. The competing offer is described by the average price per unit of content and by how the actual price can differ from the average price dependent on the future market conditions, as measured by the price variance.

The figures present three scenarios. In all three scenarios the competition tries to undercut the service platform by offering about 15% higher average price to content providers for their services. The three scenarios differ by how strong the competition is, that is by its capability to maintain the price consistently higher under the changing market conditions. In scenario 1 shown by the thick solid lines the competition is strong and has its price variance about two times smaller compared with the platform offer. In scenario 2 depicted by the thick dashed lines the competition is about as strong as the platform offer and has the similar price variance. In scenario 3 shown with thin solid lines the competition is weaker than the platform and has about twice higher variability of its offer to content providers than the platform.

The results show that in scenario 1 with strong competition only economically weak content providers with small tolerance towards losses will be interested in the collaboration with the platform. Often this will correspond to

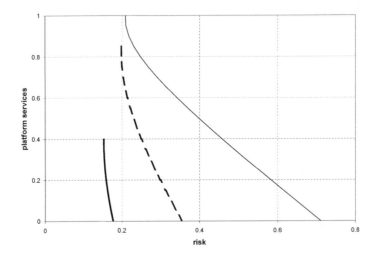

Figure 17.5.   Share of platform services in the service portfolios of content providers

small firms or even individuals who can not sustain large losses. For such entities participation in the platform means additional security and insurance against losses in the case when the strong competing offer will prove to be deceitful in reality. Even then, the interest of such firms drops sharply when their risk tolerances grow even by a small amount.

Scenario 3 corresponds to the opposite case when the platform faces aggressive but economically relatively weak competition. Its weakness manifests itself in large variability of its price offer to the content providers despite the 15% higher average price. In this case the market share of the platform services is much higher and the platform manages to attract also strong actors with higher capacities to sustain losses. Also the market share drops slower with the increase of the loss tolerance of the agents. Scenario 2 corresponds to the intermediate case when the competition is about as strong as the platform and has about the same capability to maintain its price offer to the service providers.

Similar patterns arise when the variability of the revenue steam of content providers is due not to the changes in the unit price of content but due to the variability of usage frequencies of this content. Having these predictions, the platform service provider can now realistically weight his own strength and weaknesses, invest more effort into market research and decide under which market conditions, with what kind of partners and with what kind of competition he can successfully operate the platform.

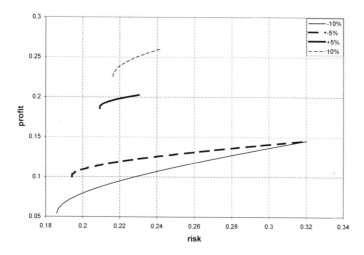

Figure 17.6. Dependence of risk/return preferences of content providers on the platform price offer

Thus, Figures 17.4 and 17.5 show the reaction of content providers to the relative strength of platform and competition expressed through the quality of revenue streams offered to the content providers. Instead, Figures 17.6 and 17.7 show how this reaction depends on the price offer of the platform and competition for the unit of content. In other words, the first case corresponds to the competition on quality while the second case to the competition on price. Four price scenarios are considered. In scenario 1 the price offer of the platform is 10% lower than the price of competition (thin solid line). In scenario 2 the platform price is 5% inferior to the competition price (thick dashed line). In scenario 3 the platform offers 5% higher price compared to the competition (thick solid line). Finally, in scenario 4 the platform offer is 10% superior to the competition. The quality of offer expressed in the terms of variability of revenue stream is about the same for the platform and the competition.

Figure 17.6 shows the efficient risk/return efficient frontiers of the content providers for this case, while Figure 17.7 depicts the projected market share of the platform depending on the risk tolerance of the participating content providers. In the case when the platform offers inferior price, the picture is similar to what we have already observed on Figures 17.4 and 17.5. Namely, the higher economic strength of the content providers expressed as their tolerance to loss, the less they are interested in cooperation with the service platform. At the same time the weaker service providers are willing to accept significant reductions in the price in return to more security which diversification brings.

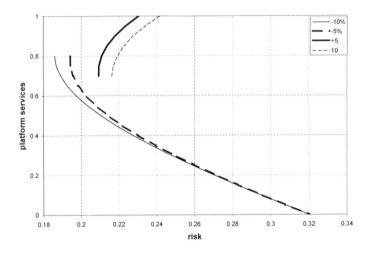

Figure 17.7.   Share of platform services in the service portfolios of content providers

The picture reverses when the service platform tries to beat the competition by offering more attractive prices compared to the competition. Now the weaker agents are willing to sacrifice part of the benefits of the platform offer by maintaining the competition in their service portfolios, while the stronger content providers prefer the exclusive arrangements with the service platform.

Finally, Figure 17.8 shows how the return of the service provider depends on the revenue sharing scheme, or, equivalently, on his price offer to the providers of other enablers. Besides the content provider and the service provider we consider here the service context provider (enabler E2 from Figure 17.2), while it is assumed that all other enablers are supplied by the service provider. Horizontal axes on this figure show the fraction of the revenue which goes to the providers of enablers E2 and E4 while the vertical axis shows the return of the service provider. Zero return means that this particular sharing scheme is not accepted by all providers and therefore the service provision does not happen. In other words, what we see on Figure 17.8 is the feasible region (23) of the optimization problem of the service provider. Such figures will be helpful in determining the room for the price maneuver which is available for the service provider.

7.   Conclusions

The notions of modern financial theory and in particular portfolio theory and risk/return trade-off constitute a powerful tool for evaluation of business

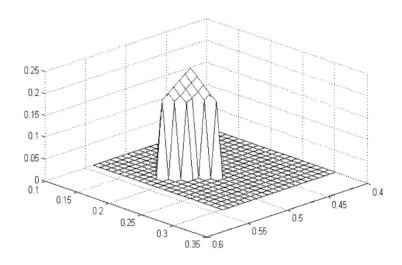

Figure 17.8. Dependence of the return of service provider on revenue sharing

models for collaborative provision of advanced mobile data services. Here we developed two models which utilize and adapt these notions for the case of multiactor environment. Many relevant issues remained beyond the scope of this paper and will be treated in our future research. These include different actor constellations, combinations of roles by an actor, evaluation of the whole service provision platform, modeling of flexibilities and uncertainties inherent in the service provision, life cycle of a service. Besides, the present paper sets the stage for further development of modeling and decision support tools for analysis of various service types, service bundles, service subscription types as well as various business model types.

Acknowledgement.   Part of this work is performed within the project IST-2005-027617 SPICE, partly funded by the European Union. We would like to thank the SPICE project partners for collaboration. Development of some of the algorithms greatly benefited from support by COST Action 293 *Graphs and algorithms in communication networks (GRAAL).*   Part of this work is financed by the ISIS project (Infrastructure for Integrated Services), financed by Norwegian Research Council (NFR # 180122). This project also provided practical cases for the techno-business analysis. Last but not least, we are grateful to three anonymous referees who helped us to improve the paper by providing thoughtful and challenging comments.

References

[1] Amendment to the capital accord to incorporate market risks. Bank for International Settlements, 1996.

[2] Jan-Arild Audestad, Alexei A. Gaivoronski, and Adrian Werner. Extending the stochastic programming framework for the modeling of several decision makers: Pricing and competition in the telecommunication sector. *Annals of Operations Research*, 142:19–39, 2006.

[3] John R. Birge and Francois Louveaux. *Introduction to Stochastic Programming*. Springer, New York, 1997.

[4] Benoît Colson, Patrice Marcotte, and Gilles Savard. Bilevel programming: A survey. *4OR*, 3(2):87–107, 2005.

[5] S. Dempe. *Foundations of Bilevel Programming*. Kluwer Academic Publishers, Dordrecht, 2002.

[6] E. Faber, P. Ballon, H. Bouwman, T. Haaker, O. Rietkerk, and M. Steen. Designing business models for mobile ICT services. In *Proceedings of 16th Bled E-Commerce Conference*, Bled, Slovenia, June 2003.

[7] A. A. Gaivoronski. SQG: Stochastic programming software environment. In S.W. Wallace and W.T. Ziemba, editors, *Applications of Stochastic Programming*. SIAM & MPS, 2005.

[8] Alexei A. Gaivoronski. Stochastic optimization in telecommunications. In M. G. C. Resende and P. M. Pardalos, editors, *Handbook of Optimization in Telecommunications*, chapter 27, pages 761–799. Springer, 2006.

[9] T. Haaker, B. Kijl, L. Galli, U. Killström, O. Immonen, and M. de Reuver. Challenges in designing viable business models for context-aware mobile services. In *CICT Conference Papers*, Copenaghen, 2006.

[10] P. Kall and S. Wallace. *Stochastic Programming*. John Wiley and Sons, New York, 1994.

[11] David G. Luenberger. *Investment Science*. Oxford University Press, 1998.

[12] H. Markowitz. *Portfolio Selection*. Blackwell, second edition, 1991.

[13] D. Mitra, K. G. Ramakrishnan, and Q. Wang. Combined economic modeling and traffic engineering: Joint optimization of pricing and routing in multi-service networks. In *Proceedings of 17th International Teletraffic Congress, Salvador, Brasil*, Amsterdam, 2001. Elsevier.

[14] Michael Patriksson and Laura Wynter. Stochastic mathematical programs with equilibrium constraints. *Operations Research Letters*, 25(4):159–167, 1999.

[15] S. Scholtes and M. Stöhr. Exact penalization of mathematical programs with equilibrium constraints. *SIAM Journal on Control and Optimization*, 37:617–652, 1999.

[16] Oz Shy. *The Economics of Network Industries*. Cambridge University Press, 2001.

[17] L. Trigeorgis. *Real Options : Managerial Flexibility and Strategy in Resource Allocation*. MIT Press, Cambridge, Mass., 1996.

[18] J. Zoric, Nj. A. Gjermundshaug, and S. Alapnes. Experiments with semantic support in mobile service architectures. In *65th IEEE Vehicular Technology Conference, 23-25 April 2007, Dublin, Ireland*.

[19] J. Zoric, Nj. A. Gjermundshaug, and S. Alapnes. Service mobility - a challenge for semantic support. In *16th IST Mobile & Wireless Communications Summit, Budapest, Hungary*, 1-5 July, 2007.

Early Titles in
OPERATIONS RESEARCH/COMPUTER SCIENCE INTERFACES

Greenberg /*A Computer-Assisted Analysis System for Mathematical Programming Models and Solutions: A User's Guide for ANALYZE*

Greenberg / *Modeling by Object-Driven Linear Elemental Relations: A Users Guide for MODLER*

Brown & Scherer / *Intelligent Scheduling Systems*

Nash & Sofer / *The Impact of Emerging Technologies on Computer Science & Operations Research*

Barth / *Logic-Based 0-1 Constraint Programming*

Jones / *Visualization and Optimization*

Barr, Helgason & Kennington / *Interfaces in Computer Science & Operations Research: Advances in Metaheuristics, Optimization, & Stochastic Modeling Technologies*

Ellacott, Mason & Anderson / *Mathematics of Neural Networks: Models, Algorithms & Applications*

Woodruff / *Advances in Computational & Stochastic Optimization, Logic Programming, and Heuristic Search*

Klein / *Scheduling of Resource-Constrained Projects*